Bookkeeping & Accounting

ALL-IN-ONE

FOR DUMMIES®

A Wiley Brand

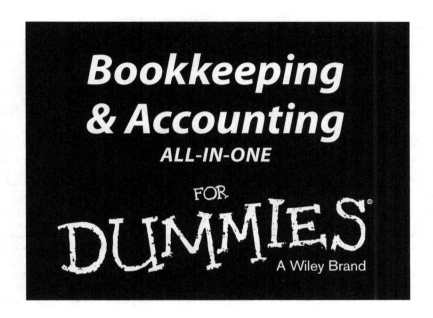

Bookkeeping & Accounting

ALL-IN-ONE

FOR DUMMIES®

A Wiley Brand

by Colin Barrow, Paul Barrow, Lita Epstein, Jane Kelly, ACMA, and John A. Tracy

Edited by Jane Kelly, ACMA

Bookkeeping & Accounting All-in-One For Dummies®

Published by: **John Wiley & Sons, Ltd.,** The Atrium, Southern Gate, Chichester, www.wiley.com

This edition first published 2015

© 2015 John Wiley & Sons, Ltd, Chichester, West Sussex.

Registered office

John Wiley & Sons Ltd, The Atrium, Southern Gate, Chichester, West Sussex, PO19 8SQ, United Kingdom

For details of our global editorial offices, for customer services and for information about how to apply for permission to reuse the copyright material in this book please see our website at www.wiley.com.

Wiley publishes in a variety of print and electronic formats and by print-on-demand. Some material included with standard print versions of this book may not be included in e-books or in print-on-demand. If this book refers to media such as a CD or DVD that is not included in the version you purchased, you may download this material at www.dummies.com. For more information about Wiley products, visit www.wiley.com.

Designations used by companies to distinguish their products are often claimed as trademarks. All brand names and product names used in this book are trade names, service marks, trademarks or registered trademarks of their respective owners. The publisher is not associated with any product or vendor mentioned in this book.

For general information on our other products and services, please contact our Customer Care Department within the U.S. at 877-762-2974, outside the U.S. at (001) 317-572-3993, or fax 317-572-4002. For technical support, please visit www.wiley.com/techsupport.

For technical support, please visit www.wiley.com/techsupport.

A catalogue record for this book is available from the British Library.

ISBN 978-1-119-02653-2 (paperback); ISBN 978-1-119-02660-0 (ebk); ISBN 978-1-119-02661-7 (ebk)

10 9 8 7 6 5 4 3 2 1

Contents at a Glance

Table of Contents

Book IV: Working to Prepare Financial Statements 209

Introduction

· ·

*W*elcome to *Bookkeeping & Accounting All-in-One For Dummies!* This book explains the different roles that both bookkeepers and accountants take on within a business. If you're a one-man or one-woman band, however, don't worry; within these pages you too can find out how to do the bookkeeping basics and see the ways in which an accountant can assist you further.

About This Book

This book aims to help you understand the bookkeeping tasks that need to be done within your business and to demonstrate how an accountant can help your business to set targets that will hopefully expand and grow.

Bookkeeping & Accounting All-in-One For Dummies is divided into six separate books. Each book is split into several chapters that tackle key aspects of bookkeeping and accounting functions. The Table of Contents gives you more detail of what is contained within each chapter. Each chapter presents information in a modular fashion so that you get all the information you need to accomplish a task in one place. You don't need to remember things from different parts of the book; if another chapter has information relevant to the discussion at hand, you'll find a cross reference telling you where to find it, so you don't have to read the chapters in order. You can read the chapters or sections that interest you when it suits you.

If you end up reading all that there is to read in this book, but find you still want more, check out the extra information in these *For Dummies* titles (all published by Wiley):

- ✔ *Bookkeeping For Dummies* (Jane Kelly, Paul Barrow & Lita Epstein)
- ✔ *Understanding Business Accounting For Dummies* (John A. Tracy & Colin Barrow)
- ✔ *Accounting Workbook For Dummies* (Jane Kelly & John A. Tracy)

Foolish Assumptions

Bookkeeping & Accounting All-in-One For Dummies makes some key assumptions about who you are and why you picked up this book, and assumes that you fall into one of the following categories:

- ✔ You're a member of staff in a small business who's been employed to undertake the bookkeeping and accounting function.

- ✔ You're a small business owner who currently doesn't have the funds to employee an individual. Therefore, you need to understand the basics of bookkeeping to enable you to deal with the day-to-day paperwork, with a view to perhaps using an accountant at year-end.

- ✔ You're a small-business owner who is thinking of employing a bookkeeper but wants to know the differences between what a bookkeeper can do for your business and what an accountant can offer.

If any – or all – of these assumptions accurately describes you, then you've come to the right book!

Icons Used in This Book

Every *For Dummies* book uses icons to highlight especially important, interesting or useful information. The icons used in this book are:

Look at this icon for practical information that you can use straightaway to help you to run your bookkeeping and accounting systems in the most effective way.

This icon indicates any items you need to remember after reading the book – and sometimes throughout it.

This icon calls your attention to examples of specific tasks that you can undertake to help you perform the bookkeeping or accounting skills explained in this book.

The paragraphs next to this icon contain information that is, er, slightly technical in nature. You don't *need* to know the information here to get by, but it helps.

This bombshell alerts you to potential problems you may create for yourself without realising it. Don't ignore this icon!

Beyond the Book

At www.dummies.com/extras/bookkeepingaccountingaio you can access some online extras, just in case you need a bit more help and guidance! You can also find the handy cheat sheet at www.dummies.com/cheatsheet/bookkeepingaccountingaio.

Where to Go from Here

You're now ready to enter the world of bookkeeping and accounting. If you're a complete beginner, starting at the beginning and gradually working through from there is probably the best approach. If you have some experience, but are a little rusty in certain areas, you can pick and choose the chapters that are most relevant to you. After all, this book is designed for you to dip in and out of as you like. I hope that you find it a useful tool for developing and managing your business.

Book I
Basic Bookkeeping

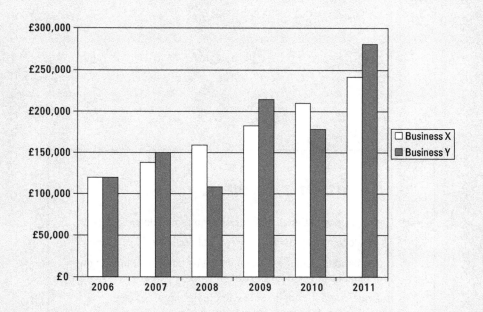

In this book...

- Get to grips with the basic bookkeeping terminology.
- Take a look at the double entry rules of bookkeeping.
- Understand the Chart of Accounts to see how it impacts on the Profit and Loss and Balance Sheet.
- See how the different ledgers work together to make your accounting system work for your business.

Chapter 1

So You Want to Do the Books

In This Chapter

▶ Introducing bookkeeping and its basic purpose

▶ Maintaining a paper trail

▶ Managing daily business finances

▶ Making sure that everything's accurate

*F*or many small business owners, while they love working in their chosen field using the skills they know and love, they don't always like to perform 'bookkeeping' duties. Most company owners prefer to employ the skills of a qualified bookkeeper. Some may, perhaps, prefer to give their bag-full of receipts to their accountant and simply hope that a useful set of accounts comes out of the end of the accounting sausage machine!

In this chapter we help to demystify the role of a bookkeeper. It may be that you're just starting off in business and, as a result, can't afford the services of a bookkeeper just yet! Think of this chapter as a checklist of jobs that need to be done.

Throughout the book, we introduce Have a Go sections, which are practical exercises aimed at helping you understand the bookkeeping principles we discuss. Feel free to draw all over these sections of the book; we want it to be as useful for you as possible.

Delving into Bookkeeping Basics

Like most businesspeople, you probably have great ideas for running your own business and just want to get started. You don't want to be distracted by the small stuff, like keeping detailed records of every penny you spend; you just want to build a business with which you can make lots of money.

Well, slow down there – you're not in a race! If you don't carefully plan your bookkeeping system and figure out exactly how and what financial details you want to track, you've absolutely no way to measure the success (or failure, unfortunately) of your business efforts.

Bookkeeping, when done properly, gives you an excellent measure of how well you're doing and also provides lots of information throughout the year. This information allows you to test the financial success of your business strategies and make any necessary course corrections early in the year to ensure that you reach your year-end profit goals.

Looking at basic accounting methods

You can't keep books unless you know how to go about doing so. The two basic accounting methods are *cash-based accounting* and *accrual accounting*. The key difference between the two methods is the point at which you record sales and purchases in your books. If you choose cash-based accounting, you only record transactions when cash changes hands. If you use accrual accounting, you record a transaction on its completion, even if cash doesn't change hands.

For example, suppose that your business buys products to sell from a supplier but doesn't actually pay for those products for 30 days. If you're using cash-based accounting, you don't record the purchase until you actually lay out the cash to the supplier. If you're using accrual accounting, you record the purchase when you receive the products, and you also record the future debt in an account called Trade Creditors.

HM Revenue & Customs, who has an interest in every business in the UK, accept only the accrual accounting method. So, in reality you can't use cash-based accounting. However, a special concession for smaller businesses allows them to use a form of cash-based accounting for value-added tax (VAT) purposes (which is covered in Book III, Chapter 1). In essence, you can complete your VAT return on a cash-based accounting method, which HM Revenue & Customs refers to as cash accounting.

We talk about the pros and cons of each type of accounting method in Book I, Chapter 2.

Understanding assets, capital and liabilities

Every business has three key financial parts that must be kept in balance: assets, capital and liabilities. Of course, for some of you these may be alien concepts, so maybe a quick accounting primer is in order.

We use buying a house with a mortgage as an example. The house you're buying is an *asset*; that is, something of value that you own. In the first year of the mortgage, you don't own all of it, but by the end of the mortgage period (typically 25 years) you will. The mortgage is a *liability*, or a debt that you owe. As the years roll on and you reduce the mortgage (liability), your *capital* or ownership of the asset increases. That's it in a nutshell.

- ✔ **Assets** include everything the business owns, such as cash, stock, buildings, equipment and vehicles.
- ✔ **Capital** includes the claims that owners have on the assets based on their portion of ownership in the business.
- ✔ **Liabilities** include everything the business owes to others, such as supplier bills, credit card balances and bank loans.

The formula for keeping your books in balance involves these three elements:

Assets = Capital + Liabilities

Because this equation is so important, we talk a lot about how to keep your books in balance throughout this book. You can find an initial introduction to this concept in Book I, Chapter 2.

Introducing debits and credits

To keep the books, you need to revise your thinking about two common financial terms: debits and credits. Most non-bookkeepers and non-accountants think of debits as subtractions from their bank accounts. The opposite is true with credits – people usually see credits as additions to their accounts, in most cases in the form of refunds or corrections in favour of the account holders.

Well, forget all you think that you know about debits and credits. Debits and credits are totally different animals in the world of bookkeeping. Because keeping the books involves a method called *double-entry bookkeeping*, you have to make at least two entries – a debit and a credit – into your bookkeeping system for every transaction. Whether that debit or credit adds or subtracts from an account depends solely upon the type of account.

We know all this debit, credit and double-entry stuff sounds confusing, but we promise that this system is going to become much clearer as you work through this book. We start explaining this important concept in Book I, Chapter 2.

Book I

Basic Book-keeping

Charting your bookkeeping course

You can't just enter transactions in the books willy-nilly. You need to know exactly where those transactions fit into the larger bookkeeping system. To know where everything goes, you use your *Chart of Accounts*, which is essentially a list of all the accounts that your business has and the types of transactions that go into each one. (We talk more about the Chart of Accounts in Book I, Chapter 3.)

Discovering different business types

Before you start up in business, you're wise to sit down and have a think about the structure of your business.

For example, if you're a window cleaner, and only ever see yourself doing your own rounds and not working with anyone else, then sole trader status would be more than adequate. However, if you're planning to be much bigger and take on staff, then you need to read Book V, Chapter 1 to see how you should structure your business and what sort of advice you may need.

Planning and controlling your activities

Many businesses just start up and trade from day to day, without any real planning or control of the activities they undertake. Often, businesspeople become so busy that they're fire-fighting continually and lack any real direction. We like using checklists, because they help to organise your bookkeeping activities in a methodical and orderly manner. This level of organisation means that you can pick up and put down the accounts from day to day or even week to week. You can always start from where you left off, quickly and easily, by simply adopting some of the hints and tips contained within Book II, Chapter 1.

Instituting internal controls

Every business owner needs to be concerned with keeping tight controls on business cash and how that cash is used. One way to institute this control is by placing internal restrictions on who can enter information into your books and who has the necessary access to use that information.

Keeping an accurate paper trail

Keeping the books is all about creating an accurate paper trail. A computerised accounting system would refer to this trail as the *Audit Trail*. You want to keep track of all your business's financial transactions so that if a question comes up at a later date, you can turn to the books to figure out what went wrong. We're big fans of using checklists, so you know exactly where you are in the monthly accounting cycle. We introduce our monthly checklist in Book II, Chapter 1.

All your business's financial transactions are summarised in the Nominal Ledger, and

journals keep track of the tiniest details of each transaction. Information can be gathered quickly by using a computerised accounting system, which gives you access to your financial information in many different report formats. Controlling who enters this financial information into your books and who can access it afterwards is smart business practice, and involves critical planning on your part. We address all these concepts in the following sections.

You also need to control carefully who has the ability to accept cash receipts and spend your business's cash. Separating duties appropriately helps you to protect your business's assets from error, theft and fraud. We talk more about controlling your cash and protecting your financial records in Book II, Chapter 1.

Defining and Maintaining a Ledger

You may get confused by terms such as *books*, *ledgers*, *journals* and *accounts*. Most of these words evolved from traditional bookkeeping methods, where accounts were handwritten in huge leather-bound ledgers. These looked like books, hence the name *bookkeeping* – simply, keeping financial records in the books!

The books are also known as *journals* or *ledgers* (we told you it was a bit confusing!). You'd normally have one book for your sales, one for purchases and then a general one used for everything (often known as the *General Ledger*). Sometimes, businesses would also keep a separate cash book, which would record cash received and cash paid.

Nowadays, most people use computers to do their accounts (anything to make our busy lives easier). The most simplistic set of accounts can be done on a spreadsheet, although we don't recommend it because mistakes can easily be made and you'll struggle to find an efficient way to make sure that the books balance.

In this book we demonstrate the use of ledgers using Sage 50 Accounts. However, it's worth pointing out at this stage that if your budget is low and you're a micro business (for example, a one-man band), you may find Sage One useful. Sage One is a new online accounting service developed by Sage that's simple and easy to use. Refer to *Sage One For Dummies* by Jane Kelly to find out more.

Most computerised accounting systems use the term *ledger*, so you usually find the following:

- ✔ **Sales Ledger:** A ledger that holds all the individual customer accounts and their balances. This ledger is sometimes known as the *Customer Ledger* or the *Debtors Ledger*.

- ✔ **Purchase Ledger:** A ledger that holds all the individual supplier accounts and their balances. This ledger is sometimes known as the *Suppliers Ledger* or *Creditors Ledger*.

- ✔ **Nominal Ledger:** A ledger that includes balances and activities for all the Nominal accounts used to run the business. We discuss Nominal accounts in Book I, Chapter 4. This ledger is also known as the *General Ledger*.

- ✔ **Cashbook, or Bank:** In Sage, in particular, you can have numerous Bank current accounts and Petty Cash accounts all under the general 'Bank' heading. Any cash received or paid is recorded in this part of the accounting system.

- ✔ **Accounts:** Simply a collective term for all the ledgers.

The pinnacle of your bookkeeping system is the *Nominal Ledger.* In this ledger, you keep a summary of all your accounts and the financial activities that took place involving those accounts throughout the year.

The sum of each Nominal Ledger account can be used to develop your financial reports on a monthly, quarterly or annual basis. You can also use these account summaries to develop internal reports that help you to make key business decisions. We talk more about developing Profit and Loss statements and Balance Sheets in Book I, Chapter 3, when we introduce the *Chart of Accounts.*

We explain more about developing and maintaining the Nominal Ledger in Book I, Chapter 4. We also discuss the importance of journals and talk about the accounts commonly journalised in Book I, Chapter 4.

Using Bookkeeping Tools to Manage Daily Finances

After you set up your business's books and put in place your internal controls, you're ready to use the systems you've established to manage the day-to-day operations of your business. A well-designed bookkeeping system quickly makes the job of managing your business's finances much easier.

Tracking sales

Everyone wants to know how well sales are doing. If you keep your books up-to-date and accurate, you can easily get those numbers on a daily basis. You can also watch sales trends as often as you think necessary: daily, weekly or monthly.

Use the information collected by your bookkeeping system to monitor sales, review discounts offered to customers and track the return of products. All three elements are critical to monitoring the success of the sales of your products.

If you find that you need to offer discounts more frequently in order to increase sales, you may need to review your pricing, and you definitely need to do market research to determine the cause of this sales weakness. The cause may be the new activities of an aggressive competitor, or simply a slowdown in your particular market. Either way, you need to understand the problem and work out how to maintain your profit objectives in spite of any obstacles.

When sales tracking reveals an increase in the number of your products being returned, you need to find the reason for the increase. Perhaps the quality of the product you're selling is declining, and you need to find a new supplier. Whatever the reason, an increased number of product returns is usually a sign of a problem that needs to be researched and corrected.

We talk more about how to use the bookkeeping system for tracking sales, discounts and returns in Book II, Chapter 2.

Keeping stock

If your business keeps stock on hand or in warehouses, tracking the costs of the products you plan to sell is critical for managing your profit potential. When you see stock costs escalating, you may need to adjust your own prices in order to maintain your profit margin. You certainly don't want to wait until the end of the year to find out how much your stock cost you.

You also must keep careful watch on how much stock you have on hand and how much was sold. Stock can get damaged, discarded or stolen, meaning that your physical stock counts may differ from the counts you have in your books. Do a physical count periodically – at least monthly for most businesses and possibly daily for active retail stores.

In addition to watching for signs of theft or poor handling of stock, make sure that you've enough stock on hand to satisfy your customers' needs. We explain how to use your bookkeeping system to manage stock in Book II, Chapter 3.

If you run a service-based business, you can count yourself lucky because stock isn't as significant a cost in your business. You're predominantly selling time and using stocks of materials as a part of your service. However, you can't ignore your material costs, so the same lessons on stock control apply to you.

Running Tests for Accuracy

Tracking your transactions is a waste of time if you don't periodically test to be sure that you've entered those transactions accurately. The old adage 'Garbage in, garbage out' is particularly true for bookkeeping: if the numbers you put into your bookkeeping system are garbage, the reports you develop from those numbers are also garbage.

Checking the cash and bank

The first step in testing your books includes proving that your cash transactions are accurately recorded. This process involves checking a number of different transactions and elements, including the cash taken in on a daily basis by your staff and the accuracy of your bank account(s). We talk about all the necessary steps you can take to prove that your cash is correct in Book II, Chapter 4.

Testing your balance

After you prove that your cash is right (see Book II, Chapter 4), you can check that you've recorded everything else in your books just as precisely. Review the accounts for any glaring errors and then test whether or not they're in balance by doing a Trial Balance. You can find out more about Trial Balances in Book III, Chapter 3.

Understanding your VAT

For those of you who are VAT registered, you know that you need to submit a regular VAT return, usually on a quarterly basis. In Book III, Chapter 1 we talk about how you can easily do this return using a computerised accounting system.

Doing bookkeeping corrections

After you've entered your normal day-to-day transactions, you find you need to make additional adjustments, such as accruals, prepayments and depreciation. In Book III, Chapter 3, we explain some of these adjustments required, as you close your books at the end of an accounting period.

Preparing financial reports

Most businesses prepare at least two key financial reports: the Balance Sheet and the Profit and Loss statement. These reports can be shown to business outsiders, including the financial institutions from which the business borrows money and the business's investors.

The *Balance Sheet* is a snapshot of your business's financial health as of a particular date, and ideally it shows that your business's assets are equal to the value of your liabilities and your capital. The Balance Sheet is so-called because of its balanced formula:

Assets = Capital + Liabilities

The *Profit and Loss statement* summarises your business's financial transactions for a particular time period, such as a month, quarter or year. This financial statement starts with your sales, subtracts the costs of goods sold and then subtracts any expenses incurred in operating the business. The bottom line of the Profit and Loss statement shows how much profit your business made during the accounting period. If you haven't done well, the Profit and Loss statement shows how much you've lost.

We explain how to prepare a Balance Sheet in Book IV, Chapter 4, and we talk more about developing a Profit and Loss statement in Book IV, Chapter 1.

Computers now play an important part in creating your reports. Provided that you've set up your nominal codes correctly, you can easily prepare reports at the click of a button! Having said all this, you need to understand the bookkeeping rules of *double entry*, which we explain in Book I, Chapter 2. So, when you need to make an adjustment to your accounts, you'll have the necessary confidence to complete journals by applying the rules of double-entry bookkeeping.

Throughout the book, we demonstrate using Sage software and you'll be pleased to know that the majority of double-entry bookkeeping is done automatically for you. For example, when you create a sales invoice on the system, Sage debits the Debtors Control account and credit the individual Sales account with the net value of the invoice. It also posts the VAT element (assuming that you're VAT registered) to the VAT Control account.

Handling payroll

Payroll can be a huge nightmare for many businesses. It requires you to comply with loads of government and tax regulations and complete a lot of paperwork. You also have to worry about collecting and paying over such things as Pay As You Earn (PAYE) and National Insurance. And if you pay employee benefits, you've yet another layer of record-keeping to deal with.

We talk more about managing payroll and government requirements, particularly with the introduction of the recent RTI (Real Time Information) system, in Book III, Chapter 2.

Working with your accountant

The majority of the tasks that we discuss in the first three books can be carried out by a bookkeeper, but some tasks perhaps require the skills of an accountant. We cover the areas in which an accountant can help you and your business (as well as work with your bookkeeper) in Books V and VI.

Most bookkeepers are adept at preparing a Profit and Loss statement and a Balance Sheet, but they may not get involved with the choice of accounting methods that a business uses, such as stock valuation and calculating the cost of goods sold. We cover these areas in Book V, Chapter 1. We also look at costing methods (particularly for manufacturing businesses) in Book V, Chapter 4, and budgets in Book V, Chapter 5. The last book discusses how the business may need external accountants and the kind of role that they may play.

Having said all this, the business relies first and foremost on a good-quality bookkeeper to maintain its financial records. The bookkeeper may well be the business owner to start with. If that's you then buckle up: we're going on a bookkeeping journey!

Book I

Basic Book-keeping

Chapter 2

Getting Down to Bookkeeping Basics

*A*ll businesses need to keep track of their financial transactions, which is why bookkeeping and bookkeepers are so important. Without accurate records, how can you tell whether your business is making a profit or taking a loss?

In this chapter, we cover the key aspects of bookkeeping: we introduce you to the language of bookkeeping, familiarise you with how bookkeepers manage the accounting cycle and show you how to understand the more complex type of bookkeeping – double-entry bookkeeping.

Bookkeeping: The Record-Keeping of the Business World

Bookkeeping, the methodical way in which businesses track their financial transactions, is rooted in accounting. *Accounting* is the total structure of records and procedures used to record, classify and report information about a business's financial transactions. Bookkeeping involves the recording of that financial information into the accounting system while maintaining adherence to solid accounting principles.

The bookkeeper's job is to work day in and day out to ensure that she records transactions accurately. Bookkeepers need to be detail-oriented and love working with numbers, because they deal with numbers and accounts all day long.

Bookkeepers don't need to belong to any recognised professional body, such as the Institute of Chartered Accountants of England and Wales. You can recognise a chartered accountant by the letters *ACA* after the name, which indicates that she is an Associate of the Institute of Chartered Accountants. If she's been qualified much longer, she may use the letters *FCA*, which indicate that the accountant is a Fellow of the Institute of Chartered Accountants.

Of course, both Scotland and Ireland have their own chartered accountant bodies with their own designations. Other accounting qualifications exist, offered by the Institute of Chartered Management Accountants (ACMA and FCMA), the Institute of Chartered Certified Accountants (ACCA and FCMA) and the Chartered Institute of Public Finance Accountants (CIPFA).

The Association of Accounting Technicians offers a bookkeeping certificate (ABC) programme that provides a good grounding in this subject. In reality, most bookkeepers tend to be qualified by experience.

If you're after an accountant to help your business, use the appropriate chartered accountant or a chartered certified accountant because they have the most relevant experience.

On starting up their businesses, many small-business owners serve as their own bookkeepers until the business is large enough to hire a dedicated person to keep the books. Few small businesses have accountants on the payroll to check the books and prepare official financial reports; instead, they have bookkeepers (on the payroll or hired on a self-employed basis) who serve as the outside accountants' eyes and ears. Most businesses do seek out an accountant, usually a chartered accountant (ACA or FCA), but they do so typically to submit annual accounts to the Inland Revenue, which is now part of HM Revenue & Customs.

In many small businesses today, a bookkeeper enters the business transactions on a daily basis while working inside the business. At the end of each month or quarter, the bookkeeper sends summary reports to the accountant, who then checks the transactions for accuracy and prepares financial statements such as the Profit and Loss (see Book IV, Chapter 1), and Balance Sheet (see Book IV, Chapter 2) statements.

In most cases, the accounting system is initially set up with the help of an accountant. The aim is to ensure that the system uses solid accounting principles and that the analysis it provides is in line with that required by the business, the accountant and HM Revenue & Customs. That accountant periodically reviews the system's use to make sure that staff are handling transactions properly.

Accurate financial reports are the only way to ensure that you know how your business is doing. Your business develops these reports using the information that you, as the bookkeeper, enter into your accounting system. If that information isn't accurate, your financial reports are meaningless: remember, 'garbage in, garbage out'.

Wading through Basic Bookkeeping Lingo

Before you can take on bookkeeping and start keeping the books, you first need to get a handle on the key accounting terms. This section describes the main terms that all bookkeepers use on a daily basis.

Accounts for the Balance Sheet

Here are a few terms that you need to know:

- **Balance Sheet**: The financial statement that presents a snapshot of the business's financial position (assets, liabilities and capital) as of a particular date in time. The Balance Sheet is so-called because the things owned by the business (assets) must equal the claims against those assets (liabilities and capital).

  On an ideal Balance Sheet, the total assets need to equal the total liabilities plus the total capital. If your numbers fit this formula, the business's books are in balance. (We discuss the Balance Sheet in greater detail in Book IV, Chapter 2.)

- **Assets:** All the items a business owns in order to run successfully, such as cash, stock, debtors, buildings, land, tools, equipment, vehicles and furniture.

- **Liabilities:** All the debts the business owes, such as mortgages, loans and unpaid bills.

✔ **Capital:** All the money the business owners invest in the business. When one person (sole trader) or a group of people (partnership) own a small business, the owners' capital is shown in a Capital account. In an incorporated business (limited company), the owners' capital is shown as shares.

Another key Capital account is *Retained Earnings*, which shows all business profits that have been reinvested in the business rather than paid out to the owners by way of dividends. Unincorporated businesses show money paid out to the owners in a Drawings account (or individual Drawings accounts in the case of a partnership), whereas incorporated businesses distribute money to the owners by paying *dividends* (a portion of the business's profits paid out to the ordinary shareholders, typically for the year).

Accounts for the Profit and Loss statement

Following are a few terms related to the Profit and Loss statement that you need to know:

✔ **Profit and Loss statement:** The financial statement that presents a summary of the business's financial activity over a certain period of time, such as a month, quarter or year. The statement starts with Sales made, subtracts out the Costs of Goods Sold and the Expenses, and ends with the bottom line – Net Profit or Loss. (We show you how to develop a Profit and Loss statement in Book IV, Chapter 1.)

✔ **Income:** All sales made in the process of selling the business's goods and services. Some businesses also generate income through other means, such as selling assets that the business no longer needs or earning interest from investments. (We discuss how to track income in Book II, Chapter 2.)

✔ **Cost of Goods Sold:** All costs incurred in purchasing or making the products or services a business plans to sell to its customers. (We talk about purchasing goods for sale to customers in Book II, Chapter 3. We also talk about how the accountant would use different accounting methods to determine the cost of goods sold in Book V, Chapter 2.)

✔ **Expenses:** All costs incurred to operate the business that aren't directly related to the sale of individual goods or services. (We review common types of expenses in Book I, Chapter 3.)

Other common terms

Some other common terms include the following:

- **Accounting period:** The time for which financial information is being prepared. Most businesses monitor their financial results on a monthly basis, so each accounting period equals one month. Some businesses choose to do financial reports on a quarterly basis, so the accounting period is three months. Other businesses only look at their results on a yearly basis, so their accounting period is 12 months. Businesses that track their financial activities monthly usually also create quarterly and *annual reports* (a year-end summary of the business's activities and financial results) based on the information they gather.

- **Accounting year-end:** In most cases a business accounting year is 12 months long and ends 12 months on from when the business started or at some traditional point in the trading cycle for that business. Many businesses have year-ends of 31 March (to tie in with the tax year) and 31 December (to tie in with the calendar year). You're allowed to change your business year-end to suit your business.

  For example, if you started your business on July 1, your year-end is 30 June (12 months later). If, however, your industry traditionally has 31 December as the year-end, you're quite in order to change to this date. For example, most retailers have 31 December as their year-end. You do, of course, have to let HM Revenue & Customs know and get its formal acceptance.

- **Trade Debtors (also known as Accounts Receivable):** The account used to track all customer sales made on credit. *Credit* refers not to credit-card sales, but to sales in which the business gives a customer credit directly, and which the business needs to collect from the customer at a later date. (We discuss how to monitor Trade Debtors in Book II, Chapter 2.)

- **Trade Creditors (also known as Accounts Payable):** The account used to track all outstanding bills from suppliers, contractors, consultants and any other businesses or individuals from whom the business buys goods or services. (We talk about managing Trade Creditors in Book II, Chapter 3.)

- **Depreciation:** An accounting method used to account for the ageing and use of assets. For example, if you own a car, you know that the value of the car decreases each year (unless you own one of those classic cars that goes up in value). Every major asset a business owns ages and eventually needs replacement, including buildings, factories, equipment and other key assets. (We discuss the basics of depreciation in Book III, Chapter 3, and then discuss how your accountant decides on which depreciation method to use in Book V, Chapter 2).

✔ **Nominal (or General) Ledger:** A ledger that summarises all the business's accounts. The Nominal Ledger is the master summary of the bookkeeping system. (We discuss posting to the Nominal Ledger in Book I, Chapter 4.)

✔ **Stock (or Inventory):** The account that tracks all products sold to customers. (We review stock valuation and control in Book II, Chapter 3.)

✔ **Journals:** Where bookkeepers keep records (in chronological order) of daily business transactions. Each of the most active accounts, including Cash, Trade Creditors and Trade Debtors, has its own journal. (We discuss entering information into journals in Book I, Chapter 4.)

✔ **Payroll:** The way a business pays its employees. Managing payroll is a key function of the bookkeeper and involves reporting many aspects of payroll to HM Revenue & Customs, including Pay As You Earn (PAYE) taxes to be paid on behalf of the employee and employer, and National Insurance Contributions (NICs). In addition, a range of other payments such as Statutory Sick Pay (SSP) and maternity/paternity pay may be part of the payroll function. (We discuss employee payroll in Book III, Chapter 2, including the recent Real Time Information scheme.)

✔ **Trial Balance:** How you test to ensure that the books are in balance before pulling together information for the financial reports and closing the books for the accounting period. (We discuss the Trial Balance in Book III, Chapter 3.)

Pedalling through the Accounting Cycle

As a bookkeeper, you complete your work by completing the tasks of the accounting cycle, so-called because the workflow is circular: entering transactions, manipulating the transactions through the accounting cycle, closing the books at the end of the accounting period and then starting the entire cycle again for the next accounting period.

The accounting cycle has six basic steps, shown in Figure 2-1.

1. **Transactions:** Financial transactions start the process. Transactions can include the sale or return of a product; the purchase of supplies for business activities or any other financial activity that involves the exchange of the business's assets; the establishment or payoff of a debt; or the deposit from or payout of money to the business's owners. All sales and expenses are transactions that must be recorded. We cover transactions in greater detail throughout the book as we discuss how to record the basics of business activities – recording sales, purchases, asset acquisition or disposal, taking on new debt or paying off debt.

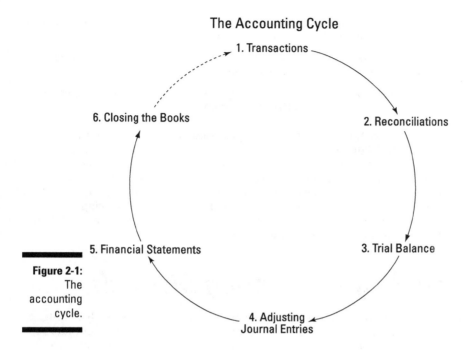

Figure 2-1:
The
accounting
cycle.

You post the transactions to the relevant account. These accounts are part of the *Nominal Ledger*, where you can find a summary of all the business's accounts. A computerised accounting system automatically journals the appropriate debits and credits to the correct accounts. For example, if a purchase invoice for British Telecom is entered as a transaction, the Creditors Ledger will be credited and the telephone Nominal account will be debited.

2. **Reconciliations:** Once you've entered all your transactions, you need to reconcile your bank account(s) to ensure that all your banking entries have been recorded correctly.

3. **Trial Balance:** At the end of the accounting period (which may be a month, quarter or year depending on your business's practices), you prepare a trial balance. You must then review each account on the Trial Balance to ensure accuracy.

4. **Adjusting journal entries:** Having reviewed the Trial Balance, you may need to make adjustments to some of the accounts in order to make corrections. You also need to account for the depreciation of assets and to adjust for one-time payments (such as insurance). These need to be allocated on a monthly basis, in order to match monthly expenses with

monthly revenues more accurately. After you make the adjustments, run another Trial Balance to ensure that you're happy with the accounts.

5. **Financial statements:** You run the Balance Sheet and Profit and Loss statement using the corrected account balances.

6. **Closing the books:** You close the books for the Revenue and Expense accounts and begin the entire cycle again.

At the end of the accounting year (year-end) you close off all the accounting ledgers. This situation means that Revenue and Expense accounts must start with a zero balance at the beginning of each new accounting year. In contrast, you carry over Asset, Liability and Capital account balances from year to year, because the business doesn't start each cycle by getting rid of old assets and buying new assets, paying off and then taking on new debt, or paying out all claims to owners and then collecting the money again.

Understanding Accounting Methods

Many not-for-profit organisations, such as sports clubs, have really simple accounting needs. These organisations aren't responsible to shareholders to account for their financial performance, though they're responsible to their members for the safe custody of their subscriptions and other funds. Consequently, the accounting focus isn't on measuring profit but more on accounting for receipts and payments. In these cases, a simple cash-based accounting system may well suffice, which allows for only cash transactions – giving or receiving credit is not possible.

However, complications may arise when members don't pay their subscriptions during the current accounting year, and the organisation needs to reflect this situation in its accounts. In this case, the accrual accounting method is best (see the later section 'Recording right away with accrual accounting').

A few businesses operate on a cash basis, and their owners can put forward a good case for using this method. However, most accountants and HM Customs & Revenue don't accept this method because it doesn't give an accurate measure of profit (or loss) for accounting periods.

In the next sections, we briefly explain how cash-based accounting works before dismissing it in favour of the more accepted and acceptable accrual method.

Realising the limitations of cash-based accounting

With *cash-based accounting*, you record all transactions in the books when cash actually changes hands, which means when the business receives cash payment from customers or pays out cash for purchases or other services. Cash receipt or payment can be in the form of cash, cheque, credit card, electronic transfer or other means used to pay for an item.

Cash-based accounting can't be used when a business sells products on credit and collects the money from the customer at a later date. No provision exists in the cash-based accounting method to record and track money due from customers at some point in the future.

This situation also applies for purchases. With the cash-based accounting method, the business only records the purchase of supplies or goods that are to be sold later when it actually pays cash. When the business buys goods on credit to be paid later, it doesn't record the transaction until the cash is actually paid out.

Depending on the size of your business, you may want to start out with cash-based accounting. Many small businesses run by a sole proprietor or a small group of partners use the easier cash-based accounting system. When your business model is simple – you carry no stock, start and finish each job within a single accounting period, and pay and get paid within this period – the cash-based accounting method can work for you. But as your business grows, you may find it necessary to switch to accrual accounting in order to track revenues and expenses more accurately and to satisfy the requirements of the external accountant and HM Revenue & Customs. The same basic argument also applies to not-for-profit organisations.

Cash-based accounting does a good job of tracking cash flow, but the system does a poor job of matching revenues earned with money laid out for expenses. This deficiency is a problem particularly when, as often happens, a business buys products in one month and sells those products in the next month.

Say you buy products in June paying £1,000 cash, with the intent to sell them that same month. You don't sell the products until July, which is when you receive cash for the sales. When you close the books at the end of June, you have to show the £1,000 expense with no revenue to offset it, meaning that you have a loss that month. When you sell the products for £1,500 in July, you have a £1,500 profit. So, your monthly report for June shows a £1,000 loss, and your monthly report for July shows a £1,500 profit, when in reality you had revenues of £500 over the two months. Using cash-based accounting, you can never be sure that you have an accurate measure of profit or loss – but because cash-based accounting is for not-for-profit organisations, this isn't surprising.

Because accrual accounting is the only accounting method acceptable to accountants and HM Revenue & Customs, we concentrate on this method throughout the book. If you choose to use cash-based accounting because you have a cash-only business and a simple trading model, don't panic: most of the bookkeeping information here is still useful, but you don't need to maintain some of the accounts, such as Trade Debtors and Trade Creditors, because you aren't recording transactions until cash actually changes hands. When you're using a cash-based accounting system and you start to sell things on credit, though, you'd better have a way to track what people owe you!

Our advice is to use the accrual accounting method right from the beginning. When your business grows and your business model changes, you need the more sophisticated and legally required accrual accounting.

Recording right away with accrual accounting

With *accrual accounting*, you record all transactions in the books when they occur, even when no cash changes hands. For example, when you sell on credit, you record the transaction immediately and enter it into a Trade Debtors account until you receive payment. When you buy goods on credit, you immediately enter the transaction into a Trade Creditors account until you pay out cash.

Like cash-based accounting, accrual accounting has drawbacks: it does a good job of matching revenues and expenses, but a poor job of tracking cash. Because you record income when the transaction occurs and not when you collect the cash, your Profit and Loss statement can look great even when you don't have cash in the bank. For example, suppose you're running a contracting business and completing jobs on a daily basis. You can record the revenue upon completion of the job even when you haven't yet collected the cash. When your customers are slow to pay, you may end up with lots of income but little cash. Remember – *never* confuse profit and cash. In the short term, cash flow is often more important than profit, but in the long term profit becomes more important. But don't worry just yet; in Book II, Chapter 2 we tell you how to manage your Trade Debtors so that you don't run out of cash because of slow-paying customers.

Many businesses that use the accrual accounting method monitor cash flow on a weekly basis to be sure that they've enough cash on hand to operate the business. If your business is seasonal, such as a landscaping business with little to do during the winter months, you can establish short-term lines of credit through your bank to maintain cash flow through the lean times.

Seeing Double with Double-Entry Bookkeeping

All businesses use *double-entry bookkeeping* to keep their books, whether they use the cash-based accounting method or the accrual accounting method. Double-entry bookkeeping – so-called because you enter all transactions twice – helps to minimise errors and increase the chance that your books balance.

When it comes to double-entry bookkeeping, the key formula for the Balance Sheet (Assets = Liabilities + Capital) plays a major role.

Golden rules of bookkeeping

You have some simple rules to remember when getting to grips with double-entry bookkeeping.

Double-entry bookkeeping goes way back

No one's really sure who invented double-entry bookkeeping. The first person to put the practice on paper was Benedetto Cotrugli in 1458, but mathematician and Franciscan monk Luca Pacioli is most often credited with developing double-entry bookkeeping. Although Pacioli is called the Father of Accounting, accounting actually occupies only one of five sections of his book, *Everything About Arithmetic,* *Geometry and Proportions*, which was published in 1494.

Pacioli didn't actually *invent* double-entry bookkeeping; he just described the method used by merchants in Venice during the Italian Renaissance period. He's most famous for his warning to bookkeepers: 'A person should not go to sleep at night until the debits equal the credits!'

First of all, remember that a debit is on the left side of a transaction and a credit is on the right side of a transaction. Then apply the following rules:

✔ If you want to increase an asset, you must debit the Assets account.

✔ To decrease an asset, you must credit the Assets account.

✔ To increase a liability, you credit the Liabilities account.

✔ To decrease a liability, you debit the Liabilities account.

✔ If you want to record an expense, you debit the Expense account.

✔ If you need to reduce an expense, you credit the Expense account.

✔ If you want to record income, you credit the Income account.

✔ If you want to reduce income, you debit the Income account.

Copy Table 2-1 and have it on your desk when you start keeping your own books (a bit like the chief accountant in the 'Sharing a secret' sidebar). We guarantee that the table can help to keep your debits and credits straight.

Believe it or not, identifying the difference becomes second nature as you start making regular entries in your bookkeeping system. But, to make things easier for you, Table 2-1 is a chart that bookkeepers and accountants commonly use. Everyone needs help sometimes!

Table 2-1	How Credits and Debits Impact Your Accounts	
Account Type	*Debits*	*Credits*
Assets	Increase	Decrease
Liabilities	Decrease	Increase
Income	Decrease	Increase
Expenses	Increase	Decrease

Here's an example of the practice in action. Suppose that you purchase a new desk for your office that costs £1,500. This transaction actually has two parts: you spend an asset (cash) to buy another asset (furniture). So, you must adjust two accounts in your business's books: the Cash account and the Furniture account. The transaction in a bookkeeping entry is as follows (we talk more about how to do initial bookkeeping entries in Book I, Chapter 4):

Account	*Debit*	*Credit*
Furniture	£1,500	
Cash		£1,500

To purchase a new desk for the office

In this transaction, you record the accounts impacted by the transaction. The debit increases the value of the Furniture account, and the credit decreases the value of the Cash account. For this transaction, both accounts impacted are Asset accounts. So looking at how the Balance Sheet is affected, you can see that the only changes are to the asset side of the Balance Sheet equation:

Assets = Liabilities + Capital

Furniture increase = No change to this side of the equation

Cash decrease

In this case, the books stay in balance because the exact pounds sterling amount that increases the value of your Furniture account decreases the value of your Cash account. At the bottom of any journal entry, include a brief explanation that explains the purpose of the entry. In the first example, we indicate that this entry was 'To purchase a new desk for the office'.

Practising with an example

To show you how you record a transaction that impacts both sides of the Balance Sheet equation, here's an example that records the purchase of stock. Suppose that you purchase £5,000 worth of widgets on credit. (Have you always wondered what widgets are? Can't help you. They're just commonly used in accounting examples to represent something purchased where what's purchased is of no real significance.) These new widgets add value to your Stock Asset account and also add value to your Trade Creditors account. (Remember, the Trade Creditors account is a Liability account where you track bills that need to be paid at some point in the future.) The bookkeeping transaction for your widget purchase looks as follows:

Account	*Debit*	*Credit*
Stock	£5,000	
Trade Creditors		£5,000

To purchase widgets for sale to customers

This transaction affects the Balance Sheet equation as follows:

Assets = Liabilities + Capital

Stock increases = Creditor increases + No change

In this case, the books stay in balance because both sides of the equation increase by £5,000.

Sharing a secret

Don't feel embarrassed if you forget which side the debits go on and which side the credits go on. One often-told story is of a young clerk in an accounts office plucking up the courage to ask the chief accountant, who was retiring that day, why for 30 years he had at the start of each day opened up his drawer and read the contents of a piece of paper before starting work.

The chief accountant at first was reluctant to spill the beans, but ultimately decided he had to pass on his secret – and who better than an up-and-coming clerk? Swearing the young clerk to secrecy, he took out the piece of paper and showed it to him. The paper read: 'Debit on the left and credit on the right.'

You can see from the two example transactions how double-entry bookkeeping helps to keep your books in balance – as long as you make sure that each entry into the books is balanced. Balancing your entries may look simple here, but sometimes bookkeeping entries can get complex when the transaction impacts more than two accounts.

Have a Go

In this section you can practise double-entry bookkeeping by having a go at the next few exercises. You can find the answers at the end of the chapter. Good luck! By the way, if you get stuck, remember to look back at the section 'Golden rules of bookkeeping', earlier in this chapter.

1. **Have a look at the following list and decide whether the items described belong in the Profit and Loss statement or the Balance Sheet.**

Item	*Profit and Loss or Balance Sheet?*
Telephone bill	
Purchase of motor vehicles	
Bank loan	
Petty cash	
Sales	
Materials purchased for resale	

2. **Write the journal entry for the following, as shown in the furniture example in the previous section:**

   On 15 February, you buy new products (to be sold in your shop) on credit for £3,000. How would you enter this transaction in your books?

Date	*Account*	*Debit*	*Credit*

3. **Write down the journal entry for the following transaction:**

   On 31 March, you sell £5,000 worth of goods and receive £5,000 in cash.

Date	*Account*	*Debit*	*Credit*

4. **Write down the journal entry for the following transaction:**

   On 30 June, you sell £3,000 worth of goods on credit. You don't get cash. Customers will pay you after you bill them. How do you record the sales transaction?

Date	*Account*	*Debit*	*Credit*

5. **Write down the journal entry for the following transaction:**

   On 30 September, you buy office supplies for £500 using a cheque. How do you record the transaction?

Date	*Account*	*Debit*	*Credit*

6. **In which two accounts would you record the cash purchase of products (stock)?**

7. In which two accounts would you record the purchase of furniture for your office using a credit card?

8. In which two accounts would you record the payment of rent to your landlord in cash?

9. If your accountant wants to know how many products are still on the shelves after you closed the books for an accounting period, which account would you show?

10. If a customer buys your product on credit, in which account would you record the transaction?

11. You receive an invoice for some goods received. Where do you record the invoice in the accounting system, so that you can pay it in the future?

12. Which report would you run to ensure that your accounts are in balance?

13. If you find a mistake, what type of entry would you make to get your books back in balance?

Answering the Have a Go Questions

1. **Telephone bill:** A telephone bill is usually considered to be an overhead of the business. As such, it would be included in the Profit and Loss account and classified as an expense.

   Purchase of motor vehicle: A motor vehicle is likely to be kept in the business for a long period of time, usually 3–4 years or more. This is categorised as a fixed asset and would be included in the Balance Sheet.

   Bank loan: The owner or directors of the business may have taken out a bank loan to provide funds for a large purchase. A bank loan is something that the business owes to a third party, and it's considered to be a liability. As such, it'll be shown in the Balance Sheet.

   Petty cash: Although it may be a small amount of money held in a petty cash tin, it's still considered to be an asset. It'll therefore be shown as an asset in the Balance Sheet.

   Sales: Once your business starts generating income through sales, this must be entered into a Profit and Loss account. Sales is the first category of a Profit and Loss statement; when you deduct costs from this, a profit or loss can be calculated.

   Materials purchased for resale: You may buy goods and sell them on in their present state, or you may buy materials that can be used to manufacture a product. Either way, these costs are considered to be *direct costs* (they're directly attributed to making the products you sell) and as such they need to be shown as Cost of Goods Sold in the Profit and Loss account.

2. **In this transaction, you'd debit the Purchases account to show the additional purchases made during that period and credit the Creditors account.**

   Remember, if you're increasing a liability (such as Creditors) you must credit that account. When recording an expense such as Purchases, you should debit that account. Because you're buying the goods on credit, that means you have to pay the bill at some point in the future.

Date	*Account*	*Debit*	*Credit*
15 Feb	Purchases	£3,000	
15 Feb	Creditors		£3,000

3. **As you think about the journal entry, you may not know whether something is a credit or a debit.**

As you know from our discussions earlier in the chapter, cash is an asset, and if you increase the value of an asset, you debit that account. In this question, because you received cash, you know that the Cash account needs to be a debit. So your only choice is to make the Sales account the account to be credited. This is correct because all Income accounts are increased by a credit. If you're having trouble figuring these entries out, look again at Table 2-1.

Date	Account	Debit	Credit
31 March	Cash	£5,000	
31 March	Sales		£5,000

4. In this question, rather than taking in cash, the customers are allowed to pay on credit, so you need to debit the Asset account Debtors.

(Remember: When increasing an asset, you debit that account.) You'll credit the Sales account to track the additional revenue. (When recording income, you credit the Income account.)

Date	Account	Debit	Credit
30 June	Debtors	£3,000	
30 June	Sales		£3,000

5. In this question, you're paying with a cheque, so the transaction is recorded in your Cash account.

The Cash account tracks the amount in your bank account. Any cash, cheques, debit cards or other types of transactions that are taken directly from your bank account are always entered as a credit. This is because you're decreasing an asset (say, cash); therefore, you must credit the Cash account. All money paid out for expenses is always a debit. When recording an expense, always post a debit to the Expense account.

Date	Account	Debit	Credit
30 Sept	Office Supplies	£500	
30 Sept	Cash		£500

6. In which two accounts would you record the cash purchase of products (stock)?

Record the cash spent in the Cash account. The product cost should be recorded in the Stock account, until the products are sold. A business acquires products either by buying them (retailers) or by producing them (manufacturers). After the product is sold, the product cost should be taken out of Stock and added to the Cost of Goods Sold expense account. The unsold units are left in Stock, and this Stock is checked periodically, when a physical count of the stock is done. Most businesses have an automatic stock update facility, which makes it easy to manage. If in doubt, check with an accountant first and she will be able to advise on the best method to use.

7. **Record the furniture in an Asset account called Furniture and record the credit card transaction in a Liability account called Credit Card.**

   You'd record the charge on the credit card in a Liability account called Credit Card. Cash wouldn't be paid until the credit card bill is due to be paid. Furniture is always listed as an asset on your Balance Sheet. Anything you buy that you expect to use for more than one year is a fixed asset, rather than an expense.

8. **Record the rent payment in an Expense account called Rent.**

   Record the cash used in a Current Asset account called Cash. Cash is always a Current Asset account (unless your bank account is overdrawn and then it would be considered a liability and would be shown in Current Liabilities). Rent is always an expense.

9. **Stock account.**

   The Stock account is adjusted at the end of each accounting period to show the total number of products remaining to be sold at the end of the period.

10. **Debtors Ledger.**

    This is the account that is used to track all customer purchases bought on credit. In addition to this account, which summarises all products bought on credit, you'd also need to enter the purchases into the individual accounts of each of your customers so you can bill them and track their payments.

11. **Creditors Ledger.**

    You record all unpaid invoices in Trade Creditors.

12. **You would run a Trial Balance.**

    The Trial Balance is a working tool that helps you test whether your books are in balance before you prepare your financial statements.

13. **A journal.**

    At the end of an accounting period you correct any mistakes by entering journals. These entries also need to be in balance. You'll always have at least one account that's a debit and one that's a credit.

Chapter 3

Outlining Your Financial Roadmap with a Chart of Accounts

Can you imagine what a mess your cheque book would be if you didn't record each cheque you write? Like us, you've probably forgotten to record a cheque or two on occasion, but you certainly found out quickly enough when an important payment bounced as a result. Yikes!

Keeping the books of a business can be a lot more difficult than maintaining a personal cheque book. Each business transaction must be carefully recorded to make sure that it goes into the right account. This careful bookkeeping gives you an effective tool for working out how well the business is doing financially.

As a bookkeeper, you need a roadmap to help you determine where to record all those transactions. This roadmap is called the Chart of Accounts. In this chapter, we tell you how to set up the Chart of Accounts, which includes many different accounts. We also review the types of transactions you enter into each type of account in order to track the key parts of any business – assets, liabilities, capital, income and expenses.

Getting to Know the Chart of Accounts

The *Chart of Accounts* is the roadmap that a business creates to organise its financial transactions. After all, you can't record a transaction until you know where to put it! Essentially, this chart is a list of all the accounts a business has, organised in a specific order; each account has a description that includes the type of account and the types of transactions to be entered into that account. Every business creates its own Chart of Accounts based on how the business is operated, so you're unlikely to find two businesses with the exact same Charts of Accounts.

However, you find some basic organisational and structural characteristics in all Charts of Accounts. The organisation and structure are designed around two key financial reports: the *Balance Sheet*, which shows what your business owns and what it owes, and the *Profit and Loss statement*, which shows how much money your business took in from sales and how much money it spent to generate those sales. (You can find out more about Profit and Loss statements in Book IV, Chapter 1 and Balance Sheets in Book IV, Chapter 2.)

The Chart of Accounts starts with the balance sheet accounts, which include the following:

- **Fixed assets:** Includes all accounts that show things the business owns that have a lifespan of more than 12 months, such as buildings, furniture, plant and equipment, motor vehicles and office equipment.

- **Current assets:** Includes all accounts that show things the business owns and expects to use in the next 12 months, such as cash, Trade Debtors (also known as Accounts Receivable, which is money due from customers), prepayments and stock.

- **Current liabilities:** Includes all accounts that show debts that the business must repay over the next 12 months, such as Trade Creditors (also known as Accounts Payable, which is bills from suppliers, contractors and consultants), hire purchase and other loans, value-added tax (VAT) and income/corporation tax, accruals and credit cards payable.

- **Long-term liabilities:** Includes all accounts that show debts that the business must pay over a period of time longer than the next 12 months, such as mortgages repayable and longer-term loans that are repayable.

- **Capital:** Includes all accounts that show the owners of the business and their claims against the business's assets, including any money invested in the business, any money taken out of the business and any earnings that have been reinvested in the business.

The rest of the chart is filled with Profit and Loss statement accounts, which include the following:

- ✓ **Income:** Includes all accounts that track sales of goods and services as well as revenue generated for the business by other means.

- ✓ **Cost of Goods Sold:** Includes all accounts that track the direct costs involved in selling the business's goods or services.

- ✓ **Expenses:** Includes all accounts that track expenses related to running the businesses that aren't directly tied to the sale of individual products or services.

When developing the Chart of Accounts, start by listing all the Asset accounts, the Liability accounts, the Capital accounts, the Revenue accounts and, finally, the Expense accounts. All these accounts feed into two statements: the Balance Sheet and the Profit and Loss statement.

In this chapter, we review the key account types found in most businesses, but this list isn't cast in stone. You need to develop an account list that makes the most sense for how you're operating your business and the financial information you want to track. As we explore the various accounts that make up the Chart of Accounts, we point out how the structure may differ for different types of businesses.

The Chart of Accounts is a money-management tool that helps you follow your business transactions, so set it up in a way that provides you with the financial information you need to make smart business decisions. You're probably going to tweak the accounts in your chart annually and, if necessary, you may add accounts during the year if you find something for which you want more detailed tracking. You can add accounts during the year, but don't delete accounts until the end of a 12-month reporting period. We discuss adding and deleting accounts from your books in Book III, Chapter 3.

Starting with the Balance Sheet Accounts

The first part of the Chart of Accounts is made up of Balance Sheet accounts, which break down into the following three categories:

- ✓ **Assets:** These accounts show what the business owns. Assets include cash on hand, furniture, buildings and vehicles.

- ✓ **Liabilities:** These accounts show what the business owes or, more specifically, claims that lenders have against the business's assets.

For example, mortgages on buildings and long-term loans are two common types of liabilities. Also, a mortgage (a legal charge) is a good example of a claim that the lender (bank or building society) has over a business asset (in this case, the premises being bought through the mortgage).

✔ **Capital:** These accounts show what the owners put into the business and the claims the owners have against the business's assets. For example, shareholders are business owners that have claims against the business's assets.

The Balance Sheet accounts, and the financial report they make up, are so-called because they have to *balance* out. The value of the assets must be equal to the claims made against those assets. (Remember, these claims are liabilities made by lenders and capital made by owners.)

We discuss the Balance Sheet in greater detail in Book IV, Chapter 2, including how to prepare and use it. This section, however, examines the basic components of the Balance Sheet, as reflected in the Chart of Accounts.

Tackling assets

The accounts that track what the business owns – its assets – are always the first category on the chart. The two types of asset accounts are fixed assets and current assets.

Fixed assets

Fixed assets are assets that you anticipate your business is going to use for more than 12 months. This section lists some of the most common fixed assets, starting with the key accounts related to buildings and business premises that the business owns:

✔ **Land and Buildings:** This account shows the value of the land and buildings the business owns. The initial value is based on the cost at the time of purchase, but this asset can be (and often is) revalued as property prices increase over time. Because of the virtually indestructible nature of this asset, it doesn't depreciate at a fast rate. *Depreciation* is an accounting method that reduces the value of a fixed asset over time. We discuss depreciation in Book III, Chapter 3, and in Book V, Chapter 2 where we see how the accountant determines what depreciation method to use.

✔ **Accumulated Depreciation – Land and Buildings:** This account shows the cumulative amount this asset has depreciated over its useful lifespan.

✓ **Leasehold Improvements:** This account shows the value of improvements to buildings or other facilities that a business leases rather than purchases. Frequently, when a business leases a property, it must pay for any improvements necessary in order to use that property as the business requires. For example, when a business leases a shop, the space leased is likely to be an empty shell or filled with shelving and other items that don't match the particular needs of the business. As with land and buildings, leasehold improvements depreciate as the value of the asset ages – usually over the remaining life of the lease.

✓ **Accumulated Depreciation – Leasehold Improvements:** This account tracks the cumulative amount depreciated for leasehold improvements.

The following are the types of accounts for smaller long-term assets, such as vehicles and furniture:

✓ **Vehicles:** This account shows any cars, lorries or other vehicles owned by the business. The initial value of any vehicle is listed in this account based on the total cost paid to put the vehicle into service. Sometimes this value is more than the purchase price if additions were needed to make the vehicle usable for the particular type of business. For example, when a business provides transportation for the handicapped and must add additional equipment to a vehicle in order to serve the needs of its customers, that additional equipment is added to the value of the vehicle. Vehicles also depreciate through their useful lifespan.

✓ **Accumulated Depreciation – Vehicles:** This account shows the depreciation of all vehicles owned by the business.

✓ **Furniture and Fixtures:** This account shows any furniture or fixtures purchased for use in the business. The account includes the value of all chairs, desks, store fixtures and shelving needed to operate the business. The value of the furniture and fixtures in this account is based on the cost of purchasing these items. Businesses depreciate these items during their useful lifespan.

✓ **Accumulated Depreciation – Furniture and Fixtures:** This account shows the accumulated depreciation of all furniture and fixtures.

✓ **Plant and Equipment:** This account shows equipment that was purchased for use for more than 12 months, such as process-related machinery, computers, copiers, tools and cash registers. The value of the equipment is based on the cost to purchase these items. Equipment is also depreciated to show that over time it gets used up and must be replaced.

✓ **Accumulated Depreciation – Plant and Equipment:** This account tracks the accumulated depreciation of all the equipment.

The following accounts show the fixed assets that you can't touch (accountants refer to these assets as *intangible assets*), but that still represent things of value owned by the business, such as start-up costs, patents and copyrights. The accounts that track them include:

- **Start-up Costs:** This account shows the initial start-up expenses to get the business off the ground. Many such expenses can't be set off against business profits in the first year. For example, special licences and legal fees must be written off over a number of years using a method similar to depreciation, called *amortisation*, which is also tracked.

- **Amortisation – Start-up Costs:** This account shows the accumulated amortisation of these costs during the period in which they're being written-off.

- **Patents:** This account shows the costs associated with *patents*, which are grants made by governments that guarantee to the inventor of a product or service the exclusive right to make, use and sell that product or service over a set period of time. Like start-up costs, patent costs are amortised. The value of this asset is based on the expenses the business incurs to get the right to patent its product.

- **Amortisation – Patents:** This account shows the accumulated amortisation of a business's patents.

- **Copyrights:** This account shows the costs incurred to establish *copyrights*, the legal rights given to an author, playwright, publisher or any other distributor of a publication or production for a unique work of literature, music, drama or art.

- **Goodwill:** This account is needed only if a business buys another business for more than the actual value of its tangible assets. Goodwill reflects the intangible value of this purchase for things like business reputation, store locations, customer base and other items that increase the value of the business bought. The value of goodwill isn't everlasting and so, like other intangible assets, must be amortised.

- **Research and Development:** This account shows the investment the business has made in future products and services, which may not see the light of day for several years. These costs are written off (amortised) over the life of the products and services as and when they reach the marketplace.

If you hold a lot of assets that aren't of great value, you can also set up an Other Assets account to show those assets that don't have significant business value. Any asset you show in the Other Assets account that you later want to show individually can be shifted to its own account. We discuss adjusting the Chart of Accounts in Book III, Chapter 3.

Current assets

Current assets are the key assets that your business uses up within a 12-month period and are likely not to be there the next year. The accounts that reflect current assets on the Chart of Accounts are

- ✓ **Current account:** This account is the business's primary bank account for operating activities, such as depositing receipts and paying expenses. Some businesses have more than one account in this category; for example, a business with many divisions may have an account for each division.

- ✓ **Deposit account:** This account is used for surplus cash. Any cash not earmarked for an immediate plan is deposited in an interest-earning savings account. In this way, the cash earns interest while the business decides what to do with it.

- ✓ **Cash on Hand:** This account is used to record any cash kept at retail stores or in the office. In retail stores, cash must be kept in registers in order to provide change to customers. In the office, petty cash is often kept for immediate cash needs that pop up from time to time. This account helps you keep track of the cash held outside the various bank and deposit accounts.

- ✓ **Trade Debtors:** This account shows the customers who still owe you money if you offer your products or services to customers on credit (by which we mean *your* own credit system).

    Trade Debtors isn't used to show purchases made on other types of credit cards, because your business gets paid directly by banks, not customers, when customers use credit cards. Check out Book II, Chapter 2 to read more about this scenario and the corresponding type of account.

- ✓ **Stock:** This account shows the value of the products you have on hand to sell to your customers. The value of the assets in this account varies depending upon the way you decide to track the flow of stock into and out of the business. We discuss stock valuation and recording in greater detail in Book II, Chapter 3.

- ✓ **Prepayments:** This account shows goods or services you pay for in advance: the payment is credited as it gets used up each month. For example, say that you prepay your property insurance on a building that you own one year in advance. Each month you reduce the amount that you prepaid by one-twelfth as the prepayment is used up. We discuss prepayments in Book III, Chapter 3.

Depending upon the type of business you're setting up, you may have other current Asset accounts to set up. For example, say that you're starting a service business in consulting. You're likely to have an account called Consulting Fees for tracking cash collected for those services.

Laying out your liabilities

After you deal with assets, the next stop on the bookkeeping journey is the accounts that show what your business owes to others. These others can include suppliers from whom you buy products or supplies, financial institutions from which you borrow money and anyone else who lends money to your business. Like assets, you lump liabilities into current liabilities and long-term liabilities.

Current liabilities

Current liabilities are debts due in the next 12 months. Some of the most common types of current liabilities accounts that appear on the Chart of Accounts are as follows:

- ✔ **Trade Creditors:** This account shows money that the business owes to suppliers, contractors and consultants that must be paid in less than 12 months. Most of these liabilities must be paid in 30 to 90 days from initial invoicing.

- ✔ **Value-Added Tax (VAT):** This account shows your VAT liability. You may not think of VAT as a liability, but because the business collects the tax from the customer and doesn't pay it immediately to HM Customs & Revenue, the taxes collected become a liability. Of course you're entitled to offset the VAT that the business has been charged on its purchases before making a net payment. A business usually collects VAT throughout the month and then pays the net amount due on a quarterly basis. We discuss paying VAT in greater detail in Book III, Chapter 1.

- ✔ **Accrued Payroll Taxes:** This account shows payroll taxes, such as Pay As You Earn (PAYE) and National Insurance, collected from employees and the business itself, which have to be paid over to HM Revenue & Customs. Businesses don't have to pay these taxes over immediately and may pay payroll taxes on a monthly basis. We discuss how to handle payroll taxes in Book III, Chapter 2.

- ✔ **Credit Cards Payable:** This account shows all credit card accounts for which the business is liable. Most businesses use credit cards as short-term debt and pay them off completely at the end of each month, but some smaller businesses carry credit card balances over a longer period of time. In Chart of Accounts, you can set up one Credit Card Payable account, but you may want to set up a separate account for each card your business holds to improve your ability to track credit card usage.

The way you set up your current liabilities – and how many individual accounts you establish – depends upon the level of detail that you want to use to track each type of liability.

Long-term liabilities

Long-term liabilities are debts due in more than 12 months. The number of long-term liability accounts you maintain on your Chart of Accounts depends on your debt structure. For example, if you've several different loans, then set up an account for each one. The most common type of long-term liability accounts is Loans Payable. This account tracks any long-term loans, such as a mortgage on your business building. Most businesses have separate Loans Payable accounts for each of their long-term loans. For example, you can have *Loans Payable – Mortgage Bank* for your building and *Loans Payable – Vehicles* for your vehicle loan.

In addition to any separate long-term debt that you may want to track in its own account, you may also want to set up an account called *Other Liabilities*. You can use this account to track types of debt that are so insignificant to the business that you don't think they need their own accounts.

Controlling the capital

Every business is owned by somebody. *Capital accounts* track owners' contributions to the business as well as their share of ownership. For a limited company, ownership is tracked by the sale of individual shares because each stockholder owns a portion of the business. In smaller businesses owned by one person or a group of people, capital is tracked using capital and drawing accounts. Here are the basic capital accounts that appear in the Chart of Accounts:

- ✔ **Ordinary Share Capital:** This account reflects the value of outstanding ordinary shares sold to investors. A business calculates this value by multiplying the number of shares issued by the value of each share of stock. Only limited companies need to establish this account.

- ✔ **Retained Earnings:** This account tracks the profits or losses accumulated since a business opened. At the end of each year, the profit or loss calculated on the Profit and Loss statement is used to adjust the value of this account. For example, if a business made a £100,000 profit after tax in the past year, the Retained Earnings account is increased by that amount; if the business lost £100,000, that amount is subtracted from this account. Any dividends paid to shareholders reduce the profit figure transferred to Retained Earnings each year.

- ✔ **Capital:** This account is only necessary for small, unincorporated businesses, such as sole traders or partnerships. The Capital account reflects the amount of initial money the business owner contributed to the business as well as any additional contributions made after initial start-up. The value of this account is based on cash contributions and other assets contributed by the business owner, such as equipment, vehicles or buildings. When a small company has several different partners, each partner gets his own Capital account to track his contributions.

✔ **Drawing:** This account is only necessary for businesses that aren't incorporated. The Drawing account tracks any money that a business owner takes out of the business. If the business has several partners, each partner gets his own Drawing account to track what he takes out of the business.

Keeping an Eye on the Profit and Loss Statement Accounts

The Profit and Loss statement is made up of two types of accounts:

✔ **Expenses:** These accounts track all costs that a business incurs in order to keep itself afloat.

✔ **Revenue:** These accounts track all income coming into the business, including sales, interest earned on savings and any other methods used to generate income.

The bottom line of the Profit and Loss statement shows whether your business made a profit or a loss for a specified period of time. We discuss how to prepare and use a Profit and Loss statement in greater detail in Book IV, Chapter 1.

This section examines the various accounts that make up the Profit and Loss statement portion of the Chart of Accounts.

Recording the profit you make

Accounts that show revenue coming into the business are first up in the Profit and Loss statement section of the Chart of Accounts. If you choose to offer discounts or accept returns, then that activity also falls within the revenue grouping. The most common income accounts are

✔ **Sales of Goods or Services:** This account, which appears at the top of every Profit and Loss statement, shows all the money that the business earns selling its products, services or both.

✓ **Sales Discounts:** This account shows any reductions to the full price of merchandise (necessary because most businesses offer discounts to encourage sales).

✓ **Sales Returns:** This account shows transactions related to returns, when a customer returns a product.

When you examine a Profit and Loss statement from a business other than the one you own or are working for, you usually see the following accounts summarised as one line item called *Revenue* or *Net Revenue*. Because not all income is generated by sales of products or services, other income accounts that may appear on a Chart of Accounts include the following:

✓ **Interest Income:** This account shows any income earned by collecting interest on a business's savings accounts. If the business lends money to employees or to another business and earns interest on that money, that interest is recorded in this account as well.

✓ **Other Income:** This account shows income that a business generates from a source other than its primary business activity. For example, a business that encourages recycling and earns income from the items recycled records that income in this account.

Recording the cost of sales

Of course, before you can sell a product, you must spend money to buy or make that product. The type of account used to track the money spent on products that are sold is called a Cost of Goods Sold account. The most common cost of goods sold accounts are

✓ **Purchases:** This account shows the purchases of all items you plan to sell.

✓ **Purchase Discount:** This account shows the discounts you may receive from suppliers when you pay for your purchase quickly. For example, a business may give you a 2 per cent discount on your purchase when you pay the bill in 10 days rather than wait until the end of the 30-day payment period.

✓ **Purchase Returns:** This account shows the value of any returns when you're unhappy with a product you bought.

✓ **Freight Charges:** This account shows any charges related to shipping items that you purchase for later sale. You may or may not want to keep this detail.

✓ **Other Sales Costs:** This account is a catch-all account for anything that doesn't fit into one of the other Cost of Goods Sold accounts.

Acknowledging the other costs

Expense accounts take the cake for the longest list of individual accounts. Anything you spend on the business that can't be tied directly to the sale of an individual product falls under the Expense account category. For example, advertising a sale isn't directly tied to the sale of any one product, so the costs associated with advertising fall under the Expense account category.

The Chart of Accounts mirrors your business operations, so you decide how much detail you want to keep in your expense accounts. Most businesses have expenses that are unique to their operations, so your list is likely to be longer than the one we present here. However, you also may find that you don't need some of these accounts. Small businesses typically have expense headings that mirror those required by HM Revenue & Customs on its self-assessment returns.

On your Chart of Accounts, the Expense accounts don't have to appear in any specific order, so we list them alphabetically. The most common Expense accounts are

- ✔ **Advertising:** This account shows all expenses involved in promoting a business or its products. Expenditure on newspaper, television, magazine and radio advertising is recorded here, as well as any costs incurred to print flyers and mailings to customers. Also, when a business participates in community events such as cancer walks or craft fairs, associated costs appear in this account.

- ✔ **Amortisation:** This account is similar to the Depreciation account (see later in this list) and shows the ongoing monthly charge for the current financial year for all your intangible assets.

- ✔ **Bank Service Charges:** This account shows any charges made by a bank to service a business's bank accounts.

- ✔ **Depreciation:** This account shows the ongoing monthly depreciation charge for the current financial year for all your fixed assets – buildings, cars, vans, furniture and so on. Of course, when the individual depreciation values are large for each fixed asset category, you may open up individual depreciation accounts.

- ✔ **Dues and Subscriptions:** This account shows expenses related to business-club membership or subscriptions to magazines for the business.

- ✔ **Equipment Rental:** This account records expenses related to renting equipment for a short-term project; for example, a business that needs to rent a van to pick up new fixtures for its shop records that van rental in this account.

✔ **Insurance:** This account shows insurance costs. Many businesses break this account down into several accounts such as Building Insurance, Public Liability Insurance and Car Insurance.

✔ **Legal and Accounting:** This account shows the cost of legal or accounting advice.

✔ **Miscellaneous Expenses:** This account is a catch-all account for expenses that don't fit into one of a business's established accounts. If certain miscellaneous expenses occur frequently, a business may choose to add an account to the Chart of Accounts and move related expenses into that new account by subtracting all related transactions from the Miscellaneous Expenses account and adding them to the new account. With this shuffle, you need to carefully balance out the adjusting transaction to avoid any errors or double counting.

✔ **Office Expenses:** This account shows any items purchased in order to run an office. For example, office supplies such as paper and pens or business cards fit in this account. As with miscellaneous expenses, a business may choose to track certain office expense items in its own accounts. For example, when you find that your office is using a lot of copy paper and you want to track that separately, set up a Copy Paper Expense account. Just be sure that you really need the detail because a large number of accounts can get unwieldy and hard to manage.

✔ **Payroll Taxes:** This account records any taxes paid related to employee payroll, such as PAYE, Statutory Sick Pay (SSP) and maternity/paternity pay.

✔ **Postage:** This account shows any expenditure on stamps, express package shipping and other shipping. If your business does a large amount of shipping through suppliers such as UPS or Federal Express, you may want to track that spending in separate accounts for each supplier. This option is particularly helpful for small businesses that sell over the Internet or through mail-order sales.

✔ **Profit (or Loss) on Disposal of Fixed Assets:** This account records any profit when a business sells a fixed asset, such as a car or furniture. Make sure that you only record revenue remaining after subtracting the accumulated depreciation from the original cost of the asset.

✔ **Rent:** This account records rental costs for a business's office or retail space.

✔ **Salaries and Wages:** This account shows any money paid to employees as salary or wages.

✔ **Telephone:** This account shows all business expenses related to the telephone and telephone calls.

- ✔ **Travel and Entertainment:** This account records any expenditure on travel or entertainment for business purposes. To keep a close watch some businesses separate these expenses into several accounts, such as Travel and Entertainment – Meals; Travel and Entertainment – Travel; and Travel and Entertainment – Entertainment.

- ✔ **Utilities:** This account shows utility costs, such as electricity, gas and water.

- ✔ **Vehicles:** This account shows expenses related to the operation of business vehicles.

Setting Up Your Chart of Accounts

You can use all the lists of accounts provided in this chapter to set up your business's own Chart of Accounts. No secret method exists for creating your own chart – just make a list of the accounts that apply to your business.

When first setting up your Chart of Accounts, don't panic if you can't think of every type of account you may need for your business. You can easily add to the Chart of Accounts at any time. Just add the account to the list and distribute the revised list to any employees who use the Chart of Accounts for recording transactions into the bookkeeping system. (Employees who code invoices or other transactions and indicate the account to which those transactions are to be recorded need a copy of your Chart of Accounts as well, even if they aren't involved in actual bookkeeping.)

The Chart of Accounts usually includes at least three columns:

- ✔ **Account:** Lists the account names.

- ✔ **Type:** Lists the type of account – Asset, Liability, Capital, Income, Cost of Goods Sold or Expense.

- ✔ **Description:** Contains a description of the type of transaction that is to be recorded in the account.

Many businesses also assign numbers to the accounts, to be used for coding charges. If your company uses a computerised system, the computer automatically assigns the account number. For example, Sage 50 Accounts provides you with a standard Chart of Accounts that you can adapt to suit your business. Sage also allows you to completely customise your Chart of

Accounts to codes that suit your business; however, most businesses find that the standard Chart of Accounts is sufficient. A typical numbering system is as follows:

- ✔ Asset accounts: 0010 to 1999
- ✔ Liability accounts: 2000 to 2999
- ✔ Capital accounts: 3000 to 3999
- ✔ Sales and Cost of Goods Sold accounts: 4000 to 6999
- ✔ Expense accounts: 7000 to 9999

This numbering system matches the one used by some computerised accounting systems, so you can easily make the transition if you decide to automate your books using a computerised accounting system in the future.

One major advantage of a computerised accounting system is the number of different Charts of Accounts that have been developed based on the type of business you plan to run. When you get your computerised system, which-ever accounting software you decide to use, you can review the list of chart options included with that software for the type of business you run, delete any accounts you don't want and add any new accounts that fit your busi-ness plan.

If you're setting up your Chart of Accounts manually, be sure to leave a lot of room between accounts to add new accounts. For example, number your Trade Debtors account 1100 and then start your bank accounts from 1200. If you've a number of bank accounts, you can number them 1210, 1220, 1230 and so on. That leaves you plenty of room to add new bank accounts as well as petty cash. The same applies to your revenue accounts: you need to allow plenty of room in your codes for your business to grow. For example, 4000 may be Retail Sales from your shop, but you may start to develop an online presence and need a code to track online sales, perhaps 4050. You can add further codes for foreign online sales as opposed to UK online sales. Don't be too rigid in your choice of codes – leave as large a gap as possible between codes to give you maximum flexibility.

Figure 3-1 is a sample Chart of Accounts developed using Sage 50 Accounts, the accounts package we use throughout this book. This sample chart high-lights the standard overhead accounts that Sage has already set up for you.

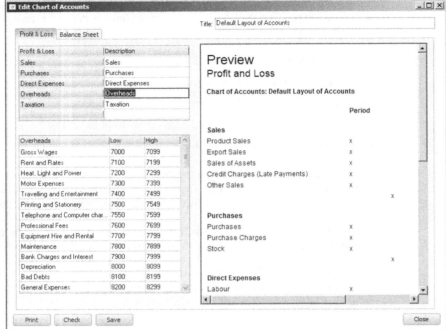

Figure 3-1:
The top portion of a sample Chart of Accounts showing overheads.

Have a Go

1. **Describe three types of current assets and state in which financial statement you'd find them.**

2. **In which financial statement would you expect to see expenses?**

   List five different types of expenses.

3. **In which financial statement would you find current liabilities?**

   Describe some of the entries you might find there.

4. **In which financial statement would you expect to find capital?**

   As well as capital introduced by the owner, what else would you expect to see there?

5. **Think about the current assets you need to track for your business, and write down the accounts in this section.**

6. **Think about the Fixed Asset accounts you need to track for your business, and write down the accounts for those assets in this section.**

7. Think about the Current Liabilities accounts you need to track for your business, and write down the accounts for those liabilities in this section.

8. Think about the Long-term Liabilities accounts you need to track for your business, and write down the accounts for those liabilities in this section.

9. Think about the Capital accounts you need to track for your business, and write down the accounts you need in this section.

10. Think about the Revenue accounts you need to track for your business, and write down those accounts in this section.

11. Think about the Cost of Goods Sold accounts you need to track for your business, and write down those accounts in this section.

12. Think about the Expense accounts you need to track for your business, and write down those accounts in this section.

Answering the Have a Go Questions

1. **You can find current assets in the Balance Sheet.**

   The usual types of current assets are

   - Stock
   - Debtors
   - Cash at bank
   - Cash in hand
   - Prepayments

   See the previous section 'Current assets' for descriptions.

2. **You can find expenses in the Profit and Loss statement.**

   Typical expenses can be

   - Wages
   - Office stationery
   - Telephone costs
   - Rent and rates
   - Heat, light and power
   - Fuel expenses

   Find more examples in 'Acknowledging the other costs'.

3. **You can find current liabilities in the Balance Sheet.**

Typical items include:

- Trade Creditors (suppliers you owe money to)
- Accrued expenses (costs you've incurred but you may not have an invoice for)
- HM Revenue & Customs payments due such as PAYE/NI and VAT
- Overdrafts

We go into more detail in the section 'Laying out your liabilities'.

4. **You find capital in the Balance Sheet.**

As well as capital introduced, you also find *drawings* (cash taken out of the business for personal use), dividends and *retained profits* (profits made from previous periods, but retained in the business). If your business is structured as a company, then you also have ordinary share capital, which reflects each individual's share of the company.

5–12. **The remaining exercises in this chapter don't have right or wrong answers.**

You need to set up your Chart of Accounts with accounts that match how your business operates.

Chapter 4

Looking at Ledgers

*I*n this chapter, we discuss the accounting ledgers. You meet the Sales Ledger, Purchase Ledger and Cashbook and discover how they interact with the Nominal Ledger. We tell you how to develop entries for the ledger and also how to enter (or post) them from the original sources. In addition, we explain how you can change already posted information or correct entries in the Nominal Ledger.

The most common ledgers include:

✔ **Sales Ledger:** This tracks day-to-day sales, and contains the accounts of debtors (customers).

✔ **Purchases Ledger:** This tracks day-to-day purchases, and contains the accounts of creditors (suppliers).

✔ **Nominal Ledger:** Sometimes called the General Ledger, this ledger is used for all the remaining accounts, such as income and expense accounts as well as including the Purchase Ledger account balance and the Sales Ledger account balance. There are also accounts for items such as stock, value-added tax (VAT) and loans. The Nominal Ledger basically contains all the transactions that a business has ever made.

✔ **Cashbook:** This tracks the daily use of cash.

If you're using a computerised accounting system, your ledgers are integrated (see Figure 4-1). This means that as you enter transactions into, say, your Sales Ledger, the Nominal Ledger is automatically updated. The same applies to entries that are made via your Cashbook or Purchase Ledger.

Your computerised system follows the principles of double-entry bookkeeping; so for every debit, you have a corresponding credit.

Keeping watch: The eyes and ears of a business

The Nominal Ledger serves as the figurative eyes and ears of bookkeepers and accountants who want to know what financial transactions have taken place historically in a business. By reading the Nominal Ledger – not exactly interesting reading unless you love numbers – you can see, account by account, every transaction that has taken place in the business.

The Nominal Ledger is the master summary of your business. You can find all the transactions that ever occurred in the history of the business in the Nominal Ledger account. In just one place you can find transactions that impact Cash, Stock, Trade Debtors (Accounts Receivable), Trade Creditors (Accounts Payable) and any other account included in your business's Chart of Accounts. (See Book I, Chapter 3 for more information about setting up the Chart of Accounts and the kinds of transactions you can find in each account.)

Figure 4-1: Showing how all ledgers are integrated in a computerised system.

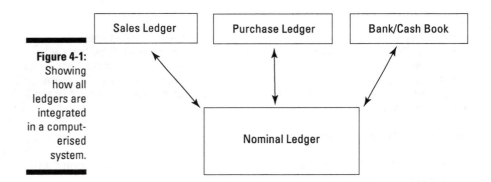

Developing Entries for the Ledger

In the next section, we take you through the process of entering transactions on each of the ledgers, and we look at the bookkeeping entries for all transactions. You can practise your double-entry bookkeeping at the end of this chapter, in the 'Have a Go' section. Because most people now use computerised accounting systems, we demonstrate the types of reports and documents that you can run off to prove your transactions. We use Sage 50 to demonstrate these reports.

You enter your transactions using source documents or other data. Source documents tend to be the following:

- ✔ Sales invoices (unless automatically generated from your accounts program)
- ✔ Sales credit notes
- ✔ Purchase invoices from your suppliers
- ✔ Purchase credit notes
- ✔ Cheque payments
- ✔ Cash receipts (from your paying-in book)
- ✔ Remittance advice slips received from customers, which usually accompany the cheque or BACs receipt confirmation
- ✔ Bank statements (to pick up other bank payments and receipts)

Posting Sales Invoices

Have a look at the bookkeeping that occurs when you post some sales invoices. Assume that the invoices aren't paid straight away; they're credit sales.

Using the double-entry bookkeeping rules from Book I, Chapter 2, you know the following:

If you want to record income, you credit the Income account.

If you want to increase an asset, you debit the Asset account.

So, if you raise an invoice for £200 (ignoring VAT for the moment), then the following bookkeeping takes place:

	Debit	Credit
Debtors	£200	
Sales		£200

Every time you post a sales invoice, this same double entry takes place.

A computerised accounting system does the double entry for you, but you still need to understand the bookkeeping rules, so that you can create journals if corrections are necessary at any point in the future. See the section 'Adjusting for Nominal Ledger Errors', later in this chapter.

In Figure 4-2, we show you the Customer Invoices Daybook for Sweet Dreams (a fictitious company). This daybook simply provides a list of sales invoices that have been entered in Sage. If you were still operating a manual system, the same information would be reflected in the Sales journal.

Make sure that you understand the bookkeeping here: you make the following double entry based on the information shown in the Customer Invoice Daybook as shown in Figure 4-2:

Account	Debit	Credit
Trade Debtors	£960	
Sales		£800
VAT		£160

Date: 22/10/2014   **Sweet Dreams**   Page: 1
Time: 13:13:46
Day Books: Customer Invoices (Detailed)

Date From:	01/06/2014							Customer From:		
Date To:	30/06/2014							Customer To:	ZZZZZZZZ	
Transaction From:	1							N/C From:		
Transaction To:	99,999,999							N/C To:	99999999	
Dept From:	0									
Dept To:	999									

Tran No.	Type	Date	A/C Ref	N/C	Inv Ref	Dept.	Details	Net Amount	Tax Amount	T/C	Gross Amount	V	B
1	SI	01/06/2014	SMITHS	4000	243	0	Sweet sales	200.00	40.00	T1	240.00	N	-
2	SI	01/06/2014	CHARLIES	4000	244	0	Machine refilled	300.00	60.00	T1	360.00	N	-
3	SI	03/06/2014	PERRYP	4000	245	0	Tuck shop stock	100.00	20.00	T1	120.00	N	-
4	SI	05/06/2014	JONESJ	4000	246	0	Machine refilled	200.00	40.00	T1	240.00	N	-
							Totals:	800.00	160.00		960.00		

Page 1 of 1   100%

Figure 4-2: Showing the Customer Invoices Daybook.

Note that this entry is balanced. You increase the Trade Debtors account to show that customers owe the business money because they bought items on credit. You increase the Sales account to show that even though no cash changed hands, the business in Figure 4-2 took in revenue. You collect cash when the customers pay their bills.

You give each transaction a reference to its original source point. For example, the first invoice listed for Smith's account has the invoice reference 243. If you went to the sales invoice file and found invoice no. 243, you'd have the original source of the transaction in your hands. This is very useful when it comes to customer queries, because you can immediately locate the invoice and check the details.

As an aside, Sage 50 also gives each transaction a unique transaction number. It's the first number in the first column of each report. If you need to make a correction to a transaction, this number is the way you'd identify that specific transaction and be able to amend it.

Posting Purchase Invoices

Your business needs to account for the invoices received from its suppliers. Often, you won't pay these invoices straight away, so you post them into the Creditors Ledger (sometimes known as the Suppliers Ledger).

Using the double-entry rules as discussed in Book I, Chapter 2, you then get the following double entry:

To increase a liability, you credit the Liabilities account.

If you want to increase an asset, you debit the Asset account.

Because you're recording a liability when you post invoices that you owe money for, you credit the Creditors Ledger. Hence, you must make the opposite debit entry to the Nominal account to which the invoice has been coded; for example, Materials Purchased.

Have a look at some purchase invoices that have been entered for Sweet Dreams. See Figure 4-3.

In Figure 4-3 Sweet Dreams has posted four purchase invoices for the gross value of £1,175.

Because this report is a Sage daybook report, you can see the nominal code that Sweet Dreams's bookkeeper, Kate, used when she entered the invoices. In this case, 5000 is the nominal code used for all invoices, which happens to be the nominal code for the Materials Purchased account.

Date: 22/10/2014
Time: 13:15:07

Sweet Dreams

Day Books: Supplier Invoices (Detailed)

Page: 1

Date From: 01/06/2014
Date To: 30/06/2014

Supplier From:
Supplier To: ZZZZZZZZ

Transaction From: 1
Transaction To: 99,999,999

N/C From:
N/C To: 99999999

Dept From: 0
Dept To: 999

Tran No.	Type	Date	A/C Ref	N/C	Inv Ref	Dept	Details	Net Amount	Tax Amount	T/C	Gross Amount	V	B
6	PI	03/06/2014	HELENS	5000	2	0	Misc items	208.33	41.67	T1	250.00	N	-
14	PI	01/06/2014	HENRYS	5000	3	0	Sweets	625.00	125.00	T1	750.00	N	-
15	PI	05/06/2014	BARRYS	5000	4	0	Boxes of sweets	83.33	16.67	T1	100.00	N	-
16	PI	08/06/2014	HELENS	5000	5	0	Paper	62.50	12.50	T1	75.00	N	-
							Totals	979.16	195.84		1,175.00		

Page 1 of 1 100%

Figure 4-3: Supplier Invoices Daybook for Sweet Dreams.

So, the double entry that Kate made for these combined transactions is as follows:

Account	*Debit*	*Credit*
Materials Purchased	£979.16	
VAT	£195.84	
Creditors Ledger		£1,175.00

Like the entry for the Sales account, this entry is balanced. The Trade Creditors account is increased to show that money is due to suppliers, and the Materials Purchased account is also increased to show that more supplies were purchased.

Note: An invoice reference number is shown on the daybook report. This relates to the sequential invoice number given to each purchase invoice. For example, the invoice posted for Henry's has a reference of 3. If you were to select the purchase invoice file and locate invoice number 3, you'd find the original purchase invoice for Henry's. This is especially important in the event of a supplier query. It provides an easy method of locating the exact invoice.

Entering Items into the Nominal Ledger

Many transactions don't impact the Sales Ledger or the Purchase Ledger, but they still have to be accounted for. The Nominal Ledger, as stated before, is the master ledger and is a place where all transactions can be found.

Figure 4-4 shows an example of a Nominal Ledger Daybook from Sage. You can see two separate transactions noted here, each with a debit entry and a credit entry.

Date:	22/10/2014				Sweet Dreams				Page:	1		
Time:	13:15:47				Day Books: Nominal Ledger							
Date From:	01/06/2014							N/C From:				
Date To:	30/06/2014							N/C To:	99999999			
Transaction From:	1							Dept From:	0			
Transaction To:	99,999,999							Dept To:	999			
No	Type	N/C	Date	Ref	Ex.Ref	Details	Dept	T/C	Debit	Credit	V	B
11	JC	1200	10/06/2014	TRANS		Paying credit card	0	T9		150.00	-	N
12	JD	1240	10/06/2014	TRANS		Paying credit card	0	T9	150.00		-	N
19	JD	0050	08/06/2014	Van		Van Purchased	0	T9	10,000.00		-	-
20	JC	3010	08/06/2014	Van		Van Purchased	0	T9		10,000.00	-	-
								Totals:	10,150.00	10,150.00		

Page 1 of 1   100%

Figure 4-4:
Showing
the Nominal
Daybook
report for
Sweet
Dreams

Neither of these transactions has impacted the Purchase Ledger or the Sales Ledger, which is why they show up here.

The first two lines show a transfer between two different bank accounts. Basically, a payment has been made from account 1200, which happens to be the Current account, and the payment has been made to 1240, which is a Credit Card account.

The second two entries show a journal that was carried out by Kate, the bookkeeper for Sweet Dreams. They show a van, which was purchased for the business using capital introduced by the owner of the company.

Cashbook Transactions

Everyone likes to be paid, and that includes suppliers. You use the Cashbook to post all transactions that relate to payments or receipts to the business.

Sage uses separate daybooks for Customer Receipts and Other Income Received, as well as Supplier Payments and Other Payments Made.

This section shows you copies of all the relevant daybooks and the bookkeeping entries that are associated with each daybook.

Bank payments

Businesses always make payments to people other than suppliers. For example, they might have salaries, loans, interest and other types of charges to pay. These payments are made from the Bank account or Cashbook, but impact the Nominal Ledger, as part of the double-entry process.

We demonstrate some bank payments that have been made by Sweet Dreams in Figure 4-5. You'll notice that we've printed the Bank Payments Daybook report. If you'd made any payments using cash, you'd also have to print out the Cash Payments Daybook report.

Date: 22/10/2014   **Sweet Dreams**   Page: 1
Time: 13:18:20   **Day Books: Bank Payments (Detailed)**

Date From:	01/06/2014							Bank From:	
Date To:	30/06/2014							Bank To:	99999999
Transaction From:	1							N/C From:	
Transaction To:	99,999,999							N/C To:	99999999
Dept From:	0								
Dept To:	999								

Bank: 1200   Currency: Pound Sterling   Bank Rec.

No	Type	N/C	Date	Ref	Details	Dept	Net £	Tax £	T/C	Gross £	V	B	Date
8	BP	7100	01/06/2014	1065	Rent	0	800.00	0.00	T9	800.00	-	N	
10	BP	7003	04/06/2014	1068	Salaries paid	0	350.00	0.00	T9	350.00	-	N	
					Totals £		1,150.00	0.00		1,150.00			

Page 1 of 1   100%

Figure 4-5:
Bank
Payments
Daybook
report.

You can see that Sweet Dreams has paid rent and some salaries. These payments have been made from the Bank account. You can see from the report that the Bank account nominal code used is 1200 (which is the default Bank account for Sage). You can also see that the nominal codes used for Rent and Salaries are 7100 and 7003 respectively.

The double-entry bookkeeping that has taken place is as follows:

Nominal Code	Account	Debit	Credit
7100	Rent	£800	
7003	Salaries	£350	
1200	Bank		£1,150

This Nominal Ledger summary balances out at £1,150 each for the debits and credits. The Bank account is decreased to show the cash outlay; the Rent and Salaries Expense accounts are increased to show the additional expenses.

Looking at the Bank Payments Daybook, you can also see a reference column. The numbers in the reference column refer to the cheque number used to make that payment. For example, cheque number 1065 was used to pay the rent.

Whether you use a computerised or a manual system, always use references to point towards the original source of the data. In this example, a cheque stub reference has been used.

Supplier payments

When businesses pay their suppliers, unless they've paid cash immediately, the two accounts that are affected are the Supplier (Creditors) Ledger and the Bank account.

Figure 4-6 shows an example of the Supplier Payments Daybook for Sweet Dreams.

You can see from the daybook report that Sweet Dreams has paid two suppliers in June 2014. It's paid Helen's £250 and Henry's £500. Therefore, Sweet Dreams has taken a total of £750 out of the bank to pay suppliers. The double entry for these two transactions can be summarised as follows:

Nominal Code	Account	Debit	Credit
2100	Creditors	£750	
1200	Bank		£750

Figure 4-6:
Supplier
Payment
Daybook.

Date:	22/10/2014		Sweet Dreams					Page:	1	
Time:	13:19:41		Day Books: Supplier Payments (Detailed)							

Date From:	01/06/2014						Bank From:			
DateTo:	30/06/2014						Bank To:	99999999		
Transaction From:	1						Supplier From:			
Transaction To:	99,999,999						Supplier To:	ZZZZZZZ		

Bank	1200	Currency	Pound Sterling							Bank Rec
No	Type	A/C	Date	Ref	Details	Net £	Tax £	T/C	Gross £ V B	Date
9	PP	HELENS	03/06/2014	1067	Purchase Payment	250.00	0.00	T9	250.00 -	N
			- 03/06/2014	2	£ 250.00 (£ 250.00) to PI 6					
13	PP	HENRYS	03/06/2014	1066	Purchase Payment	500.00	0.00	T9	500.00 -	N
			- 03/06/2014	1	£ 500.00 (£ 500.00) to PI 5					
					Totals £	750.00	0.00		750.00	

Page 1 of 1   100%

You can see that the bank has been credited, because you're reducing an asset (that is, cash), and the Creditors Account has been debited, because you're reducing a liability. Think back to your double-entry rules if you're not sure.

Bank receipts

A business receives money from a variety of sources, not just from its customers. For example, in a new business, the owners of the business may decide to introduce capital into the business to help pay the bills for the first few months until sales pick up. Perhaps they receive start-up grants, or receive interest from savings accounts. Figure 4-7 shows the daybook report for Bank Received for Sweet Dreams.

You may have noticed that some cash sales are listed here. This is money taken at the tills and paid directly into the bank account for Sweet Dreams. The owner has also introduced £15,000 of capital.

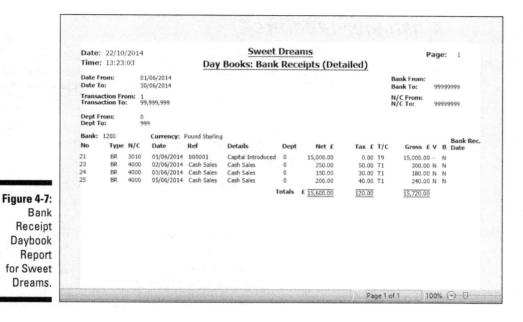

Figure 4-7:
Bank
Receipt
Daybook
Report
for Sweet
Dreams.

The transactions that are posted to the Nominal Ledger can be summarised as follows:

Nominal Code	Account	Debit	Credit
1200	Bank	£15,720	
4000	Sales		£600
3050	Capital Introduced		£15,000
2201	VAT		£120

Both sides total £15,720, so the books are in balance.

Once again, you can apply double-entry rules. You debit the bank, because an asset (the bank) is being increased, due to the money being paid in. You credit the Sales account because it's an Income account, and you also credit the Capital Introduced account, because the amount is a liability for the business. The reason is that the business technically owes the owner this money. You also credit VAT, because VAT is a liability and is money owed to HM Revenue & Customs.

Customer receipts

Obviously, you hope to be paid quite often! If you're doing a good job as a bookkeeper, you know how much money is owed to the business at any one time. You also know who's behind with their payments. We discuss how you can find out who owes you money in Book II, Chapter 2.

Receipts from customers can come in several formats. They're cash received, cheques received or a BACs payment received directly into your bank account. Either way, the money has to be accounted for.

Figure 4-8 shows an example of a Customer Receipts Daybook for Sweet Dreams.

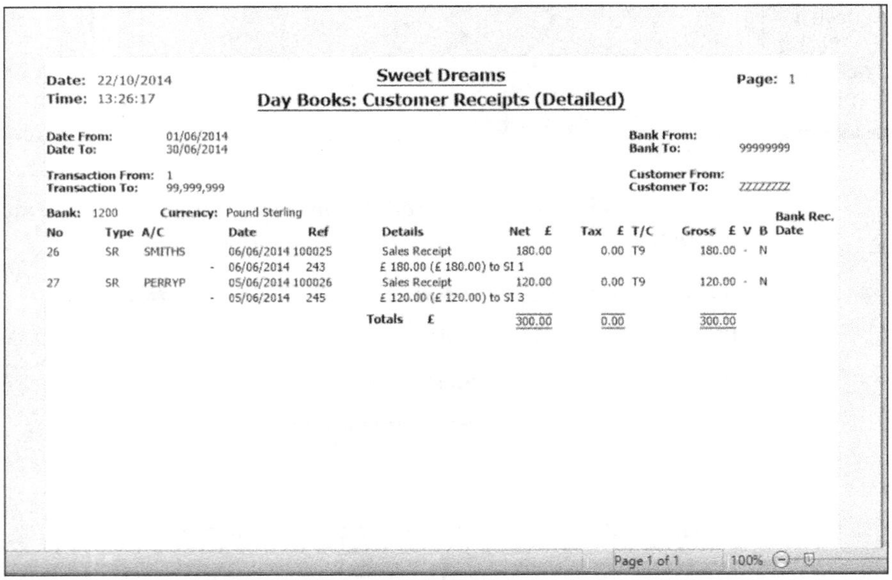

Date: 22/10/2014
Time: 13:26:17

Sweet Dreams

Day Books: Customer Receipts (Detailed)

Page: 1

Date From: 01/06/2014
Date To: 30/06/2014

Bank From:
Bank To: 99999999

Transaction From: 1
Transaction To: 99,999,999

Customer From:
Customer To: ZZZZZZZZ

Bank: 1200 Currency: Pound Sterling

No	Type	A/C		Date	Ref	Details	Net £	Tax £	T/C	Gross £	V	B	Bank Rec. Date
26	SR	SMITHS		06/06/2014	100025	Sales Receipt	180.00	0.00	T9	180.00	-	N	
			-	06/06/2014	243	£ 180.00 (£ 180.00) to SI 1							
27	SR	PERRYP		05/06/2014	100026	Sales Receipt	120.00	0.00	T9	120.00	-	N	
			-	05/06/2014	245	£ 120.00 (£ 120.00) to SI 3							
						Totals £	300.00	0.00		300.00			

Page 1 of 1 100%

Figure 4-8: Customer Receipts Daybook for Sweet Dreams.

You can see that Sweet Dreams has a couple of cheques received from customers. S. Smith paid £180 and has the reference 100025 against the sales receipt. This refers to the paying-in slip number used when paying the cheque into the bank. This is especially useful when you come to reconcile your bank account later in the accounting process. Underneath, the reference 243 is the invoice number that's being paid.

You can also see that P. Perry sent a cheque for £120. The paying-in slip reference was 100026 and the invoice being paid was 245.

This transaction can be summarised as follows:

Nominal Code	Account	Debit	Credit
1200	Bank account	£300	
1100	Debtors Ledger		£300

Following your double-entry rules, you can see that the Bank account has been debited, because you're increasing an asset, namely the Bank account balance. The Debtors Ledger has been credited, because you're also reducing an asset, namely Debtors. The books still balance, because an equal and opposite entry has been made in the accounts.

Introducing Control Accounts

So far we've discussed how you enter transactions into your bookkeeping system, and we've demonstrated the double-entry bookkeeping associated with each of the transactions.

At the end of the month, check that the Sales Ledger, the Purchase Ledger and the Nominal Ledger are in agreement. The easiest way to do this check is to perform Control account reconciliations.

'What on earth are these?' we hear you say!

Well, don't panic, they're quite straightforward, particularly in a computerised accounting system, where the double entry is all done for you!

In performing a Control account reconciliation, all you're doing is checking that the Nominal Ledger agrees with both the Debtors (Customers) and Creditors (Suppliers) Ledgers.

Debtors Control account

This account totals all the Sales Invoices, Sales Credit Notes and Customer receipts for the month and is held in the Nominal Ledger.

The Debtors Control account shows you how much is owing to your business by your customers. It can be reconciled against the Aged Debtors report for the same period to ensure accuracy of your information. This would be known as a *Debtors Control account reconciliation.*

Figure 4-9 shows you an example of Sweet Dreams Debtors Control account for the month of June 2014.

You can access the account via the Nominal Ledger and print off a nominal activity report for the month of June. See Figure 4-9.

You can see that the account balance is £600 – this sum is the total amount owed by debtors at 30 June 2014. The Debtors Control account details all the transactions that have taken place in the month of June. You can see that Kate, the Sweet Dreams bookkeeper, has raised sales invoices, created a credit note and recorded a couple of receipts from Smiths for £180, and Perry for £120.

If you want to verify the amount in the Sales Ledger, you can run an Aged Debtor report that shows all outstanding invoices for the month. We've run the report for Sweet Dreams for June 2014 (the same period as the nominal activity report shown in Figure 4-9).

Here, you can see that the total amount outstanding at 30 June 2014 was £600, as agreed with the Debtors Control account balance of the same period.

This proves that the Nominal Ledger and the Sales Ledger are in agreement. This is an important reconciliation you need to do at the end of each month, and should always form part of your bookkeeping routine.

Date:	22/10/2014			**Sweet Dreams**					Page:	1	
Time:	13:27:03			**Nominal Activity**							
Date From:		01/06/2014					N/C From:	1100			
Date To:		30/06/2014					N/C To:	1100			
Transaction From:	1										
Transaction To:	99,999,999										

N/C:	1100		Name:	Debtors Control Account			Account Balance:		600.00 DR	

No	Type	Date	Account	Ref	Details	Dept	T/C	Value	Debit	Credit	V	B
1	SI	01/06/2014	SMITHS	243	Sweet sales	0	T1	240.00	240.00		N	-
2	SI	01/06/2014	CHARLIES	244	Machine refilled	0	T1	360.00	360.00		N	-
3	SI	03/06/2014	PERRYP	245	Tuck shop stock	0	T1	120.00	120.00		N	-
4	SI	05/06/2014	JONESJ	246	Machine refilled	0	T1	240.00	240.00		N	-
17	SC	03/06/2014	SMITHS	124	Credit for faulty goods	0	T1	60.00		60.00	N	-
26	SR	06/06/2014	SMITHS	100025	Sales Receipt	0	T9	180.00		180.00	-	N
27	SR	05/06/2014	PERRYP	100026	Sales Receipt	0	T9	120.00		120.00	-	N
							Totals:		960.00	360.00		
							History Balance:		600.00			

Page 1 of 1   100% ⊖ ⊕

Figure 4-9: Debtors Control account for Sweet Dreams.

Date: 22/10/2014 Page: 1
Time: 13:27:43

Sweet Dreams

Aged Debtors Analysis (Detailed) - By Balance (Descending)

Date From: 01/06/2014 Customer From:
Date To: 30/06/2014 Customer To: ZZZZZZZZ
Include future transactions: No
Exclude later payments: No

** NOTE: All report values are shown in Base Currency, unless otherwise indicated **

A/C: CHARLIES Name: Charlies Garage Contact: Tel:

No	Type	Date	Ref	Details	Balance	Future	Current	Period 1	Period 2	Period 3	Older
2	SI	01/06/2014	244	Machine refilled	360.00	0.00	360.00	0.00	0.00	0.00	0.00
				Totals:	360.00	0.00	360.00	0.00	0.00	0.00	0.00

Turnover: 300.00 Account Balance : 360.00
Credit Limit £ 0.00

A/C: JONESJ Name: J Jones Contact: Tel:

No	Type	Date	Ref	Details	Balance	Future	Current	Period 1	Period 2	Period 3	Older
4	SI	05/06/2014	246	Machine refilled	240.00	0.00	240.00	0.00	0.00	0.00	0.00
				Totals:	240.00	0.00	240.00	0.00	0.00	0.00	0.00

Turnover: 200.00 Account Balance : 240.00
Credit Limit £ 0.00

Grand Totals:	600.00	0.00	600.00	0.00	0.00	0.00	0.00

Figure 4-10: An Aged Debtor report for Sweet Dreams for June 2014.

Creditors Control account

Similarly, the Creditors Control account shows you how much you owe your suppliers. This can be reconciled against the Aged Creditors report, to verify the accuracy of your information.

Figure 4-11 shows an example of Sweet Dreams's Creditors Control account for the month of June 2014. You can see that the balance is £725, made up of a number of purchase invoices, a credit note and a couple of payments.

You can check that the information contained in the Nominal Ledger (Creditors Control account) is accurate by running an Aged Creditors report from the Creditors Ledger.

See Figure 4-12 for an example of an Aged Creditors report for Sweet Dreams for the month of June 2014.

You can see that the balance on the Aged Creditors report is also £725, so the two reports reconcile.

In performing both of the preceding reconciliations, you're checking that the Nominal Ledger agrees with both the Debtors (customers) and Creditors (suppliers) Ledgers.

Date: 22/10/2014
Time: 13:29:57

Sweet Dreams

Nominal Activity

Page: 1

Date From: 01/06/2014
Date To: 30/06/2014

N/C From: 2100
N/C To: 2100

Transaction From: 1
Transaction To: 99,999,999

N/C: 2100 Name: Creditors Control Account Account Balance: 725.00 CR

No	Type	Date	Account	Ref	Details	Dept	T/C	Value	Debit	Credit	V	B
6	PI	03/06/2014	HELENS	2	Misc items	0	T1	250.00		250.00	N	-
9	PP	03/06/2014	HELENS	1067	Purchase Payment	0	T9	250.00	250.00		-	N
13	PP	03/06/2014	HENRYS	1066	Purchase Payment	0	T9	500.00	500.00		-	N
14	PI	01/06/2014	HENRYS	3	Sweets	0	T1	750.00		750.00	N	-
15	PI	05/06/2014	BARRYS	4	Boxes of sweets	0	T1	100.00		100.00	N	-
16	PI	08/06/2014	HELENS	5	Paper	0	T1	75.00		75.00	N	-
18	PC	05/06/2014	HENRYS	346	Returning goods	0	T1	200.00	200.00		N	-
						Totals:			950.00	1,175.00		
						History Balance:				225.00		

Page 1 of 1 100%

Figure 4-11: Creditors Control account for Sweet Dreams for June 2014.

Date: 22/10/2014
Time: 13:30:37

Sweet Dreams

Aged Creditors Analysis (Detailed)

Page: 1

Date From: 01/06/2014
Date To: 30/06/2014

Supplier From:
Supplier To: ZZZZZZZZ

Include future transactions: No
Exclude later payments: No

** NOTE: All report values are shown in Base Currency, unless otherwise indicated **

A/C: BARRYS Name: Barry's Packaging Contact: Tel:

No:	Type	Date	Ref	Details	Balance	Future	Current	Period 1	Period 2	Period 3	Older
15	PI	05/06/2014	4	Boxes of sweets	100.00	0.00	100.00	0.00	0.00	0.00	0.00
				Totals:	100.00	0.00	100.00	0.00	0.00	0.00	0.00

Turnover: 83.33
Credit Limit £ 0.00

A/C: HELENS Name: Helens Contact: Tel:

No:	Type	Date	Ref	Details	Balance	Future	Current	Period 1	Period 2	Period 3	Older
16	PI	08/06/2014	5	Paper	75.00	0.00	75.00	0.00	0.00	0.00	0.00
				Totals:	75.00	0.00	75.00	0.00	0.00	0.00	0.00

Turnover: 270.83
Credit Limit £ 0.00

A/C: HENRYS Name: Henrys Contact: Tel:

No:	Type	Date	Ref	Details	Balance	Future	Current	Period 1	Period 2	Period 3	Older
14	PI	01/06/2014	3	Sweets	750.00	0.00	750.00	0.00	0.00	0.00	0.00
18	PC	05/06/2014	346	Returning goods	-200.00	0.00	-200.00	0.00	0.00	0.00	0.00
				Totals:	550.00	0.00	550.00	0.00	0.00	0.00	0.00

Turnover: 875.00
Credit Limit £ 0.00

	Balance	Future	Current	Period 1	Period 2	Period 3	Older
Grand Totals:	725.00	0.00	725.00	0.00	0.00	0.00	0.00

Figure 4-12: Aged Creditor Report for Sweet Dreams for June 2014.

Understanding How the Ledgers Impact the Accounts

The three accounts – Cash, Trade Debtors and Trade Creditors – are part of the Balance Sheet, which we explain fully in Book IV, Chapter 2. Asset accounts on the Balance Sheet usually carry debit balances because they reflect assets (in this case, cash) that the business owns. Cash and Trade Debtors are Asset accounts. Liability and Capital accounts usually carry credit balances because Liability accounts show claims made by creditors (in other words, money the business owes to financial institutions, suppliers or others), and Capital accounts show claims made by owners (in other words, how much money the owners have put into the business). Trade Creditors is a Liability account.

Here's how these accounts impact the balance of the business:

Assets	=	*Liabilities*	+	*Capital*
Cash		Trade Creditors		
Trade Debtors		(Usually credit balance)		
(Usually debit balance)				

Here's how these accounts affect the balances of the business.

The Sales account (see Figure 4-13) isn't a Balance Sheet account. Instead, the Sales account is used to develop the Profit and Loss statement, which shows whether or not a business made a profit in the period being examined. A profit means that you earned more through sales than you paid out in costs or expenses. Expense and cost accounts usually carry a debit balance.

(For the low-down on Profit and Loss statements, see Book IV, Chapter 1.) Credits and debits are pretty straightforward in the Sales account: credits increase the account and debits decrease it. Fortunately, the Sales account usually carries a credit balance, which means that the business has income.

The Profit and Loss statement's bottom line figure shows whether or not the business made a profit. When the business makes a profit, the Sales account credits exceed Expense and Cost account debits. The profit is in the form of a credit, which gets added to the Capital account called Retained Earnings, which tracks how much of your business's profits are reinvested to grow the business. When the business loses money and the bottom line of the Profit and Loss statement shows that costs and expenses exceeded sales, the number is a debit. That debit is subtracted from the balance in Retained Earnings, to show the reduction to profits reinvested in the business.

Date: 22/10/2014   **Sweet Dreams**   Page: 1
Time: 13:32:41   **Nominal Activity**

Date From: 01/06/2014   N/C From: 4000
Date To: 30/06/2014   N/C To: 4000

Transaction From: 1
Transaction To: 99,999,999

N/C: 4000   Name: Sweet Sales   Account Balance: 1,650.00 CR

No	Type	Date	Account	Ref	Details	Dept	T/C	Value	Debit	Credit	V	B
1	SI	01/06/2014	SMITHS	243	Sweet sales	0	T1	200.00		200.00	N	-
2	SI	01/06/2014	CHARLIES	244	Machine refilled	0	T1	300.00		300.00	N	-
3	SI	03/06/2014	PERRYP	245	Tuck shop stock	0	T1	100.00		100.00	N	-
4	SI	05/06/2014	JONESJ	246	Machine refilled	0	T1	200.00		200.00	N	-
17	SC	03/06/2014	SMITHS	124	Credit for faulty goods	0	T1	50.00	50.00		N	-
23	BR	02/06/2014	1200	Cash Sales	Cash Sales	0	T1	250.00		250.00	N	N
24	BR	03/06/2014	1200	Cash Sales	Cash Sales	0	T1	150.00		150.00	N	N
25	BR	05/06/2014	1200	Cash Sales	Cash Sales	0	T1	200.00		200.00	N	N

Totals: 50.00   1,400.00
History Balance: 1,350.00

Page 1 of 1   100% ⊖ ⊽

Figure 4-13:
The Sales account for Sweet Dreams as shown in the Nominal Ledger.

When your business earns a profit at the end of the accounting period, the Retained Earnings account increases thanks to a credit from the Sales account. When you lose money, your Retained Earnings account decreases.

Because the Retained Earnings account is a Capital account and Capital accounts usually carry credit balances, Retained Earnings usually carries a credit balance as well.

Adjusting for Nominal Ledger Errors

Your entries in the Nominal Ledger aren't cast in stone. If necessary, you can always change or correct an entry with an *adjusting entry.* Four of the most common reasons for Nominal Ledger adjustments are

- **Depreciation:** A business shows the ageing of its assets through depreciation. Each year, you write off a portion of the original cost of an asset as an expense, and you note that change as an adjusting entry.

- **Prepaid expenses:** You allocate expenses that are paid up front, such as a year's worth of insurance, by the month using an adjusting entry. You usually make this type of adjusting entry as part of the closing process at the end of an accounting period. We show you how to develop entries related to prepaid expenses in Book III, Chapter 3.

✔ **Adding an account:** You can add accounts by way of adjusting entries at any time during the year. If you're creating the new account to track transactions separately that at one time appeared in another account, you must move all transactions already in the books to the new account. You do this transfer with an adjusting entry to reflect the change.

✔ **Deleting an account:** Only delete an account at the end of an accounting period.

We talk more about adjusting entries and how you can use them in Book III, Chapter 3.

Sometimes, you may simply make a mistake and need to journal a balance from one account to another. For example, you may have coded paper that you bought into the postage account in error. In order to correct this mistake, you need to carry out the following correction:

	Debit	*Credit*
Office Stationery	£30	
Postage		£30

To correct the postage account

The double entry has now corrected both accounts, but you need to have knowledge of the bookkeeping rules set out in Book I, Chapter 2 to feel confident to be able to carry out this nominal adjustment. In Sage 50, you would use a nominal journal to complete this transaction, as shown in Figure 4-14.

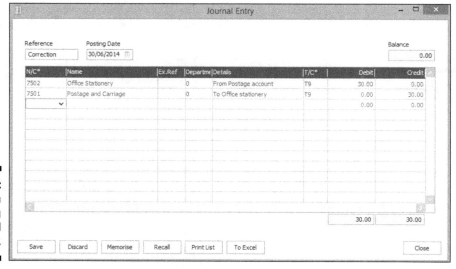

Figure 4-14: Showing a correcting journal entry.

Book I

Basic Book-keeping

Have a Go

Grab a piece of paper and have a go at practising how to create your own entries and how to post them to the Nominal Ledger.

1. **In which ledger would you record the purchase of new furniture for a business on credit?**

2. **In which ledger would you record the payment of invoices with cash?**

3. **In which ledger would you record the sale of goods to a customer on credit?**

4. **Using the information in Figure 4-15, how would you develop an entry for the Nominal Ledger to record transactions from the Sales Ledger for the month of July?**

5. **Using the information from Figure 4-16, how would you develop an entry for the Nominal Ledger to record purchase invoices posted for the month of July?** Assume that the invoices aren't going to be paid straight away.

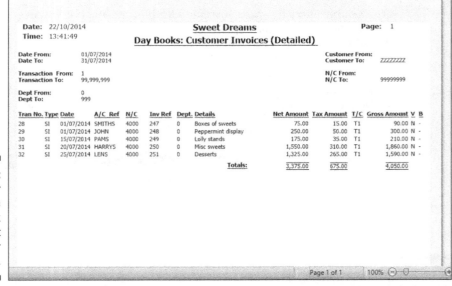

Figure 4-15: Customer Invoice Daybook for Sweet Dreams for July 2014.

Date: 22/10/2014						Sweet Dreams			Page: 1		
Time: 13:46:18						Day Books: Supplier Invoices (Detailed)					

Date From:	01/07/2014			Supplier From:	
Date To:	31/07/2014			Supplier To:	ZZZZZZZZ
Transaction From:	1			N/C From:	
Transaction To:	99,999,999			N/C To:	99999999
Dept From:	0				
Dept To:	999				

Tran No.	Type	Date	A/C Ref	N/C	Inv Ref	Dept	Details	Net Amount	Tax Amount	T/C	Gross Amount	V	B
33	PI	01/07/2014	RUTHS	5000	1801	0	Multi pack sweets	2,000.00	400.00	T1	2,400.00	N	-
34	PI	10/07/2014	HENRYS	5000	1802	0	Crates for transporting	1,500.00	300.00	T1	1,800.00	N	-
35	PI	15/07/2014	DEBS	5000	1803	0	Paper bags for shops	575.00	115.00	T1	690.00	N	-
36	PI	25/07/2014	KARENS	5000	1804	0	Multi pack sweets	175.00	35.00	T1	210.00	N	-
							Totals	4,250.00	850.00		5,100.00		

Figure 4-16:
The Supplier
Invoices
Day Book
for Sweet
Dreams for
July 2014.

Page 1 of 1   100%

6. **On 1 July, Kate the bookkeeper transfers £150 from the business Current Bank account to the Petty Cash account.** Can you confirm the double entry that takes place in the accounts system? Which accounts are debited and which are credited and why?

7. **Kate writes some cheques out as follows:**

Chq No.	Details	Amount
1069	Rent	£800
1070	Salaries	£500

Can you confirm the double entry that takes place for these two transactions?

8. **On 31 July, Kate decided to pay the following suppliers:**

Supplier	Chq No.	Amount
Barry's Packaging	1071	£100
Helen's	1072	£75
Henry's	1073	£550

Can you confirm the double entry that takes place in the accounting system?

9. **Kate receives a grant on 1 July for £200.** She pays this grant into the business current account. Can you confirm the double entry that takes place and say why?

10. **On 15 July, Kate receives a cheque from her customer J. Jones for £140.** Can you confirm the double entry that takes place in the accounts system and explain why?

11. **At the end of the month, Kate runs a copy of her Trial Balance and sees that a large balance has been coded to Materials Purchased.** Using her Sage reports, she can see a couple of items that have been coded to Materials Purchased incorrectly.

    The following two items, need to be taken out of materials purchased and coded to the following accounts:

Office Stationery	£62.50
Distribution Costs	£1,500

    Can you confirm the double entry that needs to take place to correct the accounts?

Answering the Have a Go Questions

1. **The purchase of new furniture for the business would actually be an asset and not a cost, for the purpose of purchasing or manufacturing items for sale.**

    Therefore, the following double entry would take place:

Account	*Debit*	*Credit*
Office Furniture	£xx	
Creditors Ledger		£xx

    The rules of double entry applied are

    To increase an asset (Office Furniture), you debit the Asset account.

    To increase a liability (Creditors Ledger), you credit the Liability account.

2. **Cashbook.**

    All cash payments are entered into the Cashbook as a cash payment.

3. **Sales Ledger: all sales are tracked in the Sales Ledger.**

4. **The double entry would be as follows:**

Account	Debit	Credit
Trade Debtors	£4,050	
Sales		£3,375
VAT		£675

5. **The double entry would be as follows:**

Account	Debit	Credit
Materials Purchased	£4,250	
VAT	£850	
Trade Creditors		£5,100

6. **The double entry that takes place is as follows:**

Account	Debit	Credit
Petty Cash account	£150	
Bank Current account		£150

The double entry rules that have been applied are

If you want to increase an Asset account (for example, Petty Cash), you debit that account.

To decrease an Asset account (for example, Bank Current account) you credit that account.

See Figure 4-17 for the Nominal Daybook report to see confirmation of the double entry that has taken place.

You can see that Sage 50 has debited nominal code 1230 (Petty Cash) and credited nominal code 1200 (Bank Current Account).

7. **The double entry that should take place when the bank payments are shown below. You can also see the entries shown in Figure 4-18.**

Account	Debit	Credit
Rent	£800	
Wages	£500	
Bank		£1,300

The double entry rules that have been adhered to are as follows:

To record an expense (such as Rent or Wages), you debit the Expense account.

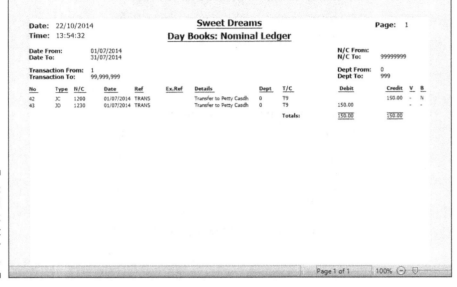

Figure 4-18:
The Bank
Payment
Day Book
for Sweet
Dreams for
July 2014.

To decrease an asset (in this case the Bank account), you credit the Asset account.

Notice that the cheque numbers have been used in the reference field, thus allowing the transaction to be traced back to the original source document.

8. **The double entry that takes place is as follows:**

Account	Debit	Credit
Creditors Ledger	£725	
Bank		£725

The double entry rules used are as follows:

To decrease a liability (Trade Creditors), you must debit the account.

To decrease an asset (Bank Current account), you must credit the account.

You can see these transactions demonstrated in the Supplier Payments Daybook shown in Figure 4-19.

Book I

Basic Book-keeping

Figure 4-19: Supplier Payments Day Book for Sweet Dreams for July 2014.

9. **The double entry should be as follows:**

Account	Debit	Credit
Bank	£200	
Other Income		£200

The double entry rules are as follows:

To increase an asset (Bank Current account), you debit the Asset account.

To record income, you credit the Income account.

10. **The double entry that takes place is as follows:**

Account	Debit	Credit
Bank	£140	
Debtors Ledger		£140

The double entry rules that are applied are as follows:

To increase an asset (such as Bank), the account is debited.

To decrease an asset (such as Debtors), the account is credited.

11. **The double entry that needs to take place to correct the materials purchased code is as follows:**

Account	Debit	Credit
Office Stationery	£62.50	
Distribution Costs	£1,500	
Materials Purchased		£1,562.50

This now corrects the appropriate codes.

Book II

Bookkeeping Day to Day

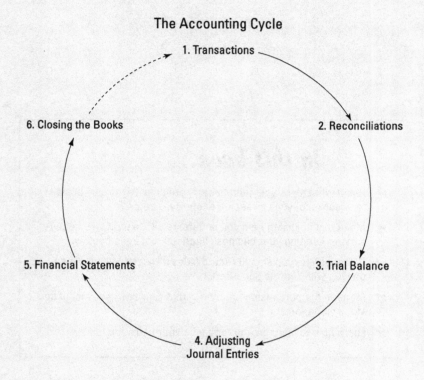

The Accounting Cycle

1. Transactions

2. Reconciliations

3. Trial Balance

4. Adjusting
Journal Entries

5. Financial Statements

6. Closing the Books

In this book...

- ✔ Know what tasks you need to carry out on a day-to-day basis to ensure that you're keeping accurate records.

- ✔ Make a checklist to help you undertake all the activities necessary for keeping your business finances running smoothly.

- ✔ Discover how you should record sales transactions, including dealing with returns and discounts.

- ✔ Manage the purchasing function within your business including stock management.

- ✔ Learn how to manage and reconcile your bank accounts.

Chapter 1

Planning and Controlling Your Workload

*A*s a bookkeeper, you need to work in an orderly manner and be aware of which jobs need doing on a daily, weekly and monthly basis, which is why checklists are so useful. You need to do certain jobs on a daily basis, depending on the size of your business; for example, entering invoices. Other jobs are done on a monthly basis, such as reconciling your bank account. Most businesses receive only one statement once a month and wait until they've received it before they reconcile their bank account.

As the company bookkeeper, you should analyse all the jobs that require completing and decide on an appropriate order in which to conduct those tasks. You then need to allocate the work to the appropriate person or department, so that everyone in the office is aware of what responsibilities they have. If your business is so small that you're the only person in it, you have to do everything. Nothing like hands-on experience!

This chapter offers hints and tips to help you process your transactions in an efficient manner.

Introducing Checklists

Having a list of all the jobs that need to be carried out in a month is always a good idea. That way, you know what you're working towards. In bookkeeping, the number of transactions that you deal with varies massively from company to company. You're reacting both to the number of invoices that a business generates itself for customers and to the invoices that it receives from its suppliers. Every business differs in the number of invoices that it handles.

Some businesses have entire departments that process just invoices. For example, you may have a department that processes just purchase invoices. The business may receive so many that you have purchase journal clerks who only process and write up purchase invoices. The bigger your company, the more likely you are to use a computerised accounting system. However, whether you use computers or not, you still benefit from using checklists to guide you through the monthly bookkeeping routine.

Figure 1-1 is an example of a checklist that we use on a monthly basis.

Figure 1-1: An example of a monthly bookkeeping checklist.

Bookkeeping Checklist	Apr	May	Jun	Jul	Aug	Sep	Oct	Nov	Dec	Jan	Feb	Mar
Monthly												
Enter Sales Invoices												
Enter Purchase Invoices												
Enter Cheque Payments												
Enter Receipts from paying in book												
Enter prepayment journals												
Enter accruals journals												
Enter wages journals												
Enter stock journal												
Enter depreciation												
Pay Inland Revenue												
Bank Reconciliation												
Quarterly												
VAT Return												

Sorting Out Your Sales Invoices

If your business produces sales invoices for customers who are buying on credit, read on! Your business may produce these invoices by hand, a word processor or a computerised system. We talk about cash sales and computer-generated invoices in Book II Chapter 2. Here we discuss the filing and management of those invoices after they've been produced.

Referring to the checklist shown in Figure 1-1, you can see that the first job on the list is entering sales invoices. Make sure that the person who produces the sales invoices puts them somewhere you can easily find them, for example, an in-tray simply for sales invoices or a concertina-style file that invoices are kept in prior to you entering them into your bookkeeping system.

If you have a computerised system that produces sales invoices automatically, you can skip this step, as the computer produces those invoices automatically and the Sales journal updated accordingly, as detailed in Book II Chapter 2.

You should find that each sales invoice has already been given an invoice number. Adopt a sequential numbering system that allows you to notice whether invoices have been missed or not. The invoice numbers can be alpha-numeric if it helps with your business, but the invoices should be filed in numerical order, so that you file and enter them into your bookkeeping system in roughly chronological order.

As you enter each invoice into your Sales Ledger, tick or mark the invoice in some way to indicate that you've posted it into your bookkeeping system so you avoid entering the same invoice twice.

File your invoices neatly in a lever arch file.

Book II

Book-keeping Day to Day

Entering Your Purchases Invoices

You receive purchase invoices in the post on an almost daily basis. Whoever opens the post needs to know where to put those invoices until it is time to enter them into the bookkeeping system. Again, as with the sales invoices, keep the purchase invoices in one dedicated place until you're ready to enter them into your Purchase Ledger.

Sequential numbering and coding

Some companies like to keep a separate lever arch file for each supplier, or at least file the invoices in supplier order. Others simply number the purchase invoices sequentially with a stamping machine and use this number within the bookkeeping system. Using this method, you can file all your purchase invoices in one file and just keep them in numerical order.

When you enter the invoice into the bookkeeping system, you need to know which nominal code to apply in order to enter the invoice. It may not be immediately obvious what the invoice is for. For example, as a bookkeeper, you need to know whether the invoice relates to a direct cost of the business or whether it is simply an overhead of the business.

Some companies use a data-entry stamp, which has spaces to enter vital information such as the date the invoice was posted, nominal code and maybe a space for the data-entry clerk to initial, to confirm that the transaction has been entered.

You may find that you're entering invoices on a daily basis. When you begin to enter invoices at the start of each day, check your bookkeeping system to see what the last invoice entered was. You can check the last invoice number used and then you know which invoice number to start with when you enter your next invoice.

If you're using a computerised system such as Sage 50 Accounts, you can check the Purchase Daybook. See Figure 1-2 for an example of the report you can run to check the last purchase invoice entered.

Notice the 'Invoice Reference' column. This column is where the sequential purchases invoice number appears.

Date: 22/10/2014						**Sweet Dreams**					Page: 1	
Time: 17:49:46						**Day Books: Supplier Invoices (Detailed)**						
Date From:	01/06/2014								Supplier From:			
Date To:	31/12/2019								Supplier To:	ZZZZZZZ		
Transaction From:	1								N/C From:			
Transaction To:	99,999,999								N/C To:	99999999		
Dept From:	0											
Dept To:	999											
Tran No.	Type	Date	A/C Ref	N/C	Inv Ref	Dept	Details	Net Amount	Tax Amount	T/C	Gross Amount	V	B
6	PI	03/06/2014	HELENS	5000	2	0	Misc items	208.33	41.67	T1	250.00	N	-
14	PI	01/06/2014	HENRYS	5000	3	0	Sweets	625.00	125.00	T1	750.00	N	-
15	PI	05/06/2014	BARRYS	5000	4	0	Boxes of sweets	83.33	16.67	T1	100.00	N	-
16	PI	08/06/2014	HELENS	5000	5	0	Paper	62.50	12.50	T1	75.00	N	-
33	PI	01/07/2014	RUTHS	5000	1801	0	Multi pack sweets	2,000.00	400.00	T1	2,400.00	N	-
34	PI	10/07/2014	HENRYS	5000	1802	0	Crates for transporting	1,500.00	300.00	T1	1,800.00	N	-
35	PI	15/07/2014	DEBS	5000	1803	0	Paper bags for shops	575.00	115.00	T1	690.00	N	-
36	PI	25/07/2014	KARENS	5000	1804	0	Multi pack sweets	175.00	35.00	T1	210.00	N	-
							Totals	5,229.16	1,045.84		6,275.00		

Figure 1-2:
Check your Purchase Daybook to see the last invoice entered.

Paying your suppliers

Although we don't include this task on the checklist, paying your suppliers on time is vital to any business. Flip to Book II Chapter 3 to see just why!

You may decide to pay your suppliers at specific times in the month, so add this task to your monthly bookkeeping routine.

Checking Cash Payments and Receipts

Book II

Book-
keeping
Day to Day

In Book II Chapter 4, we discuss the importance of ensuring that all banking entries are included in your bookkeeping system, particularly when you need to reconcile your bank account. In this chapter, we discuss the practical ways to ensure that you include all your data in your system.

Cash payments

Most businesses make payments in several ways. Cash payments include:

- ✔ Cash (naturally!) – usually from the petty cash tin
- ✔ Cheque
- ✔ Bank transfer, CHAPS or BACS, or another form of electronic payment

As a bookkeeper, make sure that you collect all the payment information from all the relevant sources. The bank reconciliation process highlighted in Book II, Chapter 4 ensures that you do this; however, here are a few more practical tips to make the reconciliation process as simple as possible.

An easy way to ensure that you've entered all your petty cash payments is to physically tick or initial the petty cash voucher or cash receipt after entering it into your bookkeeping system. You then avoid entering items twice. You can batch up your petty cash payments and give them a batch reference so that they can be easily retrieved from your filing system.

Look at Figure 1-3 to see an example of a batch entry of petty cash receipts being posted onto Sage 50 Accounts. The batch of receipts has been given the reference PC01. A separate bank account has been set up called Petty Cash.

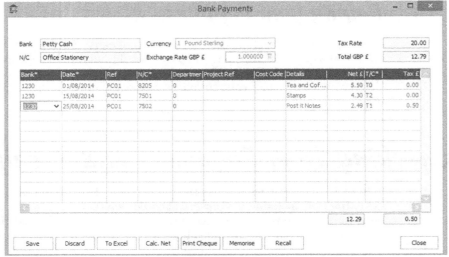

Figure 1-3:
Petty cash
payment
showing
PC01 as
a batch
reference.

To make life as easy as possible, when you write out cheques, ensure that you include clear information about who you're paying on the cheque stub. Don't attempt to write *War and Peace* here, but include the date, the payee and the amount. Write this information clearly, especially if it may not be you that ultimately writes up the Cash Payments book or enters the amount into your computerised accounting system. If you've spidery handwriting, spare a thought for the person who needs to read this information! Entering wrong amounts or the wrong account leads to problems when trying to reconcile the bank account.

At some point, you enter the information written on the cheque stub into the bookkeeping system. After you write the information up in your Cash Payments book or enter it onto your computing system, make sure that you physically tick the cheque stub. This way, you know that you've entered that information, and can easily flick through the cheque stubs at a later date and find where you last entered information.

You won't be aware of what electronic payments have been made until you see the bank statements for the month. Most businesses don't receive the previous month's statements until the end of the first week of the following month. For most businesses, this timing is impractical, so with the advent of Internet banking, most businesses can print out copies of their bank statements on a daily basis if necessary. Therefore you can reconcile your bank account on a much more regular basis than simply once a month, which was the traditional way. You can also identify your electronic payments sooner and enter them accordingly.

Again, an easy way to ensure that you're entering the information correctly is to physically tick the transaction on your copy of the bank statement.

Avoid printing too many copies of your bank statements, because doing so can lead to mistakes happening, with the same information entered twice.

Cash receipts

These transactions include:

- ✔ Items physically paid in at the bank via the paying-in book
- ✔ Electronic receipts via BACS and other electronic methods, including interest earned on the bank account

For items paid in using the paying-in book, make sure that you include as much detail as possible. If you can, include the invoice numbers that the customer is paying, so that you can easily allocate the receipt to the correct invoices. Knowing which invoices the customer is paying is crucial so that the Aged Debtor report is correct. (See Book II, Chapter 2 for more on Aged Debtor reports.)

After you've entered the information from your bank paying-in slips to your bookkeeping system, tick the stub to show that the information's been entered, so you can see at a glance where you're up to.

Reconciling Your Bank Account

Reconciling your bank account to check that your manual or computerised Cashbook matches your bank statement is usually part of your monthly accounting process. Book II, Chapter 4 shows you how to carry out the reconciliation process both manually and using computer software. Make sure that you reconcile your bank accounts, because this reconciliation ensures the accuracy of the information that has been posted to your accounting system. You should also reconcile any credit card statements that you've received; by doing this, you accurately record credit card liabilities that the business may have incurred.

Book II

**Book-
keeping
Day to Day**

Entering Your Journals

Monthly journals always need to be completed. If you refer back to the checklist shown in Figure 1-1, we refer to prepayments, accruals, wages, stock and depreciation. Your business may have some or all these journals, but you may also have additional ones that are specific to your business. Ensure that all the journals that you need to process are on your checklist so that they aren't missed out.

For more information on Accruals, Prepayments, Depreciation and Stock journals, see Book III, Chapter 3.

Controlling Your Books, Records and Money

Cash is an extremely important part of any business and you need to accurately record and monitor it. Before you take in any money, you must be sure that systems are in place to control the flow of cash in and out of the business.

Here are some tips:

✓ Initially, when your business is small, you can sign each cheque and keep control of the outflow of money. But as the business grows, you may find that you need to delegate cheque-signing responsibilities to someone else, especially if you travel frequently.

Many small business owners set up cheque-signing procedures that allow one or two of their staff to sign cheques up to a designated amount, such as £5,000. Any cheques above that designated amount require the owner's signature, or the signature of an employee and a second designated person, such as an officer of the business.

✓ A good practice is to record cheques received immediately as part of a daily morning routine. Enter the details onto the paying-in slip and update your computerised or manual accounting system at the same time. Make sure that you pay in any money received before 3:30 p.m. on the same day, to ensure that your bank account gets credit that day rather than the next.

✓ No matter how much you keep in petty cash, make sure that you set up a good control system that requires anyone who uses the cash to write a petty cash voucher specifying how much was used and why. Also ask that a cash receipt, for example from the shop or post office, is attached to the voucher in order to justify the cash withdrawal whenever possible.

In most cases, a member of staff buys something for the business and then gets reimbursed for that expense. If the expense is small enough, you can reimburse through the petty cash fund. If the expense is more than a few pounds, ask the person to fill out an expense account form and get reimbursed by cheque. Petty cash is usually used for minor expenses of £10 or less.

✓ The best way to control petty cash is to pick one person in the office to manage the use of all petty cash. Before you give that person more cash, he should be able to prove the absence of cash used and why it was used.

Dividing staff responsibilities

Your primary protection against financial crime is properly separating staff responsibilities when the flow of business cash is involved. In a nutshell, never have one person handling more than one of the following tasks:

✓ **Bookkeeping:** Involves reviewing and entering all transactions into the business's books. The bookkeeper makes sure that transactions are accurate, valid and appropriate, and have the proper authorisation. For example, if a transaction requires paying a supplier, the bookkeeper makes sure that the charges are accurate and someone with proper authority has approved the payment. The bookkeeper can review documentation of cash receipts and the overnight deposits taken to the bank, but shouldn't actually make the deposit.

Also, if the bookkeeper is responsible for handling payments from external parties, such as customers or suppliers, he shouldn't enter those transactions in the books.

✓ **Authorisation:** Involves being the manager or managers delegated to authorise expenditures for their departments. You may decide that transactions over a certain amount must have two or more authorisations before cheques can be sent to pay a bill. Spell out authorisation levels clearly and make sure that everyone follows them, even the owner or managing director of the business. (Remember, if you're the owner, you set the tone for how the rest of the office operates; when you take shortcuts, you set a bad example and undermine the system you put in place.)

✓ **Money-handling:** Involves direct contact with incoming cash or revenue, whether cheque, credit card or credit transactions, as well as outgoing cash flow. People who handle money directly, such as cashiers, shouldn't also prepare and make bank deposits. Likewise, the person writing cheques to pay business bills shouldn't be authorised to sign those cheques; to be safe, have one person prepare the cheques based on authorised documentation and a second person sign those cheques, after reviewing the authorised documentation.

When setting up your cash-handling systems, try to think like an embezzler to figure out how someone can take advantage of a system.

✔ **Financial report preparation and analysis:** Involves the actual preparation of the financial reports and any analysis of those reports. Someone who's not involved in the day-to-day entering of transactions in the books needs to prepare the financial reports. For most small businesses, the bookkeeper turns over the raw reports from the computerised accounting system to an outside accountant who reviews the materials and prepares the financial reports. In addition, the accountant does a financial analysis of the business activity results for the previous accounting period.

We realise that you may be just starting up a small business and therefore not have enough staff to separate all these duties. Until you do have that capability, make sure that you stay heavily involved in the inflow and outflow of cash in your business. At least once a month:

✔ **Open your business's bank statements and review the transactions.** Someone else can be given the responsibility of reconciling the statement, but you still need to keep an eye on the transactions listed.

✔ **Look at your business cheque book counterfoils to ensure that no cheques are missing.** A bookkeeper who knows that you periodically check the books is less likely to find an opportunity for theft or embezzlement. If you find that a cheque or page of cheques is missing, act quickly to find out whether the cheques were used legitimately. If you can't find the answer, call your bank and put a stop on the missing cheque numbers.

✔ **Observe your cashiers and managers handling cash to make sure that they're following the rules you've established.** This practice is known as *management by walking around* – the more often you're out there, the less likely you are to be a victim of employee theft and fraud.

Balancing control costs

As a small-business owner, you're always trying to balance the cost of protecting your cash and assets with the cost of adequately separating those duties. Putting in place too many controls, which end up costing you money, can be a big mistake.

For example, you may create stock controls that require salespeople to contact one particular person who has the key to your product warehouse. This kind of control may prevent employee theft, but can also result in lost sales, because salespeople can't find the key-holder while dealing with an interested customer. In the end, the customer gets mad, and you lose the sale.

When you put controls in place, talk to your staff both before and after instituting the controls to see how they're working and to check for any unforeseen problems. Be willing and able to adjust your controls to balance the business needs of selling your products, managing the cash flow and keeping your eye on making a profit. Talk to other businesspeople to see what they do and pick up tips from established best practice. Your external accountant can be a good source of valuable information.

Have a Go

Grab a pencil and some paper and test your knowledge on the best way of working as a bookkeeper.

1. **You work in the accounts department for a small business. Write a procedure for a new member of staff to follow, which shows him what to do when a cheque arrives by post into the business.**

   Consider who opens the post, who writes up the paying-in book and who ultimately takes the cheques to the bank. Try to remember that these responsibilities should be split up as much as possible to minimise any possibility of fraud.

2. **Review your petty cash procedure.**

   Decide who is responsible for maintaining the petty cash tin, and how much the petty cash float is going to be. Make sure that all staff are aware of the petty cash procedure.

3. **Imagine that you're setting up the accounting department. Jot down the types of tasks that require separation of duties.**

Answering the Have a Go Questions

1. **The following is an example of what you may have written.**

   Procedure for banking cheques:

   • The person responsible for opening the post should ensure that all cheques and notifications of payments from customers (for example, a remittance advice) are passed to the accounts department on the day that they're received.

- One person in the accounts department should be responsible for writing up the bank paying-in book and recording all the money received, along with details of the customer and which invoice they're paying. As much detail as possible should be written on the paying-in slip stub.

- If possible, a different individual should ensure that the paying-in book is taken to the bank and the money deposited, the same day it is received.

- When the bank paying-in book has been returned to the accounts department, the customer receipts should be entered into your bookkeeping system. If you have a computerised system, you should enter the customer receipts against the appropriate account, using the bank paying-in reference and details shown on the paying-in book to identify which invoices the payment should be allocated to. Tick the paying-in slip when you've entered the information into your bookkeeping system.

2. **Here are the main elements of a petty cash procedure:**

   - Designate a member of staff to be responsible for petty cash. Ensure that all members of staff know who this person is.

   - Complete petty cash vouchers for all petty cash payments detailing the type of expenditure and noting VAT if applicable. Attach the receipts to the vouchers, so that VAT may be claimed at a later date.

   - Ensure that the individual claiming money from petty cash signs the petty cash voucher to acknowledge receipt of the money and also ensure that the petty cashier authorises the payment by signing the voucher accordingly.

   - Number each petty cash voucher so that it can be filed and easily located later if necessary.

   - Write up the petty cash book, or enter the petty cash vouchers onto your computerised system, using the number mentioned in the last step as a reference.

   - Petty cash should be counted and balanced on a regular basis. This task is usually done when the float needs topping up.

3. **The following are the types of duties that you should consider separating among different members of staff.**

   Obviously, in a very small company this separation may not be possible, so let common sense prevail!

- The person who opens the post and accepts the cash should not enter the transaction in the books.

- The person who enters the data in the books on a daily basis should not prepare the financial statements.

- The person who prepares the cheques should not have the authority to sign the cheques.

- The person who pays the money into the bank should not be the person who completes the paying-in slips.

Book II

Book-keeping Day to Day

Chapter 2

Counting Your Sales

*E*very business loves to take in money, and this means that you, the bookkeeper, have lots to do to ensure that sales are properly recorded in the books. In addition to recording the sales themselves, you must monitor customer accounts, discounts offered to customers, and customer returns and allowances.

If the business sells products on credit, you have to monitor customer accounts carefully in Trade Debtors (Accounts Receivable), including monitoring whether customers pay on time and alerting the sales team when customers are behind on their bills and future purchases on credit need to be declined. Some customers never pay, and in that case you must adjust the books to reflect non-payment as a bad debt.

This chapter reviews the basic responsibilities of a business's bookkeeping and accounting staff for tracking sales, making adjustments to those sales, monitoring customer accounts and alerting management to slow-paying customers.

Collecting on Cash Sales

Most businesses collect some form of cash as payment for the goods or services they sell. Cash receipts include more than just notes and coins; you can consider cheques and credit- and debit-card payments as cash sales for bookkeeping purposes. In fact, with electronic transaction processing (when a customer's credit or debit card is swiped through a machine), a deposit is usually made to the business's bank account the same day (sometimes within seconds of the transaction, depending on the type of system the business sets up with the bank).

The only type of payment that doesn't fall under the umbrella of a cash payment is purchases made on credit. And by *credit*, we mean the credit your business offers to customers directly rather than through a third party, such as a bank credit card or loan. We talk more about this type of sale in the section 'Selling on Credit', later in this chapter.

Discovering the value of sales receipts

Modern businesses generate sales receipts in one of three ways: by the cash register, by the credit- or debit-card machine or by hand (written out by the salesperson). Whichever of these three methods you choose to handle your sales transactions, the sales receipt serves two purposes:

✔ Gives the customer proof that the item was purchased on a particular day at a particular price in your shop in case she needs to exchange or return the merchandise.

✔ Gives the shop a receipt that can be used at a later time to enter the transaction into the business's books. At the end of the day, the receipts are also used to cash up the cash register and ensure that the cashier has taken in the right amount of cash based on the sales made.

You're familiar with cash receipts, no doubt, but just to show you how much useable information can be generated for the bookkeeper on a sales receipt, Figure 2-1 shows a sample receipt from a hardware shop.

Receipts contain a wealth of information that can be collected for your business's accounting system. A look at a receipt tells you the amount of cash collected, the type of products sold, the quantity of products sold and how much value-added tax (VAT) was collected.

We're assuming that your business operates some form of computerised accounting system, but it may be that you need to journal the sales information from your till into your accounting system (unless of course you have an automated process). Either way, as a reminder, the double entry required to enter your sales information is as follows:

	Debit	*Credit*
Bank account	£26.38	
Sales		£21.98
VAT Collected account		£4.40

Sales receipts for 1 August 2014.

HANDSON'S HARDWARE

Sales receipt 01/08/2014

Item	Quantity	Price	Total
Nails	1 box	£8.99	£8.99
Picture hooks	1 pack	£2.99	£2.99
Paint	2 gallons	£10.00	£10.00
Subtotal			**£21.98**
VAT @ 20%			**£4.40**
Total Sale			**£26.38**
Paid Cash			**£26.38**

Figure 2-1:
A sales receipt from Handson's Hardware.

In this example entry, the Bank account is an Asset account shown on the Balance Sheet (see Book IV, Chapter 2 for more about the Balance Sheet), and its value increases with the debit. The Sales account is a Revenue account on the Profit and Loss statement (see Book IV, Chapter 1 for more about the Profit and Loss statement), and its balance increases with a credit, showing additional revenue. (We talk more about debits and credits in Book I, Chapter 2.) The VAT Collected account is a Liability account that appears on the Balance Sheet, and its balance increases with this transaction.

Businesses pay VAT to HM Revenue & Customs monthly or quarterly, depending on rules set by HM Revenue & Customs. Therefore, your business must hold the money owed in a Liability account so that you're certain you can pay the VAT collected from customers when due. We talk more about VAT payments in Book III, Chapter 1.

Recording cash transactions in the books

Assuming that you're using a computerised accounting system, you can enter more detail from the day's receipts and record stock sold as well. Most of the computerised accounting systems include the ability to record the sale of stock. Figure 2-2 shows you the Sage 50 Accounts Cash Sales screen that you can use to input data from each day's sales. Note that you need the Sage 50 Accounts Professional version to use the Sales Order Processing function to generate cash sales and automatically update your stock.

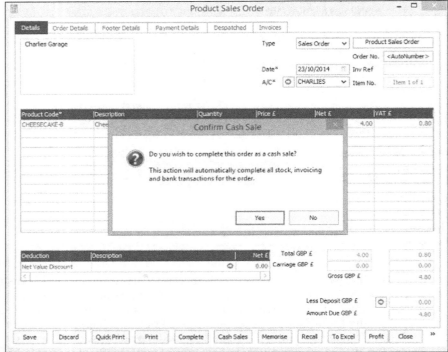

Figure 2-2:
Example of
a cash sale
in Sage 50
Accounts.

Note: A cheaper computerised option would be to use Sage One Cashbook, or Sage One Accounts, which is an online accounting service, but cheap to use. It's ideal for one-man bands and micro-businesses. Take a look at *Sage One for Dummies* by Jane Kelly (Wiley) to find out more.

In addition to the information included in the Cash Receipts book, note that Sage 50 Accounts also collects information about the items sold in each transaction. Sage 50 Accounts then automatically updates stock information, reducing the amount of stock on hand when necessary. If the cash sale in Figure 2-2 is for an individual customer, you enter her name and address in the A/C field. At the bottom of the Cash Sales screen, the Print tab takes you to a further menu where you have the option to print or email the receipt. You can print the receipt and give it to the customer or, for a phone or Internet order, email it to the customer. Using this option, payment can be made by any method such as cheque, electronic payment or credit or debit card.

Sage 50 Accounts also gives you the ability to process card payments from customers over the phone and use real-time authorisation and posting. To use Sage Pay, you need a Sage Pay account and a merchant bank account. For more information about this, please see www.sagepay.com.

If your business accepts credit cards, expect sales revenue to be reduced by the fees paid to credit card companies. Usually, you face monthly fees as well as fees per transaction; however, each business sets up individual arrangements with its bank regarding these fees. Sales volume impacts how much you pay in fees, so when researching bank services, ensure that you compare credit card transaction fees to find a good deal.

Selling on Credit

Many businesses decide to sell to customers on credit, meaning credit that the business offers and not through a bank or credit card provider. This approach offers more flexibility in the type of terms you can offer your customers, and you don't have to pay bank fees. However, credit involves more work for you, the bookkeeper, and the risk of a customer not paying what she owes.

When you accept a customer's bank-issued credit card for a sale and the customer doesn't pay the bill, you get your money; the bank is responsible for collecting from the customer, taking the loss if she doesn't pay. This doesn't apply when you decide to offer credit to your customers directly. If a customer doesn't pay, your business takes the loss.

Deciding whether to offer credit

The decision to set up your own credit system depends on what your competition is doing. For example, if you run an office supply store and all other office supply stores allow credit to make it easier for their customers to get supplies, you probably need to offer credit to stay competitive.

You need to set up some ground rules when you want to allow your customers to buy on credit. For personal customers, you have to decide

- How to check a customer's credit history
- What the customer's income level needs to be for credit approval
- How long to give the customer to pay the bill before charging interest or late fees

If you want to allow your trade or business customers to buy on credit, you need to set ground rules for them as well. The decisions you need to make include:

- ✔ Whether to deal only with established businesses. You may decide to give credit only to businesses that have been trading for at least two years.

- ✔ Whether to require *trade references*, which show that the business has been responsible and paid other businesses when they've taken credit. A customer usually provides you with the details of two suppliers that offered her credit. You then contact those suppliers directly to see whether the customer has been reliable and on time with payments.

- ✔ Whether to obtain credit rating information. You may decide to use a third-party credit-checking agency to provide a credit report on the business applying for credit. This report suggests a maximum credit limit and whether the business pays on time. Of course a fee is charged for this service, but using it may help you avoid making a terrible mistake. Asimilar service is available for individuals.

The harder you make getting credit and the stricter you make the bill-paying rules, the less chance you have of taking a loss. However, you may lose customers to a competitor with lighter credit rules.

You may require a minimum income level of £50,000 and make customers pay in 30 days to avoid late fees or interest charges. Your sales staff report that these rules are too rigid because your direct competitor down the street allows credit on a minimum income level of £30,000 and gives customers 60 days to pay before charging late fees and interest charges. Now you have to decide whether you want to change your credit rules to match those of the competition. If you do lower your credit standards to match your competitor, however, you may end up with more customers who can't pay on time (or at all) because you've qualified customers for credit at lower income levels and given them more time to pay. If you do loosen your qualification criteria and bill-paying requirements, monitor your customer accounts carefully to ensure that they're not falling behind.

The key risk you face is selling products for which you're never paid. For example, if you allow customers 30 days to pay and cut them off from buying goods when their accounts fall more than 30 days behind, the most you can lose is the amount purchased over a two-month period (60 days). But if you give customers more leniency, allowing them 60 days to pay and cutting them off after payment is 30 days late, you're faced with three months (90 days) of purchases for which you may never be paid.

Recording credit sales in the books

When sales are made on credit, you have to enter specific information into the accounting system. In addition to inputting information regarding cash receipts (see 'Collecting on Cash Sales', earlier in this chapter), you update the customer accounts to make sure that each customer is billed and the money is collected. You debit the Trade Debtors account, an Asset account shown on the Balance Sheet (see Book IV, Chapter 2), which shows money due from customers.

Figure 2-3 shows an example of a sales invoice from Simply Stationery.

Invoice

Simply Stationery

32 High Street, Benton, Digbyshire. DG17 2LD
Tel: 01234 567890 Fax: 01234 567891
Email: Sales@simplystationery.co.uk
WWW.simplystationery .co.uk
VAT Reg: 862 113 49

Invoice to:

The Village Shop,
69 Bradbury Way,
Benton,
Digbyshire
DG17 4LY

Invoice No: 105

Date: 21.04.14

Description	Qty	Price	Total	Discount	Net
A4 Copy Paper	20	£2.00	£40.00	0.00	£40.00

Terms 30 Days

Goods Total	£40.00
Less Discount	£00.00
Net Sales	£40.00
VAT @ 20%	£8.00
Total Sales	£48.00

Figure 2-3:
A sales invoice from Simply Stationery.

When the bookkeeper for Simply Stationery enters this invoice, whether on a computer or in manual ledgers, the journal entry for a credit sale would look like this:

	Debit	*Credit*
Trade Debtors	£48.00	
Sales		£40.00
VAT account		£8.00

A computerised accounting system makes this journal entry automatically, but you still need to know what the bookkeeping entries are, just in case you need to correct something. In addition to making this journal entry, your accounts package will enter the information into the customer's account so that accurate statements can be sent out at the end of the month.

When the customer pays the bill, you update the individual customer's record to show that payment has been received. Sage 50 Accounts automatically enters the following into the bookkeeping records:

	Debit	*Credit*
Trade Debtors		£48.00
Cash	£48.00	

Payment from The Village Shop

If you're using Sage 50 Accounts, you can enter credit sales on an invoice like the one in Figure 2-4.

Sage 50 Accounts uses the information on the invoice to update the following accounts:

- ✔ Trade Debtors
- ✔ Stock
- ✔ Customer's
- ✔ VAT

Print out the invoice and send it to the customer straight away. Depending on the payment terms you've negotiated with your customers, send out monthly statements to remind customers that their debt to your company is still outstanding. Regular monitoring of your Aged Debtor report ensures that you know who has not yet paid you. In order to keep these reports up to date, allocate the cash to each customer account on a regular basis.

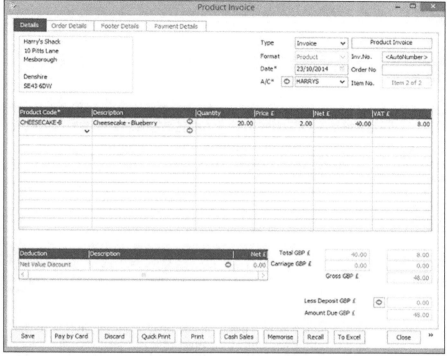

Figure 2-4:
Creating
a sales
invoice
using Sage
50 Accounts
for goods
sold on
credit.

Book II

**Book-
keeping
Day to Day**

When you receive payment from a customer, here's what to do:

1. **From the Bank module, click the Customer icon and select the customer account.**

2. **Sage 50 Accounts automatically lists all outstanding invoices. (See Figure 2-5.)**

3. **Enter how much the customer is paying in total.**

4. **Select the invoice or invoices paid.**

5. **Sage 50 Accounts updates the Trade Debtors account, the Cash account and the customer's individual account to show that payment has been received.**

If your customer is paying a lot of outstanding invoices, Sage 50 Accounts has two clever options that may save you some time. The first option, Pay in Full, marks every invoice as paid if the customer is settling up in full. The other option, Wizard, matches the payment to the outstanding invoices by starting with the oldest until it matches up the exact amount of the payment.

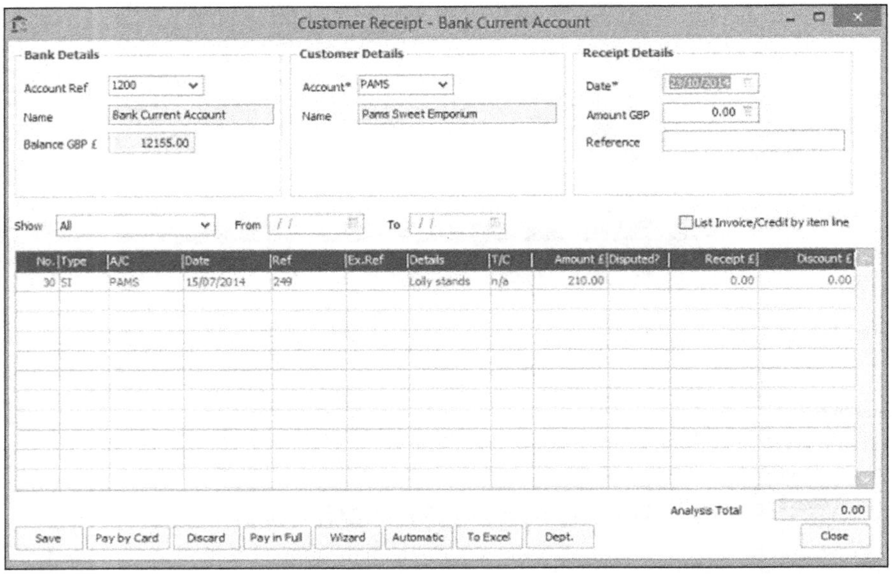

Figure 2-5:
In Sage 50 Accounts, recording payments from customers who bought on credit starts with the Customer Receipt screen.

If your business uses a point-of-sale program integrated into the computerised accounting system, recording credit transactions is even easier for you. Sales details feed into the system as each sale is made, so that you don't have to enter the detail at the end of the day. These point-of-sale programs save a lot of time, but they can get really expensive.

Even if customers don't buy on credit, point-of-sale programs provide businesses with an incredible amount of information about their customers and what they like to buy. This data can be used in the future for direct marketing and special sales to increase the likelihood of return business.

Cashing Up the Cash Register

To ensure that cashiers don't pocket a business's cash, at the end of each day cashiers must *cash up* (show that they've the right amount of cash in the register based on the sales transactions during the day) the amount of cash, cheques and credit sales they took in during the day.

This process of cashing up a cash register actually starts at the end of the previous day, when cashier John Smith and his manager agree on the amount of cash left in John's register drawer. They record cash sitting in cash registers or cash drawers as part of the Cash in Hand account.

When John comes to work the next morning, he starts out with the amount of cash left in the drawer. At the end of the business day, he or his manager run a summary of activity on the cash register for the day to produce a report of the total sales taken in by the cashier. John counts the amount of cash in his register as well as totals for the cheques, credit card receipts and credit account sales. He then completes a cash-out form that looks something like Table 2-1:

Table 2-1	Cash Register: John Smith, 25/4/2014	
Receipts	*Sales*	*Total*
Opening Cash		£100
Cash Sales	£400	
Credit Card Sales	£800	
Credit Account Sales	£200	
Total Sales		£1,400
Sales on Credit		£1,000
Cash Received		£400
Total Cash in Register		£500

A manager reviews John Smith's cash register summary (produced by the actual register) and compares it to the cash-out form. If John's ending cash (the amount of cash remaining in the register) doesn't match the cash-out form, he and the manager try to pinpoint the mistake. If they can't find a mistake, they fill out a cash-overage or cash-shortage form. Some businesses charge the cashier directly for any shortages, whereas others take the position that the cashier's fired after a certain number of shortages of a certain amount (say, three shortages of more than £10).

The manager decides how much cash to leave in the cash drawer or register for the next day and deposits the remainder. He carries out this task for each of his cashiers and then deposits all the cash and cheques from the day in a night-deposit box at the bank. He sends a report with details of the deposit to the bookkeeper so that the data appears in the accounting system. The bookkeeper enters the data on the Cash Sales screen (refer to Figure 2-2) if a computerised accounting system is being used, or into the Cash Receipts book if the books are being kept manually.

Monitoring Sales Discounts

Most businesses offer discounts at some point in time to generate more sales. Discounts are usually in the form of a sale with 10 per cent, 20 per cent or even more off purchases.

When you offer discounts to customers, monitor your sales discounts in a separate account so that you can keep an eye on how much you discount sales each month. If you find that you're losing more and more money to discounting, look closely at your pricing structure and competition to find out why you're having to lower your prices frequently to make sales. You can monitor discount information easily by using the data found on a standard sales invoice. Figure 2-6 shows an invoice from Handson's Hardware, which shows a discount.

From this example, you can see clearly that the business takes in less cash when discounts are offered. When recording the sale in the Cash Receipts book, you record the discount as a debit. This debit increases the Sales Discount account, which the bookkeeper subtracts from the Sales account to calculate the net sales. (We walk you through all these steps and calculations when we discuss preparing the Profit and Loss statement in Book IV, Chapter 1.) Here's what the bookkeeping entry would look like for Handson's Hardware. Remember, if you're using a computerised accounting system, this double entry is done automatically as you post the invoice onto the system.

	Debit	*Credit*
Bank account	£64.80	
Sales Discounts	£6.00	
Sales		£60.00
VAT		£10.80

Sales invoice no. 4567

If you use Sage 50 Accounts, you can add the sales discount as a line item on the sales receipt or invoice, and the system automatically adjusts the sales figures and updates your Sales Discount account.

Invoice

Handsons Hardware

Unit 10 Leestone Industrial Unit, Newtown, Digbyshire. DG14 7PQ
Tel: 01234 123456 Fax: 01234 123457
Email: Sales@handsonshardware.co.uk
WWW.handsonshardware.co.uk
VAT Reg: 987 654 49

Invoice to:

Invoice No: 4567
Account No: 789

Jo Tester,
74 Acacia Avenue,
Benton,
Digbyshire
DG 17 4GH

Date: 25.02.14

Description	Qty	Price	Total
Hammer	1	£15.00	£15.00
Paint brushes	5	£5.00	£25.00
Paint	2 Gall	£10.00	£20.00

Terms 30 Days

Goods Total	£60.00
Less Discount	£6.00
Net Sales	£54.00
VAT@ 20%	£10.80
Total Sales	£64.80

Figure 2-6:
A sales invoice from Handson's Hardware showing a sales discount.

Recording Sales Returns and Allowances

Most businesses deal with *sales returns* on a regular basis. Customers regularly return purchased items because the item is defective, they change their minds or for other reasons. Instituting a no-return policy is guaranteed to produce unhappy customers: ensure that you allow sales returns in order to maintain good customer relations.

Accepting sales returns can be a complicated process. Usually, a business posts a set of rules for returns that may include:

- ✔ Returns are allowed only within 30 days of purchase.
- ✔ You must have a receipt to return an item.
- ✔ When you return an item without a receipt, you can receive only a credit note.

You can set up whatever rules you want for returns. For internal control purposes, the key to returns is monitoring how your staff handle them. In most cases, ensure that a manager's approval is required on returns. Also, make sure that your employees pay close attention to how the customer originally paid for the item being returned. You certainly don't want to give a customer cash when she used credit – you're just handing over your money! After a return's approved, the cashier returns the amount paid by cash or credit card. Customers who bought the items on credit don't get any money back, because they didn't pay anything but expected to be billed later. Instead, a form is filled out so that the amount of the original purchase can be subtracted from the customer's credit account.

You use the information collected by the cashier who handled the return to input the sales return data into the books. For example, a customer returns an item worth £47 that was purchased with cash. You record the cash refund in the Cash Receipts book like this:

	Debit	*Credit*
Sales Returns and Allowances	£39.17	
VAT @ 20%	£7.83	
Bank account		£47.00
To record return of purchase		

If the item was bought with a discount, you list the discount as well and adjust the price to show that discount.

In this journal entry:

- The Sales Returns and Allowances account increases. This account normally carries a debit balance and is subtracted from the Sales account when preparing the Profit and Loss statement, thereby reducing revenue received from customers.

- The debit to the VAT account reduces the amount in that account because VAT is no longer due on the purchase.

- The credit to the Bank account reduces the amount of cash in that account.

Sales allowances (sales incentive programmes) are becoming more popular with businesses. Sales allowances are most often in the form of a gift card. A sold gift card is actually a liability for the business because the business has received cash, but no merchandise has gone out. For that reason, gift card sales are entered in the Gift Card Liability account. When a customer makes a purchase at a later date using the gift card, the Gift Card Liability account is reduced by the purchase amount. Monitoring the Gift Card Liability account allows businesses to keep track of how much is yet to be sold without receiving additional cash.

A business that sells goods on credit and then subsequently receives the goods back needs to raise a *sales credit note* within their accounting system to reverse the effect of the sales invoice that has already been generated.

Figure 2-7 shows an example of a credit note that's been raised by Handson's Hardware, because the paint that was delivered was the wrong colour. The customer has returned the paint but needs a refund against her account.

The double entry that occurs when a credit note is raised and entered into an accounting system is as follows:

	Debit	*Credit*
Sales Return account	£18.00	
VAT account	£3.60	
Debtors account		£21.60

Credit Note dated 25.02.14 to Jo Tester

CREDIT NOTE

Handsons Hardware

Unit 10 Leestone Industrial Unit, Newtown, Digbyshire. DG14 7PQ
Tel: 01234 123456   Fax: 01234 123457
Email: Sales@handsonshardware.co.uk
WWW.handsonshardware.co.uk
VAT Reg: 987 654 49

Credit:

Jo Tester,
74 Acacia Avenue,
Benton,
Digbyshire
DG17 4GH

Invoice No: 4567
Account No: 789

Date: 25.02.14

Description	Qty	Price	Total
Paint	2	£10.00	£20.00
Reason: Wrong Colour			

Terms 30   Days

Goods Total	£20.00
Less Discount	£2.00
Net Credit	£18.00
VAT@ 20%	£3.60
Total Sales	£21.60

Figure 2-7:
An example
of a credit
note raised,
annotated
with the
double-entry
transactions.

Monitoring Trade Debtors

Making sure that customers pay their bills is a crucial responsibility of the bookkeeper. Before sending out the monthly bills, you should run an *Aged Debtor report*, which lists all customers who owe money to the business and the age of each debt, as shown in Figure 2-8.

Date: 23/10/2014 Page: 1
Time: 20:05:20

Sweet Dreams
Aged Debtors Analysis (Detailed) - By Balance (Descending)

Date From:	01/01/1980	Customer From:	
Date To:	23/10/2014	Customer To:	ZZZZZZZ
Include future transactions:	No		
Exclude later payments:	No		

** NOTE: All report values are shown in Base Currency, unless otherwise indicated **

A/C: HARRYS Name: Harry's Shack Contact: Tel:

No	Type	Date	Ref	Details	Balance	Future	Current	Period 1	Period 2	Period 3	Older
31	SI	20/07/2014	250	Misc sweets	1,860.00	0.00	0.00	0.00	0.00	1,860.00	0.00
				Totals:	1,860.00	0.00	0.00	0.00	0.00	1,860.00	0.00

Turnover: 1,550.00 Account Balance: 1,860.00
Credit Limit £ 0.00

A/C: LENS Name: Len's Restaurant Contact: Tel:

No	Type	Date	Ref	Details	Balance	Future	Current	Period 1	Period 2	Period 3	Older
32	SI	26/07/2014	251	Desserts	1,590.00	0.00	0.00	0.00	0.00	1,590.00	0.00
				Totals:	1,590.00	0.00	0.00	0.00	0.00	1,590.00	0.00

Turnover: 1,325.00 Account Balance: 1,590.00
Credit Limit £ 0.00

A/C: CHARLIES Name: Charles Garage Contact: Tel:

No	Type	Date	Ref	Details	Balance	Future	Current	Period 1	Period 2	Period 3	Older
2	SI	01/06/2014	244	Machine refilled	360.00	0.00	0.00	0.00	0.00	0.00	360.00
				Totals:	360.00	0.00	0.00	0.00	0.00	0.00	360.00

Turnover: 300.00 Account Balance: 360.00
Credit Limit £ 0.00

A/C: JOHN Name: Contact: Tel:

No	Type	Date	Ref	Details	Balance	Future	Current	Period 1	Period 2	Period 3	Older
29	SI	01/07/2014	248	Peppermint display	300.00	0.00	0.00	0.00	0.00	300.00	0.00
				Totals:	300.00	0.00	0.00	0.00	0.00	300.00	0.00

Figure 2-8: An Aged Debtor report using Sage 50 software.

Book II

Book-keeping Day to Day

The Aged Debtor report quickly tells you which customers are behind in their bills. In this example, customers are put on stop when their payments are more than 60 days late, so all the accounts shown, with the exception of the John account, should be put on stop, until the invoices are paid and their accounts are brought up to date.

Give a copy of your Aged Debtor report to the sales manager so she can alert staff to problem customers. The sales manager can also arrange for the appropriate collections procedures. Each business sets up its own specific collections process, usually starting with a phone call, followed by letters and possibly legal action, if necessary.

Accepting Your Losses

You may encounter a situation in which a customer never pays your business, even after an aggressive collections process. In this case, you've no choice but to write off the purchase as a bad debt and accept the loss.

Most businesses review their Aged Debtor reports every 6 to 12 months and decide which accounts need to be written off as bad debt. Accounts written off are recorded in a Nominal Ledger account called *Bad Debt*. (See Book I, Chapter 4 for more information about the Nominal Ledger.) The Bad Debt account appears as an Expense account on the Profit and Loss statement. When you write off a customer's account as bad debt, the Bad Debt account increases and the Trade Debtors account decreases.

To give you an idea of how you write off an account, assume that one of your customers never pays £105.75 due. Here's what your journal entry looks like for this debt:

	Debit	*Credit*
Bad Debt	£105.75	
Trade Debtors		£105.75

Sage 50 Accounts has a wizard that helps you write off individual transactions as a bad debt and does all the double entry for you, so you don't need to worry!

If the bad debt included VAT, you've suffered a double loss because you've paid over the VAT to HM Revenue & Customs, even though you never received it. Fortunately, you can reclaim this VAT when you do your next VAT return.

Have a Go

The rest of this chapter gives you extra practice on double-entry bookkeeping, so that you're able to carry out adjustments to the accounts if you need to. More importantly, it means that you'll understand what your computerised accounting system is doing in the background every time you post an entry.

It may be worthwhile referring back to the golden rules of bookkeeping mentioned in Book I, Chapter 2. You see, sticking the rules up on your wall doesn't seem so daft now, does it?!

1. **Take a look at the sales receipt in Figure 2-9. How would you record this transaction in your books, if you were the bookkeeper for a hardware business?**

2. **Looking at the sales receipt in Figure 2-10, how would you record this transaction in your books, if you were a bookkeeper for this office supply business?**

HANDSON'S HARDWARE

Sales receipt 25/2/2014

Item	Quantity	Price	Total
Hammer	1	£15.00	£15.00
Paint Brushes	5	£5.00	£5.00
Paint	2 gallons	£10.00	£10.00
Subtotal			**£60.00**
VAT @ 20%			**£12.00**
Total Sale			**£72.00**
Paid Cash			**£72.00**

Figure 2-9: Sales Receipt for Handson's Hardware on 25/2/2014.

SIMPLY STATIONERY

Sales receipt 05/03/2014

Item	Quantity	Price	Total
Paper	2 boxes	£10.00	£20.00
Print Cartridge	1	£15.00	£15.00
Hanging Files	2 boxes	£5.00	£10.00
Subtotal			**£45.00**
VAT @ 20%			**£9.00**
Total Sale			**£54.00**
Paid by VISA Credit Card			**£54.00**

Figure 2-10: Sales Receipt for Simply Stationery on 05/03/2014.

3. Using the invoice shown in Figure 2-11, how would you record this credit transaction in your books, if you were the bookkeeper for Handson's Hardware?

4. Using the invoice shown in Figure 2-12, how would you record this credit transaction in your books, if you were a bookkeeper for this office supply business?

Invoice

Handsons Hardware

Unit 10 Leestone Industrial Unit ,Newtown, Digbyshire. DG14 7PQ

Tel: 01234 123456   Fax: 01234 123457

Email: Sales@handsonshardware.co.uk

WWW.handsonshardware.co.uk

VAT Reg: 987 654 49

Invoice to:

Jo Tester,
74 Acacia Avenue,
Benton,
Digbyshire
DG17 4GH

Invoice No: 4673
Account No: 823

Date: 12.05.14

Description	Qty	Price	Total	Discount	Net
Hammer	1	£15.00	£15.00	0.00	£15.00
Nails	1 box	£9.00	£9.00	0.00	£9.00
Ladder	1	£90.00	£90.00	0.00	£90.00

Terms 30 Days

Goods Total	£114.00
Less Discount	£00.00
Net Sales	£114.00
VAT @ 20%	£22.80
Total Sales	£136.80

Figure 2-11: Sales invoice for Handson's Hardware.

5. **Use the information in the cash register summary that follows to complete the blank cash summary form. Also, assume that the cash register had £100 at the beginning of the day and £426 at the end of the day. Is there a difference between how much should be in the register and how much is actually in there?**

Invoice

Simply Stationery

32 High Street, Benton, Digbyshire. DG17 2LD
Tel: 01234 567890 Fax: 01234 567891
Email: Sales@simplystationery.co.uk
WWW.simplystationery .co.uk
VAT Reg: 862 113 49

Invoice to: Invoice No: 124

Sues Insurance Agency
23 High Street
Benton
Digbyshire
DG17 4LU

Date: 05.03.14

Description	Qty	Price	Total	Discount	Net
A4 Copy Paper	2	£15.00	£30.00	0.00	£30.00
Print cartridge	1	£25.00	£25.00	0.00	£25.00
Hanging Files	2	£10.00	£20.00	0.00	£20.00

Terms 30 Days

Goods Total	£75.00
Less Discount	£00.00
Net Sales	£75.00
VAT@ 20 %	£15.00
Total Sales	£90.00

Figure 2-12:
Sales
invoice
for Simply
Stationery.

Book II

**Book-
keeping
Day to Day**

Cash Register Summary for Jane Doe on 15/3/2014

Item	Quantity	Price	Total
Paper	20 boxes	£15.00	£300.00
Print cartridges	10	£25.00	£250.00
Envelopes	10 boxes	£7.00	£70.00
Pens	20 boxes	£8.00	£160.00

(continued)

Cash Register Summary for Jane Doe on 15/3/2014 (continued)

Item	Quantity	Price	Total
Subtotal			£780.00
VAT @ 20 %			£156.00
Total cash sales			£336.00
Total credit card sales			£200.00
Total credit account sales			£400.00
Total sales			£936.00

Cash Register: _____   Date: _____

Receipts	Sales	Cash in Register
Beginning cash		_____
Cash sales	_____	
Credit card sales	_____	
Credit account sales	_____	
Total sales	_____	
Minus credit sales	_____	
Total cash received		_____
Total cash that should be in register		_____
Actual cash in register		_____
Difference		_____

6. **How would you record the following transaction in your books, if you were a bookkeeper for an office supply business? Design a sales invoice using the information supplied and show the bookkeeping transactions. Be as creative as you like with the name and address of the office supply business. Use the examples of previous sales invoices shown in Figures 2-3 and 2-6 to help you with the design of the invoice.**

Sales Receipt for 05/03/2014

Item	Quantity	Price	Total
Paper	2 boxes	£15.00	£30.00
Print cartridge	1	£15.00	£15.00

Item	Quantity	Price	Total
Hanging files	2 boxes	£5.00	£10.00
Subtotal			£55.00
Sales discount @ 20%			£11.00
Sales after discount			£44.00
VAT @ 20%			£8.80
Total cash sale			£52.80

7. **How would you record the following credit transaction in your books, if you were a bookkeeper for this office supply business?**

Sales Summary for 05/03/2014

Item	Quantity	Price	Total
Paper	10 boxes	£15.00	£150.00
Print cartridges	5	£15.00	£75.00
Hanging files	7 boxes	£5.00	£35.00
Envelopes	10 boxes	£7.00	£70.00
Pens	20 boxes	£8.00	£160.00
Subtotal			£490.00
Sales discount @ 20%			£98.00
Sales after discount			£392.00
VAT @ 20%			£78.40
Total cash sales			£145.40
Total credit card sales			£150.00
Total credit account sales			£175.00
Total sales			£470.40

8. **A customer returns a pair of trousers she bought for £35 using a credit card. She has a receipt showing when she made the original purchase. The rate of VAT is 20 per cent. How would you record this transaction in the books?**

9. **On 15 December, Jean Jones, a customer of Simply Stationery, returns a filing cabinet she bought on 1 December for £75 on credit. She's already been issued with a sales invoice, but hasn't paid for**

it yet. Design a credit note for this transaction and state how you'd record the transaction in the books.

Note: The rate of VAT is 20 per cent.

10. You discover, after compiling your Aged Debtors report for 30 June 2014, that you've an account that's more than six months past due for a total of £125.65. Your company policy is that you write off bad debt when an account is more than six months late. How would you record this transaction in your books?

Answering the Have a Go Questions

1. **Handson's Hardware would record the sales receipts transactions as follows:**

	Debit	Credit
Bank account	£72.00	
Sales		£60.00
VAT		£12.00

Cash receipts for 25/2/2014

2. **Simply Stationery would record the sales receipts information as follows:**

	Debit	Credit
Bank account	£54.00	
Sales		£45.00
VAT		£9.00

Cash receipts for 05/03/14

3. **You'd record the sales invoice details as follows:**

	Debit	Credit
Debtors	£136.80	
Sales		£114.00
VAT		£22.80

Credit receipts for 12/05/2014

4. You'd record the sales invoice details as follows:

	Debit	*Credit*
Debtors	£90.00	
Sales		£75.00
VAT		£15.00

Credit receipts for 05/03/2014

5. Here's how you'd complete the cash-out form.

Cash Register: Jane Doe, 15/3/2014

Receipts	*Sales*	*Cash in Register*
Beginning cash		£100.00
Cash sales	£336.00	
Credit card sales	£200.00	
Business credit sales	£400.00	
Total sales	£936.00	
Minus sales on credit	(£600.00)	
Total cash received		£336.00
Total cash that should be in register		£436.00
Actual cash in register		£426.00
Difference		Shortage of £10.00

The manager would need to investigate why the till was down by £10.

6. You can use Figures 2-3 and 2-6 to guide you in designing your invoice for these transactions.

The bookkeeping entry is as follows:

	Debit	*Credit*
Bank account	£52.80	
Sales Discount	£11.00	
Sales		£55.00
VAT		£8.80

Cash receipts for 05/03/14

7. **The entry would be:**

	Debit	Credit
Bank account	£295.40	
Debtors	£175.00	
Sales Discount	£98.00	
Sales		£490.00
VAT		£78.40

Cash receipts for 05/03/14

8. **The entry would be:**

	Debit	Credit
Sales Returns and Allowance	£29.17	
VAT	£5.83	
Bank account		£35.00

Even though the customer is receiving a credit on her credit card, you show this refund by crediting your Bank account. Remember, when a customer uses a credit card, the card is processed by the bank and cash is deposited in the business's bank account.

9. **The double-entry bookkeeping would be:**

	Debit	Credit
Sales Returns and Allowances	£60.00	
VAT	£15.00	
Debtors		£75.00

10. **The entry would look like this:**

	Debit	Credit
Bad Debt	£125.65	
Debtors		£125.65

*Accounts written off for
bad debt as at 30/06/14*

Chapter 3

Buying and Tracking Your Purchases

*I*n order to make money, your business must have something to sell. Whether you sell products or offer services, you have to deal with costs directly related to the goods or services being sold. Those costs primarily come from the purchase or manufacturing of the products you plan to sell or the items you need in order to provide the services.

All businesses must keep careful watch over the cost of the products they sell or the services they offer. Ultimately, your business's profits depend on how well you manage those costs, because in most cases costs increase over time rather than decrease. How often do you find a reduction in the price of needed items? It doesn't happen often. When costs increase but the price to the customer remains unchanged, the profit you make on each sale is less.

In addition to the costs to produce products or services, every business has additional expenses associated with purchasing supplies needed to run the business. The bookkeeper has primary responsibility for monitoring all these costs and expenses as invoices are paid and alerting business owners or managers when suppliers increase prices. This chapter covers how to track purchases and their costs, manage stock, buy and manage supplies, and pay the bills for the items your business buys.

Keeping Track of Stock

Products to be sold are called *stock*. As a bookkeeper, you use two accounts to track stock:

- ✔ **Purchases:** Where you record the actual purchase of goods to be sold. This account is used to calculate the *Cost of Goods Sold*, which is an item on the Profit and Loss statement (see Book IV, Chapter 1 for more on this statement).

- ✔ **Stock:** Where you track the value of stock on hand. This value is shown on the Balance Sheet as an asset in a line item called *Stock* (Book IV, Chapter 2 addresses the Balance Sheet).

Businesses track physical stock on hand using one of two methods:

- ✔ **Periodic stock count:** Conducting a physical count of the stock in the stores and in the warehouse. This count can be done daily, monthly, yearly or for any other period that best matches your business needs. (Many businesses close for all or part of a day to count stock.)

- ✔ **Perpetual stock count:** Adjusting stock counts as each sale is made. In order to use this method, you must manage your stock using a computerised accounting system tied into your point of sale (usually cash registers).

- ✔ Even if you use a perpetual stock method, periodically do a physical count of stock to ensure that the numbers match what's in your computer system. Because theft, damage and loss of stock aren't automatically entered in your computer system, the losses don't show up until you do a physical count of the stock you have on hand in your business.

When preparing your Profit and Loss statement at the end of an accounting period (whether that period is for a month, a quarter or a year), you need to calculate the Cost of Goods Sold in order to calculate the profit made.

In order to calculate the Cost of Goods Sold, you must first find out how many items of stock were sold. You start with the amount of stock on hand at the beginning of the month (called *Opening Stock*), as recorded in the Stock account, and add the amount of purchases, as recorded in the Purchases account, to find the Goods Available for Sale. Then you subtract the stock on hand at the end of the month *(Closing Stock)*, which is determined by counting remaining stock.

Here's how you calculate the number of goods sold:

> Opening Stock + Purchases = Goods Available for Sale – Closing Stock
> = Items Sold

After you determine the number of goods sold, compare that number to the actual number of items the business sold during that accounting period, which is based on sales figures collected through the month. When the numbers don't match, you've a problem. The mistake may be in the stock count, or items may be unaccounted for because someone has misplaced or damaged and discarded them. In the worst-case scenario, you may have a problem with customer or employee theft. These differences are usually tracked within the accounting system in a line item called *Stock Shortages*.

Entering initial cost

When your business first receives stock, you enter the initial cost of that stock into the bookkeeping system based on the shipment's invoice. In some cases, invoices are sent separately, and only a delivery note is included in the order. When that situation applies, you still record the receipt of the goods, because the business incurs the cost from the day it receives the goods, and you must be sure that the money is available to pay for the goods when the invoice arrives and the bill comes due. You track outstanding bills in the Trade Creditors (Accounts Payable) account. Where you only have a delivery note, use the price agreed on your purchase order (if you use purchase orders) or the price from your last invoice from that supplier.

Entering the receipt of stock is a relatively easy entry in the bookkeeping system. For example, if your business buys £1,000 of stock to be sold, you normally receive a purchase invoice for those goods. The invoice is entered into your accounting system as described in Book I, Chapter 4. The following double entry takes place:

	Debit	*Credit*
Materials Purchased	£1,000	
Trade Creditors		£1,000

The Purchases account increases by £1,000 to reflect the additional costs, and the Trade Creditors account increases by the same amount to reflect the amount of the bill that needs to be paid in the future.

When stock enters your business, in addition to recording the actual costs, you need more detail about what you've bought, how much of each item you've bought and what each item cost. You also need to track

- How much stock you have on hand
- The value of the stock you have on hand
- When you need to order more stock

Book II

Bookkeeping Day to Day

Tracking these details for each type of product bought can be a nightmare. However, a computerised accounting system simplifies this process of tracking stock. Details about stock can be entered initially into your computer accounting system in several ways:

✔ If you pay by cheque or credit card when you receive the stock, you can enter the details about each item on the cheque counterfoil or credit card slip.

✔ If you use purchase orders, you can enter the detail about each item on the purchase order, record receipt of the items when they arrive and update the information when you receive the bill.

✔ If you don't use purchase orders, you can enter the detail about the items when you receive them and update the information when you receive the bill.

To give you an idea of how this information is collected in a computerised accounting software program, Figure 3-1 shows you how to enter the details in Sage 50 Accounts. This particular form is for the receipt of stock without a purchase order and can be used when you receive a supplier invoice.

Figure 3-2 shows a stock item record in the computerised accounting system. Note that you must give the item a product code and a description. The product code is a short unique name or code to identify the stock item internally. The longer description is a more user-friendly name that can appear on customer invoices (sales transactions). You can input a cost and sales price if you want, or you can leave them at zero and enter the cost and sales prices with each transaction.

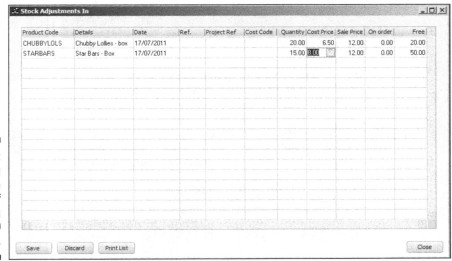

Figure 3-1: Recording of the receipt of stock using Sage 50 Accounts.

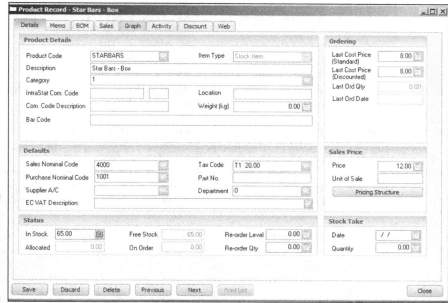

Book II

Book-keeping Day to Day

Figure 3-2: Setting up a stock item using Sage 50 Accounts.

If you've a set contract purchase price or sales price on a stock item, you can enter the price on this form to save time – you don't then have to enter the price each time you record a transaction. But if the price changes frequently, leave the space blank so that you don't forget to enter the updated price when you enter a transaction.

Notice in Figure 3-2 that you can also use this form to give you information about stock on hand and when stock needs to be reordered. To make sure that your shelves are never empty, enter a number for each item that indicates at what point you want to reorder stock. You can indicate the 'Reorder Level' in the section called 'Status'. (A nice feature of Sage 50 Accounts is that you can run a report to see which stock items have fallen below their reorder level and use that to place your next order.)

If you use the Purchase Order Processing routine and save the form that records the receipt of stock in Sage 50 Accounts, the software automatically

- ✔ Adjusts the quantity of stock you have in stock
- ✔ Increases the Asset account called Stock
- ✔ Lowers the quantity of items on order (if you initially entered the information as a purchase order)
- ✔ Averages the cost of stock on hand
- ✔ Increases the Trade Creditor account

Managing stock and its value

After you record the receipt of stock, you have the responsibility of managing the stock you have on hand. You must also know the value of that stock. You may think that as long as you know what you paid for the items, the value isn't difficult to calculate. Well, accountants can't let things be that simple, and so have five different ways to value stock:

- ✔ **LIFO (last in, first out):** You assume that the last items put on the shelves (the newest items) are the first items to be sold. Retail shops that sell non-perishable items, such as tools, are likely to use this type of system. For example, when a hardware store gets new hammers, workers probably don't unload the hammers on the shelves and put the newest items in the back. Instead, they put the new hammers in the front, so they're likely to be sold first.

- ✔ **FIFO (first in, first out):** You assume that the first items put on the shelves (the oldest items) are sold first. Shops that sell perishable goods, such as food shops, use this stock valuation method most often. For example, when new milk arrives at a shop, the person stocking the shelves unloads the older milk, puts the new milk at the back of the shelf, and then puts the older milk in front. Each carton of milk (or other perishable item) has a date indicating the last day it can be sold, so food shops always try to sell the oldest stuff first, while those items are still sellable. (They try, but how many times have you reached to the back of a food shelf to find items with the longest shelf life?)

- ✔ **Averaging:** You average the cost of goods received, to avoid worrying about which items are sold first or last. This method of stock is used most often in any retail or services environment where prices are constantly fluctuating and the business owner finds that an average cost works best for managing the Cost of Goods Sold.

- ✔ **Specific identification:** You maintain cost figures for each stock item individually. Retail outlets that sell big-ticket items such as cars, which often have a different set of extras on each item, use this type of stock valuation method.

- ✔ **LCM (lower of cost or market):** You set stock values based on whichever is lower: the amount you paid originally for the stock item (the cost) or the current market value of the item. Businesses that deal in precious metals, commodities or publicly traded securities often use this method because the prices of their products can fluctuate wildly, sometimes even in the same day.

After you choose a stock valuation method, you need to use the same method each year on your financial reports and when you file your accounts. If you decide that you want to change the method, you need to explain the reasons for the change both to HM Revenue & Customs and to your financial backers.

If you run an incorporated business in which shares have been sold, you need to explain the change to your shareholders. You also have to go back and show how the change in stock method impacts your prior financial reporting, and adjust your profit margins in previous years to reflect the new stock valuation method's impact on your long-term profit history.

Figuring out the best method for you

We're sure that you're wondering why the stock valuation method you use matters so much. The key to the choice is the impact on your bottom line as well as the tax your business pays.

Because FIFO assumes the oldest (and most likely the lowest priced) items are sold first, this method results in a lower Cost of Goods Sold number. Because Cost of Goods Sold is subtracted from sales to determine profit, a lower Cost of Goods Sold number produces a higher profit. (For more on Cost of Goods Sold, see 'Keeping Track of Stock', earlier in this chapter.)

The opposite is true for LIFO, which uses cost figures based on the last price paid for the stock (and most likely the highest price). Using the LIFO method, the Cost of Goods Sold number is higher, which means a larger sum is subtracted from sales to determine profit. Thus, the profit margin is lower. The good news, however, is that the tax bill is also low.

The Averaging method gives a business the best picture of what's happening with stock costs and trends. Rather than constantly dealing with the ups and downs of stock costs, this method smoothes out the numbers you use to calculate a business's profits. Cost of Goods Sold, taxes and profit margins for this method fall between those of LIFO and FIFO. Definitely choose this method when you're operating a business in which stock prices are constantly going up and down.

The Averaging method always falls between LIFO and FIFO as regards the Cost of Goods Sold, taxes and profit margin.

Sage 50 Accounts uses the LIFO method to calculate Cost of Goods Sold and stock line items on its financial reports, so if you choose this method, you can use Sage 50 Accounts and the financial reports it generates. However, if you choose to use one of the other four stock methods, you can't use the Sage 50 Accounts financial report numbers. Instead, you have to print out a report of purchases and calculate the accurate numbers to use on your financial reports for the Cost of Goods Sold and Stock accounts.

Check with your accountant to see which stock method is best for you given the type of business you're operating and which one is the most acceptable to HM Revenue & Customs. It's one of many accounting methods that your accountant needs to choose when setting up the stock system. We discuss the various different methods of measuring Cost of Goods Sold in Book V, Chapter 2.

Book II

Book-keeping Day to Day

Comparing the methods

To show you how much of an impact stock valuation can have on profit margin, in this section we compare three of the most common methods: FIFO, LIFO and Averaging. In this example, we assume that Business A bought the stock in question at different prices on three different occasions. Opening Stock is valued at £500 (50 items at £10 each).

Here's the calculation to determine the number of items sold (from the earlier 'Keeping Track of Stock' section):

$$\text{Opening Stock} + \text{Purchases} = \text{Goods Available for Sale} - \text{Closing Stock}$$
$$= \text{Items Sold}$$
$$50 + 500 = 550 - 75$$
$$= 475$$

Here's what the business paid to purchase the stock:

Date	Quantity	Unit Price
1 April	150	£10
15 April	150	£25
30 April	200	£30

Here's an example of how you calculate the Cost of Goods Sold using the Averaging method:

Category	Quantity (Unit Price)	Total Cost
Opening Stock	50 (£10)	£500
Purchases	150 (£10)	£1,500
	150 (£25)	£3,750
	200 (£30)	£6,000
Total Stock	550	£11,750

Now you can do other calculations:

Average Stock cost	£11,750 ÷ 550 = £21.360
Cost of Goods Sold	475 × £21.36 = £10,146
Closing Stock	75 @ £21.36 = £1,602

The Cost of Goods Sold number appears on the Profit and Loss statement and is subtracted from Sales. The Closing Stock number shows up as an asset on the Balance Sheet. This system applies to all three stock valuation methods.

Now, we demonstrate how you calculate the Cost of Goods Sold using the FIFO method. With this method, you assume that the first items you receive are the first ones you sell, and because the first items you receive here are those in Opening Stock, we start with them:

Date	Quantity (Unit Price)	Total
Opening Stock	50 (£10)	£500
1 April	150 (£10)	£1,500
15 April	150 (£25)	£3,750
30 April	125 (£30)	£3,750
Cost of Goods Sold	475	£9,500
Closing Stock	75 @ £30	£2,250

Note: Only 125 of the 200 units purchased on 30 April are used in the FIFO method. Because this method assumes that the first items into stock are the first items you sell (or take out of stock), the first items you use are those on 1 April. Then you use the 15 April items, and finally you take the remaining needed items from those bought on April 30. Because you bought 200 on April 30 and you only needed 125, 75 of the items you bought on April 30 are left in Closing Stock. The Cost of Goods Sold figure, which is £9,500, is the sum of the total values of the units that are deemed to have been sold to arrive at this figure (£500 + £1,500 + £3,750 + £3,750).

Next, calculate the Cost of Goods Sold using the LIFO method. With this method, you assume that the last items you receive are the first ones you sell, and because the last items you receive were those you purchased on April 30, we start with them:

Date	Quantity (Unit Price)	Total
30 April	200 (£30)	£6,000
15 April	150 (£25)	£3,750
1 April	125 (£10)	£1,250
Cost of Goods Sold	475	£11,000
Closing Stock	75 @ £10	£750

Note: Because LIFO assumes the last items to arrive are sold first, the Closing Stock includes the 25 remaining units (150 purchased less 125 used/sold) from the 1 April purchase plus the 50 units in Opening Stock.

Here's how the use of stock under the LIFO method impacts the business profits. We assume that you sell the items to the customers for £40 per unit, which means total sales of £19,000 for the month (£40 × 475 units sold).

In this example, we just look at the *Gross Profit*, which is the profit from Sales before considering expenses incurred for operating the business. We talk more about the different profit types and what they mean in Book IV Chapter 1. The following equation calculates Gross Profit:

Sales – Cost of Goods Sold = Gross Profit

Table 3-1 shows a comparison of Gross Profit for the three methods used in this example.

Table 3-1	Comparison of Gross Profit Based on Stock Valuation Method		
Profit and Loss Statement Line Item	**FIFO**	**LIFO**	**Averaging**
Sales	£19,000	£19,000	£19,000
Cost of Goods Sold	£9,500	£11,000	£10,146
Gross Profit	£9,500	£8,000	£8,854

Looking at the comparisons of Gross Profit, you can see that stock valuation can have a major impact on your bottom line. LIFO is likely to give you the lowest profit because the last stock items bought are usually the most expensive. FIFO is likely to give you the highest profit because the first items bought are usually the cheapest. And the profit that the Averaging method produces is likely to fall somewhere in between the two.

Buying and Monitoring Supplies

In addition to stock, all businesses must buy the supplies used to operate the business, such as paper, pens and paper clips. Supplies that businesses haven't bought in direct relationship to the manufacturing or purchasing of goods or services for sale fall into the category of *expenses*.

Just how closely you want to monitor the supplies you use depends on your business needs. The expense categories you establish may be as broad as Office Supplies and Retail Supplies, or you may want to set up accounts for each type of supply used. Each additional account is just one more thing that needs to be managed and monitored in the accounting system, so you need to determine whether keeping a particularly detailed record of supplies is worth your time.

Your best bet is to track supplies that make a big dent in your budget carefully with an individual account. For example, if you anticipate paper usage is going to be high, monitor that usage with a separate account called Paper Expenses.

Many businesses don't use the bookkeeping system to manage their supplies. Instead, they designate one or two people as office managers or supply managers and keep the number of accounts used for supplies to a minimum. Other businesses decide to monitor supplies by department or division, and set up a Supply account for each one. This system puts the burden of monitoring supplies in the hands of the department or division managers.

Staying on Top of Your Bills

Eventually, you have to pay for both the stock and the supplies you purchase for your business. In most cases, you post the bills to the Trade Creditors account when they arrive, and they're paid when due. A large chunk of the cash you pay out of your Cash account (see Book I, Chapter 4 and Book II, Chapter 1 for more information on the Cash account and handling cash) is in the form of the cheques you send out to pay bills due in Trade Creditors, so you need to have careful controls over the five key functions of Trade Creditors:

- ✔ Entering bills you need to pay into the accounting system
- ✔ Preparing cheques to pay the bills
- ✔ Signing cheques to pay the bills
- ✔ Sending out payment cheques to suppliers
- ✔ Reconciling the Bank account

In your business, the person who enters the bills to be paid into the system is likely to be the same person who also prepares the payment cheques. However, you must ensure that someone else does the other tasks. Never allow the person who prepares the cheques to review the bills to be paid and sign the cheques, unless of course that person's you, the business owner. (We talk more about cash control and the importance of separating duties in Book II, Chapter 1.)

Properly managing Trade Creditors allows you to avoid late fees or interest and take advantage of discounts offered for paying early, therefore saving your business a lot of money. If you're using a computerised accounting system, you need to enter the bill due date and any discount information at the time you receive the stock or supplies. (See Figure 3-1 for how you record this information.)

If you're working with a paper system rather than a computerised accounting system, you need to set up a way to ensure that you don't miss bill due dates. Many businesses use two accordion files: one set up by the month, and the other set up by the day. On receipt, you put a bill into the first accordion file according to the due month. On the first day of that month, the Purchase Ledger clerk pulls all the bills due that month and puts them in the daily accordion file based on the dates the bills are due. The clerk then posts payment cheques in time to arrive in the suppliers' offices by the due dates.

In some cases, businesses offer a discount if their customers pay bills early. Sage 50 Accounts allows you to set up for each supplier Settlement Due dates and Settlement Discount percentage figures. For example, if a supplier is set up as '10 days' and '2 per cent', it means that if the bill is paid in 10 days, the purchasing business can take a 2 per cent discount; otherwise, the amount due must be paid in full in 30 days. If the total amount due for a bill is £1,000 and the business pays the bill in 10 days, that business can take a 2 per cent discount, or £20. This discount may not seem like much, but if your business buys £100,000 of stock and supplies in a month and each supplier offers a similar discount, you can save £1,000. Over the course of a year, discounts on purchases can save your business a significant amount of money and improve your profits.

In addition, many businesses state that they charge interest or late fees if a bill isn't paid in 30 days (although in reality few dare make this charge if they want to retain the business).

Have a Go

Here are some exercises for you to practise the principles discussed in this chapter.

1. **Harry's Hardware started the month with 25 wrenches on the shelf, with an average per unit value of £3.25. During the month, Harry made these additional purchases:**

1 April	100 wrenches @ £3.50
10 April	100 wrenches @ £3.75
20 April	150 wrenches @ £4.00

   At the end of the month, Harry had 100 wrenches on the shelf. Calculate the value of the Closing Stock and the Cost of Goods Sold using the Averaging method.

2. **Harry's Hardware started the month with 25 wrenches on the shelf, with an average per unit value of £3.25. During the month, Harry made these additional purchases:**

1 April	100 wrenches @ £3.50
10 April	100 wrenches @ £3.75
20 April	150 wrenches @ £4.00

At the end of the month, Harry had 100 wrenches on the shelf. Calculate the value of the Closing Stock and the Cost of Goods Sold using the FIFO method.

3. **Harry's Hardware started the month with 25 wrenches on the shelf with an average per unit value of £3.25. During the month, Harry made these additional purchases:**

1 April	100 wrenches @ £3.50
10 April	100 wrenches @ £3.75
20 April	150 wrenches @ £4.00

At the end of the month, Harry had 100 wrenches on the shelf. Calculate the value of the Closing Stock and the Cost of Goods Sold using the LIFO method.

4. **Suppose your company receives an invoice for £500,000 on 31 March that says, 'Settlement discount of 3 per cent if paid within 10 days of date of invoice.' How much discount would you receive and by what date should you pay the invoice to receive this discount?**

5. **Suppose your company receives an invoice for £100,000 on 31 March that says, 'Settlement discount of 2 per cent if paid within 15 days of the date of invoice.' How much discount would you receive and by what date should you pay the invoice to receive this discount?**

6. **If you keep track of the amount of stock you have on hand by physically counting how much product is on your shop shelves and in your warehouse on a regular basis, what is this kind of stock system called?**

7. **If your stock is counted each time you ring up a sale on your register, what is this kind of stock system called?**

8. **If you work in a grocery shop and carefully place the newest loaves of bread at the back of the shelf and bring the older loaves of bread to the front, what type of stock system does your shop probably use?**

9. **If you work at a car dealership and you track the sale of a car using the original invoice price, what type of stock system does your dealership probably use?**

Answering the Have a Go Questions

1. **Here's how you'd calculate the Closing Stock and Cost of Goods Sold using the Averaging method:**

Opening Stock	25 wrenches @ £3.25	£81.25
1 April	100 wrenches @ £3.50	£350.00
10 April	100 wrenches @ £3.75	£375.00
20 April	150 wrenches @ £4.00	£600.00
Total Goods Available for Sale	375 wrenches	£1,406.25
Average Cost per Unit	£1,406.25/375	£3.75
Closing Stock	100 @ £3.75	£375.00
Cost of Goods Sold	275 @ £3.75	£1,031.25

2. **Here's how you'd calculate the Closing Stock and Cost of Goods Sold using the FIFO method:**

Opening Stock:	25 wrenches @ £3.25	£81.25
Next in:		
1 April	100 wrenches @ £3.50	£350.00
10 April	100 wrenches @ £3.75	£375.00
20 April	50 wrenches @ £4.00	£200.00
Cost of Goods Sold		£1,006.25
Closing Stock	100 wrenches @ £4.00	£400.00

3. **Here's how you'd calculate the Closing Stock and Cost of Goods Sold using the LIFO method:**

First Sold purchased 20 April:	150 @ £4.00	£600.00
Next Sold purchased 10 April:	100 @ £3.75	£375.00
Next Sold purchased 1 April:	25 @ £3.50	£87.50
Cost of Goods Sold		£1,062.50
Closing Stock		
75 from April 1	@ £3.50	£262.50
25 from beginning @ £3.25	£81.25	£343.75

4. **The company receives a 3 per cent discount if it pays the invoice in 10 days – by 10 April.** The discount is £15,000 if paid by 10 April. So, you should pay the invoice by 10 April.

5. **The company receives a 2 per cent discount if it pays the invoice in 15 days – by 15 April.** The discount is £2,000 if paid by 15 April. So you should pay the invoice by 15 April.

6. **If you physically count your stock on a regular, monthly, quarterly or yearly basis, this is known as a periodic stock count system.**

7. **If your business operates a system whereby the till adjusts your stock each time a sale is made, this is a perpetual stock system.**

8. **A grocery shop would want the first product in (oldest item) to be the first product out (first sold).** So your grocery shop is using the FIFO method.

9. **A car dealership usually wants to maintain a specific identification system because each car in the stock probably has different options and a different cost.** So your car dealership is using the Specific Identification method.

Chapter 4

Doing Your Banking

. . . .

In This Chapter

▶ Counting your business's cash

▶ Finalising the cash books

▶ Reconciling your bank accounts

▶ Posting cash-related adjustments

. . . .

*A*ll business owners – whether the business is a small family-owned shop or a major international conglomerate – periodically like to test how well their businesses are doing. They also want to make sure that the numbers in their accounting systems actually match what's physically in their shops and offices. After they check out what's in the books, these business owners can prepare financial reports to determine the business's financial success or failure during the last month, quarter or year. This process of verifying the accuracy of your books is called *checking the books*.

The first step in checking the books involves counting the business's cash and verifying that the cash numbers in your books match the actual cash on hand at a particular point in time. This chapter explains how you can test that the cash counts are accurate, finalise the cash books for the accounting period, reconcile the bank accounts and post any adjustments or corrections to the Nominal Ledger.

Checking the books: Why bother?

You're probably thinking that checking the books sounds like a huge task that takes lots of time. And you're right – but checking the books every now and then is essential to ensure that what's recorded in your accounting system realistically measures what's actually going on in your business.

Mistakes can be made with any accounting system and, unfortunately, any business can fall victim to theft or embezzlement. The only way to be sure that none of these problems exist in your business is to check the books periodically. Most businesses do this check every month.

Making Sure that the Closing Cash Is Right

Checking your books starts with counting your cash. Why start with cash? Because the accounting process starts with transactions, and transactions occur when cash changes hands to buy things you need to run the business or to sell your products or services. Before you can even begin to test whether the books are right, you need to know whether your books have captured what's happened to your business's cash and if the amount of cash shown in your books actually matches the amount of cash you have on hand.

In Book II, Chapter 2, we discuss how a business cashes up the money taken in by each cashier. That daily process gives a business good control of the point at which cash comes into the business from customers who buy the business's products or services. The process also measures any cash refunds the business gives to customers who returned items.

Producing a snapshot in time

The points of sale and return aren't the only times that cash comes into or goes out of the business. If your business sells products on credit (see Book II, Chapter 2), bookkeeping staff responsible for monitoring customer credit accounts collect some of the cash from customers at a later point in time. And when your business needs something, whether products to be sold or supplies for various departments, you must pay cash to suppliers and contractors. Sometimes cash is paid out on the spot, but often the bill is recorded in the Trade Creditors (Accounts Payable) account and paid at a later date. All these transactions involve the use of cash, so the amount of cash on hand in the business at any one time includes not only what's in the cash registers, but also what's on deposit in the business's bank accounts. You need to know the balances of those accounts and test those balances to ensure that they're accurate and match what's in your business's books. We talk more about how to do that in the section 'Reconciling Bank Accounts', later in this chapter.

So your snapshot in time includes not only the cash on hand in your cash registers, but also any cash you may have in the bank. Some departments may also have Petty Cash accounts, which you count as well. The total cash figure is what you show as an asset named 'Cash' in your business's financial statement, the *Balance Sheet*. The Balance Sheet shows all that the business owns (its assets) and owes (its liabilities), as well as the capital the owners have in the business. (We talk more about the Balance Sheet and how you prepare one in Book IV, Chapter 2.)

The actual cash you have on hand is just one tiny piece of the cash moving through your business during the accounting period. Your cash books contain the full details of the cash that flowed into and out of the business.

Closing the cash books

If you use a computerised accounting system, you don't have separate cash books: the money received into your business is recorded into the bank accounts. However, you can still check your cash received into the business by running various reports, such as Daybook reports, showing invoices paid on both the Customer and Supplier Ledgers. You can also run Aged Debtors reports to see who still owes you money, and also Aged Creditor reports to see how much money you owe to your suppliers. With Sage, you can run a month-end, which essentially automatically closes your cash books/bank for the period.

Book II

Book-keeping Day to Day

Reconciling Bank Accounts

Part of checking out the cash involves checking that what you have in your bank accounts actually matches what the bank thinks you have in those accounts. This process is called *reconciling* the accounts.

If you've done everything right, your accounting records match the bank's records of how much cash you have in your accounts. The day you close your books probably isn't the same date as the bank sends its statements, so do your best to balance the books internally without actually reconciling your bank account. Correcting any problems during the process minimises problems you may face reconciling the Cash accounts when that bank statement actually arrives.

You've probably reconciled your personal bank account at least a few times over the years, and the good news is that reconciling business accounts is a similar process. Table 4-1 shows one common format for reconciling your bank account:

Below we show you an example of a bank reconciliation:

You've just received your bank statement in the post. You find that your balance at the bank is £1,200 beginning balance, £4,000 in deposits, £4,300

Table 4-1	Bank Reconciliation			
Transactions	*Beginning Balance*	*Deposits*	*Disbursements*	*Ending Balance*
Balance per bank statement	£	£	£	£
Deposits in transit (those not shown on statement)		£		£
Outstanding cheques (cheques that haven't shown up yet)			(£)	(£)
Total	£	£	£	£
Balance per cash book or bank account (which should be the same)				£

in payments, and your ending balance is £900. You review the deposits and find that a deposit of £1,000 doesn't show on the statement. You find that cheques totalling £600 have not yet cleared. The balance in your bank account is £1,300. Does your bank account reconcile to the balance on your bank statement?

Using the bank reconciliation chart, Table 4-2 shows the answer.

Table 4-2	An Example of a Bank Reconciliation			
Transactions	*Beginning Balance*	*Deposits*	*Payments*	*Ending Balance*
Balance per bank statement	£1,200	£4,000	(£4,300)	£900
Deposits in transit (those not shown on statement)		£1,000		£1,000
Outstanding cheques (cheques that haven't shown up yet)			(£600)	(£600)
Total	£1,200	£5,000	(£4,900)	£1,300
Balance per Cash book or Bank account (which should be the same)				£1,300

The bank statement and your bank account do reconcile.

After entering all the transactions into your accounts system, the books for the period you're looking at may still be incomplete. Sometimes, adjustments or corrections must be made to the bank account before it can be reconciled. For example, monthly credit card fees and interest received from the bank may not yet be recorded in your bank account. There may also be standing orders and direct debits that come out of your bank account that need to be entered into your accounts system.

The best way to reconcile your bank account is to methodically enter all the cash you've received and cheques you've paid out using your source documents such as cheque books and paying-in books. Then, you need to work through a copy of your bank statements and see what else needs to be entered.

Looking at a practical way to reconcile your bank account

Following is the method we adopt when we reconcile bank accounts. Most people reconcile the bank account on a monthly basis, so the chances are you have a month's worth of bank statements in front of you for this task.

Follow these steps:

1. **With your bank statements in front of you, place a tick against all the items already entered into your bookkeeping system, including all cheques and items paid in via paying-in books.**

   A number of items remain unticked.

2. **Now enter all the remaining entries into your system, ticking them once after you enter them.**

   These entries include all your electronic receipts and payments, such as direct debits and BACS payments. You should now have a tick placed against all the entries on your bank statement.

3. **Work through each transaction in your cash book and match them against the bank statement as a double-check.**

   For manual bookkeeping systems, you mark the Cashbook using a tick (or perhaps a *B* for bank statement). All items that are left on the Cashbook without a tick are items that have not appeared on the bank statement. These items are your un-presented cheques or outstanding lodgements (deposits in transit). You can now easily write up your bank reconciliation, as shown in Table 4-1.

When you tick each item in the Cashbook against the bank statement entry, also place a cross against the original tick on the bank statement. You can then see at a glance on the bank statement that all transactions have been entered and also checked against the Cashbook.

The same reconciliation process can be applied to credit card statements that the business receives. However, be sure that if you're using a computerised reconciliation process you correctly enter the credit card balance as a negative figure, because this balance is money owed.

Considering credit card sales

If your business allows customers to buy your goods using a credit card, then you also need to reconcile the statements that you receive from the bank that handles your credit card sales.

You normally receive a statement listing

- ✔ All your business's transactions for the month
- ✔ The total amount your business sold through credit card sales
- ✔ The total fees charged to your account

If you find a difference between what the bank reports say you sold on credit cards and what the business's books show regarding credit card sales, you need to play detective and find the reason for the difference. In most cases, the error involves the charging back of one or more sales because a customer disputes the charge. In this case, an adjustment must be made to cash received, to reflect that loss of sale, so that the bank statement and business books match up.

For example, suppose £200 in credit card sales were disputed. The original entry of the transaction in the books looks like this:

	Debit	*Credit*
Sales	£200	
Bank		£200

To reverse disputed credit sales recorded in June.

This entry reduces the total Sales account for the month as well as the amount of the Cash account. If the dispute is resolved and the money is later retrieved, you can then re-enter the sale when the cash is received.

You also record any fees related to credit card fees as a bank payment. For example, if credit card fees for the month of June total £200, the entry in the books looks like this:

	Debit	Credit
Credit Card Fees	£200	
Bank		£200

To post credit card fees for the month of June.

Tracking down errors

Ideally, your balance and the bank's balance, adjusted by transactions not yet shown on the statement, match. If they don't, you need to find out why.

- ✔ **If the bank balance is higher than your balance,** check to ensure that all the deposits listed by the bank appear in the Cash account in your books. If you find that the bank lists a deposit that you don't have, you need to do some detective work to work out what that deposit was for and add the detail to your accounting records. Also, check to make sure that all cheques you've issued have cleared. Your balance may be missing a cheque that should have been listed in outstanding cheques.

- ✔ **If the bank balance is lower than your balance,** check to ensure that all cheques listed by the bank are recorded in your Cash account. You may have missed one or two cheques that were written but not properly recorded. You also may have missed a deposit that you've listed in your Cash account and thought the bank should already have shown as a deposit, but that isn't yet on the statement. If you notice a missing deposit on the bank statement, make sure that you have your proof of deposit and check with the bank to ensure that the cash is in the account.

- ✔ **If all deposits and cheques are correct but you still see a difference,** your only option is to check your maths and make sure that all cheques and deposits were entered correctly.

Sometimes, you have to decide whether rooting out every little difference is really worthwhile. When the amount is just a few pence, don't waste your time trying to find the error; just adjust the balance in your books. But when the difference is a significant amount for your business, try to track it down. You never know exactly what accounts are impacted by an error or how that difference may impact your profit or loss.

Using a computerised system

If you use a computerised accounting system, reconciliation is much easier than if you keep your books manually. In Sage 50 Accounts, for example, when you start the reconciliation process, a screen pops up in which you can add the ending bank statement balance and any bank fees or interest earned. Figure 4-1 shows you that screen. In this example, £930 is the ending balance.

After you click OK, you get a screen that lists all cheques written since the last reconciliation as well as all deposits. Double-click on all the items listed in the top part of your Sage screen that are also shown on your bank statement, as in Figure 4-2. Ensure that the matched balance and the statement balance are the same and the difference is zero (see the bottom right corner of the Sage screen), and then click Reconcile.

If you enter a Statement Reference in your statement summary, as shown in Figure 4-1, Sage 50 Accounts automatically provides a Bank Reconciliation report, which it saves as a PDF file in the History archive. This report is shown in Figure 4-3. You can also run reports showing un-reconciled items at the month-end.

Figure 4-1: When you start the reconciliation process in Sage 50 Accounts, you indicate the bank's ending balance and any bank service charges or interest earned on a particular account.

Statement Summary

Bank : 1200   Bank Current Account

Statement Reference : June 2011

Ending Balance : 930.00   Statement Date : 30/06/2011

Interest Earned :

Amount : 0.00   Date : 20/02/2012   NC :   TC : T2 0.00

Account Charges :

Amount : 0.00   Date : 20/02/2012   NC :   TC : T2 0.00

OK   Cancel

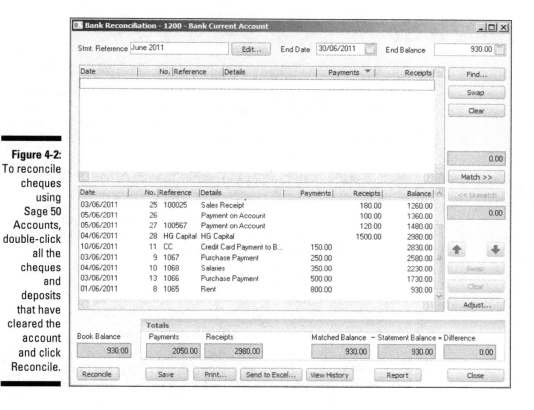

Figure 4-2:
To reconcile cheques using Sage 50 Accounts, double-click all the cheques and deposits that have cleared the account and click Reconcile.

Book II

Book-keeping Day to Day

Figure 4-3:
After reconciling your accounts, Sage 50 Accounts automatically provides a Bank Reconciliation report.

Have a Go

Your turn! Sharpen your pencil and test yourself on checking the books.

1. **Make a list of all the accounts in your business that you need to reconcile at the end of each accounting period. Remember to include all bank accounts and Petty Cash accounts, as well as any credit card accounts that have been used in the month.** (We provide a general answer at the end of this chapter.)

2. **What's the purpose of a Petty Cash account? List a few typical items that you might pay through petty cash.**

3. **If you allow customers to pay by credit card, check your system to ensure that you understand how to account for monies received by the credit card company. Have you got a system in place to be able to identify which customers are paying you?**

   For example, the credit card company probably just deposits a lump sum from credit card payments into your bank account. You need to ensure that you've a method of identifying which customers have paid you via credit card, so that you may update your accounts.

   If you don't have procedures in place, write some now.

4. **When you get your credit card sales statement, you find a total of £225 was charged in fees and you find three chargebacks for customer disputes totalling £165. How do you record this information in your books?**

5. **When you get your credit card sales statement, you find a total of £275 in chargebacks from customer disputes and £320 in fees. How do you record this information in your books?**

6. **You've just received your bank statement in the post. You find your balance at the bank is £1,500 beginning balance, £6,000 in deposits, £6,500 in payments, and your ending balance is £1,000. You review the deposits and find that a deposit of £2,000 does not show on the statement. You find that cheques totalling £1,700 haven't cleared yet. The balance in your bank account is £1,300. Does your bank account reconcile to the balance on your bank statement?**

7. **You've just received your bank statement in the post. You find your balance at the bank is £1,800 beginning balance, £7,000 in deposits, £6,500 in payments, and your ending balance is £2,300. You review the deposits and find that a deposit of £1,000 does not show on the statement. You find that cheques totalling £2,500 haven't cleared yet.**

The balance in your bank account is £1,200. Does your bank account reconcile to the balance on your bank statement?

8. **Suppose that you can't reconcile your bank statement. As you review the cheques, you see one written for £2,500 that you haven't recorded in your books. As you research the cheque, you find that it's a payment made to Olive's Office Supplies. How would you record that in the books?**

9. **Suppose you can't reconcile your bank statement and you find that a deposit of £5,300 isn't recorded. As you research the deposit, you find that the sales receipts weren't recorded for 15 May. How would you record that in the books?**

Answering the Have a Go Questions

1. **The following accounts are normally reconciled:**

   • Bank Current account

   • Bank Deposit account

   • Petty Cash account

   • Credit Card accounts

2. **Usually, small cash needs are handled using a petty cash fund. Often, an office manager handles this.** You may want to send a memo to your staff to advise them of the typical items of expenditure that are expected to be paid through petty cash. Typical petty cash items include:

   • Tea, coffee, milk

   • Postage

   • Keys cut

   • Small stationery items

   • Sundry cleaning supplies

   This list just offers a sample of the kinds of expenditure that may be posted through the Petty Cash account.

3. **Not all companies take payment via credit card from their customers.** If yours does, take the time now to reflect on the procedures surrounding the credit card receipts. Can they be improved?

4. **The bookkeeping entry to show the credit card fee is as follows:**

	Debit	*Credit*
Credit Card Fee	£225	
Bank		£225

	Debit	*Credit*
Sales	£165	
Bank		£165

5. **The bookkeeping entry for the disputed sales items is as follows:**

The bookkeeping entry to show the credit card fee is as follows:

	Debit	*Credit*
Credit Card Fee	£320	
Cash		£320

The bookkeeping entry for the sales adjustment is as follows:

	Debit	*Credit*
Sales	£275	
Cash		£275

6. **The bank statement does reconcile to the cheque book. Here's the proof:**

Transactions	Beginning Balance	Deposits	Payments	Ending Balance
Balance per bank statement	£1,500	£6,000	(£6,500)	£1,000
Deposits in transit (those not shown on statement)		£2,000		£2,000
Outstanding cheques (cheques that haven't shown up yet)			(£1,700)	(£1,700)
Total	£1,500	£8,000	(£8,200)	£1,300
Balance per Bank account or Cashbook (which should be the same)				£1,300

7. **The bank statement doesn't reconcile to the bank account. A difference is shown of £400.** You must review the bank account for possible errors. Here's the proof:

Transactions	Beginning Balance	Deposits	Payments	Ending Balance
Balance per bank statement	£1,800	£7,000	(£6,500)	£2,300
Deposits in transit (those not shown on statement)		£1,000		£1,000
Outstanding cheques (cheques that haven't shown up yet)			(£2,500)	(£2,500)
Total	£1,800	£8,000	(£9,000)	£800
Balance per Bank account or Cashbook (which should be the same)				£1,200

Book II

Book-keeping Day to Day

In the situation where the bank reconciliation doesn't balance, try the following:

- Check that you've ticked off every item on the bank statement and matched off each entry to the Cashbook.

- Ensure that you've entered the correct bank statement balance.

- Check your maths on the reconciliation.

- Check that you've entered all the items into your accounts system correctly.

Check all these things, and you'll most likely have found the problem.

8. **You need to record the office supplies expense and you need to reflect the use of cash.**

If using a computerised accounting system, you enter the invoice as a purchase invoice, to record the liability. Then you need to pay the invoice, using the bank account. The system does the double entry for you, as shown below:

The bookkeeping for the initial entry of the invoice is as follows:

	Debit	Credit
Office Supplies Expenses	£2,500	
Creditors Ledger		£2,500

You then need to process the payment, and the bookkeeping is as follows:

	Debit	Credit
Creditors Ledger	£2500	
Bank		£2500

9. **You need to record the missing sales as follows:**

	Debit	Credit
Bank	£5,300	
Sales		£5,300

Book III

Undertaking Monthly and Quarterly Tasks

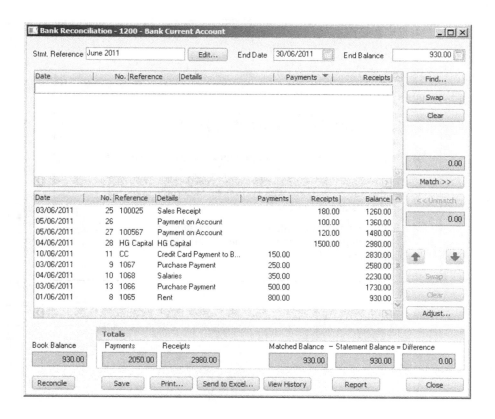

Head online and visit www.dummies.com/extras/bookkeepingaccountingaio for some free bonus articles.

In this book...

- ✔ Run and check your VAT return and know what you need to do – and when.

- ✔ Understand the RTI payroll system, an important aspect of many businesses.

- ✔ Know when an accountant may work together with the book-keeper to provide period-end adjustments, whether at month-end or year-end.

Chapter 1

Adding the Cost
of Value-Added Tax (VAT)

A lot of mystery and tales of horror surround the subject of value-added tax (VAT). Now that HM Revenue & Customs administers both tax and VAT, the average businessperson is facing an even more powerful organisation with a right to know even more about your business.

The rules governing which goods and services are subject to VAT and which items of VAT are reclaimable can be quite complex. This chapter can only scratch the surface and give a broad understanding. Contact both HM Revenue & Customs and your accountant/auditor at an early stage to find out whether all your sales are subject to VAT and how you can ensure that you're only reclaiming allowable VAT. Remember the following – get it right from the beginning.

Looking into VAT

VAT is a tax charged on most business transactions made in the UK or the Isle of Man. VAT is also charged on goods and some services imported from certain places outside the European Union and on some goods and services coming into the UK from other EU countries. VAT applies to all businesses – sole traders, partnerships, limited companies, charities and so on. In simple terms, all VAT-registered businesses act as unpaid collectors of VAT for HM Revenue & Customs.

Examples of taxable transactions are:

- ✔ Selling new and used goods, including hire purchase
- ✔ Renting and hiring out goods
- ✔ Using business stock for private purposes
- ✔ Providing a service; for example, plumbing or manicure
- ✔ Charging admission to enter buildings

As you can see, this list covers most business activities.

Certain services are exempt from VAT, including insurance, finance and credit, some property transactions, certain types of education and training, fundraising charity events and subscriptions to membership organisations. Supplies exempt from VAT don't form part of your turnover for VAT purposes.

VAT is a tax on the difference between what you buy (inputs) and what you sell (outputs), as long as these items fall within the definition of taxable transactions (see the following sections). At the end of a VAT reporting period, you pay over to HM Revenue & Customs the difference between all your output tax and input tax.

- ✔ **Input tax** is the VAT you pay out to your suppliers for goods and services you purchase for your business. You can reclaim the VAT on these goods or services coming *in* to your business. (See 'Getting VAT back', later in this chapter.) Input tax is, in effect, a tax added to all your purchases.
- ✔ **Output tax** is the VAT that you must charge on your goods and services when you make each sale. You collect output tax from your customers on each sale you make of items or services going *out* of your business. Output tax is, in effect, a tax added to all your sales.

Notice 700: The VAT Guide needs to be your bible in determining how much you need to pay and what you can reclaim. (You can find this guide at `www.hmrc.gov.uk.`)

Knowing what to charge

In addition to the obvious trading activities, you need to charge VAT on a whole range of other activities, including the following:

- ✔ **Business assets:** If you sell off any unneeded business assets, such as office equipment, commercial vehicles and so on, you must charge VAT.

✔ **Sales to staff:** Sales to staff are treated no differently than sales to other customers. Therefore you must charge VAT on sales such as canteen meals, goods at reduced prices, vending machines and so on.

✔ **Hire or loans:** If you make a charge for the use of a business asset, this amount must incur VAT.

✔ **Gifts:** If you give away goods that cost more than £50, you must add VAT. Treat gifts as if they're a sale for your VAT records.

✔ **Goods for own use:** Anything you or your family take out of the business must go on the VAT return. HM Revenue & Customs doesn't let you reclaim the VAT on goods or services that aren't used for the complete benefit of the business.

HM Revenue & Customs is really hot on using business stock for your own use, which is common in restaurants, for example. HM Revenue & Customs knows that you do it and has statistics to show how much on average businesses 'take out' this way. If you don't declare this item when you've used business stock, be prepared to have HM Revenue & Customs jump on you from a great height.

✔ **Commission earned:** If you sell someone else's goods or services and get paid by means of a commission, you must include VAT on this income.

✔ **Bartered goods:** If you swap your goods or services for someone else's goods or services, you must account for VAT on the full value of your goods or services that are part of this arrangement.

✔ **Advance payments:** If a customer gives you any sum of money, you must account for VAT on this amount and the balance when he collects the goods. If, for example, you accept payment by instalments, you collect VAT on each instalment.

✔ **Credit notes:** These items are treated exactly like negative sales invoices, so make sure that you include VAT so that you can effectively reclaim the VAT on the output that you're going to pay, or may have already paid.

In general you don't have to charge VAT on goods you sell to a VAT-registered business in another European Community (EC) member state. However, you must charge UK VAT if you sell goods to private individuals.

Knowing how much to charge

The rate of VAT applicable to any transaction is determined by the nature of that transaction. The 20 per cent rate applies to most transactions. The type

Book III

Undertaking Monthly and Quarterly Tasks

of business (size or sector) generally has no bearing on the VAT rates. Three rates of VAT currently exist in the UK:

- ✔ **A standard rate of 20 per cent:** This is the rate at which most businesses should add VAT to products and services that they sell.

- ✔ **A reduced rate, currently 5 per cent:** Some products and services have a lower rate of VAT, including domestic fuel, energy-saving installations and the renovation of dwellings.

- ✔ **A zero per cent rate:** Many products and services are given a zero rating, including some foods, books and children's clothing. A zero rating for a product or service isn't the same as a total exemption.

You can view a list of business areas where sales are reduced-rated or zero-rated in *Notice 700*, which you can download from www.hmrc.gov.uk. You can call the VAT helpline on 0845 010 9000 if you have queries about the list.

Registering for VAT

First of all you need to register for VAT so that you can charge VAT on your sales and reclaim VAT on your purchases.

The current VAT registration threshold is £81,000 (this threshold changes each year, so check with HM Revenue & Customs for the current threshold). So if your annual UK turnover (sales, not profit) is less than this figure, you don't have to register for VAT.

You may find it advantageous to register for VAT even though your sales fall below the VAT registration threshold (and may never exceed it). Registering for VAT gives your business increased credibility – if your customers are large businesses, they expect their suppliers to be VAT registered. Also, you can't reclaim VAT if you're not registered. If your business makes zero-rated supplies but buys in goods and services on which you pay VAT, you want to be able to reclaim this VAT.

As your business grows, it may be difficult to know whether you've broken through the VAT registration threshold. HM Revenue & Customs states that you must register for VAT if

- ✔ At the end of any month the total value of the sales you made in the past 12 months (or less) is more than the current threshold.

- ✔ At any time you have reasonable grounds to expect your sales to be more than the threshold in the next 30 days.

After you register for VAT, you're on the VAT treadmill and have to account for output tax on all your sales, keep proper VAT records and accounts, and send in VAT returns regularly.

Paying in and Reclaiming VAT

HM Revenue & Customs adopts a simple process, laying down and policing the rules in two ways:

- ✔ Businesses must file periodic returns to the VAT Central Unit (see the later section 'Completing Your VAT Return' for when to file VAT payments).
- ✔ Businesses receive periodic enquiries and visits from HM Revenue & Customs to verify that these returns are correct.

VAT returns must be completed by the due date, which is shown on the form, and is usually one month after the period covered by the return. Yes, this schedule means that you've one month to complete your VAT return. Any payment due to HM Revenue & Customs must be sent electronically. As long as you complete your VAT return on time and don't arouse the suspicions of HM Revenue & Customs, you may not meet the staff for many years.

You face a financial penalty if your return is late and/or seriously inaccurate. HM Revenue & Customs can and does impose hefty fines on businesses that transgress. Also, offenders who previously had the luxury of quarterly VAT returns often find themselves having to complete monthly VAT returns. Don't mess around with HM Revenue & Customs!

HM Revenue & Customs targets certain business sectors. In general, businesses structured in a complex manner (such as offshore companies) that involve a lot of cash are likely to come in for extra scrutiny. Experience tells HM Revenue & Customs that looking closely at certain types of businesses often yields extra revenues. Also, businesses that submit VAT returns late on a regular basis attract fines and may be forced to submit monthly VAT returns together with payments on account.

Paying VAT online

HM Revenue & Customs has phased out paper VAT returns, and (apart from a small number of exceptions) you need to file your VAT return online and pay your VAT electronically. The advantage of paying online is that you qualify

Book III

Undertaking Monthly and Quarterly Tasks

for seven additional calendar days after the date shown on your return to pay. Visit the HM Revenue & Customs website at www.hmrc.gov.uk and click VAT Online Services to find out about doing your VAT return online. Here's how it works:

1. **Fill in the appropriate boxes on your VAT return, using 0.00 for nil amounts.**

2. **Make any payment due by electronic methods (BACS, CHAPS or bank giro).**

3. **Wait for the acknowledgement that your electronic return was received.**

4. **Keep a copy of the electronic acknowledgement page for your records.**

Getting help for small businesses

HM Revenue & Customs has some arrangements to make VAT accounting easier for small businesses. The accounting method that your business uses determines when you pay VAT:

- ✔ **Annual Accounting:** If you use the Annual Accounting scheme, you make interim payments, either three or nine, spread across the year, towards an estimated annual VAT bill. This arrangement evens out VAT payments and helps to smooth cash flow. At the end of the year, you submit a single annual return and settle up for any balance due (or maybe receive a cheque back from HM Revenue & Customs). In effect, you complete one annual VAT return at the end of the year but make periodic payments on account (you agree with HM Revenue & Customs how many payments per year you want).

   This arrangement may suit the disorganised business that struggles to complete the more traditional four quarterly VAT returns.

   You can use this scheme if you don't expect your annual sales (excluding VAT) to exceed £1.35 million (or in special cases £1.6 million).

   The range is based on estimates of your total sales. If your sales have a boost and exceed £1.35 million, you can stay on this scheme just as long as sales don't go beyond £1.6 million. If sales exceed £1.6 million, you must come off this scheme.

- ✔ **Cash Accounting:** If you use the Cash Accounting scheme, your business accounts for income and expenses when they're actually incurred. Therefore, you don't pay HM Revenue & Customs VAT until your customers pay you. This arrangement may suit a business that has regular slow-paying customers. You can use this scheme if your estimated VAT taxable turnover isn't more than £1.35 million.

✔ **Flat Rate Scheme:** This arrangement makes VAT much simpler by allowing you to calculate your VAT payment as a flat percentage of your turnover. The percentage is determined according to the trade sector in which your business operates.

Under this scheme you can't reclaim any VAT on your actual purchases, which may mean that you lose out if your business is significantly different to the business model HM Revenue & Customs applies to you. Also, if your business undertakes a large capital spend that has a lot of VAT on it, you're unlikely to get the entire amount back under this scheme.

You can use this scheme if your annual sales (excluding VAT) aren't expected to exceed £150,000.

✔ **Retail Schemes:** If you make lots of quite small sales to the public, you may find it difficult to issue a VAT invoice for each sale. Several available retail schemes may help. For example, you can use a simpler receipt that a till can print out.

To find out more about the numerous retail schemes, visit the HM Revenue & Customs website (www.hmrc.gov.uk) and click the link for VAT, under Businesses and Corporations. Then click on 'Getting Started with VAT', followed by 'Accounting schemes' to simplify VAT accounting or save money, and scroll down the screen and select 'VAT retail scheme'.

Getting VAT back

When you're completing your VAT return, you want to reclaim the VAT on every legitimate business purchase. However, you must make sure that you only reclaim legitimate business purchases. The following is the guidance that HM Revenue & Customs gives:

✔ **Business purchases:** You can reclaim the VAT on all business purchases and expenses, not just on the raw materials and goods you buy for resale. These purchases include things like business equipment, telephone and utility bills, and payments for other services such as accountants' and solicitors' fees.

You can't deduct your input tax for certain purchases, including cars, business entertainment and second-hand goods that you bought under one of the VAT second-hand schemes.

✔ **Business/private use:** If you use services for both business and private purposes, such as your telephone, you can reclaim VAT only on the business use. No hard and fast rules exist on how you split the bill – your local HM Revenue & Customs office is likely to consider any reasonable method.

✔ **Pro-forma invoice:** If a supplier issues a pro-forma invoice, which includes VAT that you have to pay before you're supplied with the goods or service, you can't deduct this amount from your VAT bill on your next return. You can only deduct VAT when you get the proper invoice.

✔ **Private motoring:** If you use a business car for both business and private use, you can reclaim all the VAT as input tax, but you have to account for tax on any private motoring using a scale charge (see the later section 'Using fuel for private motoring').

✔ **Lost invoices:** You can't reclaim any VAT on non-existent invoices. If you do and you get a VAT visit, you're in for the high jump!

✔ **Bad-debt relief:** Occasionally, customers don't pay you, and if you've already paid over to HM Revenue & Customs the output VAT on this sale, you're going to be doubly annoyed. Fortunately, HM Revenue & Customs isn't totally heartless – you can reclaim this VAT on a later VAT return.

Completing Your VAT Return

You need to submit your VAT return online. To do so, go to www.hmrc.gov.uk and click on the link 'Register (new users)' in the box called 'Do it online' on the top-left side of the page. The site guides you through the setup process. Ensure that you allow plenty of time to register, because it involves receiving user IDs and passwords through the post.

Letting your accounting software complete your VAT return is the easiest method. Sage 50 Accounts does VAT returns as a matter of routine, picking up all the necessary information automatically. You just need to tell the program when to start and when to stop picking up the invoice information. Sage 50 Accounts even prints out the VAT return in a format similar to HM Revenue & Customs' own VAT return form. Figure 1-1 shows the Sage 50 Accounts VAT return.

Filling in the boxes

At last we come to the nitty-gritty of what figures go into each of the nine boxes on the VAT return. Table 1-1 helps keep the process simple.

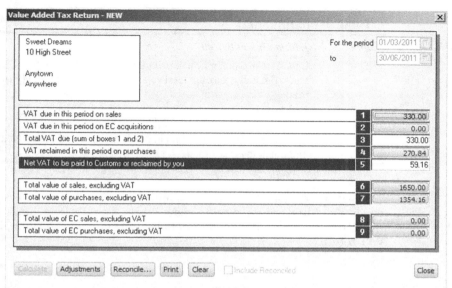

Figure 1-1:
The Sage 50
Accounts
VAT return.

Book III

Undertaking
Monthly and
Quarterly
Tasks

Table 1-1	VAT Return Boxes
Box	**Information Required**
1	VAT due on sales and other outputs in the period. *Notice 700: The VAT Guide* gives further help.
2	VAT due from you on acquisitions of goods from other EC Member States. *Notice 725 VAT: The Single Market* gives further help.
3	For paper returns, enter the sum of boxes 1 and 2. The electronic form handles all the maths needed to complete the form.
4	The input tax you're entitled to claim for the period.
5	The difference between the figures from boxes 3 and 4. Deduct the smaller from the larger. If the figure in box 3 is more than the figure in box 4, you owe this amount to HM Revenue & Customs. If the figure in box 3 is less than the figure in box 4, HM Revenue & Customs owes you this amount.
6	Your total sales/outputs excluding any VAT.
7	Your total purchases/inputs excluding any VAT.
8	Complete this box only if you supplied goods to another EC member state. Put in this box the total value of all supplies of goods (sales) to other member states. *Note:* If you include anything in box 8, make sure that you include the amount in the box 6 total.

(continued)

Table 1-1 (continued)

Box	Information Required
9	Complete this box only if you acquired goods from another EC member state. Put in this box the total value of all goods acquired (purchases) from other member states. *Note:* If you include anything in box 9, make sure that you include the amount in the box 7 total.

We deliberately keep this process simple, but remember that behind every box is a multitude of traps set to ensnare you. The HM Revenue & Customs website, www.hmrc.gov.uk, has detailed notes to help you complete your VAT return.

Glancing at problem areas

Not all businesses are entirely straightforward for VAT purposes. Some business activities have their own unique rules and regulations. The list below outlines the exceptions to the rule:

- ✔ **Building developer:** See *VAT Notice 708: Buildings and construction* about non-deductible input tax on fixtures and fittings. Also look at *Notice 742 Land and Property*, regarding land and new-build property sales.

- ✔ **Tour operator:** See *VAT Notice 709/5: Tour operators' margin scheme* about VAT you can't reclaim on margin scheme supplies.

- ✔ **Second-hand dealer:** See *VAT Notice 718: margin schemes for second-hand goods, works of art, antiques and collectors' items* about VAT you can't reclaim on second-hand dealing.

Using fuel for private motoring

If your business pays for non-business fuel for company car users, you must reduce the amount of VAT you reclaim on fuel by means of the scale charge.

Notice 700/64: Motoring expenses gives full details. If you use the scale charge, you can recover all the VAT charged on road fuel without having to split your mileage between business and private use. A *scale charge* is a method of accounting for output VAT on road fuel bought by a business that is then used for private mileage. The scale charge is based on the CO_2 emissions of each vehicle. You can obtain your CO_2 emissions from your vehicle registration certificate (for cars registered after 2001). The HMRC website offers full details of all CO_2 emissions and the associated fuel scale charge. See www.hmrc.gov.uk for further details.

Leasing a motor car

You may find that you're able to claim only 50 per cent of the input tax on contract hire rentals in certain situations. If you lease a car for business purposes, you normally can't recover 50 per cent of the VAT charged. The 50 per cent block is to cover the private use of the car. You can reclaim the remaining 50 per cent of the VAT charged. If you lease a qualifying car that you use exclusively for business purposes and not for private use, you can recover the input tax in full.

Filing under special circumstances

If you're filing your first VAT return, your final return or a return with no payment, bear a few things in mind:

- ✔ **First return:** On your first return, you may want to reclaim VAT on money you spent prior to the period covered by your first VAT return. In general, you can recover VAT on capital and pre-start-up costs and expenses incurred before you registered for VAT as long as they're VAT qualifying. For further help on this, refer to *Notice 700: The VAT Guide*, available from HM Revenue & Customs.

  If you're completing a VAT return for the first time, go to the HM Revenue & Customs website for help (www.hmrc.gov.uk) and/or speak with your accountant. You may be missing a trick in not reclaiming VAT on something you bought but didn't reclaim the VAT on. More importantly, you may be reclaiming VAT on something that the tax authority doesn't permit you to reclaim.

- ✔ **Final return:** For help with your final return, read *Notice 700/11: Cancelling your registration*. If you've any business assets, such as equipment, vehicles or stock on which you previously reclaimed VAT, you must include these items in your final VAT return. In effect, HM Revenue & Customs wants to recover this VAT (unless the amount is less than £1,000) in your last return.

  As soon as your business circumstances change, you must inform HM Revenue & Customs, which has specified time limits, depending on the circumstances. If you ignore these time limits, you may incur penalties. If in doubt, contact the VAT helpline on 0845 010 9000.

Book III

Undertaking Monthly and Quarterly Tasks

✔ **Nil return:** You can file a nil return if you:

- Have not traded in the period covered by the VAT return *and*
- No VAT exists on purchases (inputs) to recover *or*
- No VAT exists on sales (outputs) to declare.

Complete all boxes on the return as 'None' on your paper-based return or '0.00' on your electronic return.

Correcting mistakes

HM Revenue & Customs accepts the fact that people make mistakes (after all, we're only human!) and it doesn't expect perfection. However, it does have strict rules concerning mistakes. If you find a mistake on a previous return, you may be able to adjust your VAT account and include the value of that adjustment on your current VAT return. You can only do this if the mistake is found to be genuine and not deliberate, and is also below the error-correcting threshold (currently £10,000). If the amount is payable to HM Revenue & Customs, include it in the total for box 1 or box 2 (acquisitions). If the amount is repayable to you, include it in the total for box 4.

If you make a bigger mistake (the net value of the mistake is more than £10,000), *do not* include the amount on your current return. Inform your local VAT Business Advice Centre by letter or on form *VAT 652: Voluntary disclosure of errors on VAT returns*. The centre then issues a Notice of Voluntary Disclosure showing only the corrections to the period in question, and you become liable for the under-declared VAT and interest. Under these circumstances, no mis-declaration penalty is applied. Form *Notice 700/45: How to correct VAT errors and make adjustments or claims* helps you.

If you discover that an error has been made, you must disclose it to HM Revenue & Customs immediately. You cannot adjust these errors in a later VAT return.

Pursuing Payments and Repayments

Your completed VAT return results in one of two outcomes: you owe HM Revenue & Customs money or it owes you money – unless of course you complete a nil return, in which case you and HM Revenue & Customs are quits.

If you owe VAT but can't afford to pay by the due date, still send in your completed VAT return, and then contact the Business Payment Support Service on 0300 200 3835. This service was set up on 24 November 2008 to meet the needs of businesses and individuals affected by the current economic downturn. You can discuss temporary options with the service, such as extending the period of payment.

If you're owed money, you should receive a repayment about two weeks after you submit your VAT return. If after three weeks you haven't received your repayment, contact the Customs and Excise National Advice Service on 0845 010 9000.

If your business is due a repayment of VAT on a regular basis and you're on quarterly VAT returns, switch to monthly VAT returns at the earliest opportunity. Under a monthly system, you wait only two weeks for your VAT repayment rather than an additional two months.

If for any reason you receive a 'Notice of assessment and/or over-declaration' as a result of a mistake found by a visiting officer, don't wait until your next VAT return to rectify the issue. If you owe VAT, send your payment and the remittance advice in the envelope provided. If HM Revenue & Customs owes you, suppress a large smile and pay in the cheque, or check your bank account if you normally pay electronically.

Book III

Undertaking Monthly and Quarterly Tasks

Chapter 2

Employee Payroll and Benefits

In This Chapter

▶ Preparing to pay your employees

▶ Operating the new real-time information system

▶ Calculating taxes

▶ Dealing with benefits

▶ Posting payroll

▶ Paying HM Revenue & Customs

*U*nless your business employs just one person (you, the owner), you probably need to hire employees, and that means that you have to pay them, offer benefits and manage a payroll.

Human resources staff and bookkeeping staff usually share responsibilities for hiring and paying employees. As the bookkeeper, you must make sure that all HM Revenue & Customs tax-related forms are completed, and you need to manage all payroll responsibilities including paying employees, collecting and paying employee taxes, collecting and managing employee benefit contributions and paying benefit providers.

Before you proceed any further, visit the HM Revenue & Customs website at www.hmrc.gov.uk and click on the Employers link to go to the help area for new employers. There's a wealth of information to assist you in setting up a payroll and what to do on an ongoing basis. Alternatively, phone the Employer Helpline on 0300 200 3200 and let them talk you through the process.

This chapter examines the various employee staffing issues that bookkeepers need to be able to manage.

Staffing Your Business

After you decide that you want to hire employees for your business, you must be ready to deal with a lot of official paperwork. In addition to paperwork, you're faced with many decisions about how employees are to be paid and who's going to be responsible for maintaining the paperwork that HM Revenue & Customs requires.

Knowing what needs to be done to satisfy these officials isn't the only issue you must consider before you hire the first person; you also need to decide how frequently you're going to pay employees and what type of wage and salary scales you want to set up.

Obtaining an employer's PAYE reference

Every business must have an employer's Pay As You Earn (PAYE) reference in order to hire employees. Without this reference, you can't legally pay staff and deduct PAYE tax and National Insurance Contributions (NICs).

Luckily, HM Revenue & Customs makes it straightforward to obtain an employer's PAYE reference, which is typically a three-digit number (to identify the tax office) followed by four alpha characters (to identify the employer). The fastest way is to call HM Revenue & Customs' Employer Helpline on 0300 200 3200 and complete the form by telephone. Be prepared to provide the following information:

- ✔ **General business information:** Business name, trading address, name and address of employer, National Insurance number and Unique Taxpayer Reference of employer, contact telephone number, contact email address if registering using email and nature of business.

- ✔ **Employee information:** The date you took on (or intend to take on) your first employee(s), how many employees you intend to have, the date you intend to pay them for the first time and how often you intend to pay them.

If your business is a partnership or a limited company, you need to give additional information:

- ✔ **Partnership:** Names and addresses of any business partners, National Insurance numbers and Unique Taxpayer References of any business partners and your LLP number if you're a Limited Liability Partnership (LLP).

- ✔ **Limited company:** The company's registered address, company registration number and date of incorporation; and the names, addresses, private telephone numbers, National Insurance numbers and Unique Taxpayer References of the company directors.

Note: You can now register as a new employer online. A few exceptions exist, so check the website and follow the online instructions. Click on the Employers tab on the HM Revenue & Customs website at www.hmrc.gov.uk, followed by the 'I want to register as an Employer' link.

After you register, you receive an employer's registration letter, which includes your accounts office reference and your PAYE reference. This is a particularly important document, so keep it safe! You use your accounts office reference when you make payments to the HM Revenue & Customs and your PAYE reference in all other contact with HM Revenue & Customs. The letter includes a web address giving you access to the *Getting Started* guide, which can help you begin your payroll.

Starting a new employee

Every person you hire should bring a P45 from her previous employer. The *P45* is a record of the employee's taxable earnings, PAYE deducted and tax code for the current tax year. This form gives you the information you need as the new employer to make sure that you can deduct the correct amount of PAYE and National Insurance from the new employee.

It's no longer necessary to submit P45 parts to HM Revenue & Customs. You simply include the new start information as part of your Full Payment Submission (FPS), which is the submission that you must make every time you pay your employees.

Many new employees don't have P45s, perhaps because they've lost the form, or this is their first job, or maybe they're keeping another job as well as working for you. You need to obtain the following information from a worker without a P45:

Book III

Undertaking Monthly and Quarterly Tasks

- ✔ Full name
- ✔ Gender
- ✔ Date of birth
- ✔ Full address including post code
- ✔ National Insurance number (if known)

Some employers may find it easier to use the HM Revenue & Customs's Starter Checklist, which replaces the old form P46. You can download this form from the Employers section on the HM Revenue & Customs website. The form asks questions such as whether this is your first job, whether you have any other job, whether you claim Job Seekers' Allowance and whether you're paying off a student loan. The checklist should be completed by the employee and handed to the new employer, not sent to HM Revenue & Customs.

Picking pay periods

Deciding how frequently to pay your employees is an important point to work out before hiring staff. Most businesses choose one of these two pay periods:

- ✓ **Weekly:** You pay employees every week, which means you must do payroll 52 times a year.

- ✓ **Monthly:** You pay employees once a month, which means you must do payroll 12 times a year.

You can choose to use either pay period, and you may even decide to use more than one type. For example, some businesses pay hourly employees (employees paid by the hour) weekly, and pay salaried employees (employees paid by a set salary regardless of how many hours they work) monthly.

Determining wage and salary scales

You have a lot of leeway regarding the level of wages and salary that you pay your employees, but you still have to follow some rules laid out by the government. Under the National Minimum Wage Regulations, employers must pay workers a minimum amount as defined by law. These rules apply to businesses of all sizes and in all industries.

The levels of minimum wage rates from October 2014 are as follows:

- ✓ £6.50 per hour for workers aged 21 years and older

- ✓ £5.13 per hour for workers aged 18 to 20 years old

- ✓ £3.79 per hour for workers aged between 16 and 17

- ✓ £2.73 per hour for apprentices

Don't assume that the minimum wage isn't going to change, though: check the HM Revenue & Customs website periodically to get the current wage rates.

Making statutory payments

As well as guaranteeing minimum wage payments for workers, government statutes provide other benefits:

- ✓ **Sick pay:** Employees who are off sick for more than four consecutive work days, known as a period of incapacity for work (PIW), are entitled to receive Statutory Sick Pay (SSP). Of course, a sick employee must inform you as soon as possible and supply you with evidence of her sickness.

In many cases, the business continues to pay employees for short periods of sickness as part of good employment practice. However, if you don't pay employees when they're off sick for more than four days, they can claim SSP, which is based on their average earnings. As an employer, you may be able to recover some of the SSP you've paid against your NIC amounts. (***Note:*** The first three days that the employee is away from work are called *waiting days* and don't qualify for SSP.)

Different employment types, such as casual employment or term-time employment, may affect the rates that are paid.

✔ **Parental pay:** If employees qualify for Statutory Maternity Pay (SMP), they're paid for a maximum of 39 weeks. For the first six weeks, an employee is entitled to 90 per cent of her average wage. For the other weeks, she's entitled to £138.18 per week or 90 per cent of average earnings if this amount is less than £138.18.

New dads are entitled to Statutory Paternity Pay (SPP). The statutory weekly rate of Ordinary Paternity Pay and Additional Paternity Pay is £138.18 per week.

Most employees who adopt children are entitled to Statutory Adoption Pay (SAP), which is payable for up to 39 weeks at the lower rate of £138.18 per week or 90 per cent of average weekly wages if this amount is less.

All these statutory payments are offset against the NICs that the business has to pay over each month. For example, if the business was due to pay over £1,000 in NICs but paid out recoverable SSP of £108.85, it makes a net payment of £891.15. The payslip has room for you to show this adjustment. For more information on statutory benefits, visit www.gov.uk.

Using the Real-Time Information System

From April 2013 businesses have to report their payroll information in real time. That means that HM Revenue & Customs collects PAYE information more regularly. A business reports PAYE, NICs and student loans information every time it pays its employees, and not just annually when it provides an end-of-year tax return.

One of the key reasons for introducing the RTI system is to support the introduction of Universal Credits, which will overhaul the state benefits system by simplifying benefits into one payment. The RTI system will provide the Department of Work and Pensions with up-to-date information about the claimants' employment income. The claimant will no longer have to provide the information herself. The idea is that fraud will be reduced and people will receive the money that they're entitled to.

One of the main changes with this new system is that employers no longer have to submit P35s and P14s at the year-end. The following sections introduce to the basics of the RTI system.

Operating your RTI payroll system

All payroll software now uses the RTI processing system. Although PAYE is operated in the same way, the reporting process has changed. You must submit the payroll information to HM Revenue & Customs *on or before the day that you pay the employee*. This means that if you have a combination of weekly and monthly staff payments, you must make a Full Payment Submission (FPS) for each payment.

Many different payroll systems are on the market, some free and others not, but all must enable you to operate the RTI and submit your payroll details online. HM Revenue & Customs provides a free Basic PAYE Tool that enables you to process your payroll online. It also offers a list of HM Revenue & Customs-recognised payroll systems that you can review. Go to www.hmrc.gov.uk and click on the Employers tab, followed by 'Tell me about . . . Software packages and other payroll options'.

RTI Reports

Your chosen payroll software enables you to submit the following required reports:

- ✔ **Full Payment Submission (FPS):** This is one of the new forms used to report the payment information to HM Revenue & Customs. Prior to submitting this information, your payroll system asks for the following information:

    - Starter and leaver information

    - The employee's full name

    - Employee National Insurance number

    - Tax code

    - Gender

    - Employee address

    - Payment information

    - PAYE and NICs

  HM Revenue & Customs uses the data that you've submitted to calculate the PAYE and NICs liability due in each tax month.

✓ **Employer Payment Summary (EPS):** You submit an EPS only when you need to advise HM Revenue & Customs of an alteration to the PAYE and NICs liability; for example, if the business made no payment to an employee in that pay period. You can also use the EPS to recover statutory payments and Construction Industry Scheme (CIS) deductions suffered.

In addition, you may need to make other submissions during the course of the payroll year.

✓ **Employer Alignment Submission (EAS):** This is only required by employers with more than 250 employees and where two or more payroll systems may be in operation. The purpose of the EAS is to align the employee records to the HM Revenue & Customs records before the employer submits any other information.

✓ **National Insurance Verification (NVR):** When you set up a new employee, you may need to verify the National Insurance number to ensure it's correct. An incorrect NI number can result in the employer deducting the wrong amounts of National Insurance from an employee, which can subsequently affect her state pension and/or her entitlement to benefits.

If you don't have a National Insurance number for an employee then when you send your first FPS that includes payment details for that individual you must leave the National Insurance number blank.

You can't submit an NVR until you've sent at least one FPS and started submitting payroll reports in real time. HM Revenue & Customs recommends that you wait at least two weeks after sending your first FPS before you submit an NVR.

✓ **Earlier Year Update (EYU):** You can use this report after 19 April to correct any previous year-to-date totals submitted in your final FPS for the previous tax year. It applies only to the years after you started to send submissions in real time.

Collecting Employee Taxes

As the bookkeeper, you must be familiar with how to calculate the PAYE tax and NICs that you must deduct from each employee's wage or salary.

Although you can run a manual payroll, the calculation of PAYE and NICs is a monumental nightmare, demanding the most accurate and methodical approach to using the tables that HM Revenue & Customs provides each tax year. As well as getting the calculations correct, you have to record this information on a Deductions Working Sheet for each employee, which is very time consuming.

Save yourself a lot of grief and use a payroll bureau to run your weekly and monthly payroll and end-of-tax-year returns. If you employ more than 30 employees, this method saves you a lot of time and the cost isn't all that high. If you employ fewer than 30 employees and have the time to spare, use the P11 Calculator that HM Revenue & Customs provides online as part of the Basic PAYE toolkit, or buy an off-the-shelf payroll package.

Calculating NICs

NICs are made up of two elements:

✔ Employee contributions, which you deduct from your employees' pay

✔ Employer contributions, which your business must pay

Several different categories of NICs exist depending on the employee's age and sex. For most men aged 16 or over and under the male state pension age and most women aged 16 or over and under the female state pension age, you use Category A, which is referred to later as Table A. If you're unsure about which category your employee falls into, contact your local HM Revenue & Customs office or go to the website at www.hmrc.gov.uk.

Each year HM Revenue & Customs sets new Lower Earnings Limits (LEL) below which no NICs are payable by an employee. It also sets an Upper Earnings Limit (UEL) above which no more NICs are payable.

The employer pays NICs when the employee's earnings exceed the Secondary Threshold (ST – currently £153 weekly or £663 monthly). The employee pays NICs when her earnings exceed the Primary Threshold (PT – currently £153 weekly or £663 monthly).

Employers and their employees who are members of a contracted-out state pension scheme pay a reduced NIC contracted-out rate up to the Upper Accrual Point (UAP) – which is currently £770 weekly or £3,337 monthly. They then pay NICs at a higher standard rate on employee earnings between the Upper Accrual Point and the Upper Earnings Limit.

For the latest information about NICs check the HM Revenue & Customs website at www.hmrc.gov.uk.

Figuring out PAYE tax

Deducting PAYE tax is a much more complex task for bookkeepers than deducting NICs. You have to worry about an employee's tax code (of which numerous permutations exist) as well as using Table A to calculate the final tax figure to deduct.

A *tax code* is usually made up of one or more numbers followed by a letter. The number indicates the amount of pay an employee is allowed to earn in a tax year before tax becomes payable. For example, an employee with a tax code of 1000L can earn £10,000 in the current tax year before becoming liable to pay any tax at all.

A letter follows the number part of the tax code: L, P, T, V or Y. The letters show how the tax code is adjusted to take account of any budget changes.

If the tax code is followed by week 1 or month 1 or an X, instead of keeping a running total of the pay to date, you treat each pay day for that employee as if it's the first week or month of the tax year. For regular employees, you work on a running total basis of 'total pay to date' at each pay day.

Tax codes work on an annual cumulative tax allowance. For example, a tax code of 1000L means an employee can earn £10,000 tax free in a complete tax year (52 weeks or 12 months). If the employee is paid weekly, this tax-free sum adds up as the weeks go by. In this example, in week 1 the employee can earn £192.30 total pay without paying any tax (£10,000 ÷ 52). By week 8, that employee could have earned £1,538.46 total pay to date that year without paying any tax. Assuming that she's been paid in each of the intervening weeks (1 to 7), these sums earned are deducted from the total year-to-date tax-free-earnings figure to calculate how much is taxable. All this information is provided in the tax tables that you can obtain from HM Revenue & Customs.

Finally, as if all this wasn't confusing enough, an employee may have a totally different BR tax code, which stands for Basic Rate. For an employee with a BR tax code, you must deduct tax from all the pay at the basic rate – currently 20 per cent. The BR code can also be followed by a week 1 or month 1 or X, which indicates that you operate the code on a non-cumulative basis. Of course, if either week 1 or month 1 or X isn't indicated, you work on a running-total basis of total-pay-to-date at each pay day.

If you don't want to use manual tax tables, and you aren't using payroll software, then the easiest and quickest way to work out the tax deduction is to use the HM Revenue & Customs basic PAYE tools. See www.hmrc.gov.uk/paye/tools/basic-paye-tools.htm.

Determining Net Pay

Net pay is the amount a person is paid after subtracting all tax and benefit deductions from gross pay.

Book III

Undertaking Monthly and Quarterly Tasks

After you figure out all the necessary PAYE and NICs to be taken from an employee's wage or salary, you can calculate the pay amount, which is shown on the payslip. The equation you use is pretty straightforward:

Gross pay – (PAYE + NICs) = Net pay

For a sample employee, the formula may look like this:

Gross pay = £205.42

Less: PAYE tax deducted – £9.80

Less: Employee NICs – £7.13

Net pay = £188.49

This net pay calculation doesn't include any deductions for benefits. Many businesses offer their employees' health insurance, pensions, company cars and other benefits but expect the employees to share a portion of some of those costs. Most benefits are liable to PAYE tax and NICs, whereas employee contributions to pensions and some other benefits are tax deductible. To get full details on which benefits are taxable and which aren't, visit the HM Revenue & Customs website (www.hmrc.gov.uk) or ask your tax adviser.

Taxing Benefits

Many businesses offer their employees a range of benefits as well as their wage or salary. These benefits may include perks like a company car, all fuel paid for, health insurance and a business pension scheme. However, most benefits are taxable, so the employee has to pay tax on the money on the value of the benefits received. Very few benefits are non-taxable.

Fortunately, the process of collecting this tax on benefits is very straightforward. Your business informs HM Revenue & Customs what benefits each employee receives each tax year as part of the year-end process using forms P9D, P11D and P11D(B) (see the later section 'Handling Payroll Year-End'), and HMRC adjusts the employee tax code to ensure that you collect the tax due through the payroll. However, two benefits – company cars and fuel benefits – involve some additional work for you if you're involved in the payroll.

The quickest and simplest way to calculate the value of these benefits is to use the Car and Car Fuel Benefit Calculator, which you can find on the HM Revenue & Customs website. Click the 'Calculators and Tools' link on the 'Quick Link' menu on the left side of the homepage. The calculator guides you through the whole process. Also, all the monthly car magazines include the taxable benefit figures in their rating for each car reviewed.

You're responsible for working out the value of the company car benefit and telling HM Revenue & Customs. In simple terms, the car benefit charge is obtained by multiplying the list price of the car plus accessories less any capital contribution by the employee by the appropriate percentage. The *appropriate percentage* is based on the car's approved CO_2 emissions figure. The maximum appropriate percentage is 35 per cent, but you can adjust this amount depending on the type of fuel used and whether the car is electric or hybrid.

HM Revenue & Customs provides a useful helpsheet (number 203) entitled 'Car benefits and car fuel benefits' that enables you to complete your tax returns correctly using the worksheets provided.

If an employer pays for all the fuel for company car users, she can claim an additional taxable benefit called a *fuel benefit charge* for the non-business fuel used. Fortunately, this benefit is even simpler to calculate. You multiply the fixed sum of £21,100 (2014/2015 tax year) to the appropriate percentage used to calculate the car benefit. So if your car had an appropriate percentage (based on CO_2 emissions) of 24 per cent, for example, then your taxable fuel benefit charge would be £5,064 (£21,100 × 24 per cent).

When you've calculated the taxable value of the company car and fuel benefit for an employee, you must inform HM Revenue & Customs so that it can issue you with a revised tax code for that employee to collect the extra PAYE and NICs due each month. You use form P46 (Car) to notify HM Revenue & Customs of any new company cars and fuel benefits, or any changes to these benefits.

Book III

Undertaking Monthly and Quarterly Tasks

Preparing and Posting Payroll

After you deal with deductions and taxes, you have to figure out your employee's gross and net pay and post all the amounts in your journals.

Calculating payroll for hourly employees

When you're ready to prepare payroll for your hourly paid employees, the first thing you need to do is collect time records from each person being paid hourly. Some businesses use time clocks and some use timesheets to produce the required time records, but whatever the method used, usually the manager of each department reviews the time records for each employee that she supervises and then sends those time records to you, the bookkeeper.

With time records in hand, you have to calculate gross pay for each employee. For example, if an employee worked 45 hours and is paid £12 an hour, you calculate gross pay as follows:

40 standard hours × £12 per hour = £480

5 overtime hours × £12 per hour × 1.5 overtime rate = £90

£480 + £90 = £570

Doling out funds to salaried employees

You also must prepare payroll for salaried employees. You can calculate payments for salaried employees relatively easily – all you need to know is their base salaries and pay period calculations. For example, if a salaried employee is paid £15,000 per year and is paid monthly (totalling 12 pay periods), that employee's gross pay is £1,250 for each pay period (£15,000 ÷ 12).

Totalling up for commission payments

Running payroll for employees who are paid based on commission can involve complex calculations. To show you a number of variables, in this section we calculate a commission payment based on a salesperson who sells £60,000 worth of products during one month.

For a salesperson on a straight commission of 10 per cent, you calculate pay using this formula:

Total amount sold × Commission percentage = Gross pay

£60,000 × 0.10 = £6,000

For a salesperson with a guaranteed base salary of £2,000, plus an additional 5 percent commission on all products sold, you calculate pay using this formula:

Base salary + (Total amount sold × Commission percentage) = Gross pay

£2,000 + (£60,000 × 0.05) = £5,000

Although this salesperson may be happier with a base salary that she can count on each month, in this scenario she actually makes less with a base salary because the commission rate is so much lower. The salesperson makes only £3,000 in commission at 5 per cent if she sells £60,000 worth of products. Without the base pay, she'd have made 10 per cent on the £60,000, or £6,000. Therefore, taking into account her base salary of £2,000, she actually receives £1,000 less with a base pay structure that includes a lower commission pay rate.

If the salesperson has a slow sales month of just £30,000 worth of products sold, the pay is

£30,000 × 0.10 = £3,000 on straight commission of 10 per cent

and

£30,000 × 0.05 = £1,500 plus £2,000 base salary, or £3,500

For a slow month, the salesperson makes more money with the base salary rather than the higher commission rate.

You can calculate commissions in many other ways. One common way is to offer higher commissions on higher levels of sales. Using the figures in this example, this type of pay system encourages salespeople to keep their sales levels over a threshold amount to get the best commission rate.

With a graduated commission scale, a salesperson can make a straight commission of 5 per cent on the first £10,000 in sales, 7 per cent on the next £20,000 and 10 per cent on anything over £30,000. The following is what the salesperson's gross pay calculation looks like using this commission pay scale:

(£10,000 × 0.05) + (£20,000 × 0.07) + (£30,000 × 0.10) = £4,900 Gross pay

Book III

Undertaking Monthly and Quarterly Tasks

One other type of commission pay system involves a base salary plus tips. This method is common in restaurant settings in which servers receive a basic rate per hour plus tips.

Businesses must pay the minimum wage plus tips (the minimum wage is currently £6.50 for employees over 21 years of age). There's a useful guide at www.gov.uk called 'Tips at Work'.

As an employer, you must report an employee's gross taxable wages based on salary plus tips. Here's how you calculate gross taxable wages for an employee whose earnings are based on tips and wages:

Base wage + Tips = Gross taxable wages

(£3 × 40 hours per week) + £300 = £420

Checking this employee's gross wages, you see that the hourly rate earned is £10.50 per hour.

Hourly wage = £10.50 (£420 ÷ 40)

PAYE and NICs are calculated on the base wage plus tips, so the net payment you prepare for the employee in this example is for the total gross wage minus any taxes due.

Posting your payroll entries

After calculating the take-home pay for all your employees, you prepare the payroll, make the payments and post the payroll to the books. In addition to the Cash account, payroll impacts many accounts, including

- ✔ **Accrued PAYE Payable,** which is where you record the liability for tax payments
- ✔ **Accrued NICs Payable,** which is where you record the liability for NICs payments

When you post the payroll entry, you indicate the withdrawal of money from the Cash account and record liabilities for future cash payments that are due for PAYE and NICs payments. To give you an example of the proper setup for a payroll journal entry, we assume the total payroll is £10,000 with £1,000 each set aside for PAYE and NICs payable. In reality, your numbers are sure to be different, and your payments are likely to never all be the same. Table 2-1 shows what your journal entry for posting payroll looks like.

Table 2-1 shows only the entries that affect the take-home pay of the employees. The business must also make employer NICs payments. Your payroll system will calculate this amount for you. Employer NICs is a cost of employment and therefore must be treated in the books in exactly the same way as gross salaries and wages. Table 2-2 shows the journal entry to record employer NICs payments.

In this entry, you increase the Expense account for salaries and wages as well as all the accounts in which you accrue future obligations for PAYE and

Table 2-1	Payroll Journal Entry for 26 May 2014	
	Debit	*Credit*
Gross salaries and wages expense	£10,000	
Accrued PAYE payable		£1,000
Accrued NICs payable		£1,000
Cash (net payment)		£8,000

Table 2-2	Employer NICs Expenses for May	
	Debit	*Credit*
Employer NICs expense	£1,100	
Accrued employer NICs payable		£1,100

employee NICs payments. You decrease the amount of the Cash account; when cash payments are made for the PAYE and NICs payments in the future, you post those payments in the books. Table 2-3 shows an example of the entry posted to the books after making the PAYE withholding tax payment.

Table 2-3	Recording PAYE Payments for May	
	Debit	*Credit*
Accrued PAYE and NICs payable	£3,100	
Current account		£3,100

Settling Up with HM Revenue & Customs

Every month you need to pay over to HM Revenue & Customs all the PAYE and NIC amounts you deduct from your employees. To work out what you have to pay HM Revenue & Customs, add together

✔ Employee NICs

✔ Employer NICs

✔ PAYE tax

✔ Student loan repayments

These payments must be made to HM Revenue & Customs by the 19th of the following month if you're paying by cheque, or the 22nd of the month if you pay electronically. A special concession exists for small businesses to pay quarterly (5 July, 5 October, 5 January and 5 April) if the average monthly payment of PAYE and NICs is less than £1,500.

Outsourcing payroll and benefits work

If you don't want to take on payroll and benefits, you can pay for a monthly payroll service from the software company that provides your accounting software. For example, Sage provides various levels of payroll services. The Sage payroll features include calculating earnings and deductions, printing cheques or making direct deposits, providing updates to the tax tables and supplying the data needed to complete all HM Revenue & Customs forms related to payroll. The advantage of doing payroll in-house in this manner is that you can more easily integrate payroll into the business's books.

Handling Payroll Year-End

With the introduction of RTI, a much more simplified approach exists to the year-end. You no longer need to produce a P35 or P14, but you do have to produce a P60 for each employee.

You follow three steps:

1. **Enter the details of your final Full Payment Submission.** This will usually be the March payroll or last week's payroll for the tax year. Before you send this information, be sure that you've sent all previous submissions and that they were received successfully. Your payroll system should be able to help you achieve this.

2. **Confirm that this is your final submission for the tax year and then answer the additional questions required for the final submission.** These are the same type of questions that you'd have answered on the now redundant P35 form.

3. **Submit your final submission.**

As part of year-end payroll, you also issue each employee with a *P60 form*, which is a summary of payroll information for the tax year, including total tax and National Insurance deductions. The deadline for issuing this information is 31 May.

Tell employees to keep this document in a safe place, because it provides proof of income for that tax year. Mortgage companies may ask for this when employees are taking out a new mortgage or loan.

You use the following forms to report benefits provided to employees during the tax year:

✔ **P11D:** You use this form to report to HM Revenue & Customs any expenses or benefits paid to an employee who earns more than £8,500 per annum. You include items such as a company car, medical insurance and interest-free loans. If an employee was to apply for a loan or mortgage, she could use the P11D as proof of additional income.

✔ **P9D:** This form reports to HM Revenue & Customs any benefits or expenses paid to an employee who earns less than £8,500.

Add together pay and expenses and benefits to determine whether the employee is over or under the £8,500 threshold. If an employee works only part time, you should prorate the £8,500 threshold accordingly.

✔ **P11D(b):** Complete this form if you prepare more than one P11D. The form provides the total value of expenses and benefits that you've provided to your employees during the tax year that are liable to Class 1A NICs.

You must send all these forms to HM Revenue & Customs by 6 July.

Have a Go

1. **Design a payroll checklist to help you complete your monthly payroll routine.**

2. **Design a timesheet (you can use a spreadsheet for this) to calculate the gross pay for the following employee:**

    Name: Deborah Donaghue

    Department: Fixings

    Paid: Weekly

    Hours: 45

    Hourly rate: £12

    Overtime: 6 hours

    Overtime rate: £16

3. **Joe Carey is a new starter at your company. He doesn't have a P45 and has told you that he already has another part-time job. What tax code do you put him on when he starts?**

4. **You have a new sales director, Elaine Moore, starting this month. You've been told that Elaine's being paid an annual salary of £52,000. How much would her gross pay be each month?**

Answering the Have a Go Questions

1. A monthly payroll checklist would include the following items:

- Enter new starter details and set up new employees (if required).

- Process any leavers for the period, and provide a P45 for the employee.

- Using timesheets or another input mechanism to enter the pay details for the period.

- Check for any new tax codes to apply in the month, or any other legislation that may require a tax code change (for example, changes in the national budget).

- Calculate the tax and National Insurance due (if using a manual system).

- Write or print out your payslips.

- Print out any other payroll reports that you require for your records.

- Ensure that you take adequate backups of your payroll data. (If using a system such as Sage Payroll, we recommend taking a backup before updating the payroll and also after updating. This gives you an opportunity to restore the payroll, if someone has made a mistake, and re-run the update.)

- Update your payroll if you're operating a computerised system.

- Calculate the PAYE and National Insurance due to HM Revenue & Customs. Either raise a cheque or pay online, but you need to make sure that you're registered with HM Revenue & Customs to do this. See www.hmrc.gov.uk for further details about registering online.

- Ensure that you've submitted your payroll documents to HM Revenue & Customs (FPS and so on).

Design in a checklist format, so that you can tick each completed item as you go along. This is helpful if you work in a busy office and are likely to get interrupted as you're working: you can see where you've got up to and start from the appropriate point. You may want to have a list for both monthly and weekly payrolls.

2. Gross pay calculation for Deborah Donaghue:

Basic hours:	45 hours @ £12 per hour	£540
Overtime hours:	6 hours @ £16 per hour	£96
Total gross pay:		£636

3. **Joe Carey hasn't provided you with a P45. Therefore, in order to process the payroll and give him a tax code that's suitable, you should complete a new-starter checklist (see the HM Revenue & Customs website for a copy).**

   The first section of the checklist allows you to enter Joe's personal contact details and the second section allows you to complete the employee statement, which has three different options. Because Joe's told you he has another part-time job, you tick Box C, which confirms that he has another job. You can check the HM Revenue & Customs website to see what tax code you should use for an employee without a P45. It confirms that the correct tax code to use if you select statement C is BR Cumulative (Basic Rate). This means that Joe pays Basic Rate tax on all the gross pay that you've calculated. This probably means that he pays more tax than perhaps he should, but the problem will be corrected when you receive the correct code for Joe from HM Revenue & Customs. At this point you generate a refund of tax (if applicable) in the following month's payroll, as long as you apply the new tax code.

4. **The monthly gross pay for Elaine is**

Annual pay:	£52,000
Monthly pay:	£52,000 ÷ 12 = £4,333.33

   You apply the tax codes given to you from Elaine's P45.

Chapter 3

Adjusting Your Books

During an accounting period, your bookkeeping duties focus on your business's day-to-day transactions. When the time comes to report those transactions in financial statements, you must make adjustments to your books. Your financial reports are supposed to show your business's financial health, so your books must reflect any significant change in the value of your assets, even if that change doesn't involve the exchange of cash.

If you use cash-based accounting, these adjustments aren't necessary because you only record transactions when cash changes hands. We talk about accrual and cash-based accounting in Book I, Chapter 2.

If you're following the checklist we suggest in Book II, Chapter 1, we assume, in this chapter, that you've already entered/completed the following:

✔ Sale invoices

✔ Purchase invoices

✔ Bank receipts

✔ Bank payments

✔ Reconciled the bank accounts

All the above entries are routine transactions for the month. However, you also need to make some other types of adjustments. This chapter reviews the types of adjustments you need to make to the books before preparing the financial statements, including calculating depreciation, posting accruals and prepayments, updating stock figures and dealing with bad debts.

When you've posted all the necessary adjustments, print out a Trial Balance to check all the accounts and review for accuracy. We show you in the later section 'Checking your Trial Balance' how you can do this review using Sage 50 as an example.

Adjusting All the Right Areas

We look at each of the adjustments that you need to make to your books in turn. These include the following areas:

- ✔ **Asset depreciation:** To recognise the use of assets during the accounting period.

- ✔ **Accruals:** Where goods or services have been received but not invoiced, and an accrual has to be made in the accounts, so that they can be matched with revenue for the month.

- ✔ **Prepaid expenses:** To match a portion of expenses that were paid at one point during the year, but for which the benefits are used throughout the year, such as an annual insurance premium. The benefit needs to be apportioned out against expenses for each month.

- ✔ **Stock:** To update stock to reflect what you have on hand.

- ✔ **Bad debts:** To acknowledge that some customers never pay and to write off those accounts.

Depreciating assets

The largest non-cash expense for most businesses is depreciation. *Depreciation* is an important accounting exercise for every business to undertake because it reflects the use and ageing of assets. Older assets need more maintenance and repair, and eventually need to be replaced. As the depreciation of an asset increases and the value of the asset dwindles, the need for more maintenance or replacement becomes apparent. The actual time to make this adjustment to the books is when you close the books for an accounting period. (Some businesses record depreciation expenses every month to match monthly expenses with monthly revenues more accurately, but other business owners only worry about depreciation adjustments on a yearly basis, when they prepare their annual financial statements.)

Depreciation doesn't involve the use of cash. By accumulating depreciation expenses on an asset, you're reducing the value of the asset as shown on the Balance Sheet (see Book IV, Chapter 2 for the low-down on Balance Sheets).

Readers of your financial statements can get a good idea of the health of your assets by reviewing your accumulated depreciation. If financial report readers see that assets are close to being fully depreciated, they know that you probably need to spend significant funds on replacing or repairing those assets soon. As they evaluate the financial health of the business, they take that future obligation into consideration before making a decision to lend money to the business or possibly invest in it.

Usually, you calculate depreciation for accounting purposes using the *Straight-Line depreciation method.* This method is used to calculate an equal amount to be depreciated each year, based on the anticipated useful life of the asset. For example, suppose that your business purchases a car for business purposes that costs £25,000. You anticipate that the car is going to have a useful lifespan of five years and be worth £5,000 after five years. Using the Straight-Line depreciation method, you subtract £5,000 from the total car cost of £25,000 to find the value of the car during its five-year useful lifespan (£20,000). Then, you divide £20,000 by five to find your depreciation charge for the car (£4,000 per year). When adjusting the assets at the end of each year in the car's five-year lifespan, your entry to the books looks like this:

	Debit	*Credit*
Depreciation Charge	£4,000	
Accumulated Depreciation: Vehicles		£4,000
To record depreciation for Vehicles		

This entry increases depreciation charges, which appear on the Profit and Loss statement (see Book IV, Chapter 1). The entry also increases Accumulated Depreciation, which is the use of the asset and appears on the Balance Sheet directly under the Vehicles asset line. The Vehicles asset line always shows the value of the asset at the time of purchase.

You can accelerate depreciation if you believe that the business isn't going to use the asset evenly over its lifespan – namely, that the business is going to use the asset more heavily in the early years of ownership. If you use a computerised accounting system as opposed to keeping your books manually, you may or may not need to make this adjustment at the end of an accounting period. If your system is set up with an asset register feature, depreciation is automatically calculated, and you don't have to worry about it. Check with your accountant (the person who sets up the asset register feature) before calculating and recording depreciation expenses. We talk more about the different methods of depreciation in Book V, Chapter 2.

Accruing the costs

Goods and services may have been received by the business but may not have been invoiced. These costs need to be *accrued*, which means recorded in the books, so that they can be matched to the revenue for the month. These accruals are necessary only if you use the accrual accounting method. If you use the cash-based accounting method, you need to record the bills only when cash is actually paid. For more on the accrual and cash-based methods, refer to Book I, Chapter 2.

You accrue bills yet to be received. For example, suppose that your business prints and mails flyers to advertise a sale during the last week of the month. A bill for the flyers totalling £500 hasn't been received yet. Here's how you enter the bill in the books:

	Debit	Credit
Advertising	£500	
Accruals		£500

To accrue the bill from Jack's Printing for June sales flyers

This entry increases advertising expenses for the month and increases the amount due in the Accruals account. When you receive and pay the bill later, the Accruals account is debited rather than the Advertising account (to reduce the liability), and the Cash account is credited (to reduce the amount in the Cash account). You make the actual entry in the Cash Payments book when the cash is paid out.

When checking out the cash, also review any accounts in which expenses are accrued for later payment, such as Value-Added Tax Collected, to ensure that all Accrual accounts are up to date. This Tax account is actually a Liability account for taxes that you need to pay in the future. If you use the accrual accounting method, you must match the expenses related to these taxes to the revenues collected for the month in which they're incurred.

Allocating prepaid expenses

Most businesses have to pay certain expenses at the beginning of the year even though they benefit from that expense throughout the year. Insurance is a prime example of this type of expense. Most insurance businesses require you to pay the premium annually at the start of the year even though the value of that insurance protects the business throughout the year.

For example, suppose that your business's annual car insurance premium is £1,200. You pay that premium in January in order to maintain insurance cover throughout the year. Showing the full cash expense of your insurance when you prepare your January financial reports greatly reduces any profit that month and makes your financial results look worse than they actually are, which is no good. Instead, you record a large expense such as insurance or prepaid rent as an asset called *Prepaid Expenses*, and then you adjust the value to reflect that the asset is being used up.

When you record the initial invoice, you record the expense to prepayments. The double entry is as follows:

	Debit	**Credit**
Prepayments	£1,200	
Bank		£1,200

This double entry shows that you paid the original invoice by cheque and that you've coded the whole value of the invoice to prepayments.

Your £1,200 annual insurance premium is actually valuable to the business for 12 months, so you calculate the actual expense for insurance by dividing £1,200 by 12, giving you £100 per month.

Each month the Prepayment account is reduced by £100 and the cost is transferred to the Insurance Expenses account, as shown in this double entry:

	Debit	**Credit**
Insurance Expenses	£100	
Prepaid Expenses		£100

To record insurance expenses for March

This entry increases Insurance Expenses on the Profit and Loss statement and decreases the asset Prepaid Expenses on the Balance Sheet. No cash changes hands in this entry because you laid cash out when the insurance bill was paid, and the Asset account Prepaid Expenses was increased in value at the time the cash was paid.

Counting stock

Stock is a Balance Sheet asset that you need to adjust at the end of an accounting period. During the accounting period, your business buys stock and records those purchases in a Purchases account without indicating any change to stock. When the business sells the products, you record the sales in the Sales account but don't make any adjustment to the value of the stock. Instead, you adjust the stock value at the end of the accounting period because adjusting with each purchase and sale is much too time-consuming.

The steps for making proper adjustments to stock in your books are as follows:

1. **Determine the stock remaining.**

   In addition to calculating closing stock using the purchases and sales numbers in the books, also do a physical count of stock to make sure that what's on the shelves matches what's in the books.

2. **Set a value for that stock.**

   The value of closing stock varies depending on the method your business chooses for valuing stock. We talk more about stock value and how to calculate the value of closing stock in Book II, Chapter 3.

3. **Adjust the number of items remaining in stock in the Stock account and adjust the value of that account based on the information collected in Steps 1 and 2.**

If you record stock using your computerised accounting system, the system makes adjustments to stock as you record sales. At the end of the accounting period, the computer has already adjusted the value of your business's closing stock in the books. Although the work's done for you, still do a physical count of the stock to make sure that your computer records match the physical stock at the end of the accounting period.

Allowing for bad debts

No business likes to accept that money owed by some of its customers is never going to be received, but this situation is a reality for most businesses that sell items on credit. When your business determines that a customer who bought products on credit is never going to pay for them, you record the value of that purchase as a *bad debt.* (For an explanation of credit, check out Book II, Chapter 2.)

At the end of an accounting period, list all outstanding customer accounts in an *Aged Debtor report*, which is covered in Book II, Chapter 2. This report shows which customers owe how much and for how long. After a certain amount of time, you have to admit that some customers simply aren't going to pay. Each business sets its own policy of how long to wait before tagging an account as a bad debt. For example, your business may decide that when a customer is six months late with a payment, you're unlikely to ever see the money.

After you decide that an account is a bad debt, don't include its value as part of your assets in Trade Debtors (Accounts Receivable). Including bad debt value doesn't paint a realistic picture of your situation for the readers of your financial reports. Because the bad debt is no longer an asset, you adjust the value of your Trade Debtors to reflect the loss of that asset.

You can record bad debts in a couple of ways:

- ✔ **By customer:** Some businesses identify the specific customers whose accounts are bad debts and calculate the bad-debt expense for each accounting period based on specified customer accounts.

- ✔ **By percentage:** Other businesses look at their bad-debts histories and develop percentages that reflect those experiences. Instead of taking the time to identify each specific account that may be a bad debt, these businesses record bad-debt expenses as a percentage of their Trade Debtors.

- ✔ **By using a bit of both:** You can identify specific customers and write them off and apply a percentage to cover the rest.

However you decide to record bad debts, you need to prepare an adjusting entry at the end of each accounting period to record bad-debt expenses. Here's an adjusting entry to record bad-debt expenses of £1,000:

	Debit	*Credit*
Bad Debt Expense	£1,000	
Trade Debtors		£1,000

To write off customer accounts

You can't have bad-debt expenses if you don't sell to your customers on credit. You only need to worry about bad debt if you offer your customers the convenience of buying your products on credit.

If you use a computerised accounting system, check the system's instructions for how to write off bad debts. To write off a bad debt using Sage 50 Accounts, follow these steps:

1. **Open the Customers screen and select Customer Write Off/Refund from the Tasks on the left-hand side of the screen.** This screen brings up the Write Offs, Refunds and Returns Wizard (see Figure 3-1). Select the task you want to perform, such as Write Off, and then select the customer account using the drop-down arrow. Click Next to continue.

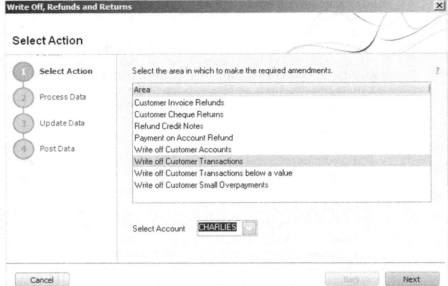

Figure 3-1:
In Sage 50 Accounts, use the Write Offs, Refunds and Returns Wizard to write off bad debts.

2. **Highlight the invoices you're writing off and click Next (see Figure 3-2).**

3. **Enter the date of the write-off and any reference you may wish to use (see Figure 3-3). Click Next to continue.**

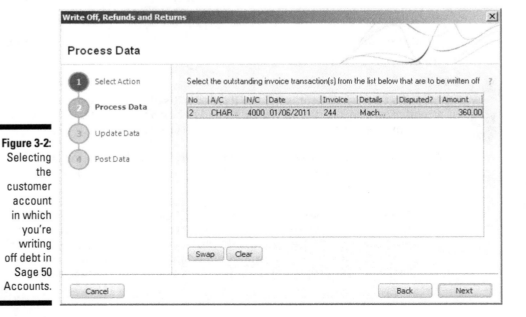

Figure 3-2:
Selecting the customer account in which you're writing off debt in Sage 50 Accounts.

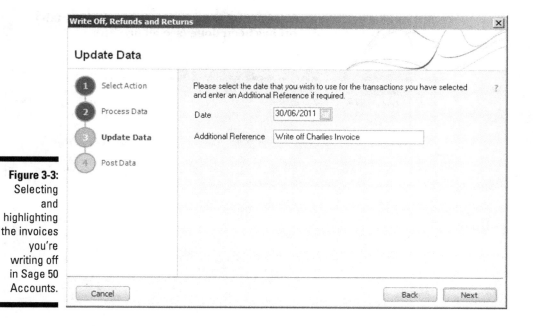

Figure 3-3:
Selecting
and
highlighting
the invoices
you're
writing off
in Sage 50
Accounts.

4. **Check the data that's about to be written off (Figure 3-4). If you're happy that the details are correct, click Post. Otherwise, click Back and redo.**

Book III

**Undertaking
Monthly and
Quarterly
Tasks**

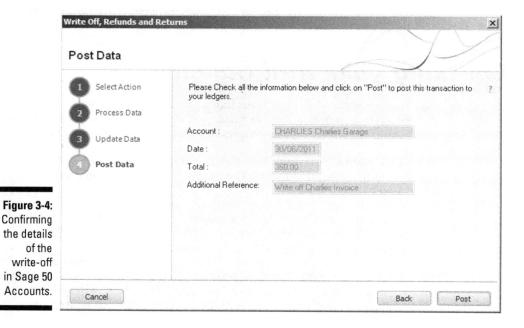

Figure 3-4:
Confirming
the details
of the
write-off
in Sage 50
Accounts.

5. **Double-click on the customer account and click the Activity tab to check that the write-off has been done (see Figure 3-5).**

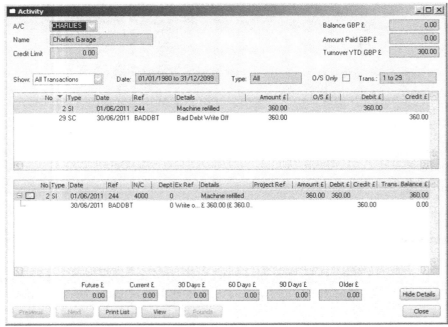

Figure 3-5:
Check that
the write-off
has been
posted
properly by
viewing the
Customer
Activity
screen.

Checking Your Trial Balance

When you've entered all your transactions and then posted your adjusting entries, such as depreciation, accruals, prepayments and so on, you need to review all your account balances to ensure the accuracy of the data.

To do this, you need to run a Trial Balance, which shows you a list of all accounts with a current balance. The report is listed in account number order as shown in Figure 3-6.

You can see from looking at the Trial Balance that it's simply a list of all the nominal accounts that contain a balance. The debit balances are shown in one column and the credit balances are shown in another. The totals of each of the columns must always be equal. If they aren't, this difference means that there's a major problem with your accounts. Computerised trial balances are always going to balance, unless there's serious corruption of data. If you're maintaining a manual Trial Balance, you must check all your figures again.

| Date: | 22/02/2012 | | Sweet Dreams | Page: | 1 |
| Time: | 16:42:16 | | Period Trial Balance | | |

To Period: Month 3, June 2011

N/C	Name	Debit	Credit
0050	Motor Vehicles	10,000.00	
1100	Debtors Control Account	140.00	
1200	Bank Current Account	930.00	
2100	Creditors Control Account		725.00
2200	Sales Tax Control Account		330.00
2201	Purchase Tax Control Account	270.84	
3010	Capital Introduced		11,500.00
4000	Sweet Sales		1,650.00
5000	Materials Purchased	1,354.16	
7003	Staff Salaries	350.00	
7100	Rent	800.00	
8100	Bad Debt Write Off	360.00	
	Totals:	14,205.00	14,205.00

Page 1 of 1   100% ⊖ ⊕

Figure 3-6:
An example
of a Trial
Balance in
Sage 50.

You may want to make further adjustments after you've reviewed your Trial Balance. Perhaps you posted items to the wrong nominal code. You need to write out correcting entries to sort this mistake out. This is where your double-entry rules come back into play.

You may want to investigate an account because the balance seems high. For example, Kate the bookkeeper wants to see what's been coded to Capital Introduced, because at £11,500 the amount seems quite high. In order to investigate this account, Kate would have to run a Nominal Activity report in Sage. This report would show her all the items that have been posted to the nominal code she's investigating. See Figure 3-7 for the Nominal Activity report that Kate has run for Capital Introduced.

Kate can see from the report that two items have been posted to Capital Introduced; one was for £10,000 and relates to the company vehicle that was bought using owner funds, and the other was cash lent to the business by the owner. Kate is happy with her findings and doesn't need to make any adjustments.

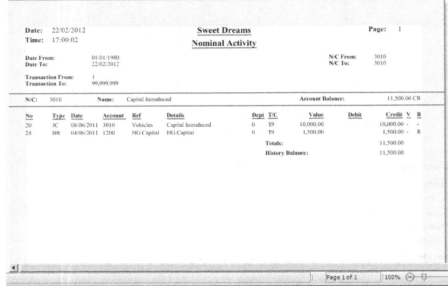

Figure 3-7:
Showing
a Nominal
Activity
report for
Capital
Introduced.

Changing Your Chart of Accounts

After you finalise your Nominal Ledger for the year, you may want to
make changes to your Chart of Accounts, which lists all the accounts in
your accounting system. (For the full story on the Chart of Accounts, see
Book I, Chapter 3.) You may need to add accounts if you think that you
need additional ones or delete accounts if you think that they're no longer
needed.

Delete accounts from your Chart of Accounts only at the end of the year. If
you delete an account in the middle of the year, your annual financial statements don't reflect the activities in that account prior to its deletion. So even
if you decide halfway through the year not to use an account, leave it on the
books until the end of the year and then delete it.

You can add accounts to your Chart of Accounts throughout the year, but
if you decide to add an account in the middle of the year in order to more
closely track certain assets, liabilities, revenues or expenses, you may need
to adjust some related entries.

Suppose that you start the year recording paper expenses in the Office Supplies Expenses account, but paper usage and its expense keeps increasing and you decide to track the expense in a separate account beginning in July.

First, you add the new account, Paper Expenses, to your Chart of Accounts. Then you prepare an adjusting entry to move all the paper expenses that were recorded in the Office Supplies Expenses account to the Paper Expenses account. In the interest of space and to avoid boring you, the adjusting entry below is an abbreviated one. In your actual entry, you'd probably detail the specific dates on which paper was bought as an office supplies expense rather than just tally one summary total.

	Debit	*Credit*
Paper Expenses	£1,000	
Office Supplies Expenses		£1,000

To move expenses for paper from the Office Supplies Expenses account to the Paper Expenses account

---

Moving beyond the catch-all Miscellaneous Expenses account

When new accounts are added to the Chart of Accounts, the account most commonly adjusted is the Miscellaneous Expenses account. In many cases, you may expect to incur an expense only one or two times during the year, therefore making it unnecessary to create a new account specifically for that expense. But after a while, you find that your 'rare' expense is adding up, and you'd be better off with a designated account, meaning that you need to create adjusting entries to move expenses out of the Miscellaneous Expenses account.

For example, suppose you think that you're going to need to rent a car for the business just once before you buy a new vehicle, and so you enter the rental cost in the books as a Miscellaneous Expense. However, after renting cars three times, you decide to start a Rental Expense account mid-year. When you add the Rental Expense account to your Chart of Accounts, you need to use an adjusting entry to transfer any expenses incurred and recorded in the Miscellaneous Expense account prior to the creation of the new account.

Book III

Undertaking Monthly and Quarterly Tasks

Have a Go

This section allows you to practise bookkeeping questions.

1. **Using the information below, and using Figure 3-6 (a Sage 50 Trial Balance) as an example of how it should look, reconstruct a Trial Balance for the end of June.**

   Your totals for each of the accounts at the end of June are:

Account	*Debit*	*Credit*
Cash Debit	£2,500	
Debtors Debit	£1,500	
Stock Debit	£1,000	
Equipment Debit	£5,050	
Vehicle Debit	£25,000	
Furniture Debit	£5,600	
Creditors Credit		£2,000
Loans Payable Credit		£28,150
Owner's Capital Credit		£5,000
Sales Credit		£27,000
Purchases Debit	£12,500	
Advertising Debit	£2,625	
Interest Expenses Debit	£345	
Office Expenses Debit	£550	
Payroll Taxes Debit	£425	
Rent Expense Debit	£800	
Salaries and Wages Debit	£3,500	
Telephone Expenses Debit	£500	
Utilities Expenses Debit	£255	

2. **Your company owns a copier that cost £30,000. Assume a useful life of five years. How much should you record for depreciation expenses for the year? What is your bookkeeping entry?**

3. Your offices have furniture that cost £200,000. Assume a useful life of five years. How much should you record for depreciation expenses for the year? What is your adjusting entry?

4. Suppose that your company pays £6,000 for an advertising campaign that covers the period 1 January to 31 December. You have already received an invoice dated 15 January, which you've paid at the end of January. You're closing the books for the month of May. How much should you have charged to the Profit and Loss account for the period to 31 May and what balance should remain in Prepayments?

5. Your accountant has prepared your year-end accounts, but hasn't sent you a bill yet! From past experience, you know that you should accrue about £2,400. What journal entry do you need to make to enter this situation into the books?

6. At the end of the month, you find that you've £9,000 in Closing Stock. You started the month with £8,000 in Opening Stock. What adjusting entry would you make to the books?

7. At the end of the month you calculate your Closing Stock and find that the value is £250 more than your Opening Stock value, which means that you purchased stock during the month that was not used. What adjusting entry should you make to the books?

8. You identify six customers that are more than six months late paying their bills, and the total amount due from these customers is £2,000. You decide to write off the debt. What adjusting entry would you make to the books?

9. Your company has determined that, historically, 5 per cent of its debtors never pay. What adjusting entry should you make to the books if your Debtors account at the end of the month is £10,000?

10. You decide that you want to track the amount that you spend on postage separately. Prior to this, you were entering these transactions in the Office Expense account. You make this decision in May, five months into your accounting year. You've already entered £1,000 for postage expenses. What would you need to do to start the account in the middle of the accounting year?

11. You decide that you want to track telephone expenses separately from other utilities. Prior to this, you were entering these transactions in the Utilities Expense account. You make this decision in July, but have already recorded transactions totalling £1,400 in your books. What do you need to do to start this new account in the middle of the accounting year?

Book III

Undertaking Monthly and Quarterly Tasks

Answering the Have a Go Questions

1. **Here's how the completed Trial Balance should look:**

Account	Debit	Credit
Cash	£2,500	
Debtors	£1,500	
Stock	£1,000	
Equipment	£5,050	
Vehicle	£25,000	
Furniture	£5,600	
Creditors		£2,000
Loans Payable		£28,150
Owner's Capital		£5,000
Sales		£27,000
Purchases	£12,500	
Advertising	£2,625	
Interest Expenses	£345	
Office Expenses	£550	
Payroll Taxes	£425	
Rent Expense	£800	
Salaries and Wages	£3,500	
Telephone Expenses	£500	
Utilities Expenses	£255	
TOTALS	£62,150	£62,150

2. **Annual depreciation expense = £30,000 ÷ 5 = £6,000**

	Debit	Credit
Depreciation expense	£6,000	
Accumulated depreciation: Office Machines		£6,000

3. **Annual depreciation expense = (£200,000) ÷ 5 = £40,000**

	Debit	*Credit*
Depreciation expense	£40,000	
Accumulated depreciation: Furniture & Fittings		£40,000

4. **The original invoice should be coded to Prepaid Expenses.** You need to calculate the monthly charge for advertising, which would be £6,000 ÷ 12 months = £500 per month. Each month, you must do the following journal:

	Debit	*Credit*
Advertising Costs	£500	
Prepaid Expenses		£500

This journal has the effect of charging the Profit and Loss account with £500 each month and reducing the prepayment in the Balance Sheet.

Therefore, in May the balances are:

- Advertising Expenses (in Profit & Loss) £2,500 (£500 × 5 months)
- Prepayment in Balance Sheet £3,500 (£6,000 − £2,500)

5. **The journal entry should be as follows:**

	Debit	*Credit*
Accountancy Costs	£2,400	
Accruals		£2,400

You could, if you wanted, prepare a monthly accrual and post a monthly charge through the accounts. To do this, simply split the £2,400 by 12 and post £200 per month. When the actual invoice comes in, it should be coded to Accruals rather than Accounting Fees.

6. **You ended the month with £1,000 more stock than you started with.** So you need to increase the Stock on hand by £1,000 and decrease the Purchases expense by £1,000, because some of the stock purchased won't be used until the next month. The entry would be:

	Debit	*Credit*
Stock	£1,000	
Purchases		£1,000

Book III

Undertaking Monthly and Quarterly Tasks

7. **Your entry would be:**

	Debit	Credit
Stock	£250	
Purchases		£250

This entry decreases the amount of the Purchases expenses because you purchased some of the Stock that you then didn't use.

8. **Your entry would be:**

	Debit	Credit
Bad Debt Expenses	£2,000	
Debtors (Accounts Receivable)		£2,000

9. **First you need to calculate the amount of the Bad Debt Expenses:**

- Bad Debt Expenses = £10,000 × 0.05 = £500

Your entry would be:

	Debit	Credit
Bad Debt Expenses	£500	
Debtors		£500

10. **First you need to establish a new account called Postage Expenses in your Chart of Accounts.**

Then you need to transfer the amount of transactions involving the payment of postage from your Office Expenses account to your new Postage Expenses account. The transaction looks like this:

	Debit	Credit
Postage Expenses	£1,000	
Office Expenses		£1,000

11. **First you need to establish a new account called Telephone Expenses in your Chart of Accounts.** Then you need to transfer the amount of transactions involving the payment of telephone bills from your Utilities Expenses account to your Telephone Expenses account. The transaction looks like this:

	Debit	Credit
Telephone Expenses	£1,400	
Utilities Expenses		£1,400

Book IV

Working to Prepare Financial Statements

In this book...

- Produce and understand the Profit and Loss statement.
- Learn about basic ratios in order to test the profits and liquidity of a business.
- Create a Balance Sheet.
- Discover the three different types of cash flow within a business, and develop your own cash flow statement.

Chapter 1

Producing a Profit and Loss Statement

*W*ithout one very important financial report tool, you can never know for sure whether or not your business is making a profit. This tool is called the *Profit and Loss statement*, and most businesses prepare this statement on a monthly basis, as well as quarterly and annually, in order to get periodic pictures of how well the business is doing financially.

Analysing the Profit and Loss statement and the details behind it can reveal lots of useful information to help you make decisions for improving your profits and business overall. This chapter covers the various parts of a Profit and Loss statement, how you develop one and examples of how you can use it to make business decisions.

Lining Up the Profit and Loss Statement

Did your business make any profit? You can find the answer in your *Profit and Loss statement*, the financial report that summarises all the sales activities, costs of producing or buying the products or services sold, and expenses incurred in order to run the business.

Profit and Loss statements summarise the financial activities of a business during a particular accounting period (which can be a month, quarter, year or some other period of time that makes sense for a business's needs).

Normal practice is to include two accounting periods on a Profit and Loss statement: the current period plus the year to date. The five key lines that make up a Profit and Loss statement are:

- ✔ **Sales or Revenue:** The total amount of invoiced sales you take in from selling the business's products or services. You calculate this amount by totalling all the sales or revenue accounts. The top line of the Profit and Loss statement is Sales or Revenue; either is okay.

- ✔ **Cost of Goods Sold:** How much you spent in order to buy or make the goods or services that your business sold during the accounting period under review. The later section 'Finding Cost of Goods Sold' shows you how to calculate Cost of Goods Sold.

- ✔ **Gross Profit:** How much your business made before taking into account operations expenses; calculated by subtracting the Cost of Goods Sold from the Sales or Revenue.

- ✔ **Operating Expenses:** How much you spent on operating the business; these expenses include administrative fees, salaries, advertising, utilities and other operations expenses. You add all your expenses accounts on your Profit and Loss statement to get this total.

- ✔ **Net Profit or Loss:** Whether or not your business made a profit or loss during the accounting period in review; calculated by subtracting total expenses from Gross Profit.

Formatting the Profit and Loss Statement

Here, we show you a simplified UK format for the Profit and Loss statement:

Revenues	
Turnover	£10,000
Cost of Goods Sold	<u>£5,000</u>
Gross Profit	£5,000
Operating Expenses	
Advertising	£700
Salaries	£1,200
Supplies	£1,500
Depreciation	<u>£500</u>
Interest Expenses	£500
Total Operating Expenses	£4,400

Revenues	
Operating Profit	£600
Other Income	
Interest Income	£200
Total Profit	£800

Preparing the Profit and Loss Statement

If you're using a computerised accounting system, the Profit and Loss report is generated at the press of a button. However, if you're operating a manual system, you need to use the figures from your Trial Balance to construct the Profit and Loss statement.

Finding Net Sales

Net Sales is a total of all your sales minus any discounts. In order to calculate Net Sales, you look at the sales account, discounts and any sales fees on your Trial Balance. For example, suppose that you have Total Sales at £20,000, discounts of £1,000 and credit card fees on sales of £125. To find your Net Sales, you subtract the discounts and credit card fees from your Total Sales amount, leaving you with £18,875.

Finding Cost of Goods Sold

Cost of Goods Sold is the total amount your business spent to buy or make the goods or services that you sold. To calculate this amount for a business that buys its finished products from another business in order to sell them to customers, you start with the value of the business's Opening Stock (the amount in the Stock account at the beginning of the accounting period), add all purchases of new stock and then subtract any Closing Stock (stock that's still on the shelves or in the warehouse; it appears on the Balance Sheet, which is covered in Book IV, Chapter 2).

The following is a basic Cost of Goods Sold calculation:

Opening Stock + Purchases = Goods Available for Sale

£100 + £1,000 = £1,100

Goods Available for Sale – Closing Stock = Cost of Goods Sold

£1,100 – £200 = £900

To simplify the example for calculating Cost of Goods Sold, these numbers assume the Opening Stock (the value of the stock at the beginning of the accounting period) and Closing Stock (the value of the stock at the end of the accounting period) values are the same. See Book II, Chapter 3 for details about calculating stock value. So to calculate Cost of Goods Sold, you need just two key lines: the purchases made and the discounts received to lower the purchase cost, as in the following example.

Purchases – Purchases Discounts = Cost of Goods Sold

£8,000 – £1,500 = £6,500

Drawing remaining amounts from your Trial Balance

After you calculate Net Sales and Cost of Goods Sold (see the preceding sections), you can use the rest of the numbers, usually overheads, from your Trial Balance to prepare your business's Profit and Loss statement. Figure 1-1 shows a sample Profit and Loss statement.

You and anyone else in-house are likely to want to see the type of detail shown in the example in Figure 1-1, but most business owners prefer not to show all their operating detail to outsiders: they like to keep the detail private. Fortunately, if you operate as a sole trader or partnership, only HM Revenue & Customs needs to see your detailed Profit and Loss figures. If your turnover is less than £79,000 per annum, HM Revenue & Customs allows you to file an abbreviated set of accounts for the purpose of completing your Self-Assessment Tax return (SA103S), only requesting the following headings:

✔ Turnover

✔ Other Income

✔ Cost of Goods Sold

✔ Car, Van and Travel Expenses (after private-use deduction)

    ✔ Wages, Salaries and Other Staff Costs

    ✔ Rent, Rates, Power and Insurance Costs

    ✔ Repairs and Renewals of Property and Equipment

    ✔ Accountancy, Legal and Other Professional Fees

    ✔ Interest, Bank and Credit Card Financial Charges

    ✔ Phone, Fax, Stationery and Other Office Costs

    ✔ Other Allowable Business Expenses

Also, if you're a small limited company, when you file your accounts at Companies House you can file abbreviated accounts, which means that you can keep your detailed Profit and Loss figures secret. Speak with your external accountant about whether you qualify as a small company because the exemption levels do change from time to time.

Profit and Loss Statement

May 2012

Month Ended	May
Revenues:	
Net Sales	£ 18,875
Cost of Goods Sold	(£ 6,500)
Gross Profit	£ 12,375
Operating Expenses:	
Advertising	£ 1,500
Bank Service Charges	£ 120
Insurance Expenses	£ 100
Interest Expenses	£ 125
Legal & Accounting Fees	£ 300
Office Expenses	£ 250
Payroll Taxes Expenses	£ 350
Postage Expenses	£ 75
Rent Expenses	£ 800
Salaries	£ 3,500
Supplies	£ 300
Telephone Expenses	£ 200
Utilities	£ 255
Total Operating Expenses	£ 7,875
Net Profit	£ 4,500

Figure 1-1:
A sample Profit and Loss statement.

Deciphering Gross Profit

Business owners must carefully watch their Gross Profit trends on monthly Profit and Loss statements. Gross Profit trends that appear lower from one month to the next can mean one of two things: sales revenue is down, or Cost of Goods Sold is up.

If revenue is down month to month, you may need to quickly find out why and fix the problem in order to meet your sales goals for the year. Or, by examining sales figures for the same month in previous years, you may determine that the drop is just a normal sales slowdown given the time of year and isn't cause to hit the panic button.

If the downward trend isn't normal, it may be a sign that a competitor's successfully drawing customers away from your business, or it may indicate that customers are dissatisfied with some aspect of the products or services you supply. Whatever the reason, preparing a monthly Profit and Loss statement gives you the ammunition you need to find and fix a problem quickly, thereby minimising any negative hit to your yearly profits.

The other key element of Gross Profit – Cost of Goods Sold – can also be a big factor in a downward profit trend. For example, if the amount you spend to purchase products that you sell goes up, your Gross Profit goes down. As a business owner, you need to do one of five things if the Cost of Goods Sold is reducing your Gross Profit:

- ✔ Find a new supplier who can provide the goods cheaper.
- ✔ Increase your prices, as long as you don't lose sales because of the increase.
- ✔ Find a way to increase your volume of sales so that you can sell more products and meet your annual profit goals.
- ✔ Find a way to reduce other expenses to offset the additional product costs.
- ✔ Accept the fact that your annual profit is going to be lower than expected.

The sooner you find out that you have a problem with costs, the faster you can find a solution and minimise any reduction in your annual profit goals.

Monitoring Expenses

The Expenses section of your Profit and Loss statement gives you a good summary of how much you spent to keep your business operating that wasn't directly related to the sale of an individual product or service. For example, businesses usually use advertising both to bring customers in and with the hope of selling many different types of products. That's why you need to list advertising as an expense rather than a Cost of Goods Sold. After all, rarely can you link an advertisement to the sale of an individual product. The same is true of all the administrative expenses that go into running a business, such as rent, wages and salaries, office costs and so on.

 Business owners watch their expense trends closely to be sure that they don't creep upwards and lower the business's bottom lines. Any cost-cutting you can do on the expense side is guaranteed to increase your bottom-line profit.

Using the Profit and Loss Statement to Make Business Decisions

Many business owners find it easier to compare their Profit and Loss statement trends using percentages rather than the actual numbers. Calculating these percentages is easy enough – you simply divide each line item by Net Sales. Figure 1-2 shows a business's percentage breakdown for one month.

Looking at this percentage breakdown, you can see that the business had a Gross Profit of 65.6 per cent, and its Cost of Goods Sold, at 34.4 per cent, accounted for just over one-third of the revenue. If the prior month's Cost of Goods Sold was only 32 per cent, the business owner needs to find out why the cost of the goods used to make this product seems to have increased. If this trend of increased Cost of Goods Sold continues through the year without some kind of fix, the business makes at least 2.2 per cent less Net Profit.

You may find it helpful to see how your Profit and Loss statement results compare to industry trends for similar businesses with similar revenues, a process called *benchmarking*. By comparing results, you can find out whether your costs and expenses are reasonable for the type of business you operate, and you can identify areas with room to improve your profitability. You also may spot red flags for line items upon which you spend much more than the national average.

Profit and Loss Statement		
May 2012		
Month Ended	**May**	
Net Sales	£ 18,875	100.0%
Cost of Goods Sold	(£ 6,500)	34.4%
Gross Profit	£ 12,375	65.6%
Operating Expenses:		
Advertising	£ 1,500	7.9%
Bank Service Charges	£ 120	0.6%
Insurance Expenses	£ 100	0.5%
Interest Expenses	£ 125	0.7%
Legal & Accounting Fees	£ 300	1.6%
Office Expenses	£ 250	1.3%
Payroll Taxes Expenses	£ 350	1.9%
Postage Expenses	£ 75	0.4%
Rent Expenses	£ 800	4.2%
Salaries	£ 3,500	18.5%
Supplies	£ 300	1.6%
Telephone Expenses	£ 200	1.1%
Utilities	£ 255	1.4%
Total Operating Expenses	£ 7,875	41.7%
Net Profit	£ 4,500	23.8%

Figure 1-2:
Percentage
breakdown
of a Profit
and Loss
statement.

To find industry trends for businesses similar to yours with similar revenues, visit www.bvdinfo.com. The FAME database contains full financial data on approximately 2 million active companies in the UK and Ireland that file their accounts at Companies House. A word of warning, though: small companies are required to file very little financial information – typically, just a Balance Sheet. This fact means that if you want to see detailed Profit and Loss information, you have to look at the big businesses with turnover above £6.5 million and a Balance Sheet greater than £3.26 million.

However, the information available for all the companies on this database is useful and can be searched in a number of ways. For example, you can compile industry-average statistics, which can be a useful way to see how your business compares with others in the same line of business. You can take this compilation a stage further and compare your business to other businesses that you already know or have found on this database.

You can also find out how your business looks to the outside world if you use FAME to dig out the financials for your business. A credit rating, details of any court judgements and other interesting information are all included in the reports.

FAME is available by subscription, which may make it expensive for the occasional user. That said, we noticed a free trial is available, so check the website for more details (www.bvdinfo.com). You may find that a regional library has FAME available to the public on a free basis or through a per-session cost. Most of the UK universities have FAME, so if you can access one of their library services you can also use this facility. This service may be available through an annual library subscription.

Testing Profits

With a completed Profit and Loss statement, you can do a number of quick ratio tests of your business's profitability. You certainly want to know how well your business did compared to other similar businesses. You also want to be able to measure your *return* (the percentage you made) on your business.

Three common tests are Return on Sales, Return on Assets and Return on Shareholders' Capital. These ratios have much more meaning if you can find industry averages for your particular type of business, so that you can compare your results. Check with your local Chamber of Commerce to see whether it has figures for local businesses, or order a report for your industry online from FAME (see the preceding section).

We look at ratios in a lot more detail in Book VI, Chapter 2, where we examine how investors typically read and interpret financial reports.

Return on Sales

The Return on Sales (ROS) ratio tells you how efficiently your business runs its operations. Using the information on your Profit and Loss statement, you can measure how much profit your business produced per pound of sales and how much extra cash you brought in per sale.

You calculate ROS by dividing Net Profit before taxes by Sales. For example, suppose that your business had a Net Profit of £4,500 and Sales of £18,875. The following shows your calculation of ROS:

Net Profit before taxes ÷ Sales = Return on Sales

£4,500 ÷ £18,875 = 23.8%

Book IV

Working to Prepare Financial Statements

As you can see, your business made 23.8 per cent on each pound of sales. To determine whether that amount calls for celebration, you need to find the ROS ratios for similar businesses. You may be able to get such information from your local Chamber of Commerce, or you can order an industry report online from FAME.

Return on Assets

The Return on Assets (ROA) ratio tests how well you're using your business's assets to generate profits. If your business's ROA is the same or higher than other similar companies, you're doing a good job of managing your assets.

To calculate ROA, you divide Net Profit by Total Assets. You find Total Assets on your Balance Sheet, which you can read more about in Book IV, Chapter 2. Suppose that your business's Net Profit was £4,500 and Total Assets were £40,050. The following shows your calculation of ROA:

Net Profit ÷ Total Assets = Return on Assets

£4,500 ÷ £40,050 = 11.2%

Your calculation shows that your business made 11.2 per cent on each pound of assets it held.

ROA can vary significantly depending on the type of industry in which you operate. For example, if your business requires you to maintain lots of expensive equipment, such as a manufacturing firm, your ROA is much lower than a service business that doesn't need as many assets. ROA can range from below 5 per cent for manufacturing businesses that require a large investment in machinery and factories, to as high as 20 per cent or even higher for service businesses with few assets.

Return on Shareholders' Capital

To measure how successfully your business earned money for the owners or investors, calculate the Return on Shareholders' Capital (ROSC) ratio. This ratio often looks better than Return on Assets (see the preceding section) because ROSC doesn't take debt into consideration.

You calculate ROSC by dividing Net Profit by Shareholders' or Owners' Capital. (You find capital amounts on your Balance Sheet; see Book IV, Chapter 2.) Suppose that your business's Net Profit was £4,500 and the Shareholders' or Owners' Capital was £9,500. Here's the formula:

Net Profit ÷ Shareholders' or Owners' Capital = Return on Shareholders' Capital

£4,500 ÷ £9,500 = 47.3%

Most business owners put in a lot of cash up front to get a business started, so seeing a business whose liabilities and capital are split close to 50 per cent each is fairly common.

Branching Out with Profit and Loss Statement Data

The Profit and Loss statement you produce for external use – financial institutions and investors – may be very different from the one you produce for in-house use by your managers. Most business owners prefer to provide the minimum amount of detail necessary to satisfy external users of their financial statements, such as summaries of expenses instead of line-by-line expense details, a Net Sales figure without reporting all the detail about discounts and fees, and a Cost of Goods Sold number without reporting all the detail about how that was calculated.

Internally, the contents of the Profit and Loss statement are a very different story. With more detail, your managers are better able to make accurate business decisions. Most businesses develop detailed reports based on the data collected to develop the Profit and Loss statement. Items such as discounts, returns and allowances are commonly pulled out of Profit and Loss statements and broken down into more detail:

- **Discounts** are reductions on the selling price as part of a special sale. They may also be in the form of volume discounts provided to customers who buy large amounts of the business's products. For example, a business may offer a 10 per cent discount to customers who buy 20 or more of the same item at one time. In order to put their Net Sales numbers in perspective, business owners and managers must monitor how much they reduce their revenues to attract sales.

- **Returns** are transactions in which the buyer returns items for any reason – not the right size, damaged, defective and so on. If a business's number of returns increases dramatically, a larger problem may be the cause; therefore business owners need to monitor these numbers carefully in order to identify and resolve any problems with the items they sell.

✔ **Allowances** cover gifts cards and other accounts that customers pay for up front without taking any merchandise. Allowances are actually a liability for a business because the customer (or the person who was given the gift card) eventually comes back to get merchandise and doesn't have to pay any cash in return.

Another section of the Profit and Loss statement that you're likely to break down into more detail for internal use is the Cost of Goods Sold. Basically, you take the detail collected to calculate that line item, including Opening Stock, Closing Stock, Purchases and Purchase discounts, and present it in a separate report. (We explain how to calculate Cost of Goods Sold in the section 'Finding Cost of Goods Sold', earlier in this chapter.)

No limit exists to the number of internal reports you can generate from the detail that goes into your Profit and Loss statement and other financial statements. For example, many businesses design a report that looks at month-to-month trends in revenue, Cost of Goods Sold and profit. In fact, you can set up your computerised accounting system (if you use one) to generate this and other custom-designed reports automatically. Using your computerised system, you can produce these reports at any time during the month if you want to see how close you are to meeting your month-end, quarter-end or year-end goal.

Many businesses also design a report that compares actual spending to the budget. On this report, each of the Profit and Loss statement line items appear with its accompanying planned budget figures and the actual figures. When reviewing this report, you flag any line item that's considerably higher or lower than expected and then research it to find a reason for the difference.

I look at budgeting in more detail in Book V, Chapter 5.

Have a Go

This section tests your knowledge about the Profit and Loss statements.

1. **Your Purchases account shows that you purchased £10,000 worth of paper goods to be sold during the accounting period. In which section of the Profit and Loss Statement would you include that account?**

2. **Your Telephone Expenses account shows that you paid a total of £2,000 for your company's telephones during the accounting period. In which section of the Profit and Loss Statement would you show that account?**

3. Your Sales Discounts account shows that you offered customers a total of $1,500 in discounts during the accounting period. In which section of the Profit and Loss Statement would you put that information?

4. In the space below, describe how you would calculate Gross Profit. Show the calculation required if it helps.

5. In the space below, explain how you would calculate Net Profit. Show the calculation required if it helps.

6. Using the figures given below, prepare a Profit and Loss statement using the format shown earlier in this chapter.

Net Sales	$50,000
Interest Profit and Loss	$1,200
Cost of Goods Sold	$20,000
Advertising	$3,000
Salaries	$5,000
Supplies	$2,500
Interest Expenses	$1,300
Depreciation	$1,500

7. Looking at your accounts, you find that you've the following balances at the end of an accounting period:

Sales of Goods	$20,000
Sales Discounts	$2,000
Sales Returns	$1,500

8. Using these figures, calculate your Net Sales in the space below.

9. Suppose that you started the month of June with $200 of stock in hand. You purchased $2,000 of stock during June and you've $500 of stock left to sell at the end of June. You're preparing a Profit and Loss statement for the month of June. What would your Cost of Goods Sold be for the month of June?

10. Suppose that you started the month of July with $500 of stock on hand. You purchased $1,500 of stock during July and you've $100 of stock left to sell at the end of July. You're preparing a Profit and Loss statement for the month of July. What would your Cost of Goods Sold be for the month of July?

11. Suppose that your company had a net Profit and Loss of $10,595 and sales of $40,500 for the month of June. Calculate the ROS ratio.

12. Suppose that your company had a net Profit and Loss of £13,565 and sales of £75,725 for the month of July. Calculate the ROS ratio.

13. Your company's Net Profit for the month of May is £5,300 and its Total Assets are £75,040. What's the ROA ratio?

14. Your company's Net Profit for the month of May is £10,700 and its Total Assets are £49,650. What's the ROA ratio?

15. Your company earned a Net Profit of £75,750 and its Shareholders' or Owner's Equity is £500,000. Calculate the Return on Equity ratio.

16. Your company earned a Net Profit of £52,500 and its Owner's Equity is £375,000. Calculate the Return on Equity ratio.

Answering the Have a Go Questions

1. Purchases are included as part of your calculation for Cost of Goods Sold.

2. Telephone Expenses are part of Operating Expenses for a business.

3. Sales Discounts are included as part of your calculation for Net Sales.

4. Gross Profit is calculated as follows:

Sales Revenue	X
Less Cost of Goods Sold	(X)
Gross Profit	X

The actual Gross Profit figure is often expressed as a percentage of sales to provide you with a Gross Profit margin.

For example:

Sales Revenue	£100,000
Cost of Goods Sold	(£75,000)
Gross Profit	£25,000

Gross Profit margin would be $25,000 \div 100,000 = 0.25$ (25 per cent expressed as a percentage).

5. Net Profit is often described as the 'bottom line', because it's the profit after all Operating Expenses have been taken from your Gross Profit.

You can express the Net Profit as a percentage of sales to provide you with a Net Profit margin.

For example:

Sales Revenue	£100,000
Cost of Goods Sold	(£75,000)
Gross Profit	£25,000
Operating Expenses	(£15,000)
Net Profit	£10,000

The Net Profit margin would be 10,000 ÷ 100,000 = 0.10 (10 per cent expressed as a percentage)

6. **Using the figures given in the example, the Profit and Loss statement would appear as follows:**

Revenues

Sales	£50,000
Cost of Goods Sold	(£20,000)
Gross Profit	£30,000
Operating Expenses	
Advertising	£3,000
Salaries	£5,000
Supplies	£2,500
Interest Expenses	£1,300
Depreciation	£1,500
Total Operating Expenses	£13,300
Operating Profit	£16,700
Other Income	
Interest Income	£1,200
Net Profit	£17,900

7. **The net sales are calculated as follows:**

Sales of Goods Sold	£20,000
Sales Discounts	(2,000)
Sales Returns	(1,500)
Net Sales	£16,500

8. **Your Cost of Goods Sold for the month of June would be:**

Opening Stock	£200
Add Purchases	£2,000
Goods Available for Sale	£2,200
Less Closing Stock	(£500)
Cost of Goods Sold	£1,700

9. **Your Cost of Goods Sold for the month of July would be:**

Opening Stock	£500
Add Purchases	£1,500
Goods Available for Sale	£2,000
Less Closing Stock	(£100)
Cost of Goods Sold	£1,900

10. **The ROS ratio would be:**

£10,595 ÷ £40,500 = 26.2%

So, in this case the company made 26.2 per cent for each pound of sales.

11. **The ROS ratio would be:**

£13,565 ÷ £75,725 = 17.9%

So, in this case the company made 17.9 per cent for each pound of sales.

12. **The ROA ratio is:**

£5,300 ÷ £75,040 = 7.06%

13. **The ROA ratio is:**

£10,700 ÷ £49,650 = 21.55%

14. **The Return on Equity ratio would be:**

£75,750 ÷ £500,000 = 15.15%

So the owner's return on his investment is 15.15 per cent.

15. **The Return on Equity ratio would be:**

£52,500 ÷ £375,000 = 14%

So the owner's return on his investment is 14 per cent.

Chapter 2

Developing a Balance Sheet

*P*eriodically, you want to know how well your business is doing. Therefore, at the end of each accounting period you draw up a Balance Sheet – a snapshot of your business's condition. This snapshot gives you a picture of where your business stands – its assets, its liabilities and how much the owners have invested in the business at a particular point in time.

This chapter explains the key ingredients of a Balance Sheet and tells you how to pull them all together. You also find out how to use analytical tools called ratios to see how well your business is doing.

Breaking Down the Balance Sheet

Basically, creating a Balance Sheet is like taking a picture of the financial aspects of your business.

The business name appears at the top of the Balance Sheet along with the ending date for the accounting period being reported. The rest of the report summarises:

✔ **The business's assets,** which include everything the business owns in order to stay in operation.

✔ **The business's debts,** which include any outstanding bills and loans that it must pay.

✔ **The owner's capital,** which is basically how much the business's owners have invested in the business.

Generating Balance Sheets electronically

If you use a computerised accounting system, you can take advantage of its report function to generate your Balance Sheets automatically. These Balance Sheets give you quick snapshots of the business's financial position, but may require adjustments before you prepare your financial reports for external use.

One key adjustment you're likely to make involves the value of your stock. Most computerised accounting systems use the averaging method to value stock. This method totals all the stock purchased and then calculates an average price for the stock (see Book II, Chapter 3 for more information on stock valuation). However, your accountant may recommend a different valuation method that works better for your business. Therefore, if you use a method other than the default averaging method to value your stock, you need to adjust the stock value that appears on the Balance Sheet generated from your computerised accounting system.

Assets, liabilities and capital probably sound familiar – they're the key elements that show whether or not your books are in balance. If your liabilities plus capital equal assets, your books are in balance. All your bookkeeping efforts are an attempt to keep the books in balance based on this formula, which we talk more about in Book I, Chapter 2.

Gathering Balance Sheet Ingredients

Most people now operate a computerised accounting system and the Balance Sheet is achieved simply by pressing a few buttons. However, you'll find it useful to know how the Balance Sheet is constructed, and this chapter shows you how, with the aid of a fictitious set of accounts.

To keep this example simple, we've selected key accounts from the company's Trial Balance as shown in Table 2-1:

Dividing and listing your assets

The first part of the Balance Sheet is the assets section. The first step in developing this section is dividing your assets into two categories: current assets and fixed assets.

Table 2-1	Balance Sheet Accounts	
Account Name	**Balance in Account**	
	Debit	Credit
Cash	£2,500	
Petty Cash	£500	
Trade Debtors (Accounts Receivable)	£1,000	
Stock	£1,200	
Equipment	£5,050	
Vehicles	£25,000	
Furniture	£5,600	
Drawings	£10,000	
Trade Creditors (Accounts Payable)		£2,200
Loans Payable		£29,150
Capital		£5,000
Net Profit for the Year		£14,500
Total	£50,850	£50,850

Current assets

Current assets are things your business owns that you can easily convert to cash and expect to use in the next 12 months to pay your bills and your employees. Current assets include cash, Trade Debtors (money due from customers) and stock. (We cover Trade Debtors in Book II, Chapter 2 and stock in Book II, Chapter 3.)

When you see Cash as the first line item on a Balance Sheet, that account includes what you have on hand in the tills and what you have in the bank, including current accounts, savings accounts and petty cash. In most cases, you simply list all these accounts as one item, Cash, on the Balance Sheet.

The current assets for the fictional business are:

Cash	£2,500
Petty Cash	£500
Trade Debtors	£1,000
Stock	£1,200

You total the Cash and Petty Cash accounts, giving you £3,000, and list that amount on the Balance Sheet as a line item called Cash.

Book IV

Working to Prepare Financial Statements

Fixed assets

Fixed assets are things your business owns that you expect to have for more than 12 months. Fixed assets include land, buildings, equipment, furniture, vehicles and anything else that you expect to have for longer than a year.

The fixed assets for the fictional business are:

Equipment	£5,050
Vehicles	£25,000
Furniture	£5,600

Most businesses have more items in the fixed assets section of a Balance Sheet than the few fixed assets we show here for the fictional business. For example:

- A manufacturing business that has a lot of tools, dies or moulds created specifically for its manufacturing processes needs to have a line item called Tools, Dies and Moulds.

- A business that owns one or more buildings needs to have a line item labelled Land and Buildings.

- A business may lease its business space and then spend lots of money doing it up. For example, a restaurant may rent a large space and then furnish it according to a desired theme. Money the restaurant spends on doing up the space becomes a fixed asset called Leasehold Improvements and is listed on the Balance Sheet in the fixed assets section.

Everything mentioned so far in this section – land, buildings, leasehold improvements and so on – is a *tangible asset*. These items are ones that you can actually touch or hold. Another type of fixed asset is the *intangible asset*. Intangible assets aren't physical objects; common examples are patents, copyrights and trademarks.

- A **patent** gives a business the right to dominate the markets for the patented product. When a patent expires (usually after 20 years), competitors can enter the marketplace for the product that was patented, and the competition helps to lower the price to consumers. For example, pharmaceutical businesses patent all their new drugs and therefore are protected as the sole providers of those drugs. When your doctor prescribes a brand-name drug, you're getting a patented product. Generic drugs are products whose patents have run out, meaning that any pharmaceutical business can produce and sell its own version of the same product.

✔ A **copyright** protects original works, including books, magazines, articles, newspapers, television shows, movies, music, poetry and plays, from being copied by anyone other than the creator(s). For example, this book is copyrighted, so no one can make a copy of any of its contents without the permission of the publisher, John Wiley & Sons, Ltd.

✔ A **trademark** gives a business ownership of distinguishing words, phrases, symbols or designs. For example, check out this book's cover to see the registered trademark, *For Dummies*, for this brand. Trademarks can last forever, as long as a business continues to use the trademark and files the proper paperwork periodically.

In order to show in financial statements that their values are being used up, all fixed assets are depreciated or amortised. Tangible assets are depreciated; see Book III, Chapter 3 for a brief overview on how to depreciate fixed assets. Intangible assets such as patents and copyrights are amortised (amortisation is similar to depreciation). Each intangible asset has a lifespan based on the number of years for which the rights are granted. After setting an initial value for the intangible asset, a business then divides that value by the number of years it has protection, and the resulting amount is then written off each year as an Amortisation Expense, which is shown on the Profit and Loss statement. You can find the total amortisation or depreciation expenses that have been written off during the life of the asset on the Balance Sheet in a line item called Accumulated Depreciation or Accumulated Amortisation, whichever is appropriate for the type of asset.

Acknowledging your debts

The liabilities section of the Balance Sheet comes after the assets section and shows all the money that your business owes to others, including banks, suppliers, contractors, financial institutions and individuals. Like assets, you divide your liabilities into two categories on the Balance Sheet:

✔ **Current liabilities section:** All bills and debts that you plan to pay within the next 12 months. Accounts appearing in this section include Trade Creditors (bills due to suppliers, contractors and others), Credit Cards Payable and the current portion of a long-term debt (for example, if you've a mortgage on your premises, the payments due in the next 12 months appear in the current liabilities section).

✔ **Long-term liabilities section:** All debts you owe to lenders that are to be paid over a period longer than 12 months. Mortgages Payable and Loans Payable are common accounts in the long-term liabilities section of the Balance Sheet.

Most businesses try to minimise their current liabilities because the interest rates on short-term loans, such as credit cards, are usually much higher than those on loans with longer terms. As you manage your business's liabilities, always look for ways to minimise your interest payments by seeking longer-term loans with lower interest rates than you can get on a credit card or short-term loan.

The fictional business used for the example Balance Sheets in this chapter has only one account in each liabilities section:

Current liabilities:

Trade Creditors   £2,200

Long-term liabilities:

Loans Payable   £29,150

Naming your investments

Every business has investors. Even a small family business requires money up front to get the business on its feet. Investments are reflected on the Balance Sheet as *capital.* The line items that appear in a Balance Sheet's capital section vary depending upon whether or not the business is incorporated. (Businesses incorporate primarily to minimise their personal legal liabilities; we talk more about incorporation in Book V, Chapter 1.)

If you're preparing the books for a business that isn't incorporated, the capital section of your Balance Sheet contains these accounts:

- ✔ **Capital:** All money invested by the owners to start up the business as well as any additional contributions made after the start-up phase. If the business has more than one owner, the Balance Sheet usually has a Capital account for each owner so that individual stakes in the business can be recorded.

- ✔ **Drawings:** All money taken out of the business by the business's owners. Balance Sheets usually have a Drawing account for each owner in order to record individual withdrawal amounts.

- ✔ **Retained Earnings:** All profits left in the business.

For an incorporated business, the capital section of the Balance Sheet contains the following accounts:

- ✔ **Shares:** Portions of ownership in the business, purchased as investments by business owners.

- ✔ **Retained Earnings:** All profits that have been reinvested in the business.

Sorting out share investments

You're probably most familiar with the sale of shares on the open market through the various stock market exchanges, such as the London Stock Exchange (LSE) and the Alternative Investment Market (AIM). However, not all companies sell their shares through public exchanges; in fact, most companies aren't public companies but rather remain private operations.

Whether public or private, people become owners in a business by buying shares. If the business isn't publicly traded, the owners buy and sell shares privately. In most small businesses, family members, close friends and occasionally outside investors buy shares, having been approached individually as a means to raise additional money to build the business.

The value of each share is set at the time the share is sold. Many businesses set the initial share value at £1 to £10.

Because the fictional business isn't incorporated, the accounts appearing in the capital section of its Balance Sheet are:

Capital	£5,000
Retained Earnings	£4,500

Pulling Together the Final Balance Sheet

After you group together all your accounts (see the preceding section 'Gathering Balance Sheet Ingredients'), you're ready to produce a Balance Sheet. Businesses in the UK usually choose between two common formats for their Balance Sheets: the horizontal format or the vertical format, with the vertical format preferred. The actual line items appearing in both formats are the same; the only difference is the way in which you lay out the information on the page.

Horizontal format

The horizontal format is a two-column layout with assets on one side and liabilities and capital on the other side.

Figure 2-1 shows the elements of a sample Balance Sheet in the horizontal format.

Book IV

Working to Prepare Financial Statements

Balance Sheet
As of 31 May 2012

Fixed Assets			Capital		
Equipment	£ 5,050		Opening balance	£ 5,000	
Furniture	£ 5,600		Net Profit for year	£ 14,500	
Vehicles	£ 25,000			£ 19,500	
		£ 35,650	Less Drawings	£ 10,000	
					£ 9,500
			Long-term Liabilities		
			Loans Payable		£ 29,150
Current Assets			**Current Liabilities**		
Stock	£ 1,200		Trade Creditors		£ 2,200
Trade Debtors	£ 1,000				
Cash	£ 3,000				
	£ 5,200				
		£ 40,850			£ 40,850

Figure 2-1: A sample Balance Sheet using the horizontal format.

Vertical format

The vertical format is a one-column layout showing assets first, followed by liabilities and then capital.

Using the vertical format, Figure 2-2 shows the Balance Sheet for a fictional business.

Whether you prepare your Balance Sheet as per Figure 2-1 or Figure 2-2, remember that Assets = Liabilities + Capital, so both sides of the Balance Sheet must balance to reflect this.

The vertical format includes:

- ✔ **Net current assets:** Calculated by subtracting current assets from current liabilities – a quick test to see whether or not a business has the money on hand to pay bills. Net current assets is sometimes referred to as *working capital*.

- ✔ **Total assets less current liabilities:** What's left over for a business's owners after all liabilities have been subtracted from total assets. Total assets less current liabilities is sometimes referred to as *net assets*.

Balance Sheet
As of 31 May 2012

Fixed Assets		
Equipment	£ 5,050	
Furniture	£ 5,600	
Vehicles	£ 25,000	
		£ 35,650
Current Assets		
Stock	£ 1,200	
Trade Debtors	£ 1,000	
Cash	£ 3,000	
	£ 5,200	
Less: Current Liabilities		
Trade Creditors	£ 2,200	
Net Current Assets		£ 3,000
Total Assets Less Current Liabilities		£ 38,650
Long-term Liabilities		
Loans Payable		£ 29,150
		£ 9,500
Capital		
Opening Balance		£ 5,000
Net Profit for Year		£ 14,500
		£ 19,500
Less Drawings		£ 10,000
		£ 9,500

Figure 2-2:
A sample Balance Sheet using the vertical format.

Putting Your Balance Sheet to Work

With a complete Balance Sheet in your hands, you can analyse the numbers through a series of ratio tests to check your cash status and monitor your debt. These tests are the type of tests that financial institutions and potential investors use to determine whether or not to lend money to or invest in your business. Therefore, a good idea is to run these tests yourself before seeking loans or investors. Ultimately, the ratio tests in this section can help you determine whether or not your business is in a strong cash position.

Book IV

Working to Prepare Financial Statements

Testing your cash

When you approach a bank or other financial institution for a loan, you can expect the lender to use one of two ratios to test your cash flow: the *current ratio* and the *acid test ratio* (also known as the *quick ratio*).

Current ratio

This ratio compares your current assets to your current liabilities and provides a quick glimpse of your business's ability to pay its bills in the short term.

The formula for calculating the current ratio is:

Current assets ÷ Current liabilities = Current ratio

The following is an example of a current ratio calculation:

£5,200 ÷ £2,200 = 2.36 (current ratio)

Lenders usually look for current ratios of 1.2 to 2, so any financial institution considers a current ratio of 2.36 a good sign. A current ratio under 1 is considered a danger sign because it indicates that the business doesn't have enough cash to pay its current bills. This rule is only a rough guide and some business sectors may require a higher or lower current ratio figure. Get advice to see what the norm is for your business sector.

A current ratio over 2.0 may indicate that your business isn't investing its assets well and may be able to make better use of its current assets. For example, if your business is holding a lot of cash, you may want to invest that money in some long-term assets, such as additional equipment, that you can use to help grow the business.

Acid test (quick) ratio

The acid test ratio uses only the Cash account and Trade Debtors in its calculation – otherwise known as *liquid assets*. Although similar to the current ratio in that it examines current assets and liabilities, the acid test ratio is a stricter test of a business's ability to pay bills. The assets part of this calculation doesn't take stock into account because it can't always be converted to cash as quickly as other current assets and because in a slow market selling your stock may take a while.

Many lenders prefer the acid test ratio when determining whether or not to give a business a loan because of its strictness.

Calculating the acid test ratio is a two-step process:

1. **Determine your quick assets.**

   Cash + Trade Debtors = Quick assets

2. **Calculate your quick ratio.**

   Quick assets ÷ Current liabilities = Quick ratio

The following is an example of an acid test ratio calculation:

£3,000 + £1,000 = £4,000 (quick assets)

£4,000 ÷ £2,200 = 1.8 (acid test ratio)

Lenders consider that a business with an acid test ratio around 1 is in good condition. An acid test ratio of less than 1 indicates that the business can't currently pay back its current liabilities.

Assessing your debt

Before you even consider whether or not to take on additional debt, always check out your debt condition. One common ratio that you can use to assess your business's debt position is the *gearing ratio*. This ratio compares what your business owes – *external borrowing* – to what your business's owners have invested in the business – *internal funds*.

Calculating your debt-to-capital ratio is a two-step process:

1. **Calculate your total debt.**

   Current liabilities + Long-term liabilities = Total debt

2. **Calculate your gearing ratio.**

   Total debt ÷ Capital = Gearing ratio

The following is an example of a debt-to-capital ratio calculation:

£2,200 + £29,150 = £31,350 (total debt)

£31,350 ÷ £9,500 = 3.3 (gearing ratio)

Lenders like to see a gearing ratio close to 1 because it indicates that the amount of debt is equal to the amount of capital. Most banks probably wouldn't lend any more money to a business with a debt to capital ratio of

3.3 until its debt levels were lowered or the owners put more money into the business. The reason for this lack of confidence may be one of two:

- ✔ They don't want to have more money invested in the business than the owners.
- ✔ They're concerned about the business's ability to service the debt.

We look at ratios in a lot more detail in Book VI, Chapter 2; skip ahead to see how investors may read the financial statements of a company.

Have a Go

The next section invites you to have a go at putting together a few Balance Sheets, so that you become more familiar with the component parts.

1. **In which part of the Balance Sheet do you find the Furniture account?**

2. **In which part of the Balance Sheet do you find the Trade Creditors (Accounts Payable) account?**

3. **Describe the Owner's Capital account.**

4. **Where do you find the Land and Buildings Account?**

5. **Whereabouts in the Balance Sheet do you find the Credit Cards Payable account?**

6. **Where do you find the Retained Earnings account?**

7. **To practise preparing a Balance Sheet in the horizontal format, use this list of accounts to prepare a Balance Sheet for the Abba Company as of the end of May 2014:**

Cash	£5,000
Debtors	£2,000
Stock	£10,500
Equipment	£12,000
Furniture	£7,800
Building	£300,000
Creditors	£5,200
Loans Payable	£250,000
Owners Capital	£52,000
Retained Earnings	£30,100

8. To practise preparing a Balance Sheet in the vertical format, use this list of accounts to prepare a Balance Sheet for the Abba Company as of the end of May 2014:

Cash	£5,000
Debtors	£2,000
Stock	£10,500
Equipment	£12,000
Furniture	£7,800
Building	£300,000
Creditors	£5,200
Loans Payable	£250,000
Owners Capital	£52,000
Retained Earnings	£30,100

9. Your Balance Sheet shows that your current assets equal £22,000 and your current liabilities equal £52,000. What is your current ratio? Is that a good or bad sign to lenders?

10. Suppose that your Balance Sheet shows that your current assets equal £32,000 and your current liabilities equal £34,000. What would your current ratio be? Is that a good or bad sign to lenders?

11. Your Balance Sheet shows that your current assets equal £45,000 and your current liabilities are £37,000. What is your current ratio? Is that a good or bad sign to lenders?

12. Your Balance Sheet shows that your Cash account equals £10,000, your Debtors account equals £25,000 and your current liabilities equal £52,000. What would your acid test ratio be? Is that a good or bad sign to lenders?

13. Suppose that your Balance Sheet shows that your Cash account equals £15,000, your Debtors equals £17,000 and your current liabilities equals £34,000. What would your acid test ratio be? Is that a good or bad sign to lenders?

14. Suppose that your Balance Sheet shows that your Cash account equals £19,000, your Debtors equals £21,000 and your current liabilities equals £37,000. What would your acid test ratio be? Is that a good or bad sign to lenders?

Book IV

Working to Prepare Financial Statements

15. A business's current liabilities are £2,200 and its long-term liabilities are £35,000. The owners' equity in the company totals £12,500. What is the debt-to-equity ratio? Is this a good or bad sign?

16. Suppose that a business's current liabilities are £5,700 and its long-term liabilities are £35,000. The owners' equity in the company totals £42,000. What is the debt-to-equity ratio? Is this ratio a good or bad sign?

17. Suppose that a business's current liabilities are £6,500 and its long-term liabilities are £150,000. The owners' equity in the company totals £175,000. What is debt-to-equity ratio? Is this ratio a good or bad sign?

Answering the Have a Go Questions

1. The Furniture account is regarded as a fixed asset because furniture is kept in the business for more than 12 months.

2. **Trade Creditors (Accounts Payable) are suppliers that the business owes money to.** This account is classified as a current liability.

3. **Owners capital can be described as the money invested in the business by the owners.** When owners put money into the business, this act can be described as capital introduced. When money is taken out, it can be taken as drawings (if the business is a sole trader or partnership) or dividends (if the business is a limited company).

4. **The Land and Buildings account is part of fixed assets because land and buildings are kept in the business for a long period of time.**

5. **The Credit Cards payable account is money owed by the business to credit cards.** This account is therefore a liability. Because the debt is due to be repaid within 12 months, the account is considered a Current Liability account.

6. **The Retained Earnings account tracks the earnings that the owners reinvest in the business each year, and are part of the owners' equity in the company.**

7. **The horizontal format would look like this:**

Abba Company Balance Sheet; as of 31 May 2014

Fixed Asset			**Capital**		
Building	£300,000		Opening balance	£52,000	
Equipment	£12,000		Net Profit for the year	£30,100	
Furniture	£7,800				£82,100
		£319,800			
Current Assets			Current Liabilities		
Stock	£10,500		Creditors	£5,200	
Debtors	£2,000				
Cash	£5,000		**Long-Term Liabilities**		
			Loans Payable	£250,000	
Total Current Assets	£17,500				
Total Assets		£337,300	Total Liabilities and Equity		£337,300

8. **Here's what the vertical format would look like:**

Abba Company Balance Sheet; as of 31 May 2014

Fixed Assets		
Building	£300,000	
Equipment	£12,000	
Furniture	£7,800	
		£319,800
Current Assets		
Stock	£10,500	
Debtors	£2,000	
Cash	£5,000	
		£17,500

(continued)

Abba Company Balance Sheet; as of 31 May 2014 (continued)

Less: Current Liabilities		
Creditors	£5,200	
Net Current Assets		£12,300
Total Assets less Current Liabilities		£332,100
Long-Term Liabilities		
Loans Payable		£250,000
		£82,100
Capital		
Opening Balance		£52,000
Retained Earnings		£30,100
Total Equity		£82,100

9. **Calculate the current ratio:**

    £22,000 ÷ £52,000 = 0.42

    This ratio is considerably below 1.2, so it would be considered a really bad sign. A ratio this low would indicate that a company may have trouble paying its bills because its current liabilities are considerably higher than the money the company has on hand in current assets.

10. **Calculate the current ratio:**

    £32,000 ÷ £34,000 = 0.94

    The current ratio is slightly below the preferred minimum of 1.2, which would be considered a bad sign. A financial institution may loan money to this company, but consider it a higher risk. A company with this current ratio would pay higher interest rates than one in the 1.2 to 2 current ratio preferred range.

11. **Calculate the current ratio:**

    £45,000 ÷ £37,000 = 1.22

    The current ratio is at 1.22, which would be considered a good sign and the company probably wouldn't have difficulty borrowing money.

12. **First you calculate your quick assets:**

    £10,000 + £25,000 = £35,000

    Then you calculate your acid test ratio:

    £35,000 ÷ £52,000 = 0.67

    An acid test ratio of less than 1 would be considered a bad sign. A company with this ratio would have a difficult time getting a loan from a financial institution.

13. **First you calculate your quick assets:**

    £15,000 + £17,000 = £32,000

    Then you calculate your acid test ratio:

    £32,000 ÷ £34,000 = 0.94

    An acid test ratio of less than 1 would be considered a bad sign. Because this company's acid test ratio is close to 1 it could probably get a loan, but would have to pay a higher interest rate because it would be considered a higher risk.

14. **First you calculate your quick assets:**

    £19,000 + £21,000 = £40,000

    Then you calculate your acid test ratio:

    £40,000 ÷ £37,000 = 1.08

    An acid test ratio of more than 1 would be considered a good sign. A company with this ratio would probably be able to get a loan from a financial institution without difficulty.

15. **First, you calculate your total debt:**

    £2,200 + £35,000 = £37,200

    Then you calculate your debt-to-equity ratio:

    £37,200 ÷ £12,500 = 2.98

    A debt-to-equity ratio of more than 1 would be considered a bad sign. A company with this ratio probably wouldn't be able to get a loan from a financial institution until the owners put more money into the business from other sources, such as family and friends or a private investor.

Book IV

Working to Prepare Financial Statements

16. **First, you calculate your total debt:**

    £5,700 + £35,000 = £40,700

    Then you calculate your debt-to-equity ratio:

    £40,700 ÷ £42,000 = 0.97

    A debt-to-equity ratio near 1 is considered a good sign. A company with this ratio is probably able to get a loan from a financial institution, but the institution may require additional funds from the owner or investors as well if the company is applying for a large, unsecured loan. A loan secured with assets, such as a mortgage, wouldn't be a problem.

17. **First, you calculate your total debt:**

    £6,500 + £150,000 = £156,500

    Then you calculate your debt-to-equity ratio:

    £156,500 ÷ £175,000 = 0.89

    A debt-to-equity ratio of less than 1 would be considered a good sign. A company with this ratio would probably be able to get a loan from a financial institution.

Chapter 3

Cash Flows and the Cash Flow Statement

In This Chapter

▶ Separating the three types of cash flows

▶ Figuring out how much actual cash increase was generated by profit

▶ Looking at a business's other sources and uses of cash

▶ Being careful about free cash flow

▶ Evaluating managers' decisions by scrutinising the cash flow statement

This chapter talks about *cash flows* – which in general refers to cash inflows and outflows over a period of time. Suppose you tell us that last year you had total cash inflows of £145,000 and total cash outflows of £140,000. We know that your cash balance increased by £5,000. But we don't know where your £145,000 cash inflows came from. Did you earn this much in salary? Did you receive an inheritance from your rich uncle? Likewise, we don't know what you used your £140,000 cash outflow for. Did you make large payments on your credit cards? Did you lose a lot of money at the races? In short, cash flows have to be sorted into different sources and uses to make much sense.

The Three Types of Cash Flow

Accountants categorise the cash flows of a business into three types:

✔ Cash inflows from making sales and cash outflows for expenses – sales and expense transactions – are called the *operating activities* of a business (although they could be called profit activities just as well, because their purpose is to make profit).

✔ Cash outflows for making investments in new assets (buildings, machinery, tools and so on) and cash inflows from liquidating old investments (assets no longer needed that are sold off); these transactions are called *investment activities*.

✔ Cash inflows from borrowing money and from the additional investment of money in the business by its owners, and cash outflows for paying off debt, returning capital that the business no longer needs to owners and making cash distributions of profit to its owners; these transactions are called *financing activities.*

The cash flow statement (or *statement of cash flows*) summarises the cash flows of a business for a period according to this three-way classification. Generally accepted accounting principles require that whenever a business reports its Profit and Loss statement, it must also report its cash flow statement for the same period – a business shouldn't report one without the other. A good reason exists for this dual financial statement requirement.

The Profit and Loss statement is based on the *accrual basis of accounting* that records sales when made, whether or not cash is received at that time, and records expenses when incurred, whether or not the expenses are paid at that time. (Book II, Chapter 2 explains accrual basis accounting.) Because accrual basis accounting is used to record profit, you can't equate bottom-line profit with an increase in cash. Suppose a business's annual Profit and Loss statement reports that it earned £1.6 million net profit for the year. This doesn't mean that its cash balance increased by £1.6 million during the period. You have to look in the cash flow statement to find out how much its cash balance increased (or, possibly, decreased!) from its operating activities (sales revenue and expenses) during the period.

In the chapter, we refer to the net increase (or decrease) in the business's cash balance that results from collecting sales revenue and paying expenses as *cash flow from profit* (the alternative term for *cash flow from operating activities*). Cash flow from profit seems more user-friendly than cash flow from operating activities, and in fact the term is used widely. In any case, don't confuse cash flow from profit with the other two types of cash flow – from the business's investing activities and financing activities during the period.

Before moving on, here's a short problem for you to solve. This summary of the business's net cash flows (in thousands) for the year just ended, which uses the three-way classification of cash flows explained earlier, has one amount missing:

(1) From profit (operating activities)	?
(2) From investing activities	– £1,275
(3) From financing activities	+ £160
Decrease in cash balance during year	– £15

Note that the business's cash balance from all sources and uses decreased by £15,000 during the year. The amounts of net cash flows from the company's investing and financing activities are given. So you can determine that the net cash flow from profit was £1.1 million for the year. Understanding cash flows from investing activities and financing activities is fairly straightforward. Understanding the net cash flow from profit, in contrast, is more challenging – but business managers and investors should have a good grip on this very important number.

Setting the Stage: Changes in Balance Sheet Accounts

The first step in understanding the amounts reported by a business in its cash flow statement is to focus on the *changes* in the business's Assets, Liabilities and Owners' Equity accounts during the period – the increases or decreases of each account from the start of the period to the end of the period. These changes are found in the comparative two-year Balance Sheet reported by a business. Figure 3-1 presents the increases and decreases during the year in the assets, liabilities and owners' equity accounts for a business example. Figure 3-1 isn't a Balance Sheet but only a summary of *changes* in account balances. We don't want to burden you with an entire Balance Sheet, which has much more detail than is needed here.

Assets	
Cash	(15)
Debtors	800
Stock	975
Prepaid Expenses	145
Fixed Assets	1,275
Accumulated Depreciation*	(1,200)
Total	1,980
Liabilities & Owners' Equity	
Creditors	80
Accrued Expenses Payable	1,20
Income Tax Payable	20
Overdraft	200
Long-term Loans	300
Owners' Invested Capital	60
Retained Earnings	1,200
Total	1,980

Figure 3-1: Changes in Balance Sheet assets and operating liabilities that affect cash flow from profit.

* Accumulated Depreciation is a negative asset account which is deducted from Fixed Assets. The negative £1,200 change increases the negative balance of the account.

Book IV

Working to Prepare Financial Statements

Take a moment to scan Figure 3-1. Note that the business's cash balance decreased by £15,000 during the year. (An increase isn't necessarily a good thing, and a decrease isn't necessarily a bad thing; it depends on the overall financial situation of the business.) One purpose of reporting the cash flow statement is to summarise the main reasons for the change in cash – according to the three-way classification of cash flows explained earlier. One question on everyone's mind is this: How much cash did the profit for the year generate for the business? The cash flow statement begins by answering this question.

Getting at the Cash Increase from Profit

Although all amounts reported on the cash flow statement are important, the one that usually gets the most attention is *cash flow from operating activities*, or *cash flow from profit* as we prefer to call it. This is the increase in cash generated by a business's profit-making operations during the year exclusive of its other sources of cash during the year (such as borrowed money, sold-off fixed assets and additional owners' investments in the business). *Cash flow from profit* indicates a business's ability to turn profit into available cash – cash in the bank that can be used for the needs of business. Cash flow from profit gets just as much attention as net profit (the bottom-line profit number in the Profit and Loss statement).

Before presenting the cash flow statement – which is a rather formidable, three-part accounting report – in all its glory, in the following sections we build on the summary of changes in the business's assets, liabilities and owners' equities shown in Figure 3-1 to explain the components of the £1.1 million increase in cash from the business's profit activities during the year. (The £1.1 million amount of cash flow from profit was determined earlier in the chapter by solving the unknown factor.)

The business in the example experienced a rather strong growth year. Its debtors and stock increased by relatively large amounts. In fact, all the relevant accounts increased; their ending balances are larger than their beginning balances (which are the amounts carried forward from the end of the preceding year). At this point, we need to provide some additional information. The £1.2 million increase in retained earnings is the net difference of two quite different things.

The £1.6 million net profit earned by the business increased retained earnings by this amount. As you see in Figure 3-1, the account increased only £1.2 million. Thus there must have been a £400,000 decrease in retained earnings during the year. The business paid £400,000 cash dividends from profit to its owners (the shareholders) during the year, which is recorded as a decrease in retained earnings. The amount of cash dividends is reported in the *Financing Activities* section of the cash flow statement. The entire amount of net profit is reported in the *Operating Activities* section of the cash flow statement.

Computing cash flow from profit

Here's how to compute cash flow from profit based on the changes in the company's Balance Sheet accounts presented in Figure 3-1:

Computation of Cash Flow from Profit (in thousands of pounds)

	Negative Cash Flow Effects	Positive Cash Flow Effects
Net profit for the year		£1,600
Debtors increase	£800	
Stock increase	£975	
Prepaid expenses increase	£145	
Depreciation expense		£1,200
Creditors increase		£80
Accrued expenses payable increase		£120
Income tax payable increase		£20
Totals	£1,920	£3,020
Cash flow from profit (£3,020 positive increases minus £1,920 negative increases)	£1,100	

Note that net profit for the year – which is the correct amount of profit based on the accrual basis of accounting – is listed in the Positive Cash Flow column. This is only the starting point. Think of this the following way: if the business had collected all its sales revenue for the year in cash, and if it had made cash payments for its expenses exactly equal to the amounts recorded for the expenses, then the net profit amount would equal the increase in cash. These two conditions are virtually never true, and they're not true in this example. So the net profit figure is just the jumping-off point for determining the amount of cash generated by the business's profit activities during the year.

We'll let you in on a little secret here. The analysis of cash flow from profit asks what amount of profit would have been recorded if the business had been on the cash basis of accounting instead of the accrual basis. This can be confusing and exasperating, because it seems that two different profit

Book IV

Working to Prepare Financial Statements

measures are provided in a business's financial report – the true economic profit number, which is the bottom line in the Profit and Loss statement (usually called *net profit*), and a second profit number called *cash flow from operating activities* in the cash flow statement.

When the cash flow statement was made mandatory, many accountants worried about this problem, but the majority opinion was that the amount of cash increase (or decrease) generated from the profit activities of a business is very important to disclose in financial reports. For reading the Profit and Loss statement you have to wear your accrual basis accounting lenses, and for the cash flow statement you have to put on your cash basis lenses. Who says accountants can't see two sides of something?

The following sections explain the effects on cash flow that each Balance Sheet account change causes (refer to Figure 3-1).

Getting specific about changes in assets and liabilities

As a business manager, you should keep a close watch on each of your assets and liabilities and understand the cash flow effects of increases (or decreases) caused by these changes. Investors should focus on the business's ability to generate a healthy cash flow from profit, so investors should be equally concerned about these changes.

Debtors increase

Remember that the *debtors* asset shows how much money customers who bought products on credit still owe the business; this asset is a promise of cash that the business will receive. Basically, *debtors* is the amount of uncollected sales revenue at the end of the period. Cash doesn't increase until the business collects money from its customers.

But the amount in debtors *is* included in the total sales revenue of the period – after all, you did make the sales, even if you haven't been paid yet. Obviously, then, you can't look at sales revenue as being equal to the amount of cash that the business received during the period.

To calculate the actual cash flow from sales, you need to subtract from sales revenue the amount of credit sales that you didn't collect in cash over the period – but you add in the amount of cash that you collected during the period just ended for credit sales that you made in the *preceding* period. Take a look at the following equation for a business example:

£25 million sales revenue – £0.8 million increase in debtors = £24.2 million cash collected from customers during the year

The business started the year with £1.7 million in debtors and ended the year with £2.5 million in debtors. The beginning balance was collected during the year but at the end of the year the ending balance had not been collected. Thus the *net* effect is a shortfall in cash inflow of £800,000, which is why it's called a negative cash flow factor. The key point is that you need to keep an eye on the increase or decrease in debtors from the beginning of the period to the end of the period.

> ✔ If the amount of credit sales you made during the period is greater than the amount collected from customers during the same period, your debtors *increased* over the period. Therefore you need to *subtract* from sales revenue that difference between start-of-period debtors and end-of-period debtors. In short, an increase in debtors hurts cash flow by the amount of the increase.

> ✔ If the amount you collected from customers during the period is greater than the credit sales you made during the period, your debtors *decreased* over the period. In this case you need to *add* to sales revenue that difference between start-of-period debtors and end-of-period debtors. In short, a decrease in debtors helps cash flow by the amount of the decrease.

In the example we've been using, debtors increased £800,000. Cash collections from sales were £800,000 less than sales revenue. Ouch! The business increased its sales substantially over last period, so you shouldn't be surprised that its debtors increased. The higher sales revenue was good for profit but bad for cash flow from profit.

An occasional hiccup in cash flow is the price of growth – managers and investors need to understand this point. Increasing sales without increasing debtors is a happy situation for cash flow, but in the real world you can't have one increase without the other (except in very unusual circumstances).

Stock increase

Stock is the next asset in Figure 3-1 – and usually the largest short-term, or *current*, asset for businesses that sell products. If the stock account is greater at the end of the period than at the start of the period – because either unit costs increased or the quantity of products increased – what the business actually paid out in cash for stock purchases (or manufacturing products) is more than the business recorded as its cost-of-goods-sold expense in the period. Therefore, you need to deduct the stock increase from net profit when determining cash flow from profit.

In the example, stock increased £975,000 from start-of-period to end-of-period. In other words, this business replaced the products that it sold during the period *and* increased its stock by £975,000. The easiest way to understand the effect of this increase on cash flow is to pretend that the business paid for all its stock purchases in cash immediately upon receiving them. The stock on hand at the start of the period had already been paid for

Book IV

Working to Prepare Financial Statements

last period, so that cost doesn't affect this period's cash flow. Those products were sold during the period and involved no further cash payment by the business. But the business did pay cash *this* period for the products that were in stock at the end of the period.

In other words, if the business had bought just enough new stock (at the same cost that it paid out last period) to replace the stock that it sold during the period, the actual cash outlay for its purchases would equal the cost-of-goods-sold expense reported in its Profit and Loss statement. Ending stock would equal the beginning stock; the two stock costs would cancel each other out and thus would have no effect on cash flow. But this hypothetical scenario doesn't fit the example because the company increased its sales substantially over the last period.

To support the higher sales level, the business needed to increase its stock level. So the business bought £975,000 more in products than it sold during the period – and it had to come up with the cash to pay for this stock increase. Basically, the business wrote cheques amounting to £975,000 more than its cost-of-goods-sold expense for the period. This step-up in its stock level was necessary to support the higher sales level, which increased profit – even though cash flow took a hit.

It's that accrual basis accounting thing again: the cost that a business pays *this* period for *next* period's stock is reflected in this period's cash flow but isn't recorded until next period's Profit and Loss statement (when the products are actually sold). So if a business paid more *this* period for *next* period's stock than it paid *last* period for *this* period's stock, you can see how the additional expense would adversely affect cash flow but wouldn't be reflected in the bottom-line net profit figure. This cash flow analysis stuff gets a little complicated, we know, but hang in there. The cash flow statement, presented later in the chapter, makes a lot more sense after you go through this background briefing.

Prepaid expenses increase

The next asset, after stock, is prepaid expenses (refer to Figure 3-1). A change in this account works the same way as a change in stock and debtors, although changes in prepaid expenses are usually much smaller than changes in those other two asset accounts.

Again, the beginning balance of prepaid expenses is recorded as an expense this period but the cash was actually paid out last period, not this period. This period, a business pays cash for next period's prepaid expenses – which affects this period's cash flow but doesn't affect net profit until next period. So the £145,000 increase in prepaid expenses from start-of-period to end-of-period in this example has a negative cash flow effect.

As it grows, a business needs to increase its prepaid expenses for such things as fire insurance (premiums have to be paid in advance of the insurance coverage) and its stocks of office and data processing supplies. Increases in debtors, stock and prepaid expenses are the price a business has to pay for growth. Rarely do you find a business that can increase its sales revenue without increasing these assets.

The simple but troublesome depreciation factor

Depreciation expense recorded in the period is both the simplest cash flow effect to understand and, at the same time, one of the most misunderstood elements in calculating cash flow from profit. To start with, depreciation is not a cash outlay during the period. The amount of depreciation expense recorded in the period is simply a fraction of the original cost of the business's fixed assets that were bought and paid for years ago. (Well, if you want to nit-pick here, some of the fixed assets may have been bought during this period, and their cost is reported in the investing activities section of the cash flow statement.) Because the depreciation expense isn't a cash outlay this period, the amount is added back to net profit in the calculation of cash flow from profit – so far so good.

When measuring profit on the accrual basis of accounting you count depreciation as an expense. The fixed assets of a business are on an irreversible journey to the junk heap. Fixed assets have a limited life of usefulness to a business (except for land); depreciation is the accounting method that allocates the total cost of fixed assets to each year of their use in helping the business generate sales revenue. Part of the total sales revenue of a business constitutes *recovery of cost invested in its fixed assets*. In a real sense, a business 'sells' some of its fixed assets each period to its customers – it factors the cost of fixed assets into the sales prices that it charges its customers. For example, when you go to a supermarket, a very small slice of the price you pay for that box of cereal goes toward the cost of the building, the shelves, the refrigeration equipment and so on. (No wonder they charge so much for a box of cornflakes!)

Each period, a business recoups part of the cost invested in its fixed assets. In other words, £1.2 million of sales revenue (in the example) went toward reimbursing the business for the use of its fixed assets during the year. The problem regarding depreciation in cash flow analysis is that many people simply add back depreciation for the year to bottom-line profit and then stop, as if this is the proper number for cash flow from profit. It ain't so. The changes in other assets as well as the changes in liabilities also affect cash flow from profit. You should factor in *all* the changes that determine cash flow from profit, as explained in the following section.

Net profit + depreciation expense doesn't equal cash flow from profit!

The business in our example earned £1.6 million in net profit for the year, plus it received £1.2 million cash flow because of the depreciation expense built into its sales revenue for the year. The sum of these figures is £2.8 million. Is £2.8 million the amount of cash flow from profit for the period? The knee-jerk answer of many investors and managers is 'yes'. But if net profit + depreciation truly equals cash flow then *both* factors in the brackets – both net profit and depreciation – must be fully realised in cash. Depreciation is, but the net profit amount is not fully realised in cash because the company's debtors, stock and prepaid expenses increased during the year, and these increases have negative impacts on cash flow.

Adding net profit and depreciation to determine cash flow from profit is mixing apples and oranges. The business didn't realise a £1.6 million cash increase from its £1.6 million net profit. The total of the increases of its debtors, stock and prepaid expenses is £1.92 million (refer to Figure 3-1), which wipes out the net profit amount and leaves the business with a cash balance hole of £320,000. This cash deficit is offset by the £220,000 increase in liabilities (explained later), leaving a £100,000 net profit *deficit* as far as cash flow is concerned. Depreciation recovery increased cash flow by £1.2 million. So the final cash flow from profit equals £1.1 million. But you'd never know this if you simply added depreciation expense to net profit for the period.

The managers didn't have to go outside the business for the £1.1 million cash increase generated from its profit for the year. Cash flow from profit is an *internal* source of money generated by the business itself, in contrast to *external* money that the business raises from lenders and owners. A business doesn't have to find sources of external money if its internal cash flow from profit is sufficient to provide for its growth.

In passing, we should mention that a business could have a negative cash flow from profit for a year – meaning that despite posting a net profit for the period, the changes in the company's assets and liabilities caused its cash balance to decrease. In reverse, a business could report a bottom line *loss* in its Profit and Loss statement yet have a *positive* cash flow from its operating activities: the positive contribution from depreciation expense plus decreases in its debtors and stock could amount to more than the amount of loss. More commonly, a loss leads to negative cash flow or very little positive cash flow.

Operating liabilities increases

The business in the example, like almost all businesses, has three basic liabilities that are inextricably intertwined with its expenses: creditors, accrued expenses payable and income tax payable. When the beginning balance of one of these liability accounts is the same as the ending balance of the same account (not too likely, of course), the business breaks even on cash flow for that account. When the end-of-period balance is higher than the start-of-period balance, the business didn't pay out as much money as was actually recorded as an expense on the period's Profit and Loss statement.

In the example we've been using, the business disbursed £720,000 to pay off last period's creditors balance. (This £720,000 was reported as the creditors balance on last period's ending Balance Sheet.) Its cash flow this period decreased by £720,000 because of these payments. But this period's ending Balance Sheet shows the amount of creditors that the business will need to pay next period – £800,000. The business actually paid off £720,000 and recorded £800,000 of expenses to the year, so this time cash flow is *richer* than what's reflected in the business's net profit figure by £80,000 – in other words, the increase in creditors has a positive cash flow effect. The increases in accrued expenses payable and income tax payable work the same way.

Therefore, liability increases are favourable to cash flow – in a sense the business borrowed more than it paid off. Such an increase means that the business delayed paying cash for certain things until next year. So you need to add the increases in the three liabilities to net profit to determine cash flow from profit, following the same logic as adding back depreciation to net profit. The business didn't have cash outlays to the extent of increases in these three liabilities.

The analysis of the changes in assets and liabilities of the business that affect cash flow from profit is complete for the business example. The final result is that the company's cash balance increased £1.1 million from profit. You could argue that cash should have increased £2.8 million – £1.6 million net profit plus £1.2 million depreciation that was recovered during the year – so the business is £1.7 million behind in turning its profit into cash flow (£2.8 million less the £1.1 million cash flow from profit). This £1.7 million lag in converting profit into cash flow is caused by the £1.92 million increase in assets less the £220,000 increase in liabilities, as shown in Figure 3-1.

Book IV

Working to Prepare Financial Statements

Presenting the Cash Flow Statement

The cash flow statement is one of the three primary financial statements that a business must report to the outside world, according to generally accepted accounting principles (GAAP). To be technical, the rule says that whenever a business reports a Profit and Loss statement, it should also report a cash flow statement. The *Profit and Loss statement* summarises sales revenue and expenses and ends with the bottom-line profit for the period. The *Balance Sheet* summarises a business's financial condition by reporting its assets, liabilities and owners' equity. (Refer to Book IV, Chapters 1 and 2 for more about these reports.)

You can probably guess what the *cash flow statement* does by its name alone: this statement tells you where a business got its cash and what the business did with its cash during the period. We prefer the name given to this statement in the old days in the US – the *Where Got, Where Gone* statement. This nickname goes straight to the purpose of the cash flow statement: asking where the business got its money and what it did with the money.

To give you a rough idea of what a cash flow statement reports, we repeat some of the questions we asked at the start of the chapter: How much money did you earn last year? Did you get all your income in cash (or did some of your wages go straight into a pension plan or did you collect a couple of IOUs)? Where did you get other money (did you take out a loan, win the lottery or receive a gift from a rich uncle)? What did you do with your money (did you buy a house, support your out-of-control Internet addiction or lose it playing bingo)?

Getting a little too personal for you? That's exactly why the cash flow statement is so important: it bares a business's financial soul to its lenders and owners. Sometimes the cash flow statement reveals questionable judgement calls that the business's managers made. At the very least, the cash flow statement reveals how well a business handles the cash increase from its profit.

The history of the cash flow statement

The cash flow statement was not required for external financial reporting until the late 1980s. Until then, the accounting profession had turned a deaf ear to calls from the investment community for cash flow statements in annual financial reports. (Accountants had presented a *funds flow statement* prior to then, but that report proved to be a disaster – the term *funds* included more assets than just cash and represented a net amount after deducting short-term liabilities from short-term, or current, assets.)

In our opinion, the reluctance to require cash flow statements came from fears that the *cash flow from profit* figure would usurp net profit – people would lose confidence in the net profit line.

Those fears have some justification, considering the attention given to cash flow from profit and what is called 'free cash flow' (discussed later in the chapter). Although the Profit and Loss statement continues to get most of the fanfare (because it shows the magic bottom-line number of net profit), cash flow gets a lot of emphasis these days.

As explained at the start of the chapter, the cash flow statement is divided into three sections according to the three-fold classification of cash flows for a business: operating activities (which we also call *cash flow from profit* in the chapter), investing activities and financing activities.

The cash flow statement reports a business's net cash increase or decrease based on these three groupings of the cash flow statement. Figure 3-2 shows what a cash flow statement typically looks like – in this example, for a *growing* business (which means that its assets, liabilities and owners' equity increase during the period).

The trick to understanding cash flow from profit is to link the sales revenue and expenses of the business with the changes in the business's assets and liabilities that are directly connected with its profit-making activities. Using this approach earlier in the chapter, we determine that the cash flow from profit is £1.1 million for the year for the sample business. This is the number you see in Figure 3-2 for cash flow from operating activities. In our experience, many business managers, lenders and investors don't fully understand

Cash Flow Statement for Year (in thousands of pounds)		
Cash Flows from Operating Activities		
Net Income		£ 1,600
Debtors	£ (800)	
Stock Increase	£ (975)	
Prepaid Expenses Increase	£ (145)	
Depreciation Expense	£ 1,200	
Creditors Increase	£ 80	
Accrued Expense Increase	£ 120	
Income Tax Payable Increase	£ 20	£ (500)
Cash Flow from Operating Activities		£ 1,100
Cash Flows from Investing Activities		
Purchases of Property, Plant & Equipment		£ (1,275)
Cash Flows from Financing Activities		
Short-term Debt Borrowing Increase	£ 200	
Long-term Debt Borrowing Increase	£ 300	
Share Issue	£ 60	
Dividends Paid Stockholders	£ (400)	£ 160
Increase (Decrease) In Cash During Year		£ (15)
Beginning Cash Balance		£ 2,015
Ending Cash Balance		£ 2,000

Figure 3-2: Cash flow statement for the business in the example.

Book IV

Working to Prepare Financial Statements

these links, but the savvy ones know to keep a close eye on the relevant Balance Sheet changes.

What do the figures in the first section of the cash flow statement (See Figure 3-2) reveal about this business over the past period? Recall that the business experienced rapid sales growth over the last period. However, the downside of sales growth is that operating assets and liabilities also grow – the business needs more stock at the higher sales level and also has higher debtors.

The business's prepaid expenses and liabilities also increased, although not nearly as much as debtors and stock. The rapid growth of the business yielded higher profit but also caused quite a surge in its operating assets and liabilities – the result being that cash flow from profit is only £1.1 million compared with £1.6 million in net profit – a £500,000 shortfall. Still, the business had £1.1 million at its disposal after allowing for the increases in assets and liabilities. What did the business do with this £1.1 million of available cash? You have to look to the remainder of the cash flow statement to answer this key question.

A very quick read through the rest of the cash flow statement (refer to Figure 3-2) goes something like this: the company used £1,275,000 to buy new fixed assets, borrowed £500,000 and distributed £400,000 of the profit to its owners. The result is that cash decreased £15,000 during the year. Shouldn't the business have increased its cash balance, given its fairly rapid growth during the period? That's a good question! Higher levels of sales generally require higher levels of operating cash balances. However, you can see in its Balance Sheet at the end of the year (refer back to Figure 3-2) that the company has £2 million in cash, which, compared with its £25 million annual sales revenue, is probably enough.

Where to put depreciation?

Where the depreciation line goes within the first section (operating activities) of the cash flow statement is a matter of personal preference – no standard location is required. Many businesses report it in the middle or toward the bottom of the changes in assets and liabilities – perhaps to avoid giving people the idea that cash flow from profit simply requires adding back depreciation to net profit.

A better alternative for reporting cash flow from profit?

We call your attention, again, to the first section of the cash flow statement in Figure 3-2. You start with net profit for the period. Next, changes in assets and liabilities are deducted or added to net profit to arrive at cash flow from operating activities (the cash flow from profit) for the year. This format is called the *indirect method.* The alternative format for this section of the cash flow statement is called the *direct method* and is presented like this (using the same business example, with pound amounts in millions):

Cash inflow from sales	£24.2
Less cash outflow for expenses	£23.1
Cash flow from operating activities	£1.1

You may remember from the earlier discussion that sales revenue for the year is £25 million, but that the company's debtors increased £800,000 during the year, so cash flow from sales is £24.2 million. Likewise, the expenses for the year can be put on a cash flow basis. But we 'cheated' here – we've already determined that cash flow from profit is £1.1 million for the year, so we plugged the figure for cash outflow for expenses. We would take more time to explain the direct approach, except for one major reason.

Although the Accounting Standards Board (ASB) expresses a definite preference for the direct method, this august rule-making body does permit the indirect method to be used in external financial reports – and, in fact, the overwhelming majority of businesses use the indirect method. Unless you're an accountant, we don't think you need to know much more about the direct method.

Sailing through the Rest of the Cash Flow Statement

After you get past the first section, the rest of the cash flow statement is a breeze. The last two sections of the statement explain what the business did with its cash and where cash that didn't come from profit came from.

Investing activities

The second section of the cash flow statement reports the investment actions that a business's managers took during the year. Investments are like tea leaves, serving as indicators regarding what the future may hold for the company. Major new investments are the sure signs of expanding or modernising the production and distribution facilities and capacity of the business. Major disposals of long-term assets and the shedding of a major part of the business could be good news or bad news for the business, depending on many factors. Different investors may interpret this information differently, but all would agree that the information in this section of the cash flow statement is very important.

Certain long-lived operating assets are required for doing business – for example, Federal Express wouldn't be terribly successful if it didn't have aeroplanes and vans for delivering packages and computers for tracking deliveries. When those assets wear out, the business needs to replace them. Also, to remain competitive, a business may need to upgrade its equipment to take advantage of the latest technology or provide for growth. These investments in long-lived, tangible, productive assets, which we call *fixed assets* in this book, are critical to the future of the business and are called *capital expenditures* to stress that capital is being invested for the long term.

One of the first claims on cash flow from profit is capital expenditure. Notice in Figure Figure 3-2 that the business spent £1,275,000 for new fixed assets, which are referred to as *property, plant and equipment* in the cash flow statement (to keep the terminology consistent with account titles used in the Balance Sheet, because the term *fixed assets* is rather informal).

Cash flow statements generally don't go into much detail regarding exactly what specific types of fixed assets a business purchased – how many additional square feet of space the business acquired, how many new drill presses it bought and so on. (Some businesses do leave a clearer trail of their investments, though. For example, airlines describe how many new aircraft of each kind were purchased to replace old equipment or expand their fleets.)

Note: Typically, every year a business disposes of some of its fixed assets that have reached the end of their useful lives and will no longer be used. These fixed assets are sent to the junkyard, traded in on new fixed assets or sold for relatively small amounts of money. The value of a fixed asset at the end of its useful life is called its *salvage value*. The disposal proceeds from selling fixed assets are reported as a source of cash in the investments section of the cash flow statement. Usually, these amounts are fairly small. In contrast, a business may sell off fixed assets because it's downsizing or abandoning a major segment of its business. These cash proceeds can be fairly large.

Financing activities

Note that in the annual cash flow statement (refer to Figure 3-2) of the business example we've been using, the positive cash flow from profit is £1.1 million and the negative cash flow from investing activities is £1,275,000. The result to this point, therefore, is a net cash outflow of £175,000 – which would have decreased the company's cash balance this much if the business didn't go to outside sources of capital for additional money during the year. In fact, the business increased its short-term and long-term debt during the year, and its owners invested additional money in the business. The third section of the cash flow statement summarises these financing activities of the business over the period.

The term *financing* generally refers to a business raising capital from debt and equity sources – from borrowing money from banks and other sources willing to loan money to the business and from its owners putting additional money into the business. In addition, the term includes making payments on debt and returning capital to owners. *Financing* also refers to cash distributions (if any) from profit by the business to its owners.

Most businesses borrow money for a short term (generally defined as less than one year), as well as for longer terms (generally defined as more than one year). In other words, a typical business has both short-term and long-term debt. The business in our example has both short-term and long-term debt. Although not a hard-and-fast rule, most cash flow statements report just the *net* increase or decrease in short-term debt, not the total amount borrowed and the total payments on short-term debt during the period. In contrast, both the total amount borrowed and the total amount paid on long-term debt during the year are reported in the cash flow statement.

For the business we've been using as an example, no long-term debt was paid down during the year, but short-term debt was paid off during the year and replaced with new short-term notes payable. However, only the net increase (£200,000) is reported in the cash flow statement. The business also increased its long-term debt by £300,000 (refer to Figure 3-2).

The financing section of the cash flow statement also reports on the flow of cash between the business and its owners (who are the stockholders of a corporation). Owners can be both a *source* of a business's cash (capital invested by owners) and a *use* of a business's cash (profit distributed to owners). This section of the cash flow statement reports capital raised from its owners, if any, as well as any capital returned to the owners. In the cash flow statement (Figure 3-2), note that the business did issue additional stock shares for £60,000 during the year, and it paid a total of £400,000 cash dividends (distributions) from profit to its owners.

Free Cash Flow: What on Earth Does That Mean?

A new term has emerged in the lexicon of accounting and finance – *free cash flow*. This piece of language is not – we repeat, *not* – an officially defined term by any authoritative accounting rule-making body. Furthermore, the term does *not* appear in the cash flow statements reported by businesses. Rather, free cash flow is street language, or slang, even though the term appears often in *The Financial Times* and *The Economist*. Securities brokers and investment analysts use the term freely (pun intended). Like most new terms being tossed around for the first time, this one hasn't settled down into one universal meaning although the most common usage pivots on cash flow from profit.

The term *free cash flow* is used to mean any of the following:

- ✔ Net profit plus depreciation (plus any other expense recorded during the period that doesn't involve the outlay of cash but rather the allocation of the cost of a long-term asset other than property, plant and equipment – such as the intangible assets of a business).
- ✔ Cash flow from operating activities (as reported in the cash flow statement).
- ✔ Cash flow from operating activities minus some or all of the capital expenditures made during the year (such as purchases or construction of new, long-lived operating assets such as property, plant and equipment).
- ✔ Cash flow from operating activities plus interest, and depreciation, and income tax expenses – or, in other words, cash flow before these expenses are deducted.

In the strongest possible terms, we advise you to be very clear on which definition of *free cash flow* the speaker or writer is using. Unfortunately, you can't always determine what the term means in any given context. The reporter or investment professional should define the term.

One definition of free cash flow, in our view, is quite useful: cash flow from profit minus capital expenditures for the year. The idea is that a business needs to make capital expenditures in order to stay in business and thrive. And to make capital expenditures, the business needs cash. Only after paying for its capital expenditures does a business have 'free' cash flow that it can use as it likes. In our example, the free cash flow is, in fact, negative – £1.1 million cash flow from profit minus £1,275,000 capital expenditures for new fixed assets equals a *negative* £175,000.

This is a key point. In many cases, cash flow from profit falls short of the money needed for capital expenditures. So the business has to borrow more money, persuade its owners to invest more money in the business or dip into its cash reserve. Should a business in this situation distribute some of its profit to owners? After all, it has a cash *deficit* after paying for capital expenditures. But many companies like the business in our example do, in fact, make cash distributions from profit to their owners.

Scrutinising the Cash Flow Statement

Analysing a business's cash flow statement inevitably raises certain questions: What would I have done differently if I were running this business? Would I have borrowed more money? Would I have raised more money from the owners? Would I have distributed so much of the profit to the owners? Would I have let my cash balance drop by even such a small amount?

One purpose of the cash flow statement is to show readers what judgement calls and financial decisions the business's managers made during the period. Of course, management decisions are always subject to second-guessing and criticising, and passing judgement based on a financial statement isn't totally fair because it doesn't reveal the pressures the managers faced during the period. Maybe they made the best possible decisions given the circumstances. Maybe not.

The business in our example (refer to Figure 3-2) distributed £400,000 cash from profit to its owners – a 25 per cent *pay-out ratio* (which is the £400,000 distribution divided by £1.6 million net profit). In analysing whether the pay-out ratio is too high, too low or just about right, you need to look at the broader context of the business's sources of, and needs for, cash.

First look at cash flow from profit: £1.1 million, which isn't enough to cover the business's £1,275,000 capital expenditures during the year. The business increased its total debt by £500,000. Given these circumstances, maybe the business should have hoarded its cash and not paid so much in cash distributions to its owners.

So does this business have enough cash to operate with? You can't answer that question just by examining the cash flow statement – or any financial statement for that matter. Every business needs a buffer of cash to protect against unexpected developments and to take advantage of unexpected opportunities, as we explain in Book V, Chapter 5 on budgeting. This particular business has a £2 million cash balance compared with £25 million annual sales revenue for the period just ended, which probably is enough. If you were the boss of this business how much working cash balance would you want? Not an easy question to answer! Don't forget that you need to look at all three primary financial statements – the Profit and Loss statement and the Balance Sheet as well as the cash flow statement – to get the big picture of a business's financial health.

You probably didn't count the number of lines of information in Figure 3-2, the cash flow statement for the business example. Anyway, the financial statement has 17 lines of information. Would you like to hazard a guess regarding the average number of lines in cash flow statements of publicly owned companies? Typically, their cash flow statements have 30 to 40 lines of information by our reckoning. So it takes quite a while to read the cash flow statement – more time than the average investor probably has. (Professional stock analysts and investment managers are paid to take the time to read this financial statement meticulously.) Quite frankly, we find that many cash flow statements aren't only rather long but also are difficult to understand – even for an accountant. We won't get on a soapbox here but we definitely think businesses could do a better job of reporting their cash flow statements by reducing the number of lines in their financial statements and making each line clearer.

Microsoft also has a comprehensive range of templates at http://office.microsoft.com/en-gb/Templates followed by a search term, in this case 'cash flow'.

Have a Go

1. **Using the information presented in the comparative Balance Sheet that follows, determine the business's cash flow from profit (operating activities) for 2014.**

   Use the method of solving for the unknown factor as demonstrated earlier in this chapter.

Assets	2013	2014	Changes
Fixed Assets			
Plant & Machinery	£897,000	£1,060,000	£163,000
Accumulated Depreciation	(£257,000)	(£318,000)	(£61,000)
Net Book Value	£640,000	£742,000	
Current Assets			
Stock	£518,000	£576,000	£58,000
Debtors	£386,000	£340,000	(£46,000)

Assets	2013	2014	Changes
Cash	£456,000	£425,000	(£31,000)
Prepaid Expenses	£46,000	£52,000	£6,000
	£1,406,000	£1,393,000	
Current Liabilities			
Creditors	£246,000	£230,000	(£16,000)
Bank Overdraft	£350,000	£300,000	(£50,000)
Accrued Expenses	£204,000	£215,000	£11,000
	£800,000	£745,000	
Long-Term Liabilities			
Long-Term Loan	£400,000	£525,000	£125,000

2. **The beginning and ending balances of certain accounts in a business's Balance Sheet are as follows:**

	Beginning Balance	*Ending Balance*	*Changes*
Stock	£780,000	£860,000	£80,000
Debtors	£500,000	£465,000	(£35,000)
Prepaid Expenses	£110,000	£105,000	(£5,000)
Creditors	£350,000	£325,000	(£25,000)
Accrued Expenses	£165,000	£175,000	£10,000

The business records £145,000 depreciation expense for the year and its net profit is £258,000 for the year. Determine its cash flow from operating activities for the year. Present your answer in the indirect format for cash flow from operating activities in the cash flow statement.

Answering the Have a Go Questions

1. **Using the method of solving for the unknown factor you set up the problem as follows:**

   Summary of Cash Flows for the Year

Cash flow from operating activities	????
Cash flow from investing activities	(£163,000)
Cash flow from financing activities	£75,000
Decrease in cash during the year	(£31,000)

   Having calculated the missing figure (i.e the one with the question marks), the cash flow from profit is £57,000 for the year.

   In the comparative Balance Sheet, you can see that the business increases cash £75,000 from its loan and overdraft transactions during the year (£125,000 increase in long-term loans – £50,000 pay-down on the overdraft = £75,000 net increase). The business doesn't raise money by issuing shares during the year and doesn't pay cash dividends during the year. Therefore, the net cash increase from its financing activities is £75,000. The firm spends £163,000 on plant and machinery. Therefore, cash flow from profit must have increased cash £57,000: £57,000 cash increase from profit – £163,000 capital expenditures + £75,000 cash from financing activities = £31,000 decrease in cash during year. We hope that you follow all this: cash flow analysis isn't for the faint-hearted, is it?

2. **Using the indirect method, the cash flow from operating activities is as follows:**

   Cash Flow from Operating Activities

Net profit	£258,000	
Stock increase	(£80,000)	
Debtors decrease	£35,000	
Prepaid expenses decrease	£5,000	
Depreciation expense	£145,000	
Creditors decrease	(£25,000)	
Accrued expenses increase	£10,000	£348,000

Here's the process broken down:

- You have the net profit figure as a starting point.

- Stock has a negative impact on cash flow, because the business has increased its stock from the prior year and has had to foot the bill for the additional stock bought.

- Debtors have decreased year on year by £35,000, which means that the business has actually had that much more cash from its customers in the year. This has a positive effect on cash flow.

- Prepaid expenses have decreased year on year by £5,000, which means that the business hasn't had to pay out as much cash, which has a positive effect on cash flow.

- Depreciation expense isn't a cash flow item and should be added back to net profit.

- Creditors have decreased by £25,000 year on year. This means that the business paid off more money to its suppliers this year, so this has a negative effect on cash flow.

- Accrued expenses have increased year on year. These are items that have been received and not paid for, and so the fact that they have increased this year means that the business hasn't paid out as much year on year, and therefore it has a positive effect on cash flow.

- The sum of all these adjustments to the Net Profit figure means that cash flow as a result of operating activities increased by £348,000.

Book IV

Working to Prepare Financial Statements

Book V

Accountants: Managing the Business

Cash Flow Statement for Year (in thousands of pounds)				
Cash Flows from Operating Activities				
Net Income			£	1,600
Debtors	£	(800)		
Stock Increase	£	(975)		
Prepaid Expenses Increase	£	(145)		
Depreciation Expense	£	1,200		
Creditors Increase	£	80		
Accrued Expense Increase	£	120		
Income Tax Payable Increase	£	20	£	(500)
Cash Flow from Operating Activities			£	1,100
Cash Flows from Investing Activities				
Purchases of Property, Plant & Equipment			£ (1,275)	
Cash Flows from Financing Activities				
Short-term Debt Borrowing Increase	£	200		
Long-term Debt Borrowing Increase	£	300		
Share Issue	£	60		
Dividends Paid Stockholders	£	(400)	£	160
Increase (Decrease) In Cash During Year			£	(15)
Beginning Cash Balance			£	2,015
Ending Cash Balance			£	2,000

Head online and visit www.dummies.com/extras/
bookkeepingaccountingaio for some free bonus articles.

In this book...

- See how an accountant can help to structure your business.

- Explore the types of accounting methods that an accountant can help you use within your accounting system.

- Look at different methods of profit performance.

- Consider costing and budgeting within your business.

- Perform ratio analysis.

Chapter 1

Discovering Different Business Types

In This Chapter

▶ Sorting out business legal structures

▶ Reporting on self-employment and partnership tax

▶ Filing taxes for limited companies

*B*efore you begin your business, cast your mind forward and determine what you think your business is going to look like over the next few years. For example, do you see yourself heading up a multinational corporation with lots of people working for you? Or, do you perhaps see yourself on your own, working the hours that suit you, picking the jobs that you want to do? Make sure that you take a few minutes to consider this, because your answers to these questions have an impact on which structure is most suitable for your business.

Whichever structure that you decide to start with determines how much administration needs to be done and who you need to inform that you've started a business. For example, paying taxes and reporting income for your business are very important jobs, and the way in which you complete these tasks depends on your business's legal structure. From sole traders (self-employment) to limited companies and everything in between, this chapter briefly reviews business types and explains how taxes are handled for each type.

Finding the Right Business Type

Business type and tax preparation and reporting go hand in hand. If you work as a bookkeeper/accountant for a small business, you need to know the business's legal structure before you can proceed with reporting and paying tax on the business income. Not all businesses have the same legal structure, so they don't all pay tax on the profits they make in the same way.

But before you get into the subject of tax procedures, you need to understand the various business structures that you may encounter. This section outlines each type of business. You can find out how these structures pay taxes in the separate sections that follow.

Sole trader

The simplest legal structure for a business is the *sole trader*, a business owned by one individual. Most new businesses with only one owner start out as sole traders, and some never change this status. Others, however, grow by adding partners and become *partnerships*. Some businesses add lots of staff and want to protect themselves from lawsuits, so they become *Limited Liability Partnerships (LLPs)*. Those seeking the greatest protection from individual lawsuits, whether they have employees or are simply single-owner companies without employees, become limited companies. We cover these other structures later in this chapter.

Partnership

HM Revenue & Customs considers any unincorporated business owned by more than one person to be a *partnership*. The partnership is the most flexible type of business structure involving more than one owner. Each partner in the business is equally liable for the activities of the business. This structure is slightly more complicated than a sole trader (see the preceding 'Sole trader' section), and partners need to work out certain key issues before the business opens its doors. These issues include:

- ✔ How are the partners going to divide the profits?
- ✔ How does each partner sell his share of the business, if he so chooses?
- ✔ What happens to each partner's share if a partner becomes sick or dies?
- ✔ How is the partnership going to be dissolved if one of the partners wants out?

Partners in a partnership don't always have to share equal risks. A partnership may have two different types of partners: general and limited. The general partner runs the day-to-day business and is held personally responsible for all activities of the business, no matter how much he's personally invested. Limited partners, on the other hand, are passive owners of the business and not involved in day-to-day operations. If someone files a claim against the business, the limited partners can be held personally liable only for the amount of money he individually invested in the business.

Limited Liability Partnerships (LLPs)

The *Limited Liability Partnership*, or LLP, is a structure that provides the owners of partnerships with some protection from being held personally liable for their business activities. This business structure is somewhere between a partnership and a limited company: the business ownership and tax rules are similar to those of a partnership, but like a limited company, if the business is sued, the owners aren't held personally liable.

Rather like forming a limited company, an LLP is formed by filing the appropriate forms with Companies House. On receipt of these forms, the Registrar of Companies issues a Certificate of Incorporation.

 Both for business and practical reasons, we recommend drawing up an agreement to establish the rights, responsibilities and duties of the partners to each other, and to outline how they're going to run the business, because few provisions are contained within the act governing these relationships.

Limited companies

If your business faces a great risk of being sued, the safest business structure for you is the *limited company*. Courts in the UK have clearly determined that a limited company is a separate legal entity (Saloman v. Saloman 1897) and that its owners' personal assets are protected from claims against the company. Essentially, an owner or shareholder in a company can't be sued or

---

Growth of the LLP

Limited Liability Partnerships are the latest business vehicle and were introduced on 6 April 2001 after the Limited Liability Partnerships Act 2000 received royal assent on 20 July 2000. Many law firms and accounting firms are set up as LLPs. More and more small-business owners are choosing this structure rather than a limited company because the LLP is easier and cheaper to maintain (it involves a lot less paperwork, plus fewer legal and accounting fees), and yet still provides personal protection from legal entanglements.

face collections because of actions taken by the company. This veil of protection is the reason that many small-business owners choose to incorporate even though it involves a lot of expense (to pay for both lawyers and accountants) and paperwork.

In a limited company, each share represents a portion of ownership, and profits must be split based on share ownership. You don't have to sell shares on the public stock markets in order to be a limited company, though. In fact, most limited companies are private entities that sell their shares privately among friends and investors.

If you're a small-business owner who wants to incorporate, first you must form a *board of directors* (see the sidebar 'Roles and responsibilities of the limited company board'). Boards can be made up of owners of the company as well as non-owners. You can even have your spouse and children on the board – bet those board meetings are interesting.

Roles and responsibilities of the limited company board

Limited companies provide a veil of protection for company owners, but in order to maintain that protection, the owners must comply with many rules unique to corporations. The *board of directors* takes on the key role of complying with these rules, and it must maintain a record of meeting minutes that prove the board is following key operating procedures, such as:

- Establishment of records of banking associations and any changes to those arrangements
- Tracking of loans from shareholders or third parties
- Selling or redeeming shares
- Payment of dividends
- Authorisation of salaries or bonuses for officers and key executives
- Undertaking of any purchases, sales or leases of corporate assets
- Buying another company
- Merging with another company
- Making changes to the Articles of Incorporation
- Election of corporate officers and directors

Corporate board minutes are considered official and must be available for review by HM Revenue & Customs and the courts. If a company's owners want to invoke the veil of protection that corporate status provides, they must prove that the board has met its obligations and that the company operated as a limited company. In other words, you can't form a board and have no proof that it ever met and managed these key functions.

Tax Reporting for Sole Traders

HM Revenue & Customs doesn't consider sole traders and partnerships to be individual legal entities, so they're not taxed as such. Instead, sole proprietors report any business earnings on their annual tax returns – that's the only financial reporting they must do. In effect, sole traders and partnerships pay income tax on their business profits. To be technical, they pay their income tax on their business profit under what is called *trading income*. A sole trader may well have another job as well, on which he pays tax under the normal Pay As You Earn (PAYE) system. All these sources (and other sources of income) are pulled together on the tax return to assess the overall income tax liability.

The basic tax return covers everything that a person in paid employment needs to tell HM Revenue & Customs to get his tax assessed correctly. The numerous pages of questions cover every aspect of tax related to normal tax life – working, receiving dividends, earning interest, paying and receiving pensions, making small capital gains – as we said, everything.

As the bookkeeper/accountant for a sole trader, you're probably responsible for pulling together the sales, cost of goods sold and expense information needed for the forms. In most cases, you send off this information to the business's accountant to fill out all the required forms.

Ultimately, because sole traders pay income tax on all their earnings, you need to note the current rates of tax for sole traders (and other unincorporated bodies) based on their taxable profits. Table 1-1 gives this information.

Table 1-1	2014/15 Taxable Profits
Tax Rate	*2014/15 Taxable Profits*
Basic rate: 20%	£0–£31,865
Higher rate: 40%	£31,866–£150,000
Additional rate: 45% from 6 April 2013	Over £150,000

Fortunately, most people have simple tax affairs. Because employment is usually taxed under the PAYE system (the employer acts as the unpaid tax collector) and most other sources of income have basic rate of tax deducted at source, you don't need to complete a tax return each year. The tax return is needed to pull all the earnings together only where an individual may have a liability to higher rate tax, for example – other earnings that have not had tax deducted at source that push their taxable earnings above the basic tax rate.

Expanding to the supplementary pages

To deal with liability at a higher tax rate or areas too complex for the standard annual tax return, you need supplementary pages. The supplementary pages cover:

- ✔ **Employment:** To cover more complicated employment situations; for example, an employee who has more than one job.

- ✔ **Share schemes:** To cover an employee who receives shares under an employee share ownership scheme.

- ✔ **Self-employment:** These pages cover business profits for the sole trader. We look at this subject more closely in the next section.

- ✔ **Partnerships:** To declare your share of any partnership profits.

- ✔ **Land and property:** For example, where any rental income is received from any property.

- ✔ **Foreign:** To cover any overseas sources of income.

- ✔ **Trusts:** To cover any income received by means of a distribution from any trust set up for you.

- ✔ **Capital gains:** To cover any gains made from the disposal of assets rather than trading income.

- ✔ **Non-residence:** To cover any income received by non-residents in the UK and thus liable to UK tax.

HM Revenue & Customs sends supplementary pages only if you ask for them or have received them before. As a taxpayer, you're responsible for asking for a tax return and completing one every year.

Filling out the self-employment supplementary pages

This section concentrates on the supplementary pages that relate to running a business. Depending on your turnover, you use one of two different self-employment supplementary pages. If your turnover is less than £79,000, you can complete the shortened version, which is only two pages long. Double-check that you're eligible to use the shortened form by referring to the guide to completing the self-employment supplementary pages. You can find it on the HMRC website, www.hmrc.gov.uk. Search for form SA103S.

On the first page, SES1, you put down details of the business name and address and when it began or ceased trading. You also use this page to enter your business income and allowable business expenses. (Refer to Book IV, Chapter 1 for a refresher.) You put your total business expenses in box 20 if your turnover is less than £79,000. On the second page, SES 2, you summarise the capital allowances that the business is claiming for any of its assets. You then calculate your taxable profits and read page SESN9 of the notes to see whether you need to make any adjustments.

Book V

Accountants: Managing the Business

Losses, Class 4 National Insurance Contributions and Construction Industry Scheme (CIS) deductions are entered in the final section. (Make sure that you read page SESN10 of the notes to help you complete this section correctly.)

Filing Tax Forms for Partnerships

If your business is structured as a partnership (meaning that it has more than one owner) and isn't a limited liability company, your business doesn't pay taxes. Instead, all money earned by the business is split up among the partners and they pay the tax due between them very much as if they were sole traders. However, a partnership is required to complete a partnership tax return to aid the assessment of the members of the partnership. Essentially, the partnership tax return is sent out to the nominated partner and he completes the partnership tax return in a manner similar to the sole trader tax return explained in the preceding sections. That partner states what profit share is attributable to each partner, and each partner is responsible for showing this profit figure in his own personal tax return.

Don't be tempted to forget to include partnership profits (or any other source of income for that matter), because HM Revenue & Customs knows from the partnership tax return what you earned in that tax year.

Paying Taxes for Limited Companies

Limited companies are more complex than sole traders and partnerships. Although many aspects of their accounting and taxation are similar, their accounts are open to public scrutiny because each year a limited company must file its accounts at Companies House, the UK government organisation responsible for tracking information about all UK limited companies. This requirement means that although only HM Revenue & Customs knows the full details of a sole trader or partnership, the whole world has access (for a fee) to a limited company's accounts.

Companies make a separate tax return, known as a CT600, to HM Revenue & Customs, in which they detail their financial affairs. As a result, the limited company pays corporation tax on its earnings (profit) as well as tax on any dividends paid out to its shareholders. This arrangement means that its shareholders receive dividends net of basic rate of income tax because the company has already paid it for them. Two forms of CT600 exist: a short version, only four pages, is sufficient for companies with straightforward tax affairs, but more complicated companies, as designated by HM Revenue & Customs, must complete the eight-page return. Check with your accountant whether you need to complete the eight-page return.

From April 2011, companies must file their corporation tax online for accounting periods ending after 31 March 2010, and pay electronically too. The HMRC website provides a lot of help and advice, so don't panic – just click on Corporation Tax on the Businesses and Corporations menu from the home page.

Corporation tax rates vary according to how much taxable profit the company makes. Although starting rates are low for a limited company, they soon escalate to the higher (main) rate. Current corporation tax rates on profits are shown in Table 1-2.

Table 1-2	Corporation Tax Rates	
Rates for financial years starting on 1 April		
Tax Rate	**2013 Taxable Profits**	**2014 Taxable Profits**
Small profits rate:	20%	20%
Small profits rate can be claimed by qualifying companies with profits not exceeding:	£300,000	£300,000
Marginal relief: lower limit	£300, 000	£300,000
Marginal relief: upper limit	£1,500,000	£1,500,000
Main rate:	23%	21%

Check with your accountant to determine whether incorporating your business makes sense for you. A strong argument exists in favour of some smaller businesses incorporating, because they pay less corporation tax than income tax at certain levels. But tax savings isn't the only issue you have to think about; operating a limited company also increases administrative, legal and accounting costs. Make sure that you understand all the costs before incorporating.

Have a Go

Try these questions to work out which type of business structure is suited to each occasion:

1. **You decide to start your own home-based business, but want protection from being held personally liable for your business's activity. Which type of business structure would you be likely to pick?**

2. **You and two of your friends decide to start a band and you need to pick a business structure. Which type of business structure would you pick if you want to keep things as simple as possible?**

3. **You decide to start your own home-based business. Which type of business structure would be easiest for you to use in order to get started?**

Answering the Have a Go Questions

1. **You'd be likely to choose a limited company.** You can be sued personally if you structure your business as a sole proprietorship, but you've additional protection with a limited company; your personal assets are protected.

2. **The simplest structure is likely to be a partnership.** However, you'd need to agree how to share profits and what would happen if a member decided to leave the band. You should set up a simple partnership agreement to avoid complications in the future.

3. **Choosing to be a sole trader is the easiest way to start up in business.** You can start trading immediately, using your own name or a trading name.

Chapter 2

Choosing Accounting Methods

In This Chapter

▶ Having a choice of accounting methods

▶ Understanding the alternatives for calculating cost of goods sold expense and stock cost

▶ Dealing with depreciation

▶ Writing down stock and debtors

▶ Keeping two sets of books

Some people put a great deal of faith in numbers: 2 + 2 = 4, and that's the end of the story. They see a number reported to the last digit on an accounting report, and they get the impression of exactitude. But accounting isn't just a matter of adding up numbers. It's not an exact science.

Accountants *do* have plenty of rules that they must follow. The official rule book of generally accepted accounting principles laid down by the Accounting Standards Board (and its predecessors) is more than 1,200 pages long and growing fast. In addition there are the rules and regulations issued by the various government regulatory agencies that govern financial reporting and accounting methods, and those issued by publicly owned companies such as the London Stock Exchange. The Institute of Chartered Accountants and the other professional accountancy institutes play a role in setting accounting standards. And accounting standards have now gone international: with the advent of the European Union and the ever-increasing amount of international trade and investing, business and political leaders in many nations recognise the need to iron out differences in accounting methods and disclosure standards from country to country. The International Accounting Standards Board (IASB) is an independent, private sector body that develops and approves International Financial Reporting Standards under the oversight of the IFRS Foundation (www.IFRS.org).

Perhaps the most surprising thing – considering that formal rule-making activity has been going on since the 1930s – is that a business still has options for choosing among alternative accounting methods. Different methods lead to inconsistent profit measures from company to company. The often-repeated goal for standardising accounting methods is to make like things look alike and different things look different – but the accounting profession hasn't reached this stage of nirvana yet. In addition, accounting methods change over the years, as the business world changes. Accounting rules too are, to one degree or another, in a state of flux.

Because the choice of accounting methods directly affects the profit figure for the year and the values reported in the ending Balance Sheet, business managers (and investors) need to know the difference between accounting methods. You don't need to probe into these accounting methods in excruciating, technical detail, but you should at least know whether one method versus another yields higher or lower profit measures and higher or lower asset values in financial statements. This chapter explains accounting choices for measuring cost of goods sold, depreciation and other expenses. Get involved in making these important accounting decisions – it's your business, after all.

Decision-Making Behind the Scenes in Profit and Loss Statements

Book IV, Chapter 1 introduces the simplified UK format for presenting Profit and Loss statements. (We also discuss this in Book V, Chapter 3, where we look at managing profit performance.) Figure 2-1 presents another Profit and Loss statement for a business – with certain modifications that you won't see in actual external Profit and Loss statements. For explaining the choices between alternative accounting methods, certain specific expenses are broken down under the company's sales, administrative and general expenses (SA&G) category in Figure 2-1. Of these particular expenses, only depreciation is disclosed in external Profit and Loss statements. Don't expect to find in external Profit and Loss statements the other expenses shown under the SA&G category in Figure 2-1. Businesses are very reluctant to divulge such information to the outside world.

Here's a quick overview of the accounting matters and choices relating to each line in the Profit and Loss statement shown in Figure 2-1, from the top line to the bottom line:

  ✔ **Sales revenue:** Timing the recording of sales is something to be aware of. Generally speaking, sales revenue timing isn't a serious accounting problem, but businesses should be consistent from one year to the next. However, for some businesses– such as software and other high-tech companies, and companies in their early start-up phases – the timing of recording sales revenue is a major problem. A footnote to the company's financial statements should explain its revenue recognition method if there's anything unusual about it.

Profit and Loss Account for Year		
Sales Revenue		£26,000,000
Cost of Goods Sold Expense		14,300,000
Gross Margin		£11,700,000
Sales, Administrative, and General Expenses:		
Stock Shrinkage and Write-downs	£378,750	
Bad Debts	385,000	
Asset Impairment Write-downs	287,000	
Depreciation	780,000	
Warranty and Guarantee Expenses	967,250	
All Other SA&G Expenses	6,302,000	
Total		9,100,000
Earnings Before Interest and Tax		£2,600,000
Interest Expense		400,000
Earnings Before Tax		£2,200,000
Corporation Tax Expense		880,000
Net Profit		£1,320,000

Figure 2-1:
A Profit
and Loss
statement
including
certain
expenses
that aren't
reported
outside the
business.

Note: If products are returnable and the deal between the seller and buyer doesn't satisfy normal conditions for a completed sale, then recognition of sales revenue should be postponed until the return privilege no longer exists. For example, some products are sold *on approval*, which means the customer takes the product and tries it out for a few days or longer to see whether she really wants it. This area is increasingly significant with the continuing rapid growth of the Internet as a medium for selling. In response, the UK introduced the Distance Selling Regulations in October 2001. These regulations give consumers additional rights to obtain full refunds on goods bought over the Internet and through mail order without having to give a reason for doing so.

✔ **Cost of goods sold expense:** Whether to use the first-in, first-out (FIFO) method, or the last-in, first-out (LIFO) method, or the average cost method (each of which is explained in the section 'Calculating Cost of Goods Sold and Cost of Stock', later in this chapter), cost of goods sold is a big expense for companies that sell products and naturally the choice of method can have a real impact.

✔ **Gross margin:** Can be dramatically affected by the method used for calculating cost of goods sold expense (and the method of revenue recognition, if this is a problem).

✔ **Stock write-downs:** Whether to count and inspect stock very carefully to determine loss due to theft, damage and deterioration, and whether to apply the net realisable value (NRV) method strictly or loosely are the two main questions that need to be answered. See 'Identifying Stock Losses: Net Realisable Value (NRV)', later in this chapter. Stock is a high-risk asset that's subject to theft, damage and obsolescence.

✔ **Bad debts expense:** When to conclude that the debts owed to you by customers who bought on credit (debtors) aren't going to be paid – the question is really when to *write down* these debts (that is, remove the amounts from your asset column). You can wait until after you've made a substantial effort to collect the debts, or you can make your decision before that time. See 'Collecting or Writing Off Bad Debts', later in this chapter.

✔ **Asset impairment write-downs:** Whether (and when) to *write down* or *write off* an asset – that is, remove it from the asset column. Stock shrinkage, bad debts and depreciation by their very nature are asset write-downs. Other asset write-downs are required when any asset becomes *impaired*, which means that it has lost some or all of its economic utility to the business and has little or no disposable value. An asset write-down reduces the book (recorded) value of an asset (and at the same time records an expense or loss of the same amount). A *write-off* reduces the asset's book value to zero and removes it from the accounts, and the entire amount becomes an expense or loss.

For example, your delivery van driver had an accident. The repair of the van was covered by insurance, so no write-down is necessary. But the products being delivered had to be thrown away and weren't insured while in transit. You write off the cost of the stock lost in the accident.

✔ **Depreciation expense:** Whether to use a short-life method and load most of the expense over the first few years, or a longer-life method and spread the expense evenly over the years. Refer to 'Appreciating Depreciation Methods', later in this chapter. Depreciation is a big expense for some businesses, making the choice of method even more important.

✔ **Warranty and guarantee (post-sales) expenses:** Whether to record an expense for products sold with warranties and guarantees in the same period that the goods are sold (along with the cost of goods sold expense, of course) or later, when customers actually return products for repair or replacement. Businesses can usually forecast the percentage of products sold that will be returned for repair or replacement under the guarantees and warranties offered to customers – although a new product with no track record can be a problem in this regard.

✔ **All other SA&G expenses:** This is the catch-all 'other expenses' line that you use if you can't categorise the item into any of the preceding items. Obviously, the expense has to relate to selling, admin or general expense types.

✔ **Earnings before interest and tax (EBIT):** This profit measure equals sales revenue less all the expenses above this line; therefore, EBIT depends on the particular choices made for recording sales revenue and expenses. Having a choice of accounting methods means that an amount of wriggle is inherent in recording sales revenue and many expenses. How much wriggle effect do all these accounting choices have on the EBIT profit figure? This is a very difficult question to answer. The business itself may not know. We would guess (and it's no more than a conjecture on our part) that the EBIT for a period reported by most businesses could easily be 10–20 per cent lower or higher if different accounting choices had been made.

✔ **Interest expense:** Usually a cut-and-dried calculation, with no accounting problems. (Well, we can think of some really hairy interest accounting problems, but we won't go into them here.)

✔ **Corporation tax expense:** You can use different accounting methods for some of the expenses reported in your Profit and Loss statement than you use for calculating taxable income. Oh, crikey! The hypothetical amount of taxable income, if the accounting methods used in the Profit and Loss statement were used in the tax return, is calculated; then the corporation tax based on this hypothetical taxable income is figured. This is the corporation tax expense reported in the Profit and Loss statement. This amount is reconciled with the actual amount of corporation tax owed based on the accounting methods used for tax purposes. A reconciliation of the two different tax amounts is provided in a rather technical footnote to the financial statements. See 'Reconciling Corporation Tax', later in this chapter.

✔ **Net profit:** Like EBIT, this can vary considerably depending on which accounting methods you use for measuring expenses. (See also Book VI, Chapter 1 on *profit smoothing*, which crosses the line from choosing acceptable accounting methods into the grey area of 'earnings management' through means of accounting manipulation.)

Whereas bad debts, post-sales expenses and asset write-downs vary in importance from business to business, cost of goods sold and depreciation methods are so important that a business must disclose which methods it uses for these two expenses in the footnotes to its financial statements. (Book VI, Chapter 1 explains footnotes to financial statements.) HM Revenue & Customs requires that a company actually records in its cost of goods sold expense and stock asset accounts the amounts determined by the accounting method it uses to determine taxable income – a rare requirement in company tax law.

Considering how important the bottom-line profit number is, and that different accounting methods can cause a major difference in this all-important number, you'd think that accountants would have developed clear-cut and definite rules so that only one accounting method would be correct for a given set of facts. No such luck. The final choice boils down to an arbitrary decision, made by top-level accountants in consultation with, and with the consent of, managers. If you own a business or are a manager in a business, we strongly encourage you to get involved in choosing which accounting methods to use for measuring your profit and for presenting your Balance Sheet. Accounting methods vary from business to business more than you'd probably suspect, even though all of them stay within the boundaries of acceptable practice. The rest of this chapter expands on the methods available for measuring certain expenses. Sales revenue accounting can be a challenge as well, but profit accounting problems lie mostly on the expense side of the ledger.

Calculating Cost of Goods Sold and Cost of Stock

One main accounting problem of companies that sell products is how to measure their *cost of goods sold expense*, which is the sum of the costs of the products sold to customers during the period. You deduct cost of goods sold from sales revenue to determine *gross margin* – the first profit line on the Profit and Loss statement (see Book IV, Chapter 1 for more about Profit and Loss statements, and Figure 1-1 there for a typical Profit and Loss statement). Cost of goods sold is therefore a very important figure, because if gross margin is wrong, bottom-line profit (net profit) is wrong.

First a business acquires products, either by buying them (retailers) or by producing them (manufacturers). Book V, Chapter 4 explains how manufacturers determine product cost; for retailers product cost is simply the purchase cost. (Well, it's not entirely this simple, but you get the point.) Product cost is entered in the stock asset account and is held there until the products are sold. Then, but not before, product cost is taken out of stock and recorded in the cost of goods sold expense account.

You must be absolutely clear on this point. Suppose that you clear £700 from your salary for the week and deposit this amount in your bank account. The money stays in there and is an asset until you spend it. You don't have an expense until you write a cheque. Likewise, not until the business sells products does it have a cost of goods sold expense. When you write a cheque, you know how much it's for – you have no doubt about the amount of the expense. But when a business withdraws products from its stock and records cost of goods sold expense, the expense amount is in some doubt. The amount of expense depends on which accounting method the business selects.

The essence of this accounting issue is that you have to divide the total cost of your stock between the units sold (cost of goods sold expense, in the Profit and Loss statement) and the unsold units that remain on hand waiting to be sold next period (stock asset, in the Balance Sheet).

For example, say you own a shop that sells antiques. Every time an item sells, you need to transfer the amount you paid for the item from the stock asset account into the cost of goods sold expense account. At the start of a fiscal period, your cost of goods sold expense is zero, and if you own a medium-sized shop selling medium-quality antiques, your stock asset account may be £20,000. Over the course of the fiscal period, your cost of goods sold expense should increase (hopefully rapidly, as you make many sales).

You probably want your stock asset account to remain fairly static, however. If you paid £200 for a wardrobe that sells during the period, the £200 leaves the stock asset account and finds a new home in the cost of goods sold expense account. However, you probably want to turn around and replace the item you sold, ultimately keeping your stock asset account at around the same level – although more complicated businesses have more complicated strategies for dealing with stock and more perplexing accounting problems.

You have three methods to choose from when you measure cost of goods sold and stock costs: You can follow a first-in, first-out (FIFO) cost sequence, follow a last-in, first-out cost sequence (LIFO), or compromise between the two methods and take the average costs for the period. Other methods are acceptable, but these three are the primary options.

Product costs are entered in the stock asset account in the order acquired, but they're not necessarily taken out of the stock asset account in this order. The different methods refer to the order in which product costs are *taken out* of the stock asset account. You may think that only one method is appropriate – that the sequence in should be the sequence out. However, generally accepted accounting principles permit other methods.

In reality, the choice boils down to FIFO versus LIFO; the average cost method runs a distant third in popularity. If you want our opinion, FIFO is better than LIFO for reasons that we explain in the next two sections. You may not agree, and that's your right. For your business, you make the call.

The FIFO method

With the FIFO method, you charge out product costs to cost of goods sold expense in the chronological order in which you acquired the goods. The procedure is that simple. It's like the first people in line to see a film get in the cinema first. The usher collects the tickets in the order in which they were bought.

We think that FIFO is the best method for both the expense and the asset amounts. We hope that you like this method, but also look at the LIFO method before making up your mind. You should make up your mind, you know. Don't just sit on the sidelines. Take a stand.

Suppose that you acquire four units of a product during a period, one unit at a time, with unit costs as follows (in the order in which you acquire the items): £100, £102, £104 and £106. By the end of the period, you've sold three of those units. Using FIFO, you calculate the cost of goods sold expense as follows:

£100 + £102 + £104 = £306

In short, you use the first three units to calculate the cost of goods sold expense. (You can see the benefit of having such a standard method if you sell hundreds or thousands of different products.)

The ending stock asset, then, is £106, which is the cost of the most recent acquisition. The £412 total cost of the four units is divided between the £306 cost of goods sold expense for the three units sold and the £106 cost of the one unit in ending stock. The total cost has been taken care of; nothing fell between the cracks.

FIFO works well for two reasons:

- In most businesses, products actually move into and out of stock in a FIFO sequence: the earlier acquired products are delivered to customers before the later acquired products are delivered, so the most recently purchased products are the ones still in ending stock to be delivered in the future. Using FIFO, the stock asset reported on the Balance Sheet at the end of the period reflects the most recent purchase cost and therefore is close to the current *replacement cost* of the product.

- When product costs are steadily increasing, many (but not all) businesses follow a FIFO sales price strategy and hold off on raising sales prices as long as possible. They delay raising sales prices until they've sold all lower-cost products. Only when they start selling from the next batch of products, acquired at a higher cost, do they raise sales prices. We strongly favour using the FIFO cost of goods sold expense method when the business follows this basic sales pricing policy because both the expense and the sales revenue are better matched for determining gross margin.

The LIFO method

Remember the cinema usher we mentioned earlier? Think about that usher going to the *back* of the line of people waiting to get into the next showing and letting them in from the rear of the line first. In other words, the later you bought your ticket, the sooner you get into the cinema. This is the LIFO method, which stands for *last-in, first-out*. The people in the front of the queue wouldn't stand for it, of course, but the LIFO method is quite acceptable for determining the cost of goods sold expense for products sold during the period. The main feature of the LIFO method is that it selects the *last* item you purchased first and then works backward until you have the total cost for the total number of units sold during the period. What about the ending stock, the products you haven't sold by the end of the year? Using the LIFO method, you never get back to the cost of the first products acquired (unless you sold out your entire stock); the earliest cost remains in the stock asset account.

Using the same example from the preceding section, assume that the business uses the LIFO method instead of FIFO. The four units, in order of acquisition, had costs of £100, £102, £104 and £106. If you sell three units during the period, LIFO gives you the following cost of goods sold expense:

£106 + £104 + £102 = £312

The ending stock cost of the one unit not sold is £100, which is the oldest cost. The £412 total cost of the four units acquired less the £312 cost of goods sold expense leaves £100 in the stock asset account. Determining which units you actually delivered to customers is irrelevant; when you use the LIFO method, you always count backward from the last unit you acquired.

If you really want to argue in favour of using LIFO – and we have to tell you that we won't back you up on this one – here's what you can say:

- ✔ Assigning the most recent costs of products purchased to the cost of goods sold expense makes sense because you have to replace your products to stay in business and the most recent costs are closest to the amount you'll have to pay to replace your products. Ideally, you should base your sales prices not on original cost but on the cost of replacing the units sold.

- ✔ During times of rising costs, the most recent purchase cost maximises the cost of goods sold expense deduction for determining taxable income, and thus minimises the taxable income. In fact, LIFO was invented for income tax purposes. True, the cost of stock on the ending Balance Sheet is lower than recent acquisition costs, but the Profit and Loss statement effect is more important than the Balance Sheet effect.

The more product cost you take out of the stock asset to charge to cost of goods sold expense, the less product cost you have in the ending stock. In maximising cost of goods sold expense, you minimise the stock cost value.

But here are the reasons why LIFO, in our view, is usually the wrong choice (the following sections of this chapter go into more details about these issues):

✔ Unless you base your sales prices on the most recent purchase costs or you raise sales prices as soon as replacement costs increase – and most businesses don't follow either of these pricing policies – using LIFO depresses your gross margin and, therefore, your bottom-line net profit.

✔ The LIFO method can result in an ending stock cost value that's seriously out-of-date, especially if the business sells products that have very long lives.

✔ Unscrupulous managers can use the LIFO method to manipulate their profit figures if business isn't going well. Refer to 'Manipulating LIFO stock levels to give profit a boost', later in the chapter.

Note: In periods of rising product costs, it's true that FIFO results in higher taxable income than LIFO does – something you probably want to avoid, we're sure. Nevertheless, even though LIFO may be preferable in some circumstances, we still say that FIFO is the better choice in the majority of situations, for the reasons discussed earlier, and you may come over to our way of thinking after reading the following sections. By the way, if the products are intermingled such that they can't be identified with particular purchases, then the business has to use FIFO for its income tax returns.

The greying of LIFO stock cost

If you sell products that have long lives and for which your product costs rise steadily over the years, using the LIFO method has a serious impact on the ending stock cost value reported on the Balance Sheet and can cause the Balance Sheet to look misleading. Over time, the cost of replacing products becomes further and further removed from the LIFO-based stock costs. Your 2014 Balance Sheet may very well report stock based on 1985, 1975 or 1965 product costs. As a matter of fact, the product costs used to value stock can go back even further.

Suppose that a major manufacturing business has been using LIFO for more than 45 years. The products that this business manufactures and sells have very long lives – in fact, the business has been making and selling many of the same products for many years. Believe it or not, the difference between its LIFO and FIFO cost values for its ending stock is about £2 billion because some of the products are based on costs going back to the 1950s, when the company first started using the LIFO method. The FIFO cost value of its ending stock is disclosed in a footnote to its financial statements; this disclosure is how you can tell the difference between a business's LIFO and FIFO cost values. The gross margin (before income tax) over the business's 45 years would have been £2 billion higher if the business had used the FIFO method – and its total taxable income over the 45 years would have been this much higher as well.

Of course, the business's income taxes over the years would have been correspondingly higher as well. That's the trade-off.

Note: A business must disclose the difference between its stock cost value according to LIFO and its stock cost value according to FIFO in a footnote on its financial statements – but, of course, not too many people outside of stock analysts and professional investment managers read footnotes. Business managers get involved in reviewing footnotes in the final steps of getting annual financial reports ready for release (refer to Book VI, Chapter 1). If your business uses FIFO, your ending stock is stated at recent acquisition costs, and you don't have to determine what the LIFO value may have been. Annual financial reports don't disclose the estimated LIFO cost value for a FIFO-based stock.

Many products and raw materials have very short lives; they're regularly replaced by new models (you know, with those 'New and Improved!' labels) because of the latest technology or marketing wisdom. These products aren't around long enough to develop a wide gap between LIFO and FIFO, so the accounting choice between the two methods doesn't make as much difference as with long-lived products.

Manipulating LIFO stock levels to give profit a boost

The LIFO method opens the door to manipulation of profit – not that you would think of doing this, of course. Certainly, most of the businesses that choose LIFO do so to minimise current taxable income and delay paying taxes on it as long as possible – a legitimate (though perhaps misguided in some cases) goal. However, some unscrupulous managers know that they can use the LIFO method to 'create' some profit when business isn't going well.

So if a business that uses LIFO sells more products than it purchased (or manufactured) during the period, it has to reach back into its stock account and pull out older costs to transfer to the cost of goods sold expense. These costs are much lower than current costs, leading to an artificially low cost of goods sold expense, which in turn leads to an artificially high gross margin figure. This dipping into old cost layers of LIFO-based stock is called a *LIFO liquidation gain.*

This unethical manipulation of profit is possible for businesses that have been using LIFO for many years and have stock cost values far lower than the current purchase or manufacturing costs of products. By not replacing all the quantities sold, they let stock fall below normal levels.

Suppose that a retailer sold 100,000 units during the year and normally would have replaced all units sold. Instead, it purchased only 90,000 replacement units. Therefore, the other 10,000 units were taken out of stock, and the accountant had to reach back into the old cost layers of stock to record some of the cost of goods sold expense. To see the impact of LIFO liquidation gain on the gross margin, check out what the gross margin would look like if this business had replaced all 100,000 units versus the gross margin for replacing only 90,000. In this example, the old units in stock carry a LIFO-based cost of only £30, whereas the current purchase cost is £65. Assume that the units have a £100 price tag for the customer.

Gross margin if the business replaced all 100,000 of the units sold

Sales revenue (100,000 units at £100 per unit)	£10,000,000
Cost of goods sold expense (100,000 units at £65 per unit)	6,500,000
Gross margin	£3,500,000

Gross margin if the business replaced only 90,000 of the units sold

Sales revenue (100,000 units at £100 per unit)		£10,000,000
Cost of goods sold expense:		
Units replaced (90,000 units at £65 per unit)	£5,850,000	
Units from stock (10,000 units at £30 per unit)	300,000	6,150,000
Gross margin		£3,850,000

The LIFO liquidation gain (the difference between the two gross margins) in this example is £350,000 – the £35 difference between the old and the current unit costs multiplied by 10,000 units. Just by ordering fewer replacement products, this business padded its gross margin – but in a very questionable way.

Of course, this business may have a good, legitimate reason for trimming stock by 10,000 units – to reduce the capital invested in that asset, for example, or to anticipate lower sales demand in the year ahead. LIFO liquidation gains may also occur when a business stops selling a product and that stock drops to zero. Still, we have to warn investors that when you see a financial statement reporting a dramatic decrease in stock and the business uses the LIFO method, you should be aware of the possible profit manipulation reasons behind the decrease.

Note: A business must disclose in the footnotes to its financial statements any substantial LIFO liquidation gains that occurred during the year. The outside auditor should make sure that the company includes this disclosure. (Book VI, Chapter 3 discusses audits of financial statements by auditors.)

The average cost method

Although not nearly as popular as the FIFO and LIFO methods, the average cost method seems to offer the best of both worlds. The costs of many things in the business world fluctuate; business managers focus on the average product cost over a time period. Also, the averaging of product costs over a period of time has a desirable smoothing effect that prevents cost of goods sold from being overly dependent on wild swings of one or two purchases.

To many businesses, the compromise aspect of the method is its *worst* feature. Businesses may want to go one way or the other and avoid the middle ground. If they want to minimise taxable income, LIFO gives the best effect during times of rising prices. Why go only halfway with the average cost method? Or if the business wants its ending stock to be as near to current replacement costs as possible, FIFO is better than the average cost method. Even using computers to keep track of averages, which change every time product costs change, is a nuisance. No wonder the average cost method isn't popular! But it *is* an acceptable method.

Identifying Stock Losses: Net Realisable Value (NRV)

Regardless of which method you use to determine stock cost, you should make sure that your accountants apply the *net realisable value (NRV)* test to stock. (Just to confuse you, this test is sometimes called the *lower of cost or market (LCM)* test.) A business should go through the NRV routine at least once a year, usually near or at year-end. The process consists of comparing the cost of every product in stock – meaning the cost that's recorded for each product in the stock asset account according to the FIFO or LIFO method (or whichever method the company uses) – with two benchmark values:

- ✔ The product's *current replacement cost* (how much the business would pay to obtain the same product right now)

- ✔ The product's *net realisable value* (how much the business can sell the product for)

If a product's cost on the books is higher than either of these two benchmark values, your accountant should decrease product cost to the lower of the two. In other words, stock losses are recognised *now* rather than *later*, when the products are sold. The drop in the replacement cost or sales value of the product should be recorded now, on the theory that it's better to take your medicine now than to put it off. Also, the stock cost value on the Balance Sheet is more conservative because stock is reported at a lower cost value.

Buying and holding stock involves certain unavoidable risks. Asset write-downs, explained in the 'Decision-Making behind the Scenes in Profit and Loss Statements' section of this chapter, are recorded to recognise the consequences of two of those risks – stock shrinkage and losses to natural disasters not fully covered by insurance. NRV records the losses from two other risks of holding stock:

- ✔ **Replacement cost risk:** After you purchase or manufacture a product, its replacement cost may drop permanently below the amount you paid (which usually also affects the amount you can charge customers for the products, because competitors will drop their prices).

- ✔ **Sales demand risk:** Demand for a product may drop off permanently, forcing you to sell the products below cost just to get rid of them.

Determining current replacement cost values for every product in your stock isn't easy! Applying the NRV test leaves much room for interpretation.

Keeping accurate track of your stock costs is important to your bottom line both now and in the future, so don't fall into the trap of doing a quick NRV scan and making a snap judgement that you don't need a stock write-down.

Some shady characters abuse NRV to cheat on their company tax returns. They *write down* their ending stock cost value – decrease ending stock cost more than can be justified by the NRV test – to increase the deductible expenses on their tax returns and thus decrease taxable income. A product may have a proper cost value of £100, for example, but a shady character may invent some reason to lower it to £75 and thus record a £25 stock write-down expense in this period for each unit – which isn't justified by the facts. But even though the person can deduct more this year, she'll have a lower stock cost to deduct in the future. Also, if the person is selected for an HM Revenue & Customs audit and the tax inspectors discover an unjustified stock write-down, the person may end up being charged with tax evasion.

Most accounting software packages either support or have plug-in modules that allow you to run all these costing methods and compare their effect on your apparent financial performance. For example, Sage 50 Accounts 2015 supports the FIFO model. This means the cost price of the oldest stock is used to calculate the cost of stock.

Managing Your Stock Position

Businesses have to carry a certain minimum amount of stock to ensure the production pipeline works efficiently and likely demand is met. So the costs associated with ordering large quantities infrequently (and so reducing the order cost but increasing the cost of holding stock) have to be balanced with placing frequent orders (which pushes the cost of orders up but reduces stock holding costs). Economic Order Quantity (EOQ) is basically an accounting formula that calculates the most cost-effective quantity to order; the point at which the combination of order costs and inventory carrying costs are at the minimum.

The formula for EOQ is

$$\text{Economic Order Quantity} = \sqrt{\frac{(2 \times R \times O)}{C}}$$

where R = annual demand in units; O = cost of placing an order; and C = cost of carrying a unit of inventory for the year.

Appreciating Depreciation Methods

We discussed depreciation earlier in Book III Chapter 3, but here we expand on the methods in a little more detail.

In theory, depreciation expense accounting is straightforward enough: you divide the cost of a fixed asset among the number of years that the business expects to use the asset. In other words, instead of having a huge lump-sum expense in the year that you make the purchase, you charge a fraction of the cost to expense for each year of the asset's lifetime. Using this method is much easier on your bottom line in the year of purchase, of course.

When calculating depreciation of your assets each year, you've a choice of two main methods: Straight Line and Reducing Balance. In this section, we explain these methods as well as the pros and cons of using each one.

Although other methods of calculating depreciation are available, for accounting purposes the two main methods are Straight Line and Reducing Balance. Both methods are acceptable, and it doesn't matter to HM Revenue & Customs which you use. In practice, a business chooses one method and sticks with it. Straight-Line suits those businesses that want to write off their assets more quickly.

To show you how the methods handle assets differently, we calculate the first year's depreciation expense using the purchase of a piece of equipment on 1 January 2014, with a cost basis of £25,000. We assume the equipment has a useful life of five years, so the annual depreciation rate is 20 per cent.

Straight-Line depreciation

When depreciating assets using the *Straight-Line method*, you spread the cost of the asset evenly over the number of years that your business is going to use the asset. Straight-Line is the most commonly used method for depreciation of assets, and the easiest one to use. The formula for calculating Straight-Line depreciation is

Cost of fixed asset × Annual depreciation rate = Annual depreciation expense

For the piece of equipment in this example, the cost basis is £25,000 and the annual depreciation rate is 20 per cent. With these figures, the calculation for finding the annual depreciation expense of this equipment based on the Straight-Line depreciation method is

£25,000 × 20% = £5,000 per annum

Each year, the business's Profit and Loss statement includes £5,000 as a depreciation expense for this piece of equipment. You add this £5,000 depreciation expense to the Accumulated Depreciation account for this asset. You show this Accumulated Depreciation account below the asset's original value on the Balance Sheet. You subtract the accumulated depreciation from the value of the asset to show a net asset value, which is the value remaining on the asset.

Reducing-Balance depreciation

The *Reducing-Balance method* of depreciation works well because it comes closest to matching the calculation of Capital Allowances, HM Revenue & Customs' version of depreciation.

The peculiarity of this method is that, unlike Straight-Line, the annual depreciation expense varies, and in theory the asset is never fully depreciated. Each year, you deduct the calculated depreciation figure from the previous year's value to calculate the new brought-forward figure. As time goes on, the annual depreciation figure gets smaller and the new brought-forward figure for the asset gets gradually smaller and smaller – but the item never fully depreciates.

Using the same asset as in the preceding section at a cost of £25,000 and depreciating at an annual rate of 20 per cent, you calculate depreciation using the Reducing-Balance method as follows:

Cost	25,000
First year: depreciation (20%)	5,000
Balance	**20,000**
Second year: depreciation (20% of £20,000)	4,000
Balance	**16,000**
Third year: deprecation (20% of £16,000)	3,200
Balance	**12,800**
Fourth year: depreciation (20% of £12,800)	2,560
Balance	**10,240**

. . . and so on, forever.

By the way, the *salvage value* of fixed assets (the estimated disposal values when the assets are taken to the junkyard or sold off at the end of their useful lives) is ignored in the calculation of depreciation for income tax. Put another way, if a fixed asset is held to the end of its entire depreciation life then its original cost will be fully depreciated, and the fixed asset from that time forward will have a zero book value. (Recall that book value is equal to the cost minus the balance in the accumulated depreciation account.) Fully depreciated fixed assets are grouped with all other fixed assets in external Balance Sheets. All these long-term resources of a business are reported in one asset account called *property, plant and equipment* (instead of fixed assets). If all its fixed assets were fully depreciated, the Balance Sheet of a company would look rather peculiar – the cost of its fixed assets would be completely offset by its accumulated depreciation. We've never seen this, but it would be possible for a business that hasn't replaced any of its fixed assets for a long time.

Comparing the methods

The Straight-Line method has strong advantages: it's easy to understand and it stabilises the depreciation expense from year to year. But many business managers and accountants favour the Reducing-Balance method. Keep in mind, however, that the depreciation expense in the annual Profit and Loss statement is higher in the early years when you use the Reducing-Balance method, and so bottom-line profit is lower until later years. Nevertheless, many accountants and businesses like the Reducing-Balance method because it paints a more conservative (a lower, or a more moderate) picture of profit performance in the early years. Who knows? Fixed assets may lose their economic usefulness to a business sooner than expected. If this happens, using the Reducing-Balance depreciation method would look good in hindsight.

Minimising taxable income and corporation tax in the early years to hang on to as much cash as possible is very important to many businesses, and they pay the price of reporting lower net profit in order to defer paying corporation tax for as long as possible. Or they may use the Straight-Line method in their financial statements even though they use the Reducing-Balance method in their annual tax returns, which complicates matters. (Refer to the section 'Reconciling Corporation Tax' for more information.)

Except for brand-new enterprises, a business typically has a mix of fixed assets – some in their early years of depreciation, some in their middle years and some in their later years. So, the overall depreciation expense for the year may not be that different than if the business had been using Straight-Line depreciation for all its fixed assets. A business does *not* have to disclose in its external financial report what its depreciation expense would have been if it had been using an alternative method. Readers of the financial statements can't tell how much difference the choice of depreciation method made in that year.

Collecting or Writing Off Bad Debts

A business that allows its customers to pay on credit granted by the business is always subject to *bad debts* – debts that some customers never pay off. You are allowed, provided that you demonstrate serious efforts to recover the money owed, to write the loss in value off against your tax bill. You may also recover any value-added tax (VAT) paid in respect of the invoice concerned. Don't forget that in your role as an unpaid tax collector you'll have charged your defaulting customer VAT, paid that over to HM Revenue & Customs as required, but failed to recover the loot from the said customer, along with the rest of the boodle owed.

Reconciling Corporation Tax

Corporation tax is a heavy influence on a business's choice of accounting methods. Many a business decides to minimise its current taxable income by recording the maximum amount of deductible expenses. Thus, taxable income is lower, corporation tax paid to the Treasury is lower and the business's cash balance is higher. Using these expense maximisation methods to prepare the Profit and Loss statement of the business has the obvious effect of minimising the profit that's reported to the owners of the business. So, you may ask whether you can use one accounting method for corporation tax but an alternative method for preparing your financial statements. Can a business eat its cake (minimise corporation tax) and have it too (report more profit in its Profit and Loss statement)?

The answer is yes, you can. You may decide, however, that using two different accounting methods isn't worth the time and effort. In other areas of accounting for profit, businesses use one method for income tax and an alternative method in the financial statements (but we don't want to go into the details here).

When recording an expense, either an asset is decreased or a liability is increased. In this example, a special type of liability is increased to record the full amount of corporation tax expense: *deferred tax payable*. This unique liability account recognises the special contingency hanging over the head of the business to anticipate the time in the future when the business exhausts the higher depreciation amounts deducted in the early years by using, for example, the Reducing-Balance method of depreciation, and moves into the later years when annual depreciation amounts are less than amounts by the Straight-Line depreciation method. This liability account doesn't bear interest. Be warned that the accounting for this liability can get very complicated. The business provides information about this liability in a footnote to its financial statements, as well as reconciling the amount of corporation tax expense reported in its Profit and Loss statement with the tax owed to the government based on its tax return for the year. These footnotes are a joy to read – just kidding.

Dealing with Foreign Exchange

Foreign exchange poses a tricky problem when it comes to accounting reports. Currencies just aren't stable and they certainly don't respect year-end. A business can have all sorts of currency swishing around: pounds, dollars, euros, yen. . . . You need to include a note in your accounts to explain the extent of your use of foreign exchange and the way in which you've handled the conversion of currencies. In this section we explain three areas to pay particular attention to.

Transaction exposure

Transaction exposure occurs when a business incurs costs or generates revenues in any currency other than the one shown in its filed accounts. Two types of event can lead to this:

- A mismatch between cost of sales (manufacturing and so on) incurred in one currency and the actual sales income generated in another
- A time lag between setting the selling price in one currency and the date the customer actually pays up

As exchange rates frequently change, you need to explain how you handled the conversions.

Translation exposure

Translation exposure refers to the effects of movements in the exchange rate on the Balance Sheet and Profit and Loss statement that occur between reporting dates on assets and liabilities denominated in foreign currencies. In practice, any company that has assets or liabilities denominated in a currency other than the currency shown on its reported accounts has to 'translate' those back into the company's reporting currency when the consolidated accounts have to be produced. This can be up to four times a year for major trading businesses. Any changes in the foreign exchange rate between the countries involved cause movements in the accounts.

Comparing performance

Exchange rate movements can make it difficult to compare one year with another; an essential accounting task if management is to keep track of how a business is performing. Accountants usually handle this movement by stating that current year revenue is compared to the prior financial year, translated on consistent exchange rates to eliminate distortions due to fluctuations in exchange rates. In any event, you need to include a note in the accounts showing how you've handled currency movements.

Two Final Issues to Consider

We think that you've been assuming all along that *all* expenses should be recorded by a business. Of course, you're correct on this score. Many accountants argue that two expenses, in fact, aren't recorded by businesses, but should be. A good deal of controversy surrounds both items. Many think one or both expenses should be recognised in measuring profit and in presenting the financial statements of a business:

✔ **Share options:** As part of their compensation packages, many public companies award their high-level executives share options, which give them the right to buy a certain number of shares at fixed prices after certain conditions are satisfied (years of service and the like). If the market price of the company's shares in the future rises above the exercise (purchase) prices of the share options – assuming the other conditions of these contracts are satisfied – the executives use their share options to buy shares below the going market price of the shares.

Should the difference between the going market price of the shares and the exercise prices paid for the shares by the executives be recognised as an expense? Generally accepted accounting principles don't require that such an expense be recorded (unless the exercise price was below the market price at the time of granting the share option). However, the business must present a footnote disclosing the number of shares and exercise prices of its stock options, the theoretical cost of the share options to the business, and the dilution effect on earnings per share that exercising the share options will have. But this is a far cry from recording an expense in the Profit and Loss statement. Many persons, including Warren Buffett, who's chair of Berkshire Hathaway, Inc, are strongly opposed to share options, thinking that the better alternative is to pay the executives in cash and avoid diluting earnings per share, which depresses the market value of the shares.

In brief, the cost to shareholders of share options is off the books. The dilution in the market value of the shares of the corporation caused by its share options is suffered by the shareholders, but doesn't flow through the Profit and Loss statement of the business.

✔ **Purchasing power of pound loss caused by inflation:** Due to inflation, the purchasing power of one pound today is less than it was one year ago, two years ago and so on back in time. Yet accountants treat all pounds the same, regardless of when the pound amounts were recorded on the books. The cost balance in a fixed asset account (a building, for instance) may have been recorded 10 or 20 years ago; in contrast, the cost balance in a current asset account (stock, for instance) may have been recorded only one or two months ago (assuming the business uses the FIFO method). So, depreciation expense is based on very old pounds that had more purchasing power back then, and cost of goods sold expense is based on current pounds that have less purchasing power than in earlier years.

Stay tuned for what might develop in the future regarding these two expenses. If we had to hazard a prediction, we'd say that the pressure for recording the expense of share options will continue and might conceivably succeed – although we'd add that powerful interests oppose recording share options expense. On the other hand, the loss of purchasing power of the pound caused by inflation has become less important in an era signified by low inflation rates around the world. However, an enormous increase in the rate of inflation would resurrect this argument, and with rates of 5 per cent and more prevailing in some parts of 'new' Europe, 7 per cent in India, 10 per cent in Russia and 11 per cent in Turkey, the beast isn't quite as dead as economists would like us to believe.

Have a Go

1. Table 2.1 presents the stock acquisition history of a business for its first year. The business sells 158,100 units during the year. Using the FIFO method, determine its cost of goods sold expense for the year and its cost of ending stock.

Table 2-1	History of Stock Acquisitions During the First Year		
	Quantity (Units)	**Cost Per Unit**	**Total Cost**
First purchase	14,200	£25.75	£365,650
Second purchase	42,500	£23.85	£1,013,625
Third purchase	16,500	£24.85	£410,025
Fourth purchase	36,500	£23.05	£841,325
Fifth purchase	6,100	£26.15	£159,515
Sixth purchase	52,000	£23.65	£1,229,800
Seventh purchase	18,200	£26.00	£473,200
Totals	186,000		£4,493,140

2. The business in Table 2-1 sells 158,100 units during the year. Using the LIFO method, determine its cost of goods sold expense for the year and its cost of ending stock.

3. Calculate the annual depreciation expense for a copier with a cost basis of £5,000 and a depreciation rate of 20 per cent using the Straight-Line depreciation method.

4. Calculate the annual depreciation expense for a computer with a cost basis of £1,500 and a useful life of three years using the Straight-Line depreciation method.

5. John has just bought a photocopier costing £8,000. He intends to depreciate it at a rate of 20 per cent, using the Reducing-Balance method. Calculate the depreciation charges for the next three years and then write down the net book value at the end of the three-year period.

6. If you wanted to apply an even amount of depreciation each year against your asset, which depreciation method would you use?

7. If you have a machine with a useful life of four years, and you want to use the Straight-Line method of depreciation, what depreciation rate do you use?

8. How do you calculate net book value?

Answering the Have a Go Questions

1. Using the information given in table 2-1 above, you can determine the cost of goods sold expense with the FIFO method as shown in Table 2-2.

   The business purchased 186,000 units of goods and these were acquired in seven different batches, as I outline in Table 2-1. The business actually sold 158,000 of those units. Using a first-in, first-out method, the business would calculate the cost of goods sold, as being all of the first five batches purchased, plus 42,300 of the 52,000 units of purchase no. 6. This would enable you to calculate the cost of 158,000 units sold by summing the individual costs of each batch of goods purchased, as I show in Table 2-2.

Table 2-2	Cost of Goods Sold Expense Calculation Using the FIFO Method		
	Quantity (Units)	*Cost Per Unit*	*Total Cost*
First purchase	14,200	£25.75	£365,650
Second purchase	42,500	£23.85	£1,013,625
Third purchase	16,500	£24.85	£410,025
Fourth purchase	36,500	£23.05	£841,325
Fifth purchase	6,100	£26.15	£159,515
Sixth purchase	42,300	£23.65	£1,000,395
Totals	158,100		£3,790,535

The cost of ending stock includes some units from the sixth purchase and all units from the seventh purchase, which is summarised in Table 2-3.

Table 2-3	The cost of the remaining stock unsold (FIFO method)		
	Quantity (Units)	*Cost Per Unit*	*Total Cost*
Sixth purchase	9,700	£23.65	£229,405
Seventh purchase	18,200	£26.00	£473,200
Totals	27,900		£702,605

2. You determine the cost of goods sold expense with the LIFO as shown in Table 2-4.

   Reversing the dates of stock purchased, you can see in Table 2-4 that for the last-in, first-out (LIFO) calculation, all of batches three to seven are sold and only 28,800 units out of 42,500 units from the second batch purchased are sold. None of the first batch of purchases are sold. Calculating the cost of each of these batches allows you to find the total cost of goods sold using this method (see Table 2-4).

Table 2-4   Cost of Goods Sold Expense Calculation Using the LIFO Method

	Quantity (Units)	Cost Per Unit	Total Cost
Seventh purchase	18,200	£26.00	£473,200
Sixth purchase	52,000	£23.65	£1,229,800
Fifth purchase	6,100	£26.15	£159,515
Fourth purchase	36,500	£23.05	£841,325
Third purchase	16,500	£24.85	£410,025
Second purchase	28,800	£23.85	£686,880
Totals	158,100		£3,800,745

The cost of ending stock includes all the units from the first purchase and some from the second purchase, as summarised in Table 2-5.

Table 2-5   Cost of stock remaining that is unsold (LIFO method)

	Quantity (Units)	Cost Per Unit	Total Cost
Sixth purchase	13,700	£23.85	£326,745
Seventh purchase	14,200	£25.75	£365,650
Totals	27,900		£692,395

3. The annual depreciation cost for the copier is as follows:

   Cost price of photocopier   £5,000

   Depreciation (0.20 × £5,000)   **£1,000**

4. **The annual depreciation expense for the computer is as follows:**

    Cost price of computer £1,500

    Depreciation (£1,500 ÷ 3 years) £500

    This equates to a depreciation rate of 33.33 per cent (100% ÷ 3 years).

5. **Using the Reducing Balance method, here's what to do:**

    Year 1

Cost of photocopier	£8,000
Depreciation at 20 per cent	£1,600 (0.20 × £8,000)
Net book value	£6,400

    Year 2

Depreciation at 20 per cent	£1,280 (20 per cent of £6,400)
Net book value	£5,120 (£6,400 – £1,280)

    Year 3

Depreciation at 20 per cent	£1,024 (20 per cent of £5,120)
Net book value	£4,096 (£5,120 – £1,024)

6. **Straight Line.**

7. **You use 25 per cent (100 per cent ÷ four years).**

8. **Cost of fixed assets less accumulated depreciation.**

Chapter 3

Managing Profit Performance

*A*s a manager you get paid to make profit happen. That's what separates you from the non-manager employees at your business. Of course, you have to be a motivator, innovator, consensus builder, lobbyist and maybe sometimes a babysitter too. But the real purpose of your job is to control and improve the profit of your business. No matter how much your staff love you (or do they love those doughnuts you bring in every Monday?), if you don't meet your profit goals, you're facing the unemployment line.

You have to be relentless in your search for better ways to do things. Competition in most industries is fierce, and you can never take profit performance for granted. Changes take place all the time – changes initiated by the business and changes pressured by outside forces. Maybe a new superstore down the street is causing your profit to fall off, and you decide that you'll have a huge sale, complete with splashy ads on TV, to draw customers into the shop.

Slow down; not so fast! First make sure that you can afford to cut prices and spend money on advertising and still turn a profit. Maybe price cuts and splashy ads will keep your cash register singing and the kiddies smiling, but you need to remember that making sales doesn't guarantee that you make a profit. As all you experienced business managers know, profit is a two-headed beast – profit comes from making sales *and* controlling expenses.

So how do you determine what effect price cuts and advertising costs may have on your bottom line? By turning to your beloved accounting staff, of course, and asking for some *what-if* reports (like 'What if we offer a 15 per cent discount?').

This chapter shows you how to identify the key variables that determine what your profit would be if you changed certain factors (such as prices).

Redesigning the External Profit and Loss Statement

To begin, Figure 3-1 presents the Profit and Loss statement of a business (the same example is used in Book VI, Chapter 1). Figure 3-1 shows an *external Profit and Loss statement* – the Profit and Loss statement that's reported to the outside investors and creditors of the business. The expenses in Figure 3-1 are presented as they're usually disclosed in an external statement.

The managers of the business should understand this Profit and Loss statement, of course. But the external Profit and Loss statement isn't entirely adequate for management decision-making; this profit report falls short of providing all the information about expenses needed by managers.

Before moving on to the additional information managers need, take a quick look at the external Profit and Loss statement (Figure 3-1). Here are some key points:

(Amounts in thousands)

External Profit and Loss Account For Year

Sales Revenue	£ 52,000
Cost of Goods Sold Expense	31,200
Gross Margin	£ 20,800
Sales, Administration, and General Expenses	15,600
Depreciation Expense	1,650
Earnings Before Interest and Tax	£ 3,550
Interest Expense	750
Earnings Before Tax	£ 2,800
Tax Expense	900
Net Profit	£ 1,900

Figure 3-1: Example of a business's external Profit and Loss statement.

✔ The business represented by this Profit and Loss statement sells products and therefore has a *cost of goods sold expense.* In contrast, companies that sell services (airlines, cinemas, consultants and so on) don't have a cost of goods sold expense, because all their sales revenue goes toward meeting operating expenses and then providing profit.

✔ The external Profit and Loss statement shown in Figure 3-1 is prepared according to authorised accounting methods and disclosure standards, but keep in mind that these financial reporting standards are designed for reporting information *outside* the business. After a Profit and Loss statement is released to people outside the business, a business has no control over the circulation of its statement. The accounting profession, in deciding on the information for disclosure in external Profit and Loss statements, has attempted to strike a balance. On the one side are the needs of those who have invested capital in the business and have loaned money to the business; clearly they have the right to receive enough information to evaluate their investments in the business and their loans to the business. On the other side is the need of the business to keep certain information confidential and out of the hands of its competitors. What it comes down to is that certain information that outside investors and creditors might find interesting and helpful doesn't, in fact, legally have to be disclosed.

✔ The Profit and Loss statement doesn't report the *financial effects* of the company's profit-making activities – that is, the increases and decreases in its assets and liabilities caused by revenue and expenses. Managers need to control these financial effects, for which purpose they need the complete financial picture provided by the two other primary financial statements (the Balance Sheet and the cash flow statement) in addition to the Profit and Loss statement. See Book IV, Chapters 2 and 3 for more about these two other primary financial statements.

Basic Model for Management Profit and Loss Account

Figure 3-2 presents a model for a *management* Profit and Loss statement using the same business as the example whose external Profit and Loss statement is shown in Figure 3-1. Many lines of information are exactly the same – sales revenue and cost of goods sold expense for instance – and thus gross margins are the same. The last five lines in the two statements are the same, starting with operating profit (earnings before interest and corporation tax) down to the bottom line. In other respects, however, there are critical differences between the two profit reports.

First, note that total *unit sales volume* and *per unit amounts* are included in the management Profit and Loss statement (Figure 3-2). The business appears to sell only one product; the 520,000 units total sales volume is from sales of this product. In fact, most businesses sell a mix of many different products. The company's various managers need detailed sales revenue and

Management Profit and Loss Account For Year		
(Amounts in thousands)	Totals for Period	Per Unit
Unit Sales Volume =	520,000	
Sales Revenue	£52,000	£100
Cost of Goods Sold Expense	31,200	60
Gross Margin	£20,800	£40
Revenue-driven Operating Expenses	4,160	8
Contribution Margin	£16,640	£32
Fixed Operating Expenses	13,090	
Operating Profit, or Earnings Before Interest and Tax Expenses (EBIT)	£ 3,550	
Interest Expense	750	
Earnings Before Tax	£ 2,800	
Tax Expense	900	
Net Profit	£ 1,900	

Figure 3-2: Management Profit and Loss statement model.

cost information for each product, or product line, or segment of the business they're responsible for. To keep the illustration easy to follow we've collapsed the business's entire sales into one 'average' product. Instead of grappling with 100 or 1,000 different products, we condensed them all into one proxy product. The main purpose of Figure 3-2 is to show a basic template, or model, that can be used for the more detailed reports to different managers in the business organisation.

Variable versus fixed operating expenses

Another fundamental difference between the external profit report (Figure 3-1) and the internal profit report (Figure 3-2) is that the company's *operating expenses* (sales, administration and general expenses plus depreciation expense) are separated into two different categories in the management report:

✔ **Variable expenses:** The *revenue-driven expenses* that depend directly on the total sales revenue amount for the period. These expenses move in step with changes in total sales revenue. Commissions paid to salespersons based on a percentage of the amount of sales are a common example of variable operating expenses.

✔ **Fixed expenses:** The operating expenses that are relatively fixed in amount for the period, regardless of whether the company's total unit sales (sales volume) had been substantially more, or substantially less, than the 520,000 units that it actually sold during the year. An example of a fixed operating expense is the annual business rates on the company's property. Also, depreciation is a fixed expense; a certain amount of depreciation expense is recorded to the year regardless of actual sales volume.

The management Profit and Loss statement does not, we repeat *not*, present different profit numbers for the year compared with the profit numbers reported in the company's external Profit and Loss statement. Note that operating profit for the year (or earnings before interest and tax expenses) is the same as reported outside the business – in Figures 3-1 and 3-2 this number is the same. And in reading down the rest of the two Profit and Loss statements, note that earnings before tax and bottom-line net profit are the same in both the external and internal reports. The external Profit and Loss statement of the business reports a broad, all-inclusive group of 'Sales, Administration and General Expenses', and a separate expense for depreciation. In contrast, the management Profit and Loss statement reveals information about *how the operating expenses behave relative to the sales of the business*. The actual reporting of expenses in external Profit and Loss statements varies from business to business – but you never see Profit and Loss statements in which operating expenses are sorted between variable and fixed.

Virtually every business has *variable operating expenses*, which move up and down in tight proportion to changes in unit sales volume or sales revenue. Here are some examples of common variable operating expenses:

✔ Cost of goods sold expense – the cost of the products sold to customers

✔ Commissions paid to salespeople based on their sales

✔ Transportation costs of delivering products to customers

✔ Fees that a business pays to a bank when a customer uses a credit card such as Visa, MasterCard or American Express

The management Profit and Loss statement (Figure 3-2) can be referred to as the *internal profit report*, because it's for management eyes only and doesn't circulate outside the business – although it may be the target of industrial intelligence gathering and perhaps even industrial espionage by competitors. Remember that in the external Profit and Loss statement only one lump sum for the category of sales, administrative and general (SA&G) expenses is reported – a category for which some of the expenses are fixed but some are variable. What you need to do is have your accountant carefully examine these expenses to determine which are fixed and which are variable.

(Some expenses may have both fixed and variable components, but we don't go into these technical details.)

Further complicating the matter somewhat is the fact that the accountant needs to divide variable expenses between those that vary with sales *volume* (total number of units sold) and those that vary with sales *revenue* (total pounds of sales revenue). The following examples outline this important distinction:

✔ An example of an expense driven by sales volume is the cost of shipping and packaging. This cost depends strictly on the *number* of units sold and generally is the same regardless of how much the item inside the box costs.

✔ An example of an expense driven by sales revenue is the sales commission paid to salespersons, which directly depends on the amount of sales made to customers. Other examples are franchise fees based on total sales revenue of retailers, business premises rental contracts that include a clause that bases monthly rent on sales revenue, and royalties that are paid for the right to use a well-known name or a trademarked logo in selling the company's products and that are based on total sales revenue.

The business represented in Figure 3-2 has just one variable operating expense – an 8 per cent sales commission, resulting in an expense total of £4.16 million (£52 million sales revenue × 8 per cent). Of course, a real business probably would have many different variable operating expenses, some driven by unit sales volume and some driven by total sales revenue pounds. But the basic idea is the same for all of them and one variable operating expense serves the purpose here. Also, cost of goods sold expense is itself a sales volume driven expense (see Book V, Chapter 2 regarding different accounting methods for measuring this expense). The example shown in Figure 3-2 is a bit oversimplified – the business sells only one product and has only one variable operating expense – but the main purpose is to present a general template that can be tailored to fit the particular circumstances of a business.

Fixed operating expenses are the many different costs that a business is obliged to pay and can't decrease over the short run without major surgery on the human resources and physical facilities of the business. You must distinguish fixed expenses from your variable operating expenses.

As an example of fixed expenses, consider a typical self-service car wash business – you know, the kind where you drive in, put some coins in a box and use the water spray to clean your car. Almost all the operating costs of this business are fixed: rent on the land, depreciation of the structure and the equipment, and the annual insurance premium cost don't depend on the number of cars passing through the car wash. The only variable expenses are probably the water and the soap.

If you want to decrease fixed expenses significantly, you need to downsize the business (lay off workers, sell off property and so on). When looking at the various ways you have for improving your profit, significantly cutting down on fixed expenses is generally the last-resort option. Refer to 'Improving profit', later in this chapter, for the better options.

Better than anyone else, managers know that sales for the year could have been lower or higher. A natural question is, 'What difference in the profit would there have been at the lower or higher level of sales?' If you'd sold 10 per cent fewer total units during the year, what would your net profit (bottom-line profit) have been? You might guess that profit would have slipped 10 per cent but that would *not* have been the case. In fact, profit would have slipped by much more than 10 per cent. Are you surprised? Read on for the reasons.

Why wouldn't profit fall the same percentage as sales? The answer is because of the nature of fixed expenses – just because your sales are lower doesn't mean that your expenses are lower. *Fixed expenses* are the costs of doing business that, for all practical purposes, are stuck at a certain amount over the short term. Fixed expenses don't react to changes in the sales level. Here are some examples of fixed expenses:

- ✔ Interest on money that the business has borrowed
- ✔ Employees' salaries and benefits
- ✔ Business rates
- ✔ Fire insurance

A business can downsize its assets and therefore reduce its fixed expenses to fit a lower sales level, but that can be a drastic reaction to what may be a temporary downturn. After deducting cost of goods sold, variable operating expenses and fixed operating expenses, the next line in the management Profit and Loss statement is operating profit, which is also called *earnings before interest and tax* (or *EBIT*). This profit line in the report is a critical juncture that managers need to fully appreciate.

From operating profit (EBIT) to the bottom line

After deducting all operating expenses from sales revenue, you get to earnings before interest and tax (EBIT), which is £3.55 million in the example. *Operating* is an umbrella term that includes cost of goods sold expense and all other expenses of making sales and operating your business – but not interest and tax. Sometimes EBIT is called *operating profit*, or *operating earnings*, to emphasise that profit comes from making sales and controlling operating expenses. This business earned £3.55 million operating profit from its £52 million sales revenue – which seems satisfactory. But is its £3.55 million EBIT really good enough? What's the reference for answering this question?

The main benchmark for judging EBIT is whether this amount of profit is adequate to cover the *cost of capital* of the business. A business must secure money to invest in its various assets – and this capital has a cost. A business has to pay interest on its debt capital, and it should earn enough after-tax net profit (bottom-line profit) to satisfy its owners who have put their capital in the business. See the sidebar 'How much net profit is needed to make owners happy?' in this chapter.

Nobody – not even the most die-hard humanitarian – is in business to make a zero EBIT. You simply can't do this, because profit is an absolutely necessary part of doing business, and recouping the cost of capital is why profit is needed.

Don't treat the word *profit* as something that's whispered in the hallways. Profit builds owners' value and provides the basic stability for a business. Earning a satisfactory EBIT is the cornerstone of business. Without earning an adequate operating profit, a business couldn't attract capital, and you can't have a business without capital.

Travelling Two Trails to Profit

How is the additional information in the management Profit and Loss statement useful? Well, with this information you can figure out how the business earned its profit for the year. We're not referring to how the company decided which products to sell, and the best ways to market and advertise its products, and how to set sales prices, and how to design an efficient and smooth-running organisation, and how to motivate its employees, and all the other things every business has to do to achieve its financial goals. We're talking about an *accounting explanation of profit* that focuses on methods for

How much net profit is needed to make owners happy?

People who invest in a business usually aren't philanthropists who don't want to make any money on the deal. No, these investors want a business to protect their capital investment, earn a good bottom-line profit for them and enhance the value of their investment over time. They understand that a business may not earn a profit but suffer a loss – that's the risk they take as owners.

How much of a business's net profit (bottom-line profit) is distributed to the owners depends on the business and the arrangement that it made with the owners. But regardless of how much money the owners actually receive, they still have certain expectations of how well the business will do – that is, what the business's earnings before interest and tax will be. After all, they've staked their money on the business's success.

One test of whether the owners will be satisfied with the net profit (after interest and tax) is to compute the *return on equity* (ROE), which

is the ratio of net profit to total owners' equity (net profit ÷ owners' equity). In this chapter's business example, the bottom-line profit is £1.9 million. Suppose that the total owners' equity in the business is £15.9 million; thus the ROE is 12 per cent (£1.9 million ÷ £15.9 million). Is 12 per cent a good ROE? Well, that depends on how much the owners could earn from an alternative investment. We'd say that a 12 per cent ROE isn't bad. By the way, ROE is also known as ROSI: *return on shareholders' investment.*

Note: ROE doesn't imply that all the net profit was distributed in cash to the owners. Usually, a business needs to retain a good part of its bottom-line net profit to provide capital for growing the business. Suppose, in this example, that none of the net profit is distributed in cash to its owners. The ROE is still 12 per cent; ROE doesn't depend on how much, if any, of the net profit is distributed to the owners. (Of course, the owners may prefer that a good part of the net profit be distributed to them.)

calculating profit – going from the basic input factors of sales price, sales volume and costs to arrive at the amount of profit that results from the interaction of the factors. Business managers should be familiar with these accounting calculations. They're responsible for each factor and for profit, of course. With this in mind, therefore: how did the business earn its profit for the year?

First path to profit: Contribution margin minus fixed expenses

We can't read your mind. But if we had to hazard a guess regarding how you'd go about answering the profit question, we'd bet that, after you had the chance to study Figure 3-2, you'd do something like the following, which is correct as a matter of fact:

Computing Profit Before Tax

Contribution margin per unit	£32
× Unit sales volume	520,000
Equals: Total contribution margin	£16,640,000
Less: Total fixed operating expenses	£13,090,000
Equals: Operating profit (EBIT)	£3,550,000
Less: Interest Expense	£750,000
Equals: Earnings before tax	£2,800,000

Note that we stop at the *earnings before tax* line in this calculation. You're aware, of course, that business profit is subject to tax. This chapter focuses on profit above the taxation expense line.

Contribution margin is what's left over after you subtract cost of goods sold expense and other variable expenses from sales revenue. On a *per unit* basis the business sells its product for £100, its variable product cost (cost of goods sold) is £60 and its variable operating cost per unit is £8 – which yields £32 contribution margin per unit. *Total* contribution margin for a period equals contribution margin per unit times the units sold during the period – in the business example, £32 × 520,000 units, which is £16.64 million total contribution margin. Total contribution margin is a measure of profit *before fixed expenses are deducted*. To pay for its fixed operating expenses and its interest expense, a business needs to earn a sufficient amount of total contribution margin. In the example, the business earned more total contribution margin than its fixed expenses, so it earned a profit for the year.

How variable expenses mow down your sales price

Consider a retail hardware store that sells, say, a lawnmower to a customer. The purchase cost per unit that the retailer paid to the lawnmower manufacturer when the retailer bought its shipment is the *product cost* in the contribution margin equation. The retailer also provides one free servicing of the lawnmower after the customer has used it for a few months (cleaning it and sharpening the blade) and also pays its salesperson a commission on the sale. These two additional expenses, for the service and the commission, are examples of variable expenses in the margin equation.

Here are some other concepts associated with the term *margin* that you're likely to encounter:

Book V

Accountants: Managing the Business

- ✔ **Gross margin, also called gross profit:** Gross margin = sales revenue – cost of goods sold expense. Gross margin is profit from sales revenue *before* deducting the other variable expenses of making the sales. So gross margin is one step short of the final contribution margin earned on making sales. Businesses that sell products must report gross margin on their *external* Profit and Loss statements. However, generally accounting standards do *not* require that you report other variable expenses of making sales on external Profit and Loss statements. In their external financial reports, very few businesses divulge other variable expenses of making sales. In other words, managers don't want the outside world and competitors to know their contribution margins. Most businesses carefully guard information about contribution margins because the information is very sensitive.

- ✔ **Gross margin ratio:** Gross margin ratio = gross margin ÷ sales revenue. In the business we use as an example in this chapter, the gross margin on sales is 40 per cent. Gross margins of companies vary from industry to industry, from over 50 per cent to under 25 per cent – but very few businesses can make a bottom-line profit with less than a 20 per cent gross margin.

- ✔ **Markup:** Generally refers to the amount added to the product cost to determine the sales price. For example, suppose a product that cost £60 is marked up (based on cost) by 66⅔ per cent to determine its sales price of £100 – for a gross margin of £40 on the product. *Note:* The markup based on *cost* is 66⅔ per cent (£40 markup ÷ £60 product cost). But the gross margin ratio is only 40 per cent, which is based on *sales price* (£40 ÷ £100).

Second path to profit: Excess over break-even volume × contribution margin per unit

The second method of computing a company's profit starts with a particular sales volume as the point of reference. So, the first step is to compute this specific sales volume of the business (which isn't its actual sales volume for the year) by dividing its total annual fixed expenses by its contribution margin per unit. Interest expense is treated as a fixed expense (because for all practical purposes it's more or less fixed in amount over the short run). For the business in the example, the interest expense is £750,000 (see Figure 3-2), which, added to the £13.09 million fixed operating expenses, gives total fixed expenses of £13.84 million. The company's *break-even point*, also called its *break-even sales volume*, is computed as follows:

£13,840,000 total annual fixed expenses for year ÷ £32 contribution margin per unit = 432,500 units break-even point (or, break-even sales volume) for the year

In other words, if you multiply £32 contribution margin per unit by 432,500 units you get a total contribution margin of £13.84 million, which exactly equals the company's total fixed expenses for the year. The business actually sold more than this number of units during the year, but if it had sold only 432,500 units, the company's profit would have been exactly zero. Below this sales level the business suffers a loss, and above this sales level the business makes profit. The break-even sales volume is the crossover point from the loss column to the profit column. Of course, a business's goal is to do better than just reaching its break-even sales volume.

Calculating its break-even point calls attention to the amount of fixed expenses hanging over a business. As explained earlier, a business is committed to its fixed expenses over the short run and can't do much to avoid these costs – short of breaking some of its contracts and taking actions to downsize the business that could have disastrous long-run effects. Sometimes the total fixed expenses for the year are referred to as the 'nut' of the business – which may be a hard nut to crack (by exceeding its break-even sales volume).

In the example (see Figure 3-2) the business actually sold 520,000 units during the year, which is 87,500 units more than its break-even sales volume (520,000 units sold minus its 432,500 break-even sales volume). Therefore, you can determine the company's earnings before tax as follows:

Second Way of Computing Profit

Contribution margin per unit	£32
× Units sold in excess of break-even point	87,500
Equals: Earnings before tax	£2,800,000

This second way of analysing profit calls attention to the need of the business to achieve and exceed its break-even point to make profit. The business makes no profit until it clears its break-even hurdle, but when over this level of sales it makes profit hand over fist because the units sold from here on aren't burdened with any fixed costs, which have been covered by the first 432,500 units sold during the year. Be careful in thinking that only the last 87,500 units sold during the year generate all the profit for the year. The first 432,500 units sold are necessary to get the business into position in order for the next 87,500 units to make profit.

The key point is that when the business has reached its break-even sales volume (thereby covering its annual fixed expenses), each additional unit sold brings in pre-tax profit equal to the contribution margin per unit. Each additional unit sold brings in 'pure profit' of £32 per unit, which is the company's contribution margin per unit. A business has to get into this upper region of sales volume to make a profit for the year.

Calculating the margin of safety

The *margin of safety* is the excess of its actual sales volume over a company's break-even sales volume. This business sold 520,000 units, which is 87,500 units above its break-even sales volume – a rather large cushion against any downturn in sales. Only a major sales collapse would cause the business to fall all the way down to its break-even point, assuming that it can maintain its £32 contribution margin per unit and that its fixed costs don't change. You may wonder what a 'normal' margin of safety is for most businesses. Sorry, we can't give you a definitive answer on this. Due to the nature of the business, or industry-wide problems, or due to conditions beyond its control, a business may have to operate with a smaller margin of safety than it would like.

Doing What-If Analysis

Managing profit is like driving a car – you need to be glancing in the rear-view mirror constantly as well as looking ahead through the windscreen. You have to know your profit history to see your profit future. Understanding the past is the best preparation for the future.

The model of a *management Profit and Loss statement* shown in Figure 3-2 allows you to compare your actual profit with what it would've looked like if you'd done something differently – for example, raised prices and sold fewer units. With the profit model, you can test-drive adjustments before putting them into effect. It lets you plan and map out your profit strategy for the *coming* period. Also, you can analyse why profit went up or down from the *last* period, using the model to do hindsight analysis.

The management Profit and Loss statement profit model focuses on the key factors and variables that drive profit. Here's what you should know about these factors:

- ✔ Even a small decrease in the contribution margin per unit can have a drastic impact on profit because fixed expenses don't go down over the short run (and may be hard to reduce even over the long run).

✔ Even a small increase in the contribution margin per unit can have a dramatic impact on profit because fixed expenses won't go up over the short run – although they may have to be increased in the long run.

✔ Compared with changes in contribution margin per unit, sales volume changes have secondary profit impact; sales volume changes aren't trivial, but even relatively small margin changes can have a bigger effect on profit.

✔ You can, perhaps, reduce fixed expenses to improve profit, but you have to be very careful to cut fat and not muscle; reducing fixed expenses may very well diminish the capacity of your business to make sales and deliver a high-quality service to customers.

The following sections expand on these key points.

Lower profit from lower sales – but that much lower?

The management Profit and Loss statement shown in Figure 3-2 is designed for managers to use in profit analysis – to expose the critical factors that drive profit. Remember what information has been added that isn't included in the external Profit and Loss statement:

✔ **Unit sales volume** for the year

✔ **Per-unit values**

✔ **Fixed versus variable** operating expenses

✔ **Contribution margin** – total and per unit

Handle this information with care. The contribution margin per unit is confidential, for your eyes only. This information is limited to you and other managers in the business. Clearly, you don't want your competitors to find out your margins. Even within a business, the information may not circulate to all managers – just those who need to know.

The contribution margin per unit is one of the three most important determinants of profit performance, along with sales volume and fixed expenses – as shown in the upcoming sections.

With the information provided in the management Profit and Loss statement, you're ready to paint a what-if scenario. We're making you the chief executive officer of the business in this example. What if you'd sold 5 per cent fewer units during this period? In this example, that would mean you'd sold only 494,000 units rather than 520,000 units, or 26,000 units less. The following computation shows you how much profit damage this seemingly modest drop in sales volume would have caused.

Impact of 5 Per Cent Lower Sales Volume on Profit

Contribution margin per unit	£32
× 26,000 fewer units sold	26,000
Equals: Decrease in earnings before tax	£832,000

By selling 26,000 fewer units you missed out on the £832,000 profit that these units would have produced – this is fairly straightforward. What's not so obvious, however, is that this £832,000 decrease in profit would have been a 30 per cent drop in profit: £832,000 decrease ÷ £2.8 million profit = 30 per cent decrease. Lose just 5 per cent of your sales and lose 30 per cent of your profit? How can such a thing happen? The next section expands on how a seemingly small decrease in sales volume can cause a stunning decrease in profit. Read on.

Violent profit swings due to operating leverage

First, the bare facts for the business in the example: the company's contribution margin per unit is £32 and, before making any changes, the company sold 520,000 units during the year, which is 87,500 units in excess of its break-even sales volume. The company earned a total contribution margin of £16.64 million (see Figure 3-2), which is its contribution per unit times its total units sold during the year. If the company had sold 5 per cent less during the year (26,000 fewer units), you'd expect its total contribution margin to decrease 5 per cent, and you'd be absolutely correct – £832,000 decrease ÷ £16.64 million = 5 per cent decrease. Compared with its £2.8 million profit before tax, however, the £832,000 drop in total contribution margin equals a *30 per cent* fall-off in profit.

The main focus of business managers and investors is on profit, which in this example is profit before tax. Therefore, the 30 per cent drop in profit would get more attention than the 5 per cent drop in total contribution margin. The much larger percentage change in profit caused by a relatively small change in sales volume is the effect of *operating leverage*. Leverage means that there's a multiplier effect – that a relatively small percentage change in one factor can cause a much larger change in another factor. A small push can cause a large movement – this is the idea of leverage.

In the preceding scenario for the 5 per cent, 26,000 units decrease in sales volume, note that the 5 per cent is based on the total 520,000 units sales volume of the business. But if the 26,000 units decrease in sales volume is divided by the 87,500 units in excess of the company's break-even point – which are the units that generate profit for the business – the sales volume decrease equals 30 per cent. In other words, the business lost 30 per cent of its profit layer of sales volume and, thus, the company's profit would have dropped 30 per cent. This dramatic drop is caused by the operating leverage effect.

Note: If the company had sold 5 per cent *more* units, with no increase in its fixed expenses, its pre-tax profit would have *increased* by 30 per cent, reflecting the operating leverage effect. The 26,000 additional units sold at a £32 contribution margin per unit would increase its total contribution margin by £832,000, and this increase would increase profit by 30 per cent. You can see why businesses are always trying to increase sales volume.

Cutting sales price, even a little, can gut profit

So what effect would a 5 per cent decrease in the sales price have caused? Around a 30 per cent drop similar to the effect of a 5 per cent decrease in sales volume? Not quite. Check out the following computation for this 5 per cent sales price decrease scenario:

Impact of 5 Per Cent Lower Sales Price on Profit

Contribution margin per unit decrease	£4.60
× Units sold during year	520,000
Equals: Decrease in earnings before tax	£2,392,000

Hold on! Earnings before tax would drop from £2.8 million at the £100 sales price (refer to Figure 3-2) to only £408,000 at the £95 sales price – a plunge of 85 per cent. What could cause such a drastic dive in profit?

The sales price drops £5 per unit – a 5 per cent decrease of the £100 sales price. But contribution margin per unit doesn't drop by the entire £5 because the variable operating expense per unit (sales commissions in this example) would also drop 5 per cent, or £40 per unit – for a net decrease of £4.60 per unit in the contribution margin per unit. (This is one reason for identifying the expenses that depend on sales revenue – as shown in the management Profit and Loss statement in Figure 3-2.) For this what-if scenario that examines the case of the company selling all units at a 5 per cent lower sales price than it did, the company's contribution margin would have been only £27.40 per unit. Such a serious reduction in its contribution margin per unit would have been intolerable.

At the lower sales price, the company's contribution margin would be £27.40 per unit (£32.00 in the original example minus the £4.60 decrease = £27.40). As a result, the break-even sales volume would be much higher, and the company's 520,000 sales volume for the year would have been only 14,891 units over its break-even point. So the lower £27.40 contribution margin per unit would yield only £408,000 profit before tax.

The moral of the story is to protect contribution margin per unit above all else. Every pound of contribution margin per unit that's lost – due to decreased sales prices, increased product cost or increases in other variable costs – has a tremendously negative impact on profit. Conversely, if you can increase the contribution margin per unit without hurting sales volume, you reap very large profit benefits, as described next.

Improving profit

The preceding sections explore the downside of things – that is, what would've happened to profit if sales volume or sales prices had been lower. The upside – higher profit – is so much more pleasant to discuss and analyse, don't you think?

Profit improvement boils down to the three critical profit-making factors, listed in order from the most effective to the least effective:

- Increasing the contribution margin per unit
- Increasing sales volume
- Reducing fixed expenses

Say you want to improve your bottom-line profit from the £1.9 million net profit you earned the year just ended to £2.1 million next year. How can you pump up your net profit by £210,000? (By the way, this is the only place in the chapter we bring the tax factor into the analysis.)

First of all, realise that to increase your net profit *after taxes* by £210,000, you need to increase your before-tax profit by much more – to provide for the amount that goes to tax. Your accountant calculates that you would need a £312,000 increase in earnings before tax next year because your tax increase would be about £102,000 on the £312,000 increase in pre-tax earnings. So you have to find a way to increase earnings, before tax, by £312,000.

You should also take into account the possibility that fixed costs and interest expense may rise next year, but for this example we're assuming that they won't. We're also assuming that the business can't cut any of its fixed operating expenses without hurting its ability to maintain and support its present sales level (and a modest increase in the sales level). Of course, in real life every business should carefully scrutinise its fixed expenses to see whether some of them can be cut.

- Increase your contribution margin per unit by £0.60, which would raise the total contribution margin by £312,000, based on a 520,000 units sales volume (£0.60 × 520,000 = £312,000).

- Sell 9,750 additional units at the current contribution margin per unit of £32, which would raise the total contribution margin by £312,000 (9,750 × £32 = £312,000).

- Use a combination of these two approaches: increase both the margin per unit and the sales volume.

The second approach is obvious – you just need to set a sales goal of increasing the number of products sold by 9,750 units. (How you motivate your already overworked sales staff to accomplish that sales volume goal is up to you.) But how do you go about the first approach, increasing the contribution margin per unit by £0.60?

The simplest way to increase contribution margin per unit by £0.60 would be to decrease your product cost per unit by £0.60. Or you could attempt to reduce sales commissions from £8 per £100 of sales to £7.40 per £100 – which may adversely affect the motivation of your sales force, of course. Or you could raise the sales price by about £0.65 (remember that 8 per cent comes off the top for the sales commission, so only £0.60 would remain from that £0.65 to improve the unit contribution margin). Or you could combine two or more such changes so that your unit contribution next year would increase by £0.60. However you do it, the improvement would increase your earnings before tax by the desired amount:

Impact of £0.60 Higher Unit Contribution Margin on Profit

Contribution margin per unit increase	£0.60
× Units sold during year	520,000
Equals: Increase in earnings before tax	£312,000

Cutting prices to increase sales volume: A very tricky game to play!

A word of warning: be sure to *run the numbers* (accountant speak for using a profit model) before deciding to drop sales prices in an effort to gain more sales volume. Suppose, for example, you're convinced that if you decrease sales prices by 5 per cent, your sales volume will increase by 10 per cent. Seems like an attractive trade-off, one that would increase both profit performance and market share. But are you sure that those positive changes are the results you'll get?

The impact on profit may surprise you. Get a piece of notepaper and do the computation for this lower sales price and higher sales volume scenario:

Lower Sales Price and Higher Sales Volume Impact on Profit

New sales price (lower)	£95.00
Less: Product cost per unit (same)	£60.00
Less: Variable operating expenses (lower)	£7.60
Equals: New unit contribution margin (lower)	£27.40
× Sales volume (higher)	572,000
Equals: Total contribution margin	£15,672,800
Less: Previous total contribution margin	£16,640,000
Equals: Decrease in total contribution margin	£967,200

Your total contribution margin wouldn't go up; instead, it would go down by £967,200! In dropping the sales price by £5, you'd give up too much of your contribution margin per unit. The increase in sales volume wouldn't make up for the big dent in unit contribution margin. You may gain more market share, but would pay for it with a £967,200 drop in earnings before tax.

To keep profit the same, you'd have to increase sales volume more than 10 per cent. By how much? Divide the total contribution margin for the 520,000 units situation by the contribution margin per unit for the new scenario:

£16,640,000 ÷ £27.40 = 607,300 units

In other words, just to keep your total contribution margin the same at the lower sales price, you'd have to increase sales volume to 607,300 units – an increase of 87,300 units, or a whopping 17 per cent. That would be quite a challenge, to say the least.

Cash flow from improving profit margin versus improving sales volume

This chapter discusses increasing profit margin versus increasing sales volume to improve bottom-line profit. Improving your profit margin is the better way to go, compared with increasing sales volume. Both actions increase profit, but the profit margin tactic is much better in terms of cash flow. When sales volume increases, so does stock. On the other hand, when you improve profit margin (by raising the sales price or by lowering product cost), you don't have to increase stock – in fact, reducing product cost may actually cause stock to decrease a little. In short, increasing your profit margin yields a higher cash flow from profit than does increasing your sales volume.

A Final Word or Two

Recently, some friends pooled their capital and opened an up-market off-licence in a rapidly growing area. The business has a lot of promise. We can tell you one thing they should have done before going ahead with this new venture – in addition to location analysis and competition analysis, of course. They should have used the basic profit model (in other words, the management Profit and Loss statement) discussed in this chapter to figure out their break-even sales volume – because we're sure they have rather large fixed expenses. And they should have determined how much more sales revenue over their break-even point that they'll need to earn a satisfactory return on their investment in the business.

During their open house for the new shop we noticed the very large number of different beers, wines and spirits available for sale – to say nothing of the different sizes and types of containers many products come in. Quite literally, the business sells thousands of distinct products. The shop also sells many products like soft drinks, ice, corkscrews and so on. Therefore, the company doesn't have a single sales volume factor (meaning the number of units sold) to work with in the basic profit model. So you have to adapt the profit model to get along without the sales volume factor.

The trick is to determine your *average contribution margin as a percentage of sales revenue*. We'd estimate that an off-licence's average gross margin (sales revenue less cost of goods sold) is about 25 per cent. The other variable operating expenses of the shop probably run about 5 per cent of sales. So the average contribution margin would be 20 per cent of sales (25 per cent gross margin less 5 per cent variable operating expenses). Suppose the total fixed operating expenses of the shop are about £100,000 per month (for rent, salaries, electricity and so on), which is £1.2 million per year. So the shop needs £6 million in sales per year just to break even:

£1.2 million fixed expenses ÷ 20% average contribution margin
= £6 million annual sales to break even

Selling £6 million of product a year means moving a lot of booze. The business needs to sell another £1 million to provide £200,000 of operating earnings (at the 20 per cent average contribution margin) – to pay interest expense and tax and to leave enough net profit for the owners who invested capital in the business and who expect a good return on their investment.

By the way, some disreputable off-licence owners are known (especially to HM Revenue & Customs) to engage in *sales skimming*. This term refers to not recording all sales revenue; instead, some cash collected from customers is put in the pockets of the owners. They don't report the profit in their tax returns or in the Profit and Loss statements of the business. Our friends who started the off-licence are honest businesspeople, and we're sure they won't engage in sales skimming – but they do have to make sure that none of their store's employees skim off some sales revenue.

When sales skimming is being committed, not all the actual sales revenue for the year is recorded, even though the total cost of all products sold during the year is recorded. Obviously, this distorts the Profit and Loss statement and throws off normal ratios of gross profit and operating profit to sales revenue. If you have the opportunity to buy a business, please be alert to the possibility that some sales skimming may have been done by the present owner. Indeed, we've been involved in situations in which the person selling the business bragged about how much he was skimming off the top.

Have a Go

1. **Using the information shown in Table 3-1, calculate the contribution Margin for Company A.**

2. **Using the information shown in Table 3-1, calculate the break-even point for Company B.**

3. **Using the information in Table 3-1, calculate the margin of safety for Company A.**

4. **Using the information in Table 3-1, calculate the gross margin ration of Company B.**

Table 3-1	Internal Profit and Loss Statement Highlighting Profit Drivers			
	Company A		Company B	
	Totals	*Per Unit*	*Totals*	*Per Unit*
Sales volume (units)	50,000		1,500,000	
Sales revenue	£15,000,000	£300.00	£36,000,000	£24.00
Cost of goods sold expense	£7,500,000	£150.00	£27,000,000	£18.00
Gross margin	£7,500,000	£150.00	£9,000,000	£6.00
Variable operating expenses	£3,750,000	£75.00	£4,200,000	£2.80
Contribution margin	£3,750,000	£75.00	£4,800,000	£3.20
Fixed operating expenses	£1,950,000	£39.00	£3,000,000	£2.00
Operating profit	£1,800,000	£36.00	£1,800,000	£1.20

5. **Using the information shown in Table 3-2, calculate the effect of Company C allowing a 10 per cent decrease in its selling price, in exchange for a 10 per cent increase in sales volume. What is the effect on the operating profit?**

Table 3-2	Operating Profit Result from 10 per cent Sales Price Decrease in Exchange for 10 per cent Sales Volume Increase		
	Company C		
	Before	*After*	*Calculate Change*
Sales price	£300.00	£270.00	??
Product cost	£150.00	£150.00	
Variable operating expenses:	£15.00	£15.00	??
Volume driven expenses	£60.00	£54.00	
Revenue driven expenses at 20 per cent			
Contribution margin per unit	£75.00	£51.00	?
Times sales volume in units	50,000	55,000	?
Equals total contribution margin	£3,750,000	£2,805,000	?
Less fixed operating expenses	£1,950,000	£1,950,000	
Operating profit	£1,800,000	£855,000	?

Answering the Have a Go Questions

1. You calculate the contribution margin by multiplying the contribution per unit by the volume of units sold. So in the case of Company A, you do this:

   • Contribution per unit = £75

   • Volume sold = 50,000 units

   • Contribution margin = £75 × 50,000 = £3,750,000

2. You calculate the break-even point by taking the total annual fixed expenses and dividing them by the contribution margin per unit. For Company B, the calculation is as follows:

   • Total fixed expenses = £3,000,000

   • Contribution per unit = £3.20

   • Break-even point = 3,000,000 ÷ £3.20 = 937,500 units

3. The margin of safety is described as the volume of sales units minus the break even number of units. In the case of Company A the calculation is as follows:

   • Sales volume = 50,000 units

   • Break-even volume = 26,000 (1,950,000 ÷ £75)

   • Margin of safety = 50,000 − 26,000 = 24,000 units

4. You calculate the gross margin ratio by dividing the gross margin by the sales revenue and multiplying by 100. So in the case of Company B, the calculation is as follows:

   • Gross margin = 9,000,000

   • Sales revenue = £36,000,000

   • Gross margin ratio = 9,000,000 ÷ 36,000,000 × 100 = 25%

5. Table 3-3 shows the completed Table 3-2.

   You can see that the operating profit decreases by £945,000, which is a decrease of more than 50 per cent prior to decreasing the selling price! The reason for this huge drop isn't immediately obvious, but here goes. . . . The 10 per cent decrease in the sales prices causes the contribution margin per unit to drop from £75 to £51, which is a plunge of 32 per cent (£24 decrease divided by £75 original contribution margin). The small 10 per cent increase in sales volume can't make up for the 32 per cent decrease in contribution margin.

Table 3-3	Operating Profit Result – Completed		
	Company C		
	Before	After	Change
Sales price	£300.00	£270.00	(£30.00)
Product cost	£150.00	£150.00	
Variable operating expenses:	£15.00	£15.00	(£6.00)
Volume driven expenses	£60.00	£54.00	
Revenue driven expenses at 20 per cent			
Contribution margin per unit	£75.00	£51.00	(£24.00)
Times sales volume in units	50,000	55,000	5,000
Equals total contribution margin	£3,750,000	£2,805,000	(£945,000)
Less fixed operating expenses	£1,950,000	£1,950,000	
Operating profit	£1,800,000	£855,000	(£945,000)

Chapter 4

Cost Conundrums

- -

- -

*M*easuring costs is the second most important thing accountants do, right after measuring profit. But really, can measuring a cost be very complicated? You just take numbers off a purchase invoice and call it a day, right? Not if your business manufactures the products you sell – that's for sure! Businesses must carefully record all their costs correctly so that profit can be determined each period, and so that managers have the information they need to make decisions and to control profit performance.

Previewing What's Coming Down the Road

One main function of accounting for a manufacturing business is measuring *product cost*. Examples are the cost of a new car just rolling off the assembly line or the cost of this book, *Bookkeeping & Accounting For Dummies, All-in-One*. Most production (manufacturing) processes are fairly complex, so measuring product cost is also fairly complex in most cases. Every step in the production process has to be tracked very carefully from start to finish. One major problem is that many manufacturing costs can't be directly matched with particular products; these are called *indirect costs*. To arrive at the *full cost* of each separate product manufactured, accountants devise methods for allocating the indirect production costs to specific products. Different accountants use different allocation methods. In other respects as well, product cost accounting is characterised by a diversity of methods. Generally accepted accounting principles (GAAP) provide very little guidance for measuring product cost.

Manufacturing businesses have a lot of leeway in how their product costs are determined; even businesses in the same industry use different product cost accounting methods.

In addition to measuring product costs of manufacturers, accountants in all businesses determine many other costs: the costs of the departments and other organisational units of the business; the cost of pensions for the company's employees; the cost of marketing initiatives and advertising campaigns; and, on occasion, the cost of restructuring the business or the cost of a major recall of products sold by the business. A common refrain among accountants is 'different costs for different purposes'. True enough, but at its core cost accounting serves two broad purposes – measuring profit and providing relevant information to managers.

This chapter covers cost concepts and cost measurement methods that are used by both retail and manufacturing businesses, along with additional stuff for manufacturers to worry about. We also discuss how having a good handle on cost issues can help you recognise when a business is monkeying around with product cost to deliberately manipulate its profit figure. Service businesses – which sell a service such as transportation or entertainment – have a break here. They don't encounter the cost-accounting problems of manufacturers, but they have plenty of cost allocation issues to deal with in assessing the profitability of each of their separate sales revenue sources.

What Makes Cost So Important?

Without good cost information, a business operates in the dark. Cost data is needed for different purposes in business, including the following:

- **Setting sales prices:** The common method for setting sales prices (known as *cost-plus* or *mark-up on cost*) starts with cost and then adds a certain percentage.

- **Measuring gross margin:** Investors and managers judge business performance by the bottom-line profit figure. This profit figure depends on the *gross margin* figure that you get when you subtract your cost of goods sold expense from your sales revenue. Gross margin (also called *gross profit*) is the first profit line in the Profit and Loss statement (see Figure 4-2).

- **Valuing assets:** The Balance Sheet reports cost values for many assets, and these values are, of course, included in the overall financial position of your business.

✔ **Making optimal choices:** You often must choose one alternative over others in making business decisions. The best alternative depends heavily on cost factors, and you have to be careful to distinguish *relevant* costs from *irrelevant* costs, as described in the section 'Relevant versus irrelevant (sunk) costs', later in this chapter.

In most situations, the book value of a fixed asset is an *irrelevant* cost. Say the book value is £35,000 for a machine used in the manufacturing operations of the business. This is the amount of original cost that hasn't yet been charged to depreciation expense since it was acquired, and it may seem quite relevant. However, in deciding between keeping the old machine or replacing it with a newer, more efficient machine, the *disposable value* of the old machine is the relevant amount, not the non-depreciated cost balance of the asset. Suppose the old machine has only a £20,000 salvage value at this time. This is the relevant cost for the alternative of keeping it for use in the future – not the £35,000 that hasn't been depreciated yet. In order to keep using it, the business forgoes the £20,000 it could get by selling the asset, and this £20,000 is the relevant cost in the decision situation. Making decisions involves looking at the future cash flows of each alternative – not looking back at historical-based cost values.

Sharpening Your Sensitivity to Costs

The following sections explain important distinctions between costs that managers should understand in making decisions and exercising control. Also, these cost distinctions help managers better appreciate the cost figures that accountants attach to products that are manufactured or purchased by the business. In a later section we focus on the special accounting methods and problems of computing product costs of *manufacturers*. Retailers purchase products in a condition ready for sale to their customers – although the products have to be removed from shipping containers and a retailer does a little work making the products presentable for sale and putting the products on display.

Manufacturers don't have it so easy; their product costs have to be 'manufactured' in the sense that the accountants have to compile production costs and compute the cost per unit for every product manufactured. We can't exaggerate the importance of correct product costs (for businesses that sell products, of course). The total cost of goods (products) sold is the first, and usually the largest, expense deducted from sales revenue in measuring profit. The bottom-line profit amount reported in the Profit and Loss statement of a business for the period depends heavily on whether its product costs have been measured properly. Also, keep in mind that product cost is the value for the stock asset reported in the Balance Sheet of a business.

Direct versus indirect costs

What's the difference between these costs? Well:

- ✔ **Direct costs** can be clearly attributed to one product or product line, or one source of sales revenue, or one organisational unit of the business, or one specific operation in a process. An example of a direct cost in the book publishing industry is the cost of the paper that a book is printed on; this cost can be squarely attached to one particular phase of the book production process.

- ✔ **Indirect costs** are far removed from and can't be obviously attributed to specific products, organisational units or activities. A book publisher's phone bill is a cost of doing business but can't be tied down to just one step in the book's editorial and production process. The salary of the purchasing officer who selects the paper for all the books is another example of a cost that's indirect to the production of particular books.

Indirect costs are allocated according to some methods to different products, sources of sales revenue, organisational units and so on. Most allocation methods are far from perfect, and in the last analysis end up being rather arbitrary. Business managers should always keep an eye on the allocation methods used for indirect costs, and take the cost figures produced by these methods with a grain of salt.

The cost of filling the fuel tank in driving your car from London to Bristol and back is a direct cost of making the trip. The annual road tax that the government charges you is an indirect cost of the trip, although it's a direct cost of having the car available during the year.

Fixed versus variable costs

Two other costs you need to know about are as follows:

- ✔ **Fixed costs** remain the same over a relatively broad range of sales volume or production output. For example, the cost of renting office space doesn't change regardless of how much a business's sales volume increases or decreases. Fixed costs are like a dead weight on the business. Its total fixed costs form the hurdle that the business must overcome by selling enough units at high enough profit margins per unit in order to avoid a loss and move into the profit zone. (Book V, Chapter 3 explains the break-even point, which is the level of sales needed to cover fixed costs for the period.)

- ✔ **Variable costs** increase and decrease in proportion to changes in sales or production level. If you increase the number of books that your business produces, the cost of the paper and ink also goes up.

Breaking even

Book V

Accountants: Managing the Business

The saying goes that every picture is worth a thousand words. Well, 'finance' and 'pictures' are words that don't come together too often, but they certainly do when you look at costings.

Take a look at Figure 4-1. The bottom horizontal axis represents volume, starting at 0 and rising as the company produces more product. The vertical axis represents value, starting at 0 and rising, as you'd expect, with any increase in volume. The horizontal line in the middle of the chart represents *fixed costs* – those costs that remain broadly unchanged with increases in volume, rents and so on. The line angling upwards from the fixed cost line represents the *variable cost* – the more we produce, the higher the cost. We arrive at the total costs by adding the fixed and variable costs together.

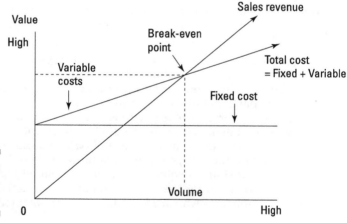

Figure 4-1:
A break-even chart.

On the hopeful assumption that our sales team has been hard at work, we should then see sales revenue kicking in. The line representing those sales starts at 0 (no sales means no money is coming in) and then rises as sales grow. The crucial information this chart shows is the *break-even point*, when total costs have been covered by the value of sales revenue and the business has started to make profit. The picture makes it easier to appreciate why lowering cost, either fixed or variable, or increasing selling prices helps a business to break even at lower volumes and hence start making profit sooner and be able to make even more profit from any given amount of assets.

Conversely, a business that only reaches break-even when sales are so high that there's virtually no spare capacity is shown as being vulnerable, because that business has a small *margin of safety* if events don't turn out as planned.

Relevant versus irrelevant (sunk) costs

Is there such a thing as an irrelevant cost in business accounting? Sure:

- ✔ **Relevant costs:** Costs that should be considered when deciding on a future course of action. Relevant costs are *future* costs – costs that you would incur, or bring upon yourself, depending on which course of action you take. For example, say that you want to increase the number of books that your business produces next year in order to increase your sales revenue, but the cost of paper has just shot up. Should you take the cost of paper into consideration? Absolutely: that cost will affect your bottom-line profit and may negate any increases in sales volume that you experience (unless you increase the sales price). The cost of paper is a relevant cost.

- ✔ **Irrelevant (or sunk) costs:** Costs that should be disregarded when deciding on a future course of action. If brought into the analysis, these costs could cause you to make the wrong decision. An irrelevant cost is a vestige of the past; that money is gone, so get over it. For example, suppose that your supervisor tells you to expect a load of new recruits next week. All your staff members use computers now, but you have loads of typewriters gathering dust in the cupboard. Should you consider the cost paid for those typewriters in your decision to buy computers for all the new staff? Absolutely not: that cost should have been written off and is no match for the cost you'd pay in productivity (and morale) for new employees who are forced to use typewriters.

Generally speaking, fixed costs are irrelevant when deciding on a future course of action, assuming that they're truly fixed and can't be increased or decreased over the short term. Most variable costs are relevant because they depend on which alternative is decided on.

 Fixed costs are usually irrelevant in decision-making because these costs will be the same no matter which course of action you decide upon. Looking behind these costs, you usually find that the costs provide *capacity* of one sort or another – so much building space, so many machine-hours available for use, so many hours of labour that will be worked and so on. Managers have to figure out the best overall way to utilise these capacities.

Separating between actual, budgeted and standard costs

Other costs to know about are:

✓ **Actual costs:** Historical costs, based on actual transactions and operations for the period just ended, or going back to earlier periods. Financial statement accounting is based on a business's actual transactions and operations; the basic approach to determining annual profit is to record the financial effects of actual transactions and allocate historical costs to the periods benefited by the costs.

✓ **Budgeted costs:** Future costs, for transactions and operations expected to take place over the coming period, based on forecasts and established goals. Note that fixed costs are budgeted differently than variable costs – for example, if sales volume is forecast to increase by 10 per cent, variable costs will definitely increase accordingly, but fixed costs may or may not need to be increased to accommodate the volume increase (see 'Fixed versus variable costs', earlier in this chapter). Book V, Chapter 5 explains the budgeting process and budgeted financial statements.

✓ **Standard costs:** Costs, primarily in manufacturing, that are carefully engineered based on detailed analysis of operations and forecast costs for each component or step in an operation. Developing standard costs for variable production costs is relatively straightforward because many of these are direct costs, whereas most fixed costs are indirect, and standard costs for fixed costs are necessarily based on more arbitrary methods (see 'Direct versus indirect costs', earlier in this chapter). *Note:* Some variable costs are indirect and have to be allocated to specific products in order to come up with a full (total) standard cost of the product.

Product versus period costs

Product costs differ from period costs:

✓ **Product costs:** Costs attached to particular products. The cost is recorded in the stock asset account until the product is sold, at which time the cost goes into the cost of goods sold expense account. One key point to keep in mind is that product cost is deferred and not recorded to expense until the product is sold.

The cost of a new car sitting on a dealer's showroom floor is a product cost. The dealer keeps the cost in the stock asset account until you buy the car, at which point the dealer charges the cost to the cost of goods sold expense.

✔ **Period costs:** Costs that are *not* attached to particular products. These costs don't spend time in the 'waiting room' of stock. Period costs are recorded as expenses immediately; unlike product costs, period costs don't pass through the stock account first. Advertising costs, for example, are accounted for as period costs and recorded immediately in an expense account. Also, research and development costs are treated as period costs.

Separating between product costs and period costs is particularly important for manufacturing businesses, as you find out in the following section.

Putting Together the Pieces of Product Cost for Manufacturers

Businesses that manufacture products have several additional cost problems to deal with. We use the term *manufacture* in the broadest sense: car makers assemble cars, beer companies brew beer, oil companies refine oil, ICI makes products through chemical synthesis and so on. *Retailers*, on the other hand, buy products in a condition ready for resale to the end consumer. For example, Levi Strauss manufactures clothing, and Selfridges is a retailer that buys from Levi Strauss and sells the clothes to the public.

The following sections describe costs that are unique to manufacturers and address the issue of determining the cost of products that are manufactured.

Minding manufacturing costs

Manufacturing costs consist of four basic types:

✔ **Raw materials:** What a manufacturer buys from other companies to use in the production of its own products. For example, The Ford Motor Company buys tyres from Goodyear (and other tyre manufacturers) that then become part of Ford's cars.

✔ **Direct labour:** The employees who work on the production line.

✔ **Variable overhead:** Indirect production costs that increase or decrease as the quantity produced increases or decreases. An example is the cost of electricity that runs the production equipment: you pay for the electricity for the whole plant, not machine by machine, so you can't attach this cost to one particular part of the process. But if you increase or decrease the use of those machines, the electricity cost increases or decreases accordingly.

✔ **Fixed overhead:** Indirect production costs that do *not* increase or decrease as the quantity produced increases or decreases. These fixed costs remain the same over a fairly broad range of production output levels (see 'Fixed versus variable costs', earlier in this chapter). Here are three significant fixed manufacturing costs:

- Salaries for certain production employees who don't work directly on the production line, such as department managers, safety inspectors, security guards, accountants, and shipping and receiving workers.

- Depreciation of production buildings, equipment and other manufacturing fixed assets.

- Occupancy costs, such as building insurance, property rental, and heating and lighting charges.

Figure 4-2 shows a sample management Profit and Loss statement for a manufacturer, including supplementary information about its manufacturing costs. Notice that the cost of goods sold expense depends directly on the product cost from the manufacturing cost summary that appears below the management profit and loss statement. A business may manufacture 100 or 1,000 different products, or even more. To keep the example easy to follow, Figure 4-2 presents a scenario for a one-product manufacturer. The example is realistic yet avoids the clutter of too much detail. The multi-product manufacturer has some additional accounting problems, but these are too technical for a book like this. The fundamental accounting problems and methods of all manufacturers are illustrated in the example.

The information in the manufacturing cost summary schedule below the profit and loss statement (see Figure 4-2) is highly confidential and for management eyes only. Competitors would love to know this information. A company may enjoy a significant cost advantage over its competitors and definitely would not want its cost data to get into the hands of its competitors.

Unlike a retailer, a manufacturer doesn't *purchase* products but begins by buying the raw materials needed in the production process. Then the

Management Profit and Loss Account for Year

Sales Volume	110,000	Units

	Per Unit	Totals
Sales Revenue	£1,400	£154,000,000
Cost of Goods Sold Expense	(760)	(83,600,000)
Gross Margin	£640	£70,400,000
Variable Operating Expenses	(300)	(33,000,000)
Contribution Margin	£340	£37,400,000
Fixed Operating Expenses	(195)	(21,450,000)
Earnings Before Interest and Tax (EBIT)	£145	£15,950,000
Interest Expense		(2,750,000)
Earnings Before Tax		£13,200,000
Corporation Tax Expense		(4,488,000)
Net Profit		£8,712,000

Manufacturing Cost Summary for Year

Annual Production Capacity	150,000	Units
Actual Output	120,000	Units

Production Cost Components	Per Unit	Totals
Raw Materials	£215	£25,800,000
Direct Labour	125	15,000,000
Variable Overhead	70	8,400,000
Total Variable Manufacturing Costs	£410	£49,200,000
Fixed Overhead	350	42,000,000
Total Manufacturing Costs	£760	£91,200,000
To 10,000 Units Stock Increase		(7,600,000)
To 110,000 Units Sold		£83,600,000

Figure 4-2: Example for determining product cost of a manufacturer.

manufacturer pays workers to operate the machines and equipment and to move the products into warehouses after they've been produced. All this is done in a sprawling plant that has many indirect overhead costs. All these different production costs have to be funnelled into the product cost so that the product cost can be entered in the stock account, and then to the cost of goods sold expense when products are sold.

Book V

Accountants: Managing the Business

Allocating costs properly: Not easy!

Two vexing issues rear their ugly heads in determining product cost for a manufacturer:

✔ **Drawing a defining line between manufacturing costs and non-manufacturing operating costs:** The key difference here is that manufacturing costs are categorised as product costs, whereas non-manufacturing operating costs are categorised as period costs (refer to 'Product versus period costs', earlier in this chapter). In calculating product cost, you factor in only manufacturing costs and not other costs. Period costs are recorded right away as an expense – either in variable operating expenses or fixed operating expenses for the example shown in Figure 4-2.

Wages paid to production-line workers are a clear-cut example of a manufacturing cost. Salaries paid to salespeople are a marketing cost and aren't part of product cost; marketing costs are treated as period costs, which means these costs are recorded immediately to the expenses of the period. Depreciation on production equipment is a manufacturing cost, but depreciation on the warehouse in which products are stored after being manufactured is a period cost. Moving the raw materials and works-in-progress through the production process is a manufacturing cost, but transporting the finished products from the warehouse to customers is a period cost. In short, product cost stops at the end of the production line – but every cost up to that point should be included as a manufacturing cost. The accumulation of direct and variable production costs starts at the beginning of the manufacturing process and stops at the end of the production line. All fixed and indirect manufacturing costs during the year are allocated to the actual production output during the year.

If you mis-classify some manufacturing costs as operating costs, your product cost calculation will be too low (refer to 'Calculating product cost', later in this chapter).

✔ **Whether to allocate indirect costs among different products, organisational units or assets:** Indirect *manufacturing* costs must be allocated among the products produced during the period. The full product cost includes both direct and indirect manufacturing costs. Coming up with a completely satisfactory allocation method is difficult and ends up being somewhat arbitrary – but must be done to determine product cost. For non-manufacturing operating costs, the basic test of whether to allocate indirect costs is whether allocation helps managers make better decisions and exercise better control. Maybe; maybe not. In any case, managers should understand how manufacturing indirect costs are allocated to products and how indirect non-manufacturing costs are allocated, keeping in mind that every allocation method is arbitrary and that a different allocation method may be just as convincing. (See the sidebar 'Allocating indirect costs is as simple as ABC – not!')

Allocating indirect costs is as simple as ABC – not!

Accountants for manufacturers have developed loads of different methods and schemes for allocating indirect overhead costs, many based on some common denominator of production activity such as direct labour hours. The latest method to get a lot of press is called *activity-based costing* (ABC).

With the ABC method, you identify each necessary, supporting activity in the production process and collect costs into a separate pool for each identified activity. Then you develop a *measure* for each activity – for example, the measure for the engineering department may be hours, and the measure for the maintenance department may be square feet. You use the activity measures as *cost drivers* to allocate cost to products. So if Product A needs 200 hours of the engineering department's time and Product B is a simple product that needs only 20 hours of engineering, you allocate ten times as much of the engineering cost to Product A.

The idea is that the engineering department doesn't come cheap – including the cost of their computers and equipment as well as their salaries and benefits, the total cost per hour for those engineers could be £100 to £200. The logic of the ABC cost-allocation method is that the engineering cost per hour should be allocated on the basis of the number of hours (the driver)

required by each product. In similar fashion, suppose the cost of the maintenance department is £10 per square foot per year. If Product C uses twice as much floor space as Product D, it will be charged with twice as much maintenance cost.

The ABC method has received much praise for being better than traditional allocation methods, especially for management decision-making, but keep in mind that it still requires rather arbitrary definitions of cost drivers – and having too many different cost drivers, each with its own pool of costs, isn't too practical. Cost allocation always involves arbitrary methods. Managers should be aware of which methods are being used and should challenge a method if they think that it's misleading and should be replaced with a better (though still somewhat arbitrary) method. We don't mean to put too fine a point on this, but to a large extent cost allocation boils down to a 'my arbitrary method is better than your arbitrary method' argument.

Note: Cost allocation methods should be transparent to managers who use the cost data provided to them by accountants. Managers should never have to guess about what methods are being used, or have to call upon the accountants to explain the allocation methods.

Calculating product cost

The basic equation for calculating product cost is as follows (using the example of the manufacturer from Figure 4-2):

£91.2 million total manufacturing costs ÷ 120,000 units production output = £760 product cost per unit

Looks pretty straightforward, doesn't it? Well, the equation itself may be simple, but the accuracy of the results depends directly on the accuracy of your manufacturing cost numbers. And because manufacturing processes are fairly complex, with hundreds or thousands of steps and operations, your accounting systems must be very complex and detailed to keep accurate track of all the manufacturing costs.

As we explain earlier, when introducing the example, this business manufactures just one product. Also, its product cost per unit is determined for the entire year. In actual practice, manufacturers calculate their product costs monthly or quarterly. The computation process is the same, but the frequency of doing the computation varies from business to business.

In this example the business manufactured 120,000 units and sold 110,000 units during the year. As just computed, its product cost per unit is £760. The 110,000 total units sold during the year is multiplied by the £760 product cost to compute the £83.6 million cost of goods sold expense, which is deducted against the company's revenue from selling 110,000 units during the year. The company's total manufacturing costs for the year were £91.2 million, which is £7.6 million more than the cost of goods sold expense. This remainder of the total annual manufacturing costs is recorded as an increase in the company's stock asset account, to recognise the 10,000-unit increase of units awaiting sale in the future. In Figure 4-2, note that the £760 product cost per unit is applied both to the 110,000 units sold and to the 10,000 units added to stock.

Note: As just mentioned, most manufacturers determine their product costs monthly or quarterly rather than once a year (as in the example). Product costs likely will vary in each successive period the costs are determined. Because the product costs vary from period to period, the business must choose which cost of goods sold and stock cost method to use – unless product cost remains absolutely flat and constant period to period, in which case the different methods yield the same results. Book V, Chapter 2 explains the alternative accounting methods for determining cost of goods sold expense and stock cost value.

Fixed manufacturing costs and production capacity

Product cost consists of two very distinct components: *variable manufacturing costs* and *fixed manufacturing costs*. In Figure 4-2 note that the company's variable manufacturing costs are £410 per unit and that its fixed manufacturing costs are £350 per unit. Now, what if the business had manufactured just one more unit? Its total variable manufacturing costs would have been £410 higher; these costs are driven by the actual number of units produced, so even one more unit would have caused the variable costs to increase. But the company's total fixed costs would have been the same if it had produced one more unit, or 10,000 more units for that matter. Variable manufacturing costs are bought on a per unit basis, as it were, whereas fixed manufacturing costs are bought in bulk for the whole period.

Fixed manufacturing costs are needed to provide *production capacity* – the people and physical resources needed to manufacture products – for the period. After the business has the production plant and people in place for the year, its fixed manufacturing costs can't be easily scaled down. The business is stuck with these costs over the short run. It has to make the best use it can from its production capacity.

Production capacity is a critical concept for business managers to grasp. You need to plan your production capacity well ahead of time because you need plenty of lead time to assemble the right people, equipment, land and buildings. When you have the necessary production capacity in place, you want to make sure that you're making optimal use of that capacity. The fixed costs of production capacity remain the same even as production output increases or decreases, so you may as well make optimal use of the capacity provided by those fixed costs.

The fixed cost component of product cost is called the *burden rate*. In our manufacturing example the burden rate is computed as follows (see Figure 4-2 for data):

£42.0 million total fixed manufacturing costs for period ÷ 120,000 units production output for period = £350 burden rate

Note that the burden rate depends on the number divided into total fixed manufacturing costs for the period; that is, the production output for the period. Now, here's a very important twist on our example: suppose the company had manufactured only 110,000 units during the period – equal exactly to the quantity sold during the year. Its variable manufacturing cost per unit would have been the same, or £410 per unit. But its burden rate would have been £381.82 per unit (computed by dividing the £42 million total fixed manufacturing costs by the 110,000 units production output). Each unit sold, therefore, would have cost £31.82 more, simply because the company produced fewer units (£381.82 burden rate at the 110,000 output level compared with the £350 burden rate at the 120,000 output level).

In this alternative scenario (in which only 110,000 units were produced), the company's product cost would have been £791.82 (£410 variable costs plus the £381.82 burden rate). The company's cost of goods sold, therefore, would have been £3.5 million higher for the year (£31.82 higher product cost × 110,000 units sold). This rather significant increase in its cost of goods sold expense is caused by the company producing fewer units, although it did produce all the units that it needed for sales during the year. The same total amount of fixed manufacturing costs would be spread over fewer units of production output.

Shifting the focus back to the example shown in Figure 4-2, the company's cost of goods sold benefited from the fact that it produced 10,000 more units than it sold during the year. These 10,000 units absorbed £3.5 million of its total fixed manufacturing costs for the year, and until the units are sold this £3.5 million stays in the stock asset account. It's entirely possible that the higher production level was justified – to have more stock on hand for sales growth next year. But production output can get out of hand – see the following section, 'Excessive production output for puffing up profit'.

For the example illustrated in Figure 4-2, the business's production capacity for the year is 150,000 units. However, this business produced only 120,000 units during the year, which is 30,000 units fewer than it could have produced. In other words, it operated at 80 per cent of production capacity, which is 20 per cent *idle capacity* (which isn't unusual):

120,000 units output ÷ 150,000 units capacity = 80% utilisation

Running at 80 per cent of production capacity, this business's burden rate for the year is £350 per unit (£42 million total fixed manufacturing costs ÷ 120,000 units output). The burden rate would have been higher if the company had produced, say, only 110,000 units during the year. The burden rate, in other words, is sensitive to the number of units produced. This can lead to all kinds of mischief, as explained next.

Excessive production output for puffing up profit

Whenever production output is higher than sales volume, be on guard. Excessive production can puff up the profit figure. How? Until a product is sold, the product cost goes in the stock asset account rather than the cost of goods sold expense account, meaning that the product cost is counted as a *positive* number (an asset) rather than a *negative* number (an expense). The burden rate is included in product cost, which means that this cost component goes into stock and is held there until the products are sold later. In short, when you overproduce, more of your fixed manufacturing costs for the period are moved to the stock asset account and less are moved into cost of goods sold expense, which is based on the number of units sold.

The actual costs / actual output method and when not to use it

To determine its product cost, the business in the Figure 4-2 example uses the *actual cost / actual output method* in which you take your actual costs – which may have been higher or lower than the budgeted costs for the year – and divide by the actual output for the year.

The actual costs / actual output method is appropriate in most situations. However, this method isn't appropriate and would have to be modified in two extreme situations:

✔ **Manufacturing costs are grossly excessive or wasteful due to inefficient production operations.** For example, suppose that the business represented in Figure 4-2 had to throw away £1.2 million of raw materials during the year. The £1.2 million is included in the total raw materials cost, but should be removed from the calculation of the raw material cost per unit. Instead, you treat it as a period cost – meaning that you take it directly into expense. Then the cost of

goods sold expense would be based on £750 per unit instead of £760, which lowers this expense by £1.1 million (based on the 110,000 units sold). But you still have to record the £1.2 million expense for wasted raw materials, so earnings before interest and taxes (EBIT) would be £100,000 lower.

✔ **Production output is significantly less than normal capacity utilisation.** Suppose that the Figure 4-2 business produced only 75,000 units during the year but still sold 110,000 units because it was working off a large stock carryover from the year before. Then its production capacity would be 50 per cent instead of 80 per cent. In a sense, the business wasted half of its production capacity, and you can argue that half of its fixed manufacturing costs should be charged directly to expense on the Profit and Loss statement and not included in the calculation of product cost.

You need to judge whether a stock increase is justified. Be aware that an unjustified increase may be evidence of profit manipulation or just good old-fashioned management bungling. Either way, the day of reckoning will come when the products are sold and the cost of stock becomes cost of goods sold expense – at which point the cost subtracts from the bottom line.

Recapping the example shown in Figure 4-2: The business manufactured 10,000 more units than it sold during the year. With variable manufacturing costs at £410 per unit, the business took on £4.1 million more in manufacturing costs than it would have if it had produced only the 110,000 units needed for its sales volume. In other words, if the business had produced 10,000 fewer units, its variable manufacturing costs would have been £4.1 million less. That's the nature of variable costs. In contrast, if the company had manufactured 10,000 fewer units, its *fixed* manufacturing costs wouldn't have been any less – that's the nature of fixed costs.

Of its £42 million total fixed manufacturing costs for the year, only £38.5 million ended up in the cost of goods sold expense for the year (£350 burden rate × 110,000 units sold). The other £3.5 million ended up in the stock asset account (£350 burden rate × 10,000 units stock increase). Let us be very clear here: we're not suggesting any malpractice. But the business did help its pre-tax profit to the amount of £3.5 million by producing 10,000 more units than it sold. If the business had produced only 110,000 units, equal to its sales volume for the year, then all the fixed manufacturing costs would have gone into cost of goods sold expense. As explained earlier, the expense would have been £3.5 million higher, and EBIT would have been that much lower.

Now suppose that the business manufactured 150,000 units during the year and increased its stock by 40,000 units. This may be a legitimate move if the business is anticipating a big jump in sales next year. But on the other hand, a stock increase of 40,000 units in a year in which only 110,000 units were sold may be the result of a serious overproduction mistake, and the larger stock may not be needed next year. In any case, Figure 4-3 shows what happens to production costs and – more importantly – what happens to profit at the higher production output level.

The additional 30,000 units (over and above the 120,000 units manufactured by the business in the original example) cost £410 per unit. (The precise cost may be a little higher than £410 per unit because as you start crowding your production capacity some variable costs may increase a little.) The business would need about £12.3 million more for the additional 30,000 units of production output:

> £410 variable manufacturing cost per unit × 30,000 additional units produced = £12,300,000 additional variable manufacturing costs invested in stock

But check out the business's EBIT in Figure 4-3: £23.65 million, compared with £15.95 million in Figure 4-2 – a £7.7 million increase, even though sales volume, sales prices and operating costs all remain the same. Whoa! What's going on here? The simple answer is that the cost of goods sold expense is £7.7 million less than before. But how can cost of goods sold expense be less? The business sells 110,000 units in both scenarios and variable manufacturing costs are £410 per unit in both cases.

The burden rate component of product cost in the first case is £350 (see Figure 4-2). In the second case the burden rate is only £280 (see Figure 4-3). Recall that the burden rate is computed by dividing total fixed manufacturing costs for the period by the production output during the period. Dividing by 150,000 units compared with 120,000 units reduces the burden rate from £350 to £280. The £70 lower burden rate multiplied by the 110,000 units sold results in a £7.7 million smaller cost of goods sold expense for the period, and a higher pre-tax profit of the same amount.

Management Profit and Loss Account for Year

Sales Volume	110,000	Units

	Per Unit	Totals
Sales Revenue	£1,400	£154,000,000
Cost of Goods Sold Expense	(690)	(75,900,000)
Gross Margin	£710	£78,100,000
Variable Operating Expenses	(300)	(33,000,000)
Contribution Margin	£410	£45,100,000
Fixed Operating Expenses	(195)	(21,450,000)
Earnings Before Interest and Tax (EBIT)	£215	£23,650,000
Interest Expense		(2,750,000)
Earnings Before Tax		£20,900,000
Corporation Tax Expense		(7,106,000)
Net Income		£13,794,000

Manufacturing Cost Summary for Year

Annual Production Capacity	150,000	Units
Actual Output	150,000	Units

Production Cost Components	Per Unit	Totals
Raw Materials	£215	£32,250,000
Direct Labour	125	18,750,000
Variable Overhead	70	10,500,000
Total Variable Manufacturing Costs	£410	£61,500,000
Fixed Overhead	280	42,000,000
Total Manufacturing Costs	£690	£103,500,000
To 40,000 Units Stock Increase		(27,600,000)
To 110,000 Units Sold		£75,900,000

Figure 4-3:
Example in which production output greatly exceeds sales volume, thereby boosting profit for the period.

In the first case the business puts £3.5 million of its total annual fixed manufacturing costs into the increase in stock (10,000 units increase × £350 burden rate). In the second case, in which the production output is at capacity, the business puts £11.2 million of its total fixed manufacturing costs into the increase in stock (40,000 units increase × £280 burden rate). Thus, £7.7 million more of its fixed manufacturing costs go into stock rather than cost of goods sold expense. But don't forget that stock increased 40,000 units, which is quite a large increase compared with the annual sales of 110,000 during the year just ended.

Who was responsible for the decision to go full blast and produce up to production capacity? Do the managers really expect sales to jump up enough next period to justify the much larger stock level? If they prove to be right, they'll look brilliant. But if the output level was a mistake and sales don't go up next year, they'll have you-know-what to pay next year, even though profit looks good this year. An experienced business manager knows to be on guard when stock takes such a big jump.

A View from the Top Regarding Costs

The CEO of a business gets paid to take the big-picture point of view. Using the business example in the chapter (refer to Figure 4-2 again), a typical CEO would study the management Profit and Loss statement and say something like the following:

> *Not a bad year. Total costs were just about 90 per cent of sales revenue. EBIT per unit was a little more than 10 per cent of sales price ($145 per unit ÷ $1,400 sales price). I was able to spread my fixed operating expenses over 110,000 units of sales for an average of $195 per unit. Compared with the $340 contribution margin per unit, this yielded $145 EBIT per unit. I can live with this.*

> *I'd like to improve our margins, of course, but even if we don't, we should be able to increase sales volume next year. In fact, I notice that we produced 10,000 units more than we sold this year. So, I'll put pressure on the sales manager to give me her plan for increasing sales volume next year.*

> *I realise that cost numbers can be pushed around by my sharp-pencil accountants. They keep reminding me about cost classification problems between manufacturing and non-manufacturing costs – but what the heck: it all comes out in the wash sooner or later. I watch the three major cost lines in my profit and loss statement – cost of goods sold, variable operating expenses and fixed operating expenses.*

> *I realise that some costs can be classified in one or another of these groupings. So, I expect my accountants to be consistent period to period, and I have instructed them not to make any changes without my approval. Without consistency of accounting methods, I can't reliably compare my expense numbers from period to period. In my view, it's better to be arbitrary in the same way, period after period, rather than changing cost methods to keep up with the latest cost allocation fads.*

Have a Go

1. **You can see in Table 4-1 that Firm X records £42 million fixed manufacturing overhead costs in the year.**

   Suppose, instead, that its fixed manufacturing overhead costs are £45.6 million for the year, which is an increase of £3.6 million. Would the business's operating profit be £3.6 million lower? (Assume that variable manufacturing costs per unit and operating expenses remain the same.)

Table 4-1	Internal Profit and Loss Statement for Firm X	
Operating Profit for Year	**Per Unit**	**Totals**
Sales volume (units)		110,000
Sales revenue	£1,400	£154,000,000
Cost of goods sold expense	(£760.00)	(£83,600,000)
Gross margin	£640.00	£70,400,000
Variable operating expenses	(£300.00)	(£33,000,000)
Contribution margin	£340.00	£37,400,000
Fixed operating expenses		(£21,450,000)
Operating profit		£15,950,000
Manufacturing Activity Summary for the Year		
Annual production capacity (units)		150,000
Actual output (units)		120,000
Raw materials	£215.00	£25,800,000
Direct labour	£125.00	£15,000,000
Variable manufacturing overhead costs	£70.00	£8,400,000
Total variable manufacturing costs	£410.00	£49,200,000
Fixed manufacturing overhead costs	£350.00	£42,000,000
Product cost and total manufacturing costs	£760.00	£91,200,000

2. **Please use the information found in Table 4-2 to answer the following:**

   Towards the end of the year, the managing director (MD) of Firm Y looks at the preliminary numbers for operating profit and doesn't like what she sees. She promised the board of directors that operating profit for the year would come in at £4.85 million. In fact, her bonus depends on hitting that operating profit target. Time is still left before the end of the year to crank up production output for the year. Therefore, she orders

Table 4-2	Internal Profit and Loss Statement for Firm Y		
		Firm Y	
Operating Profit for Year		*Per Unit*	*Totals*
Sales volume (units)			500,000
Sales revenue		£85.00	£42,500,000
Cost of goods sold expense		(£56.00)	(£28,000,000)
Gross margin		£29.00	£14,500,000
Variable operating expenses		(£12.50)	(£6,250,000)
Contribution margin		£16.50	£8,250,000
Fixed operating expenses			(£5,000,000)
Operating profit			£3,250,000
Manufacturing Activity Summary for the Year			
Annual production capacity (units)			800,000
Actual output (units)			500,000
Raw materials		£15.00	£7,500,000
Direct labour		£20.00	£10,000,000
Variable manufacturing overhead costs		£5.00	£2,500,000
Total variable manufacturing costs		£40.00	£20,000,000
Fixed manufacturing overhead costs		£16.00	£8,000,000
Product cost and total manufacturing costs		£56.00	£28,000,000

that production output be stepped up. The MD asks you, as the chief accountant, to determine what the production output level for the year would have to be in order to report £4.85 million operating profit for the year. Of course, you have ethical qualms about doing so, but you need the job. Therefore, you reluctantly decide to do the calculation. Determine the production output level that would yield £4.85 million operating profit for the year.

Answering the Have a Go Questions

1. **No, operating profit wouldn't be £3.6 million lower.**

   Table 4-3 shows that operating profit would be £3.3 million lower. The higher fixed manufacturing overhead costs drive up the product cost per unit, from £760 to £790, or £30 per unit. However, the business sells only 110,000 units, and so the £30 higher product cost per unit increases

Table 4-3	Internal Profit and Loss Statement for Firm X	
Operating Profit for Year	*Per Unit*	*Totals*
Sales volume (units)		110,000
Sales revenue	£1,400	£154,000,000
Cost of goods sold expense (see after table)	(£790.00)	(£86,900,000)
Gross margin	£610.00	£67,100,000
Variable operating expenses	(£300.00)	(£33,000,000)
Contribution margin	£310.00	£34,100,000
Fixed operating expenses		(£21,450,000)
Operating profit		£12,650,000
Manufacturing Activity Summary for the Year		
Annual production capacity (units)		150,000
Actual output (units)		120,000
Raw materials	£215.00	£25,800,000
Direct labour	£125.00	£15,000,000
Variable manufacturing overhead costs	£70.00	£8,400,000
Total variable manufacturing costs	£410.00	£49,200,000
Fixed manufacturing overhead costs	£380.00	£45,600,000
Product cost and total manufacturing costs	£790.00	£94,800,000

the cost of goods sold expense by only £3.3 million (£30 increase in product cost × 110,000 units sales volume = £3,300,000). Therefore, operating profit decreases by £3.3 million.

The operating profit decrease still leaves £300,000 of the total £3.6 million fixed manufacturing overhead costs increase to explain. The 10,000 units increase in stock absorbs this additional amount of fixed manufacturing overhead costs; including fixed manufacturing overhead costs in product cost is called *absorption costing*. Some accountants argue that product cost should include only variable manufacturing costs and not include any fixed manufacturing overhead costs. This practice is called *direct costing*, or *variable costing*, and it isn't generally accepted. GAAP require that the fixed manufacturing overhead cost must be included in product cost.

2. **In answer to question 2. The accountant has calculated that in order for the operating profit of Company Y to be £4.85Million, the business must manufacture at least 625,000 units. See Table 4-4 which shows that if the business manufactures 625,000 units, its operating profit becomes £4.85 million.**

Table 4-4	Internal Profit and Loss Report for Firm Y	
	Per Unit	**Totals**
Operating Profit Report for Year		
Sales volume (units)		500,000
Sales revenue	£85.00	£42,500,000
Cost of goods sold expense (see the product cost and total manufacturing costs in the Per Unit column)	(£52.80)	(£26,400,000)
Gross margin	£32.20	£16,100,000
Variable operating expenses	(£12.50)	(£6,250,000)
Contribution margin	£19.70	£9,850,000
Fixed operating expenses		(£5,000,000)
Operating profit		£4,850,000
Manufacturing Activity Summary for Year		
Annual production capacity (units)		800,000
Actual output (units)		625,000
Raw materials	£15.00	£9,375,000
Direct labour	£20.00	£12,500,000
Variable manufacturing overhead cost	£5.00	£3,125,000
Total variable manufacturing costs	£40.00	£25,000,000
Fixed manufacturing overhead costs	£12.80	£8,000,000
Product cost and total manufacturing costs	£52.80	£33,000,000

The MD wants £1.6 million more profit than shown in Table 4-2 (£4,850,000 profit target – £3,250,000 profit at 500,000 units production level = £1,600,000 additional profit). The only profit driver that changes with a higher production level is the burden rate, which has to decline £3.20 per unit in order to achieve the additional profit (£1,600,000 additional profit wanted ÷ 500,000 units sales volume = £3.20 decrease needed in burden rate). The burden rate has to decrease £3.20, from £16 (see Table 4-2) to £12.80. The production output level has to be 625,000 units to get the burden rate down to £12.80 (£8,000,000 fixed manufacturing overhead costs ÷ £12.80 burden rate = 625,000 units).

Whether jacking up production to 625,000 units is ethical when sales are only 500,000 units for the year is a serious question. The members of Firm Y's board of directors should definitely challenge the MD on why such a large stock increase is needed. We certainly would!

Chapter 5

Business Budgeting

A business can't open its doors each day without having some idea of what to expect. And it can't close its doors at the end of the day not knowing what happened. In the Boy Scouts, the motto is 'Be Prepared'. Likewise, a business should plan and be prepared for its future, and should control its actual performance to reach its financial goals. The only question is how.

Budgeting is one answer. Please be careful with this term. Budgeting does *not* refer to putting a financial straitjacket on a business. Instead, business budgeting refers to setting specific goals and having the detailed plans necessary to achieve the goals. Business budgeting is built on realistic forecasts for the coming period, and demands that managers develop a thorough understanding of the profit blueprint of the business as well as the financial effects of the business's profit-making activities. A business budget is an integrated plan of action – not simply a few trend lines on a financial chart. Business managers have two broad options: they can wait for results to be reported to them on a 'look back' basis, or they can look ahead and plan what profit and cash flow should be, and then compare actual results against the plan. Budgeting is the method used to enact this second option.

The financial statements included in the annual financial report of a business are prepared *after the fact*; that is, the statements are based on actual transactions that have already taken place. Budgeted financial statements, on the other hand, are prepared *before the fact*, and are based on future transactions that you expect to take place based on the business's profit and financial strategy and goals. These forward-looking financial statements are referred to as *pro forma*, which is Latin for 'provided in advance'. **Note:** Budgeted financial statements aren't reported outside the business; they're strictly for internal management use.

You can see a business's budget most easily in its set of *budgeted financial statements* – its budgeted Profit and Loss statement, Balance Sheet and cash flow statement. Preparing these three budgeted financial statements requires a lot of time and effort; managers do detailed analysis to determine how to improve the financial performance of the business. The vigilance required in budgeting helps to maintain and improve profit performance and to plan cash flow.

Budgeting is much more than slap-dashing together a few figures. A budget is an integrated financial plan put down on paper, or these days we should say entered in computer spreadsheets. Planning is the key characteristic of budgeting. The budgeted financial statements encapsulate the financial plan of the business for the coming year.

The Reasons for Budgeting

Managers don't just look out the window and come up with budget numbers. Budgeting is not pie-in-the-sky, wishful thinking. Business budgeting – to have real value – must start with a critical analysis of the most recent actual performance and position of the business by the managers who are responsible for the results. Then the managers decide on specific and concrete goals for the coming year. Budgets can be done for more than one year, but the key stepping stone into the future is the budget for the coming year – see the sidebar 'Taking it one game at a time'.

In short, budgeting demands a fair amount of management time and energy. Budgets have to be worth this time and effort. So why should a business go to the trouble of budgeting? Business managers do budgeting and prepare budgeted financial statements for three quite different reasons – distinguishing them from each other is useful.

The modelling reasons for budgeting

To construct budgeted financial statements, you need good models of the profit, cash flow and financial condition of your business. Models are blueprints, or schematics, of how things work. A business budget is, at its core, a financial blueprint of the business.

Taking it one game at a time

A company generally prepares one-year budgets, although many businesses also develop budgets for two, three and five years. However, reaching out beyond a year becomes quite tentative and very iffy. Making forecasts and estimates for the next 12 months is tough enough. A one-year budget is much more definite and detailed in comparison to longer-term budgets. As they say in the sports world, a business should take it one game (or year) at a time.

Looking down the road beyond one year is a good idea, to set long-term goals and to develop long-term strategy. But long-term planning is different to long-term budgeting.

Note: Don't be intimidated by the term *model*. It simply refers to an explicit, condensed description of how profit, cash flow, and assets and liabilities behave. For example, Book V, Chapter 3 presents a model of a management Profit and Loss statement. A model is analytical, but not all models are mathematical. In fact, none of the financial models in this book are the least bit mathematical – but you do have to look at each factor of the model and how it interacts with one or more other factors. The simple accounting equation, assets = liabilities + owners' equity, is a model of the Balance Sheet, for example. And, as Book V, Chapter 3 explains, profit = contribution margin per unit × units sold in excess of the break-even point.

Budgeting relies on financial models, or blueprints, that serve as the foundation for each budgeted financial statement. These blueprints are briefly explained, as follows:

- ✔ **Budgeted management profit and loss account:** Book V, Chapter 3 presents a design for the internal Profit and Loss statement that provides the basic information that managers need for making decisions and exercising control. This internal (for managers only) profit report contains information that isn't divulged outside the business. The management Profit and Loss statement shown in Figure 3-2 in Book V, Chapter 3 serves as a hands-on profit model – one that highlights the critical variables that drive profit. This management Profit and Loss statement separates variable and fixed expenses and includes sales volume, contribution margin per unit and other factors that determine profit performance. The management Profit and Loss statement is like a schematic that shows the path to the bottom line. It reveals the factors that must be improved in order to improve profit performance in the coming period.

- ✔ **Budgeted Balance Sheet:** The key connections and ratios between sales revenue and expenses and their related assets and liabilities are the elements of the basic model for the budgeted Balance Sheet.

✔ **Budgeted cash flow statement:** The changes in assets and liabilities from their balances at the end of the year just concluded and the balances at the end of the coming year determine cash flow from profit for the coming year. These changes constitute the basic model of cash flow from profit, which Book IV, Chapter 3 explains (a comparative Balance Sheet, which can be used to provide information for the cash flow statement, can be found in the 'Have a Go' section). The other sources and uses of cash depend on managers' strategic decisions regarding capital expenditures that will be made during the coming year, and how much new capital will be raised by increased debt and from owners' additional investment of capital in the business.

In short, budgeting requires good working models of profit performance, financial condition (assets and liabilities) and cash flow from profit. Constructing good budgets is a strong incentive for businesses to develop financial models that not only help in the budgeting process but also help managers make day-to-day decisions.

Planning reasons for budgeting

One main purpose of budgeting is to develop a definite and detailed financial plan for the coming period. To do budgeting, managers have to establish explicit financial objectives for the coming year and identify exactly what has to be done to accomplish these financial objectives. Budgeted financial statements and their supporting schedules provide clear destination points – the financial flight plan for a business.

The process of putting together a budget directs attention to the specific things that you must do to achieve your profit objectives and to optimise your assets and capital requirements. Basically, budgets are a form of planning, and planning pushes managers to answer the question: 'How are we going to get there from here?'

Budgeting also has other planning-related benefits:

✔ **Budgeting encourages a business to articulate its vision, strategy and goals.** A business needs a clearly-stated strategy guided by an overarching vision, and should have definite and explicit goals. It's not enough for business managers to have strategy and goals in their heads – and nowhere else. Developing budgeted financial statements forces managers to be explicit and definite about the objectives of the business, and to formulate realistic plans for achieving the business objectives.

✔ **Budgeting imposes discipline and deadlines on the planning process.**
Many busy managers have trouble finding enough time for lunch, let alone
planning for the upcoming financial period. Budgeting pushes managers
to set aside time to prepare a detailed plan that serves as a road map for
the business. Good planning results in a concrete course of action that
details how a company plans to achieve its financial objectives.

Management control reasons for budgeting

Budgets can be and usually are used as a means of *management control*,
which involves comparing budgets against actual performance and holding
individual managers responsible for keeping the business on schedule in
reaching its financial objectives. The board of directors of a corporation
focus their attention on the master budget for the whole business: the
budgeted management Profit and Loss statement, the budgeted Balance
Sheet and the budgeted cash flow statement for the coming year.

The chief executive officer and the chairman of the business focus on the
master budget. They also look at how each manager in the organisation is
doing on his part of the master budget. As you move down the organisation
chart of a business, managers have narrower responsibilities – say, for the
business's north-eastern territory or for one major product line; therefore,
the master budget is broken down into parts that follow the business's organisational structure. In other words, the master budget is put together from
many pieces, one for each separate organisational unit of the business. So,
for example, the manager of one of the company's far-flung warehouses has a
separate budget for expenses and stock levels for his area.

By using budget targets as benchmarks against which actual performance
is compared, managers can closely monitor progress toward (or deviations
from) the budget goals and timetable. You use a budget plan like a navigation
chart to keep your business on course. Significant variations from budget
raise red flags, in which case you can determine that performance is off course
or that the budget needs to be revised because of unexpected developments.

For management control, the annual budgeted management Profit and Loss
statement is divided into months or quarters. The budgeted Balance Sheet
and budgeted cash flow statement are also put on a monthly or quarterly
basis. The business should not wait too long to compare budgeted sales
revenue and expenses against actual performance (or to compare actual
cash flows and asset levels against the budget timetable). You need to take
prompt action when problems arise, such as a divergence between budgeted
expenses and actual expenses. Profit is the main thing to pay attention to, but
debtors and stock can get out of control (become too high relative to actual
sales revenue and cost of goods sold expense), causing cash flow problems.

(Book IV, Chapter 3 explains how increases in debtors and stock are negative factors on cash flow from profit.) A business can't afford to ignore its Balance Sheet and cash flow numbers until the end of the year.

Other benefits of budgeting

Budgeting has advantages and ramifications that go beyond the financial dimension and have more to do with business management in general. These points are briefly discussed as follows:

- **Budgeting forces managers to do better forecasting.** Managers should constantly scan the business environment to identify sea changes that can impact the business. Vague generalisations about what the future might hold for the business aren't quite good enough for assembling a budget. Managers are forced to put their predictions into definite and concrete forecasts.

- **Budgeting motivates managers and employees by providing useful yardsticks for evaluating performance and for setting managers' compensation when goals are achieved.** The budgeting process can have a good motivational impact on employees and managers by involving managers in the budgeting process (especially in setting goals and objectives) and by providing incentives to managers to strive for and achieve the business's goals and objectives. Budgets can be used to reward good results. Budgets provide useful information for superiors to evaluate the performance of managers. Budgets supply baseline financial information for incentive compensation plans. The profit plan (budget) for the year can be used to award year-end bonuses according to whether designated goals are achieved.

- **Budgeting is essential in writing a business plan.** New and emerging businesses must present a convincing *business plan* when raising capital. Because these businesses may have little or no history, the managers and owners of a small business must demonstrate convincingly that the company has a clear strategy and a realistic plan to make money. A coherent, realistic budget forecast is an essential component of a business plan. Venture capital sources definitely want to see the budgeted financial statements of the business.

In larger businesses, budgets are typically used to hold managers accountable for their areas of responsibility in the organisation; actual results are compared against budgeted goals and timetables, and variances are highlighted. Managers don't mind taking credit for *favourable* variances, or when actual comes in better than budget. Beating the budget for the period, after all, calls attention to outstanding performance. But *unfavourable* variances are a different matter. If the manager's budgeted goals and targets are fair and reasonable, the manager should carefully analyse what went wrong and what needs to be improved. But if the manager perceives the budgeted goals and targets to be arbitrarily imposed by superiors and not realistic, serious motivational problems can arise.

In reviewing the performance of their subordinates, managers should handle unfavourable variances very carefully. Stern action may be called for, but managers should recognise that the budget benchmarks may not be entirely fair, and should make allowances for unexpected developments that occur after the budget goals and targets are established.

Budgeting and Management Accounting

What we say earlier in the chapter can be likened to an advertisement for budgeting – emphasising the reasons for and advantages of budgeting by a business. So every business does budgeting, right? Nope. Smaller businesses generally do little or no budgeting – and even many larger businesses avoid budgeting. The reasons are many, and mostly practical in nature.

Some businesses are in relatively mature stages of their life cycle or operate in an industry that is mature and stable. These companies don't have to plan for any major changes or discontinuities. Next year will be a great deal like last year. The benefits of going through a formal budgeting process don't seem worth the time and cost to them. At the other extreme, a business may be in a very uncertain environment; attempting to predict the future seems pointless. A business may lack the expertise and experience to prepare budgeted financial statements, and it may not be willing to pay the cost for an accountant or outside consultant to help.

Every business – whether it does budgeting or not – should design internal accounting reports that provide the information managers need to control the business. Obviously, managers should keep close tabs on what's going on throughout the business. A business may not do any budgeting, and thus it doesn't prepare budgeted financial statements. But its managers should receive regular Profit and Loss statements, Balance Sheets and cash flow statements – and these key internal financial statements should contain detailed management control information. Other specialised accounting reports may be needed as well.

Most business managers, in our experience, would tell you that the accounting reports they get are reasonably good for management control. Their accounting reports provide the detailed information they need for keeping a close watch on the thousand and one details about the business (or their particular sphere of responsibility in the business organisation). Their main criticisms are that too much information is reported to them and all the information is flat, as if all the information is equally relevant. Managers are very busy people, and have only so much time to read the accounting reports coming to them. Managers have a valid beef on this score, we think. Ideally, significant deviations and problems should be highlighted in the accounting reports they receive – but separating the important from the not-so-important is easier said than done.

If you were to ask a cross-section of business managers how useful their accounting reports are for making decisions, you would get a different answer than how good the accounting reports are for management control. Business managers make many decisions affecting profit: setting sales prices, buying products, determining wages and salaries, hiring independent contractors and purchasing fixed assets are just a few that come to mind. Managers should carefully analyse how their actions would impact profit before reaching final decisions. Managers need internal Profit and Loss statements that are good profit models – that make clear the critical variables that affect profit (see Figure 3-2 in Book V, Chapter 3 for an example). Well-designed management Profit and Loss statements are absolutely essential for helping managers make good decisions.

Keep in mind that almost all business decisions involve non-financial and non-quantifiable factors that go beyond the information included in management accounting reports. For example, the accounting department of a business can calculate the cost savings of a wage cut, or the elimination of overtime hours by employees, or a change in the retirement plan for employees – and the manager would certainly look at this data. But such decisions must consider many other factors such as effects on employee morale and productivity, the possibility of the union going out on strike, legal issues and so on. In short, accounting reports provide only part of the information needed for business decisions, though an essential part for sure.

Needless to say, the internal accounting reports to managers should be clear and straightforward. The manner of presentation and means of communication should be attention getting. A manager shouldn't have to call the accounting department for an explanation. Designing management accounting reports is a separate topic – one beyond the limits of this book.

In the absence of budgeting by a business, the internal accounting reports to its managers become the major – often the only – regular source of financial information to them. Without budgeting, the internal accounting reports have to serve a dual function – both for control and for planning. The managers use the accounting reports to critically review what's happened (control), and use the information in the reports to make decisions for the future (planning).

Before leaving the topic, we have one final observation to share with you. Many management accounting reports that we've seen could be improved. Accounting systems, unfortunately, give so much attention to the demands of preparing external financial statements and tax returns that the needs managers have for good internal reports are too often overlooked or ignored. The accounting reports in many businesses don't speak to the managers receiving them – the reports are too voluminous and technical, and aren't focused on the most urgent and important problems facing the managers. Designing good internal accounting reports for managers is a demanding task, to be sure. Every business should take a hard look at its internal management accounting reports and identify what needs to be improved.

Budgeting in Action

Suppose you're the general manager of one of a large company's several divisions. You have broad authority to run this division, as well as the responsibility for meeting the financial expectations for your division. To be more specific, your profit responsibility is to produce a satisfactory annual operating profit, or earnings before interest and tax (EBIT). (Interest and tax expenses are handled at a higher level in the organisation.)

The CEO has made clear to you that he expects your division to increase EBIT during the coming year by about 10 per cent (£256,000, to be exact). In fact, he's asked you to prepare a budgeted management Profit and Loss statement showing your plan for increasing your division's EBIT by this target amount. He's also asked you to prepare a budgeted cash flow from profit based on your profit plan for the coming year.

Figure 5-1 presents the management Profit and Loss statement of your division for the year just ended. The format of this accounting report follows the profit model discussed in Book V, Chapter 3, which explains profit behaviour and how to increase profit. Note that fixed operating expenses are separated from the two variable operating expenses. To simplify the discussion, we've significantly condensed your management Profit and Loss statement. (Your actual reports would include much more detailed information about sales and expenses.) Also, we assume that you sell only one product, to keep the number crunching to a minimum.

Most businesses, or the major divisions of a large business, sell a mix of several different products. General Motors, for example, sells many different makes and models of cars and commercial vehicles, to say nothing about its other products. The next time you visit your local hardware store, look at the number of products on the shelves. The assortment of products sold by a business and the quantities sold of each that make up its total sales revenue

	Totals for Period	Per Unit
Unit Sales Volume =	26,000	
Sales Revenue	£ 26,000,000	£1,000.00
Cost of Goods Sold Expense	14,300,000	550.00
Gross Margin	£ 11,700,000	£450.00
Revenue-driven Operating Expenses	2,080,000	80.00
Volume-driven Operating Expenses	1,300,000	50.00
Contribution Margin	£ 8,320,000	£320.00
Fixed Operating Expenses	5,720,000	
Operating Profit	£ 2,600,000	

Figure 5-1: Management Profit and Loss statement for year just ended.

is referred to as its *sales mix*. As a general rule, certain products have higher profit margins than others. Some products may have extremely low profit margins; these are called *loss leaders*. The marketing strategy for loss leaders is to use them as magnets to get customers to buy your higher-profit-margin products along with their purchase of the loss leaders. Shifting the sales mix to a higher proportion of higher-profit-margin products has the effect of increasing the average profit margin on all products sold. (A shift to lower-profit-margin products would have the opposite effect, of course.) Budgeting sales revenue and expenses for the coming year must include any planned shifts in the company's sales mix.

Developing your profit strategy and budgeted Profit and Loss statement

Suppose that you and your managers, with the assistance of your accounting staff, have analysed your fixed operating expenses line by line for the coming year. Some of these fixed expenses will actually be reduced or eliminated next year. But the large majority of these costs will continue next year, and most are subject to inflation. Based on careful studies and estimates, you and your staff forecast that your total fixed operating expenses for next year will be £6,006,000 (including £835,000 depreciation expense, compared with the £780,000 depreciation expense for last year).

Thus, you will need to earn £8,862,000 total contribution margin next year:

£2,856,000	EBIT goal (£2,600,000 last year plus £256,000 budgeted increase)
+ 6,006,000	Budgeted fixed operating expenses next year
£8,862,000	Total contribution margin goal next year

This is your main profit budget goal for next year, assuming that fixed operating expenses are kept in line. Fortunately, your volume-driven variable operating expenses shouldn't increase next year. These are mainly transportation costs, and the shipping industry is in a very competitive 'hold-the-price-down' mode of operations that should last through the coming year. The cost per unit shipped shouldn't increase, but if you sell and ship more units next year, the expense will increase in proportion.

You've decided to hold the revenue-driven operating expenses at 8 per cent of sales revenue during the coming year, the same as for the year just ended. These are sales commissions, and you've already announced to your sales staff that their sales commission percentage will remain the same during the coming year. On the other hand, your purchasing manager has told you to plan on a 4 per cent product cost increase next year – from £550 per unit to £572 per unit, or an increase of £22 per unit. Thus, your unit contribution margin would drop from £320 to £298 (if the other factors that determine margin remain the same).

One way to attempt to achieve your total contribution margin objective next year is to load all the needed increase on sales volume and keep sales price the same. (We're not suggesting that this strategy is a good one, but it's a good point of departure.) At the lower unit contribution margin, your sales volume next year would have to be 29,738 units:

£8,862,000 total contribution margin goal ÷ £298 contribution margin per unit = 29,738 units sales volume

Compared with last year's 26,000 units sales volume, you would have to increase your sales by over 14 per cent. This may not be feasible.

After discussing this scenario with your sales manager, you conclude that sales volume can't be increased by 14 per cent. You'll have to raise the sales price to provide part of the needed increase in total contribution margin and to offset the increase in product cost. After much discussion, you and your sales manager decide to increase the sales price by 3 per cent. Based on the

3 per cent sales price increase and the 4 per cent product cost increase, your unit contribution margin next year is determined as follows:

Unit Contribution Margin Next Year	
Sales price	£1,030.00
Less: Product cost	£572.00
Less: Revenue-driven operating expenses	£82.40
Less: Volume-driven variable operating expenses	£50.00
Equals: Contribution margin per unit	£325.60

At this £325.60 budgeted contribution margin per unit, you determine the total sales volume needed next year to reach your profit goal as follows:

£8,862,000 total contribution margin goal next year ÷ £325.60 contribution margin per unit = 27,217 units sales volume

This sales volume is about 5 per cent higher than last year (1,217 additional units over the 26,000 sales volume last year = about 5 per cent increase).

If you don't raise the sales price, your division has to increase sales volume by 14 per cent (as calculated earlier). If you increase the sales price by just 3 per cent, the sales volume increase you need to achieve your profit goal next year is only 5 per cent. Does this make sense? Well, this is just one of many alternative strategies for next year. Perhaps you could increase sales price by 4 per cent. But, you know that most of your customers are sensitive to a sales price increase, and your competitors may not follow with their own sales price increase.

After lengthy consultation with your sales manager, you finally decide to go with the 3 per cent sales price increase combined with the 5 per cent sales volume growth as your official budget strategy. Accordingly, you forward your budgeted management Profit and Loss statement to the CEO. Figure 5-2 summarises this profit budget for the coming year. This summary-level budgeted management Profit and Loss statement is supplemented with appropriate schedules to provide additional detail about sales by types of customers and other relevant information. Also, your annual profit plan is broken down into quarters (perhaps months) to provide benchmarks for comparing actual performance during the year against your budgeted targets and timetable.

	Totals for Period	Per Unit
Unit Sales Volume =	27,217	
Sales Revenue	£ 28,033,968	£1,030.00
Cost of Goods Sold Expense	15,568,378	572.00
Gross Margin	£ 12,465,590	£458.00
Revenue-driven Operating Expenses	2,242,717	82.40
Volume-driven Operating Expenses	1,360,872	50.00
Contribution Margin	£ 8,862,000	£325.60
Fixed Operating Expenses	6,006,000	
Operating Profit	£ 2,856,000	

Figure 5-2:
Budgeted
Profit
and Loss
statement
for coming
year.

Budgeting cash flow from profit for the coming year

The budgeted profit plan (refer to Figure 5-2) is the main focus of attention, but the CEO also requests that all divisions present a *budgeted cash flow from profit* for the coming year. **Remember:** The profit you're responsible for as general manager of the division is earnings before interest and tax (EBIT) – not net income after interest and tax.

Book IV, Chapter 3 explains that increases in debtors, stock and prepaid expenses *hurt* cash flow from profit and that increases in creditors and accrued liabilities *help* cash flow from profit. You should compare your budgeted management Profit and Loss statement for the coming year (Figure 5-2) with your actual statement for last year (Figure 5-1). This side-by-side comparison (not shown here) reveals that sales revenue and all expenses are higher next year.

Therefore, your short-term operating assets, as well as the liabilities that are driven by operating expenses, will increase at the higher sales revenue and expense levels next year – unless you can implement changes to prevent the increases.

For example, sales revenue increases from £26,000,000 last year to the budgeted £28,033,968 for next year – an increase of £2,033,968. Your debtors balance was five weeks of annual sales last year. Do you plan to tighten up the credit terms offered to customers next year – a year in which you'll raise the sales price and also plan to increase sales volume? We doubt it. More likely, you'll keep your debtors balance at five weeks of annual sales.

Assume that you decide to offer your customers the same credit terms next year. Thus, the increase in sales revenue will cause debtors to increase by £195,574 ($\frac{5}{52}$ × £2,033,968 sales revenue increase).

Last year, stock was 13 weeks of annual cost of goods sold expense. You may be in the process of implementing stock reduction techniques. If you really expect to reduce the average time stock will be held in stock before being sold, you should inform your accounting staff so that they can include this key change in the Balance Sheet and cash flow models. Otherwise, they'll assume that the past ratios for these vital connections will continue next year.

Figure 5-3 presents a summary of your budgeted cash flow from profit (the EBIT for your division) based on the information given for this example and using the ratios explained in Book IV, Chapter 3 for short-term operating assets and liabilities. For example, debtors increases by £195,574, as just explained. And stock increases by £317,095 ($\frac{13}{52}$ × £1,268,378 cost of goods sold expense increase). *Note:* Increases in accrued interest payable and income tax payable aren't included in your budgeted cash flow. Your profit responsibility ends at the operating profit line, or earnings before interest and income tax expenses.

You submit this budgeted cash flow from profit statement (Figure 5-3) to top management. Top management expects you to control the increases in your short-term assets and liabilities so that the actual cash flow generated by your division next year comes in on target. The cash flow from profit of your division (minus the small amount needed to increase the working cash balance held by your division for operating purposes) will be transferred to the central treasury of the business.

Figure 5-3:
Budgeted
cash flow
from profit
statement
for coming
year.

Budgeted Operating Profit (See Figure 10-2)	£2,856,000
Accounts Receivable Increase	(195,574)
Inventory Increase	(317,095)
Prepaid Expenses Increase	(26,226)
Depreciation Expense	835,000
Accounts Payable Increase	34,968
Accrued Expenses Payable Increase	52,453
Budgeted Cash Flow From Operating Profit	£3,239,526

Business budgeting versus government budgeting: Only the name is the same

Business and government budgeting are more different than alike. Government budgeting is preoccupied with allocating scarce resources among many competing demands. From national agencies down to local education authorities, government entities have only so much revenue available. They have to make very difficult choices regarding how to spend their limited tax revenue.

Formal budgeting is legally required for almost all government entities. First, a budget request is submitted. After money is appropriated, the budget document becomes legally binding on the government agency. Government budgets are legal straitjackets; the government entity has to stay within the amounts appropriated for each expenditure category. Any changes from the established budgets need formal approval and are difficult to get through the system.

A business isn't legally required to use budgeting. A business can use its budget as it pleases and can even abandon its budget in midstream. Unlike the government, the revenue of a business isn't constrained; a business can do many things to increase sales revenue. In short, a business has much more flexibility in its budgeting. Both business and government should apply the general principle of cost/benefits analysis to make sure that they're getting the best value for money. But a business can pass its costs to its customers in the sales prices it charges. In contrast, government has to raise taxes to spend more.

Capital Budgeting

This chapter focuses on profit budgeting for the coming year, and budgeting the cash flow from that profit. These two are hardcore components of business budgeting – but not the whole story. Another key element of the budgeting process is to prepare a *capital expenditures budget* for top management review and approval. A business has to take a hard look at its long-term operating assets – in particular, the capacity, condition and efficiency of these resources – and decide whether it needs to expand and modernise its fixed assets. In most cases, a business would have to invest substantial sums of money in purchasing new fixed assets or retrofitting and upgrading its old fixed assets. These long-term investments require major cash outlays. So, a business (or each division of the business) prepares a formal list of the fixed assets to be purchased or upgraded. The money for these major outlays comes from the central treasury of the business. Accordingly, the capital expenditures budget goes to the highest levels in the organisation for review and final approval. The chief financial officer, the CEO and the board of directors of the business go over a capital expenditure budget request with a fine-tooth comb.

At the company-wide level, the financial officers merge the profit and cash flow budgets of all divisions. The budgets submitted by one or more of the divisions may be returned for revision before final approval is given. One main concern is whether the collective total of cash flow from all the units provides enough money for the capital expenditures that have to be made during the coming year for new fixed assets – and to meet the other demands for cash, such as for cash distributions from profit. The business may have to raise more capital from debt or equity sources during the coming year to close the gap between cash flow from profit and its needs for cash. The financial officers need to be sure that any proposed capital expenditures make good business sense. We look at this in the next three sections. If the expenditure is worthwhile, they may need to raise more money to pay for it.

Deducing payback

The simplest way to evaluate an investment is to calculate *payback* – how long it takes you to get your money back. Figure 5-4 shows an investment that calls for £20,000 cash up front in the expectation of getting £25,000 cash back over the next five years. The investment is forecasted to return a total of £20,000 by the end of year 4, so we say that this investment has a four-year payback.

When calculating the return on long-term investments, we use cash rather than profit. This is because we need to compare like with like: investments are paid for in cash or by committing cash, so we need to calculate the return using cash too.

Let's suppose that we have two competing projects from which we have to choose only one. Figure 5-5 sets out the maths. Both projects have a four-year payback, in that the outlay is recovered in that period; so this technique tells us that both projects are equally acceptable, as long as we're content to recover our outlay by year 4.

	£
Initial cost of investment	20,000
Annual net cash inflows	
Year 1	1,000
Year 2	4,000
Year 3	8,000
Year 4	7,000
Year 5	5,000
Total cash in	25,000

Figure 5-4: Calculating payback.

	£ Project 1	£ Project 2
Initial cost of investment	20,000	20,000
Annual net cash inflows		
Year 1	1,000	3,000
Year 2	4,000	5,000
Year 3	8,000	8,000
Year 4	7,000	8,000
Year 5	5,000	10,000
Total cash in	25,000	34,000

Figure 5-5: Comparing investments using payback.

However, this is only part of the story. We can see at a glance that Project 2 produces £9,000 more cash over five years than Project 1 does. We also get a lot more cash back in the first two years with Project 2, which must be better – as well as safer for the investor. Payback fails to send those signals, but is still a popular tool because of its simplicity.

Discounting cash flow

A pound today is more valuable than a pound in one, two or more years' time. For us to make sound investment decisions, we need to ask how much we would pay now to get a pound back at some date in the future. If we know we can earn 10 per cent interest from a bank then we would only pay out 90p now to get that pound in one year's time. The 90p represents the *net present value* (NPV) of that pound – the amount we would pay now to get the cash at some future date.

In effect what we're doing is discounting the future cash flow using a percentage that equates to the minimum return that we want to earn. The further out that return, the less we would pay now in order to get it.

The formula we use to discount the cash flow is

$$\text{Present value } (PV) = \pounds P \times 1/(1+r)^n$$

where $\pounds P$ is the initial investment, r is the interest expressed as a decimal and n is the year when the cash will flow in. (For example, in year 1 $n = 1$, in year 2 it will be 2 and so on). So if we require a 15 per cent return, we should only be prepared to pay 87p now to get £1 in one year's time, 76p for a pound in two years' time and just 50p now for a pound coming in five years' time.

Take a look at Figure 5-6. If we use a discount rate of 15 per cent (which is a very average return on capital for a business), the picture doesn't look so rosy. Far from paying back in four years and producing £25,000 cash for an outlay of £20,000, Project 1 is actually paying out less money (£15,642) in real terms, allowing for the time value of money, than we'ave paid out.

Figure 5-6:
Comparing cash with the net present value of that cash at 15 per cent discount rate.

	Year 1	Year 2	Year 3	Year 4	Year 5	Total
Cash in	1,000	4,000	8,000	7,000	5,000	25,000
NPV of cash	870	3,025	5,260	4,002	2,486	15,642

Calculating the internal rate of return

NPV is a powerful concept, though a slightly esoteric one. All we know so far about our attempt to evaluate Project 1 is that if we aim for a return of 15 per cent, our returns will be disappointing. So, we move on to the next stage in our quest for a sound way to appraise capital investment proposals – calculating exactly what the return on investment will be.

To arrive at this figure we need to calculate the actual return the project made on the discounted cash flow – the *internal rate of return* (IRR). To do this, we need to find the value for '*r*' in the NPV formula (see the section 'Discounting cash flow') that ensures the present value of the future cash flow equals the cost of the investment. In the case of Project 1, the IRR is just short of 7 per cent.

The IRR is a number you can use to compare one project with another to assess quickly which is superior from a financial point of view. For example, Project 2 has an IRR of 17 per cent, which is clearly better than that of Project 1, a fact not revealed by using the payback method.

Arriving at the cost of capital

No new capital investment would make much sense if it didn't at least cover the cost of the capital used to finance it. This cost is known in the trade as the *hurdle rate*, because that is the level of return any project has to beat. Say you've worked out the cost of equity as being 15 per cent. That should cover the dividends and the fairly high costs associated with raising the dosh. Next comes the cost of borrowed capital (and that of any other long-term source of finance such as hire purchase or mortgages). That figure is usually fairly self-evident because the lender will state this up front; however, you may have to make a judgement call here if your loans have a *variable rate of interest*; that is, one that can go up and down with the general bank rate. Then you have to make an educated guess as to what that might be over the life of the loan.

Next you need to combine the cost of equity and debt capital into one overall cost of capital figure; in essence, your hurdle rate.

An average cost is required because you don't usually identify each individual project with one particular source of finance. Generally, businesses take the view that all projects have been financed from a common pool of money except for the relatively rare case when project specific finance is raised.

Assume your company intends to keep the gearing ratio of borrowed capital to equity in the proportion of 20:80. (Push ahead to Book VI, Chapter 2 if gearing isn't a term in your Scrabble vocabulary.) The cost of new capital from these sources has been assessed, say, at 10 per cent and 15 per cent respectively, and corporation tax is 30 per cent. The calculation of the overall weighted average cost is as follows:

Type of capital	Proportion (a)	After-tax cost (b)	Weighted cost (a x b)
10% loan capital	0.20	7.0%	1.4%
Equity	0.80	15.0%	12.0%
			13.4%

The resulting weighted average cost of 13.4 per cent is the minimum rate that this company should accept on proposed investments. Any investment that isn't expected to achieve this return isn't a viable proposition.

Reporting on Variances

Any performance needs to be carefully monitored and compared against the budget as the year proceeds, and corrective action must be taken where necessary to keep the two consistent. This has to be done on a monthly basis (or using shorter time intervals if required), showing both the company's performance during the month in question and throughout the year so far.

Looking at Figure 5-7, you can see at a glance that the business is behind on sales for this month, but ahead on the yearly target. The convention is to put all unfavourable variations in brackets. Hence, a higher-than-budgeted sales figure doesn't have brackets, but a higher materials cost does. You can also see that profit is running ahead of budget but the profit margin is slightly behind (–0.30 per cent). This is partly because other direct costs, such as labour and distribution in this example, are running well ahead of budgeting variances.

Figure 5-7: Fixed budget – note that figures rounded up and down to nearest thousand may affect percentages.

Heading	Month			Year to date		
	Budget	**Actual**	**Variance**	**Budget**	**Actual**	**Variance**
Sales	805*	753	(52)	6,358	7,314	956
Materials	627	567	60	4,942	5,704	(762)
Materials margin	178	186	8	1,416	1,610	194
Direct costs	74	79	(5)	595	689	(94)
Gross profit	104	107	3	820	921	101
Percentage	**12.92**	**14.21**	**1.29**	**12.90**	**12.60**	**(0.30)**

Flexing your budget

A budget is based on a particular set of sales goals, few of which are likely to be met exactly in practice. Figure 5-7 shows that the business has used £762,000 more materials than budgeted. Because more has been sold, this is hardly surprising. The way to manage this situation is to flex the budget to show what would be expected to happen to expenses, given the sales that actually occurred. This is done by applying the budget ratios to the actual data. For example, materials were planned to be 22.11 per cent of sales in the budget. By applying that to the actual month's sales, you arrive at a materials cost of £587,000.

Looking at the flexed budget in Figure 5-8, you can see that the business has spent £19,000 more than expected on the material given the level of sales actually achieved, rather than the £762,000 overspend shown in the fixed budget. The same principle holds for other direct costs, which appear to be running £94,000 over-budget for the year. When you take into account the extra sales shown in the flexed budget, you can see that the company has actually spent £4,000 over-budget on direct costs. This is serious, but it isn't as serious as the fixed budget suggests. The flexed budget allows you to concentrate your efforts on dealing with true variances in performance.

Figure 5-8:
Flexed budget – note that figures rounded up and down to nearest thousand may affect percentages.

Heading	Month			Year to date		
	Budget	**Actual**	**Variance**	**Budget**	**Actual**	**Variance**
Sales	753*	753	–	7,314	7,314	–
Materials	587	567	20	5,685	5,704	(19)
Materials margin	166	186	20	1,629	1,610	(19)
Direct costs	69	79	(10)	685	689	(4)
Gross profit	97	107	10	944	921	(23)
Percentage	**12.92**	**14.21**	**1.29**	**12.90**	**12.60**	**(0.30)**

Staying Flexible with Budgets

One thing never to lose sight of is that budgeting is a *means to an end*. It's a tool for doing something better than you could without the tool. Preparing budgeted financial statements isn't the ultimate objective; a budget isn't an end in itself. The budgeting process should provide definite benefits, and businesses should use their budgeted financial statements to measure progress toward their financial objectives – and not just file them away someplace.

Budgets aren't the only tool for management control. Control means accomplishing your financial objectives. Many businesses don't use budgeting and don't prepare budgeted financial statements. But they do lay down goals and objectives for each period and compare actual performance against these targets. Doing at least this much is essential for all businesses.

Keep in mind that budgets aren't the only means for controlling expenses. Actually, we shy away from the term *controlling* because we've found that, in the minds of most people, *controlling* expenses means minimising them. The *cost/benefits* idea captures the better view of expenses. Spending more on advertising, for example, may have a good payoff in the additional sales volume it produces. In other words, it's easy to cut advertising to zero if you really want to minimise this expense – but the impact on sales volume may be disastrous.

Business managers should eliminate any *excessive* amount of an expense – the amount that really doesn't yield a benefit or add value to the business. For example, it's possible for a business to spend too much on quality inspection by doing unnecessary or duplicate steps, or by spending too much time testing products that have a long history of good quality. But this doesn't mean that the business should eliminate the expense entirely. Expense control means trimming the cost down to the right size. In this sense, expense control is one of the hardest jobs that business managers do, second only to managing people, in our opinion.

Have a Go

Use the following figures to answer the questions in this section:

Volume: 30,000 units	*£/Unit*	
Sales revenue	£30,000,000	£1,000
Cost of goods sold expense	(£15,600,000)	(£520)
Gross margin	£14,400,000	£480
Revenue-driven operating expense	£2,400,000	£80
Volume-driven operating expense	£1,500,000	£50
Contribution margin	£10,500,000	£350
Fixed operating expenses	(£6,250,000)	
Operating profit	£4,250,000	

You're the divisional manager of a large corporation and responsible for the budget of that division. The CEO of your company wants you to increase your EBIT by 15 per cent (£637,500 to be exact). Revenue- and volume-driven expenses remain the same for this year, but you and your staff forecast that fixed overheads are likely to rise by approximately 5 per cent to £6,562,500.

Have a go at these questions:

1. **Calculate the total contribution margin for your division, given the increase in fixed overheads and the increased EBIT that your CEO wants you to achieve.**

2. **Your new production manager tells you that costs per unit are going to increase by £20 per unit. Recalculate your contribution per unit and then calculate the additional number of units that you'd need to sell to achieve the new EBIT with the revised production costs.**

3. **Your sales manager tells you that his team can't achieve the budgeted increase in sales of 15 per cent. So you decide to make a 5 per cent sales price increase as well. Calculate the revised contribution per unit, to include the new 5 per cent sales price increase.**

4. **Now that you've calculated your revised contribution per unit (taking into account the increased sales price and increased production costs), calculate the number of the units that need to be sold to achieve the new contribution margin that your CEO requires.**

5. **What is the budgeted profit for the year, given the revised contribution per unit and the newly calculated sales volume of 33,092 units?**

Answering the Have a Go Questions

1. **The new EBIT is calculated as the existing operating profit plus the budgeted increase of £637,500:**

   £4,887,500 (£4,250,000 + £637,500)

   You calculate the new contribution margin as follows:

   EBIT + budgeted fixed operating expenses (£6,250,000 + 5%)

   = £4,887,500 + £6,562,500

   = £11,450,000

2. **Using the original figures given for these questions, you can see that the contribution per unit started at £350. If the production cost of each unit increases by £20, this decreases the contribution per unit to £330 (£350 – £20).**

   To calculate the number of units required to be sold to achieve the contribution margin of £11,450,000 (as calculated in the first question):

   Total contribution ÷ Revised contribution per unit

£11,450,000 ÷ £330

= 34,697 units

An increase of 4,697 (15.5% increase) units need to be sold to achieve the new contribution margin that the CEO requires.

3. **You calculate the revised contribution per unit to include the new 5 per cent sales price increase as follows:**

   Revised sales revenue £1,050 (£1,000 + 5%)

   Less production cost   (£570) (£550 + £20 increase)

   Less revenue-driven expense   (£84) (£80 + 5% increase)

   Less volume-driven expense   (£50)

   Contribution per unit **£346**

4. **You calculate the number of the units that need to be sold to achieve the new contribution margin that your CEO requires as follows:**

   Total contribution margin ÷ Revised contribution per unit

   £11,450,000 ÷ £346

   = 33,092 units to sell

   This is 3,092 units more than originally sold (a 10 per cent sales volume increase).

5. **The budgeted profit for the year is as follows:**

Volume: 33,092	*£/Unit*	
Sales revenue	£34,746,600	£1,050
Cost of goods sold	(£18,862,440)	(£570)
Gross margin	£15,884,160	
Revenue-driven operating expense	(£2,779,728)	(£84)
Volume-driven operating expense	(£1,654,600)	(£50)
Contribution margin	£11,449,832*	
Fixed operating expenses	(£6,562,500)	
Operating profit	**£4,887,332**	

*A slight rounding exists on the contribution margin, due to the way that I rounded up the sales volume.

Book VI

Accountants: Working with the Outside World

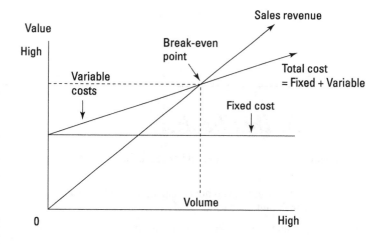

In this book...

- ✔ Know how an accountant would prepare the accounts for a larger business.
- ✔ Think like an investor: see how an investor reads the accounts of a business and uses ratios.
- ✔ Work with auditors and know what they actually do.

Chapter 1

Getting a Financial Report Ready for Prime Time

*T*he primary financial statements of a business are:

✓ **Profit and Loss statement:** Summarises sales revenue inflows and expense outflows for the period and ends with the bottom-line profit, which is the net inflow for the period (a loss is a net outflow).

✓ **Balance Sheet:** Summarises the financial condition at the end of the period, consisting of amounts for assets, liabilities and owners' equity at that instant in time.

✓ **Cash flow statement:** Summarises the net cash inflow (or outflow) from profit for the period plus the other sources and uses of cash during the period.

An annual financial report of a business contains more than just these three financial statements. The business manager plays an important role – which outside investors and lenders should understand. The manager should do certain critical things before the financial report is released to the outside world.

1. **The manager should review with a critical eye the *vital connections* between the items reported in all three financial statements.**

All amounts have to fit together like the pieces of a jigsaw. The net cash increase (or decrease) reported at the end of the cash flow statement, for instance, has to tie in with the change in cash reported in the Balance Sheet. Abnormally high or low ratios between connected accounts should be scrutinised carefully.

2. **The manager should carefully review the *disclosures* in the financial report** (all information in addition to the financial statements) to make sure that disclosure is adequate according to financial reporting standards, and that all the disclosure elements are truthful but not damaging to the interests of the business.

This disclosure review can be compared with the notion of *due diligence*, which is done to make certain that all relevant information is collected, that the information is accurate and reliable, and that all relevant requirements and regulations are being complied with. This step is especially important for public corporations whose securities (shares and debt instruments) are traded on national securities exchanges.

3. **The manager should consider whether the financial statement numbers need *touching up*** to smooth the jagged edges off the company's year-to-year profit gyrations or to improve the business's short-term solvency picture. Although this can be described as putting your thumb on the scale, you can also argue that sometimes the scale is a little out of balance to begin with and the manager is adjusting the financial statements to jibe better with the normal circumstances of the business.

In discussing the third step later in the chapter, we walk on thin ice. Some topics are, shall we say, rather delicate. The manager has to strike a balance between the interests of the business on the one hand and the interests of the owners (investors) and creditors of the business on the other. The best analogy we can think of is the advertising done by a business. Advertising should be truthful but, as we're sure you know, businesses have a lot of leeway in how to advertise their products and they have been known to engage in hyperbole. Managers exercise the same freedom in putting together their financial reports.

Reviewing Vital Connections

Business managers and investors read financial reports because these reports provide information regarding how the business is doing. When reviewing the annual financial report before releasing it outside the business, the top managers of the business should keep in mind that a financial report is designed to answer certain basic financial questions:

✔ Is the business making a profit or suffering a loss, and how much?

✔ How do assets stack up against liabilities?

✔ Where did the business get its capital and is it making good use of the money?

✔ Is profit generating cash flow?

✔ Did the business reinvest all its profit or distribute some of the profit to owners?

✔ Does the business have enough capital for future growth?

 As a hypothetical but realistic business example, Figure 1-1 highlights some of the vital connections – the lines connect one or more Balance Sheet accounts with sales revenue or an expense in the Profit and Loss statement. The savvy manager or investor checks these links to see whether everything is in order or whether some danger signals point to problems. (We should make clear that these lines of connection don't appear in actual financial reports.)

In the following list, we briefly explain these five connections, mainly from the manager's point of view. Book VI, Chapter 2 explains how investors might read a financial report and compute certain ratios. (Investors are on the outside looking in; managers are on the inside looking out.)

Note: We cut right to the chase in the following brief comments and we don't illustrate the calculations behind the comments. The purpose here is to emphasise why managers should pay attention to these important ratios.

Book VI

Accountants: Working with the Outside World

(Amounts in thousands)		Balance Sheet at End of Year	
		Assets	
Profit and Loss Account for Year		Cash	£ 3,500
Sales Revenue	£ 52,000	Debtors	5,000
Cost of Goods Sold Expense	31,200	Stock	7,800
Gross Margin	£ 20,800	Prepaid Expenses	900
Sales, Administration, and General Expenses	15,600	Fixed Assets	19,500
Depreciation Expense	1,650	Accumulated Depreciation	(6,825)
Earnings Before Interest and Income Tax	£ 3,550	Total Assets	£ 29,875
Interest Expense	750	Liabilities	
Earnings Before Income Tax	£ 2,800	Creditors	£ 1,500
Income Tax Expense	900	Accrued Expenses Payable	2,400
Net Profit	£ 1,900	Income Tax Payable	75
		Overdraft	4,000
		Long Term Loans	6,000
		Owners' Equity	
		Share Capital	4,000
		Retained Earnings	11,900
		Liabilities and Owners' Equity	£ 29,875

Figure 1-1: Vital connections between the Profit and Loss statement and the Balance Sheet.

1. **Sales Revenue and Debtors:** This business's ending balance of debtors is five weeks of its annual sales revenue. The manager should compare this ratio to the normal credit terms offered to the business's customers. If the ending balance is too high, the manager should identify which customers' accounts are past due and take actions to collect these amounts, or perhaps shut off future credit to these customers. An abnormally high balance of debtors may signal that some of these customers' amounts owed to the business should be written off as uncollectable bad debts.

2. **Cost of Goods Sold Expense and Stock:** This business's ending stock is 13 weeks of its annual cost of goods sold expense. The manager should compare this ratio to the company's stock policies and objectives regarding how long stock should be held awaiting sale. If stock is too large the manager should identify which products have been in stock too long; further purchases (or manufacturing) should be curtailed. Also, the manager may want to consider sales promotions or cutting sales prices to move these products out of stock faster.

3. **Sales, Administration and General (SA&G) Expenses and Prepaid Expenses:** This business's ending balance of prepaid expenses is three weeks of the total of these annual operating expenses. The manager should know what the normal ratio of prepaid expenses should be relative to the annual SA&G operating expenses (excluding depreciation expense). If the ending balance is too high, the manager should investigate which costs have been paid too far in advance and take action to bring these prepaids back down to normal.

4. **Sales, Administration and General (SA&G) Expenses and Creditors:** This business's ending balance of creditors is five weeks of its annual operating expenses. Delaying payment of these liabilities is good from the cash flow point of view (refer to Book IV, Chapter 3) but delaying too long may jeopardise the company's good credit rating with its key suppliers and vendors. If this ratio is too high, the manager should pinpoint which specific liabilities haven't been paid and whether any of these are overdue and should be paid immediately. Or, the high balance may indicate that the company is in a difficult short-term solvency situation and needs to raise more money to pay the amounts owed to suppliers and vendors.

5. **Sales, Administration and General (SA&G) Expenses and Accrued Expenses Payable:** This business's ending balance of this operating liability is eight weeks of the business's annual operating expenses. This ratio may be consistent with past experience and the normal lag before paying these costs. On the other hand, the ending balance may be abnormally high. The manager should identify which of these unpaid costs are higher than they should be. As with creditors, inflated amounts of accrued liabilities may signal serious short-term solvency problems.

These five key connections are very important ones, but the manager should scan all basic connections to see whether the ratios pass the common sense test. For example, the manager should make a quick eyeball test of interest expense compared with interest-bearing debt. In Figure 1-1, interest expense is £750,000 compared with £10 million total debt, which indicates a 7.5 per cent interest rate. This seems okay. But if the interest expense were more than £1 million, the manager should investigate and determine why it's so high.

There's always the chance of errors in the accounts of a business. Reviewing the vital connections between the Profit and Loss statement items and the Balance Sheet items is a very valuable final check before the financial statements are approved for inclusion in the business's financial report. After the financial report is released to the outside world, it becomes the latest chapter in the official financial history of the business. If the financial statements are wrong, the business and its top managers are responsible.

Statement of Changes in Owners' Equity and Comprehensive Income

In many situations a business needs to prepare one additional financial statement – the *statement of changes in owners' equity*. Owners' equity consists of two fundamentally different sources – capital invested in the business by the owners, and profit earned by and retained in the business. The specific accounts maintained by the business for its total owners' equity depend on the legal organisation of the business entity. One of the main types of legal organisation of business is the *company*, and its owners are *shareholders* because the company issues ownership *shares* representing portions of the business. So, the title *statement of changes in shareholders' equity* is used for companies. (Book V, Chapter 1 explains the corporation and other legal types of business entities.)

First, consider the situation in which a business does *not* need to report this statement – to make clearer why the statement is needed. Suppose a company has only one class of share and it didn't buy any of its own shares during the year and it didn't record any gains or losses in owners' equity during the year due to *other comprehensive income* (explained later in this section). This business doesn't need a statement of changes in shareholders' equity. In reading the financial report of this business you'd see in its cash flow statement whether the business raised additional capital from its owners during the year and how much in *cash dividends* (distributions from profit) was paid to the owners during the year. The cash flow statement contains all the changes in the owners' equity accounts during the year.

In sharp contrast, larger businesses – especially publicly traded corporations – generally have complex ownership structures consisting of two or more classes of shares; they usually buy some of their own shares and they have one or more technical types of gains or losses during the year. So, they prepare a statement of changes in stockholders' equity to collect together in one place all the changes affecting the owners' equity accounts during the year. This particular 'mini' statement (that focuses narrowly on changes in owners' equity accounts) is where you find certain gains and losses that increase or decrease owners' equity but that are *not* reported in the Profit and Loss statement. Basically, a business has the option to bypass the Profit and Loss statement and, instead, report these gains and losses in the statement of changes in owners' equity. In this way the gains or losses don't affect the bottom-line profit of the business reported in its Profit and Loss statement. You have to read this financial summary of the changes in the owners' equity accounts to find out whether the business had any of these gains or losses and the amounts of the gains or losses.

The special types of gains and losses that can be reported in the statement of owners' equity (instead of the Profit and Loss statement) have to do with foreign currency translations, unrealised gains and losses from certain types of securities investments by the business, and changes in liabilities for unfunded pension fund obligations of the business. *Comprehensive income* is the term used to describe the normal content of the Profit and Loss statement *plus* the additional layer of these special types of gains and losses. Being so technical in nature, these gains and losses fall in a 'twilight zone', as it were, in financial reporting. The gains and losses can be tacked on at the bottom of the Profit and Loss statement or they can be put in the statement of changes in owners' equity – it's up to the business to make the choice. If you encounter these gains and losses in reading a financial report, you'll have to study the footnotes to the financial statements to learn more information about each gain and loss.

Keep on the lookout for the special types of gains and losses that are reported in the statement of changes in owners' equity. A business has the option to tack such gains and losses onto the bottom of its Profit and Loss statement – below the net income line. But most businesses put these income gains and losses in their statement of changes in shareholders' equity, or in a note or notes to their accounts. So watch out for any large amounts of gains or losses that are reported in the statement of changes in owners' equity.

The general format of the statement of changes in shareholders' equity includes a column for each class of stock (ordinary shares, preference shares and so on); a column for any shares of its own that the business has purchased and not cancelled; a column for retained earnings; and one or more columns for any other separate components of the business's owners' equity. Each column starts with the beginning balance and then shows the increases or decreases in the account during the year. For example, a comprehensive gain is shown as an increase in retained earnings and a comprehensive loss as a decrease. The purchase of its own shares is shown as an increase in the relevant column, and if the business reissued some of these shares (such as for stock options exercised by executives), the cost of these shares reissued is shown as a decrease in the column.

We have to admit that reading the statement of changes, or *notes to the accounts*, in shareholders' equity can be heavy going. The professionals – stock analysts, money and investment managers and so on – carefully read through and dissect this statement, or at least they should. The average non-professional investor should focus on whether the business had a major increase or decrease in the number of shares during the year, whether the business changed its ownership structure by creating or eliminating a class of stock, and the impact of stock options awarded to managers of the business.

Book VI

Accountants:
Working
with the
Outside
World

Making Sure that Disclosure Is Adequate

The primary financial statements (including the statement of changes in owners' equity, if reported) are the backbone of a financial report. In fact, a financial report isn't deserving of the name if the primary financial statements aren't included. But, as mentioned earlier, there's much more to a financial report than the financial statements. A financial report needs disclosures. Of course, the financial statements provide disclosure of the most important financial information about the business. The term *disclosures*, however, usually refers to additional information provided in a financial report. In a nutshell, a financial report has two basic parts: (1) the primary financial statements and (2) disclosures.

The chief officer of the business (usually the CEO of a publicly owned company, the president of a private corporation or the managing partner of a partnership) has the primary responsibility to make sure that the financial statements have been prepared according to prevailing accounting standards and that the financial report provides adequate disclosure. He works with the chief financial officer of the business to make sure that the financial report meets the standard of adequate disclosure. (Many smaller businesses hire an independent, qualified accountant to advise them on their financial statements and other disclosures in their financial reports.)

Types of disclosures in financial reports

For a quick survey of disclosures in financial reports – that is to say, the disclosures in addition to the financial statements – the following distinctions are helpful:

- ✔ **Footnotes** provide additional information about the basic figures included in the financial statements. Virtually all financial statements need footnotes to provide additional information for the account balances in the financial statements.

- ✔ **Supplementary financial schedules and tables** provide more details than can be included in the body of financial statements.

- ✔ A wide variety of **other information** may be included, some of which is required if the business is a company quoted on a stock market subject to government regulations regarding financial reporting to its shareholders and other information that's voluntary and not strictly required legally or according to generally accepted accounting principles.

Footnotes: Nettlesome but needed

Footnotes appear at the end of the primary financial statements. Within the financial statements you see references to particular footnotes. And at the bottom of each financial statement, you find the following sentence (or words to this effect): 'The footnotes are integral to the financial statements.' You should read all footnotes for a full understanding of the financial statements.

Footnotes come in two types:

- ✔ One or more footnotes must be included to identify the **major accounting policies and methods** that the business uses. (Book V, Chapter 2 explains that a business must choose among alternative accounting methods for certain expenses, and for their corresponding operating assets and liabilities.) The business must reveal which accounting methods it uses for its major expenses. In particular, the business must identify its cost of goods sold expense (and stock) method and its depreciation methods.

- ✔ Other footnotes provide **additional information and details** for many assets and liabilities. Details about share option plans for key executives are the main type of footnote to the capital stock account in the owners' equity section of the Balance Sheet.

One problem that most investors face when reading footnotes – and, for that matter, many managers who should understand their own footnotes but find them a little dense – is that footnotes often deal with complex issues (such as lawsuits) and rather technical accounting matters. Let us offer you one footnote that brings out this latter point. This footnote is taken from the recent financial report of a well-known manufacturer that uses a very conservative accounting method for determining its cost of goods sold expense and stock cost value. (Book V, Chapter 2 explains accounting methods.) We want you to read the following footnote from the 2011 Annual Report of this manufacturer and try to make sense of it (amounts are in thousands).

> *D. Inventories: Inventories are valued principally by the LIFO (last-in, first-out) method. If the FIFO (first-in, first-out) method had been in use, inventories would have been £2,000 million and £1,978 million higher than reported at December 31, 2010 and 2011, respectively.*

Yes, these amounts are in *millions* of pounds. The company's stock cost value at the end of 2010 would have been £2 billion higher if the FIFO method had been used. Of course, you have to have some idea of the difference between the two methods, which we explain in Book V, Chapter 2.

You may wonder how different the company's annual profits would have been if the alternative method had been in use. A manager can ask the accounting department to do this analysis. But as an outside investor, you would have to compute these amounts. Businesses disclose which accounting methods they use but they don't have to disclose how different annual profits would have been if the alternative method had been used – and very few do.

Other disclosures in financial reports

The following discussion includes a fairly comprehensive list of the various types of disclosures found in annual financial reports of larger, publicly owned businesses – in addition to footnotes. A few caveats are in order. First, not every public company includes every one of the following items, although the disclosures are fairly common. Second, the level of disclosure by private businesses – after you get beyond the financial statements and footnotes – is much less than in public companies. Third, tracking the actual disclosure practices of private businesses is difficult because their annual financial reports are circulated only to their owners and lenders. A private business may include any or all of the following disclosures, but by and large it's not legally required to do so. The next section further explains the differences between private and public businesses regarding disclosure practices in their annual financial reports.

Warren Buffett's annual letter to shareholders

We have to call your attention to one notable exception to the generally self-serving and slanted writing found in the letter to shareholders by the chief executive officer of the business in annual financial reports. The annual letter to stockholders of Berkshire Hathaway, Inc. is written by Warren Buffett, the chairman and CEO. Mr Buffett has become very well known – he's called the 'Oracle of Omaha'. In the annual ranking of the world's richest people by *Forbes* magazine he's near the top of the list – right behind people like Bill Gates, the co-founder of Microsoft. If you'd invested £1,000 with him in 1960, your investment would be worth well over £1 million today. Even in the recent financial meltdown Berkshire Hathaway stock delivered a return of nearly 80 per cent over the period 2000–2011 compared to a negative 12 per cent return for the S&P 500. Mr Buffett's letters are the epitome of telling it like it is; they're very frank and quite humorous.

You can go to the website of the company (www.berkshirehathaway.com) and download his most recent letter. You'll learn a lot about his investing philosophy and the letters are a delight to read.

Public corporations typically include most of the following disclosures in their annual financial reports to their shareholders:

- **Cover (or transmittal) letter:** A letter from the chief executive of the business to the shareholders.

- **Highlights table:** A short table that presents the shareholder with a financial thumbnail sketch of the business.

- **Management discussion and analysis (MD&A):** Deals with the major developments and changes during the year that affected the financial performance and situation of the business.

- **Segment information:** The sales revenue and operating profits are reported for the major divisions of the organisation or for its different markets (international versus domestic, for example).

- **Historical summaries:** Financial history that extends back beyond the years (usually three but can be up to five or six) included in the primary financial statements.

- **Graphics:** Bar charts, trend charts and pie charts representing financial conditions; photos of key people and products.

- **Promotional material:** Information about the company, its products, its employees and its managers, often stressing an over-arching theme for the year.

✔ **Profiles:** Information about members of top management and the board of directors.

✔ **Quarterly summaries of profit performance and share prices and dividends:** Shows financial performance for all four quarters in the year and share price ranges for each quarter.

✔ **Management's responsibility statement:** A short statement that management has primary responsibility for the accounting methods used to prepare the financial statements and for providing the other disclosures in the financial report.

✔ **Independent auditor's report:** The report from the accounting firm that performed the audit, expressing an opinion on the fairness of the financial statements and accompanying disclosures. (Book VI, Chapter 3 discusses the nature of audits.) Public companies are required to have audits; private businesses may or may not have their annual financial reports audited, depending on their size.

✔ **Company contact information:** Information on how to contact the company, the website address of the company, how to get copies of the reports filed with the London Stock Exchange, the Securities Exchange Commission, the stock transfer agent and registrar of the company, and other information.

Managers of public corporations rely on lawyers, auditors and their financial and accounting officers to make sure that everything that should be disclosed in the business's annual financial reports is included and that the exact wording of the disclosures isn't misleading, inaccurate or incomplete. This is a tall order. The field of financial reporting disclosure changes constantly. Laws and authoritative accounting standards have to be observed. Inadequate disclosure in an annual financial report is just as serious as using wrong accounting methods for measuring profit and for determining values for assets, liabilities and owners' equity. A financial report can be misleading because of improper accounting methods or because of inadequate or misleading disclosure. Both types of deficiencies can lead to nasty lawsuits against the business and its managers.

Companies House provides forms showing how the Companies Act requires Balance Sheets and Profit and Loss statements to be laid out. To access the guidance, go to www.companieshouse.gov.uk/forms/introduction. shtml. All the statutory forms are available on request and free of charge.

Keeping It Private versus Going Public

Compared with their big brothers and sisters, privately owned businesses provide very little additional disclosures in their annual financial reports. The primary financial statements and footnotes are pretty much all you get.

The annual financial reports of publicly owned corporations include all, or nearly all, of the disclosure items listed earlier. Somewhere in the range of 3,000 companies are publicly owned, and their shares are traded on the London Stock Exchange, NASDAQ or other stock exchanges. Publicly owned companies must file annual financial reports with the Stock Exchange, which is the agency that makes and enforces the rules for trading in securities and for the financial reporting requirements of publicly owned corporations. These filings are available to the public on the London Stock Exchange's website (www.londonstockexchange.com) or for US companies on the SEC's EDGAR database at the SEC's website (www.sec.gov/edgar/searchedgar/cik.htm).

Both privately held and publicly owned businesses are bound by the same accounting rules for measuring profit, assets, liabilities and owners' equity in annual financial reports to the owners of the business and in reports that are made available to others (such as the lenders to the business). There aren't two different sets of accounting rules – one for private companies and another one for public businesses. The accounting measurement and valuation rules are the same for all businesses. However, *disclosure* requirements and practices differ greatly between private and public companies.

Publicly owned businesses live in a fish bowl. When a company goes public with an *IPO* (initial public offering of shares), it gives up a lot of the privacy that a closely held business enjoys. Publicly owned companies whose shares are traded on national stock exchanges live in glass houses. In contrast, privately owned businesses lock their doors regarding disclosure. Whenever a privately owned business releases a financial report to its bank in seeking a loan, or to the outside non-management investors in the business, it should include its three primary financial statements and footnotes. But beyond this, it has much more leeway and doesn't have to include the additional disclosure items listed in the preceding section.

A private business may have its financial statements audited by a professional accounting firm. If so, the audit report is included in the business's annual financial report. The very purpose of having an audit is to reassure shareholders and potential investors in the business that the financial statements can be trusted. But as we look up and down the preceding list of disclosure items we don't see any other absolutely required disclosure item for a privately held business. The large majority of closely held businesses guard their financial information like Fort Knox.

The less information divulged in the annual financial report, the better – that's the thinking of closely held businesses. And we don't entirely disagree. The shareholders don't have the liquidity for their shares that shareholders of publicly held corporations enjoy. The market prices of public companies are everything, so information is made publicly available so that market prices are fairly determined. The shares of privately owned businesses are rarely traded, so there's not such an urgent need for a complete package of information.

A private company could provide all the disclosures given in the preceding list – there's certainly no law against this. But usually they don't. Investors in private businesses can request confidential reports from managers at the annual shareholders' meetings, but doing so isn't practical for a shareholder in a large public corporation.

Book VI

Accountants: Working with the Outside World

Nudging the Numbers

This section discusses two accounting tricks that business managers and investors should know about. We don't endorse either technique, but you should be aware of both of them. In some situations, the financial statement numbers don't come out exactly the way the business wants. Accountants use certain tricks of the trade – some would say sleight-of-hand – to move the numbers closer to what the business prefers. One trick improves the appearance of the *short-term solvency* of the business, in particular the cash balance reported in the Balance Sheet at the end of the year. The other device shifts profit from one year to the next to make for a smoother trend of net income from year to year.

Not all businesses use these techniques, but the extent of their use is hard to pin down because no business would openly admit to using these manipulation methods. The evidence is fairly convincing, however, that many businesses use these techniques. We're sure you've heard the term *loopholes* applied to income tax accounting. Well, some loopholes exist in financial statement accounting as well.

Fluffing up the cash balance by 'window dressing'

Suppose you manage a business and your accountant has just submitted to you a preliminary, or first draft, of the year-end Balance Sheet for your review. Your preliminary Balance Sheet includes the following:

Preliminary Balances, Before Window Dressing

Cash	£0	Creditors	£235,000
Debtors	£486,000	Accrued expenses payable	£187,000
Stock	£844,000	Income tax payable	£58,000
Overdraft	£200,000		
Prepaid expenses	£72,000		
Current assets	£1,402,000	Current liabilities	£680,000

You start reading the numbers when something strikes you: a zero cash balance? How can that be? Maybe your business has been having some cash flow problems and you've intended to increase your short-term borrowing and speed up collection of debtors to help the cash balance. But that plan doesn't help you right now, with this particular financial report that you must send out to your business's investors and your banker. Folks generally don't like to see a zero cash balance – it makes them kind of nervous, to put it mildly, no matter how you try to cushion it. So what do you do to avoid alarming them?

Your accountant is probably aware of a technique known as *window dressing*, a very simple method for making the cash balance look better. Suppose your financial year-end is October 31. Your accountant takes the cash receipts from customers paying their bills that are actually received on November 1, 2 and 3, and records them as if these cash collections had been received on October 31. After all, the argument can be made that the customers' cheques were in the mail – that money is yours, as far as the customers are concerned, so your reports should reflect that cash inflow.

What impact does window dressing have? It reduces the amount in Debtors and increases the amount in Cash by the same amount – it has absolutely no effect on the profit figure. It just makes your cash balance look a touch better. Window dressing can also be used to improve other accounts' balances, which we don't go into here. All these techniques involve holding the books open to record certain events that take place after the end of the financial year (the ending Balance Sheet date) to make things look better than they actually were at the close of business on the last day of the year.

Sounds like everybody wins, doesn't it? Your investors don't panic and your job is safe. We have to warn you, though, that window dressing may be the first step on a slippery slope. A little window dressing today and tomorrow, who knows? Maybe giving the numbers a nudge will lead to serious financial fraud. Any way you look at it, window dressing is deceptive to your investors, who have every right to expect that the end of your fiscal year as stated on your financial reports is truly the end of your fiscal year. Think about it this way: if you've invested in a business that has fudged this data, how do you know what other numbers on the report are suspect?

Smoothing the rough edges off profit

Managers strive to make their numbers and to hit the milestone markers set for the business. Reporting a loss for the year, or even a dip below the profit trend line, is a red flag that investors view with alarm.

Managers can do certain things to deflate or inflate profit (the net profit) recorded in the year that are referred to as *profit-smoothing* techniques. Profit smoothing is also called *income smoothing*. Profit smoothing isn't nearly as serious as *cooking the books*, or *juggling the books*, which refers to deliberate, fraudulent accounting practices such as recording sales revenue that hasn't happened or not recording expenses that have happened. Cooking the books is very serious; managers can go to jail for fraudulent financial statements. Profit smoothing is more like a white lie that's told for the good of the business, and perhaps for the good of managers as well. Managers know that there's always some noise in the accounting system. Profit smoothing muffles the noise.

Managers of publicly owned companies whose shares are actively traded are under intense pressure to keep profits steadily rising. Security analysts who follow a particular company make profit forecasts for the business, and their buy-hold-sell recommendations are based largely on these earnings forecasts. If a business fails to meet its own profit forecast or falls short of analysts' forecasts, the market price of its shares suffers. Share option and bonus incentive compensation plans are also strong motivations for achieving the profit goals set for the business.

The evidence is fairly strong that publicly owned businesses engage in some degree of profit smoothing. Frankly, it's much harder to know whether private businesses do so. Private businesses don't face the public scrutiny and expectations that public corporations do. On the other hand, key managers in a private business may have incentive bonus arrangements that depend on recorded profit. In any case, business investors and managers should know about profit smoothing and how it's done.

Most profit smoothing involves pushing revenue and expenses into other years than they would normally be recorded. For example, if the president of a business wants to report more profit for the year, he can instruct the chief accountant to accelerate the recording of some sales revenue that normally wouldn't be recorded until next year, or to delay the recording of some expenses until next year that normally would be recorded this year. The main reason for smoothing profit is to keep it closer to a projected trend line and make the line less jagged.

Book V, Chapter 2 explains that managers choose among alternative accounting methods for several important expenses. After making these key choices the managers should let the accountants do their jobs and let the chips fall where they may. If bottom-line profit for the year turns out to be a little short of the forecast or target for the period, so be it. This hands-off approach to profit accounting is the ideal way. However, managers often use a hands-on approach – they intercede (one could say interfere) and override the normal accounting for sales revenue or expenses.

Both managers who do it and investors who rely on financial statements in which profit smoothing has been done should definitely understand one thing – these techniques have robbing-Peter-to-pay-Paul effects. Accountants refer to these as *compensatory effects*. The effects on next year's statement simply offset and cancel out the effects on this year. Less expense this year is counterbalanced by more expense next year. Sales revenue recorded this year means less sales revenue recorded next year.

Two profit histories

Figure 1-2 shows, side by side, the annual profit histories of two different companies over six years. Business X shows a nice, steady, upward trend of profit. Business Y, in contrast, shows somewhat of a rollercoaster ride over the six years. Both businesses earned the same total profit for the six years – in this case, £1,050,449. Their total six-year profit performance is the same, down to the last pound. Which company would you be more willing to risk your money in? We suspect that you'd prefer Business X because of the steady, upward slope of its profit history.

Question: Does Figure 1-2 really show two different companies – or are the two profit histories actually alternatives for the same company? The year-by-year profits for Business X could be the company's *smoothed* profit, and the annual profits for Business Y could be the *actual* profit of the same business – the profit that would have been recorded if smoothing techniques had not been applied.

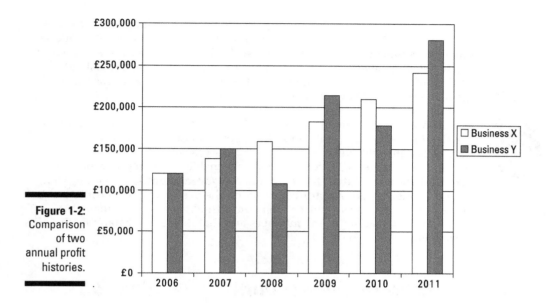

Book VI

Accountants: Working with the Outside World

Figure 1-2:
Comparison of two annual profit histories.

For the first year in the series, 2006, no profit smoothing occurred. Actual profit is on target. For each of the next five years, the two profit numbers differ. The under-gap or over-gap of actual profit compared with smoothed profit for the year is the amount of revenue or expenses manipulation that was done in the year. For example, in 2007 actual profit would have been too high, so the company moved some expenses that normally would be recorded the following year into 2007. In contrast, in 2008 actual profit was running too low, so the business took action to put off recording some expenses until 2011.

If a business has a particularly bad year, all the profit-smoothing tricks in the world won't close the gap. But several smoothing techniques are available for filling the potholes and straightening the curves on the profit highway.

Profit-smoothing techniques

One common technique for profit smoothing is *deferred maintenance.* Many routine and recurring maintenance costs required for vehicles, machines, equipment and buildings can be put off, or deferred, until later. These costs aren't recorded to expense until the actual maintenance is done, so putting off the work means that no expense is recorded. Or a company can cut back on its current year's outlays for market research and product development. Keep in mind that most of these costs will be incurred next year, so the effect is to rob Peter (make next year absorb the cost) to pay Paul (let this year escape the cost).

A business can ease up on its rules regarding when slow-paying customers are decided to be bad debts (uncollectable debtors). A business can put off recording some of its bad debts expense until next year. A fixed asset out of active use may have very little or no future value to a business. Instead of writing off the non-depreciated cost of the *impaired asset* as a loss this year, the business may delay the write-off until next year.

So, managers have control over the timing of many expenses, and they can use this discretion for profit smoothing. Some amount of expenses can be accelerated into this year or deferred to next year in order to make for a smoother profit trend. Of course, in its external financial report a business doesn't divulge the extent to which it has engaged in profit smoothing. Nor does the independent auditor comment on the use of profit-smoothing techniques by the business – unless the auditor thinks that the company has gone too far in massaging the numbers and that its financial statements are misleading.

Sticking to the accounting conventions

Over time, a generally accepted approach to the boundaries of acceptable number nudging has been arrived at. This hinges on the use of three conventions: conservatism, materiality and consistency.

Conservatism

Accountants are often viewed as merchants of gloom, always prone to taking a pessimistic point of view. The fact that a point of view has to be taken at all is the root of the problem. The convention of *conservatism* means that given a choice the accountant takes the figure that will result in a lower end profit. This might mean, for example, taking the higher of two possible expense figures. Few people are upset if the profit figure at the end of the day is higher than earlier estimates. The converse is never true.

Materiality

A strict interpretation of depreciation could lead to all sorts of trivial paperwork. For example, pencil sharpeners, staplers and paper clips, all theoretically items of fixed assets, should be depreciated over their working lives. This is obviously a useless exercise and in practice these items are written off when they're bought.

Clearly, the level of *materiality* is not the same for all businesses. A multinational may not keep meticulous records of every item of machinery under £1,000. For a small business this may represent all the machinery it has.

Consistency

Even with the help of those concepts and conventions, there's a fair degree of latitude in how you can record and interpret financial information. You need to choose the methods that give the fairest picture of how the firm is performing and stick with them. Keeping track of events in a business that's always changing its accounting methods is very difficult. This doesn't mean that you're stuck with one method forever. Any change, however, is an important step.

Browsing versus Reading Financial Reports

Very few people have the time to carefully read all the information in an annual financial report – even if the report is relatively short.

Annual financial reports are long and dense documents – like lengthy legal contracts in many ways. Pick up a typical annual financial report of a public corporation: you'd need many hours (perhaps the whole day) to thoroughly read everything in the report. You'd need at least an hour or two just to read and absorb the main points in the report. How do investors in a business deal with the *information overload* of annual financial reports put out by businesses?

An annual financial report is like the Sunday edition of *The Times* or *The Telegraph*. Hardly anyone reads every sentence on every page of these Sunday papers – most people pick and choose what they want to read. Investors read annual financial reports like they read Sunday newspapers. The information is there if you really want to read it, but most readers pick and choose which information they have time to read.

Annual financial reports are designed for archival purposes, not for a quick read. Instead of addressing the needs of investors and others who want to know about the profit performance and financial condition of the business – but have only a very limited amount of time to do so – accountants produce an annual financial report that is a voluminous financial history of the business. Accountants leave it to the users of annual reports to extract the main points from an annual report. So, financial statement readers use relatively few ratios and other tests to get a feel for the financial performance and position of the business. Some businesses (and non-profit organisations in reporting to their members and other constituencies) don't furnish an annual financial report. They know that few people have the time or the technical background to read through their annual financial reports. Instead, they provide relatively brief summaries that are boiled-down versions of their official financial statements. Typically, these summaries don't provide footnotes or the other disclosures that are included in annual financial reports. These *condensed financial statements*, without footnotes, are provided by several non-profit organisations – credit unions, for instance. If you really want to see the complete financial report of the organisation you can ask its headquarters to send you a copy.

You should keep in mind that annual financial reports do not report everything of interest to owners, creditors and others who have a financial interest in the business. *Annual* reports, of course, come out only once a year – usually two months or so after the end of the company's fiscal (accounting) year. You have to keep abreast of developments during the year by reading financial newspapers or through other means. Also, annual financial reports present the 'sanitised' version of events; they don't divulge scandals or other negative news about the business.

Finally, not everything you may like to know as an investor is included in the annual financial report. For example, for US companies, information about salaries and incentive compensation arrangements with the top-level managers of the business are disclosed in the proxy statement, not in the annual financial report of the business. A *proxy statement* is the means by which the corporation solicits the votes of shareholders on issues that require their approval – one of which is compensation packages of top-level managers. In the US, proxy statements are filed with the SEC and are available on its EDGAR database, www.sec.gov/edgar/searchedgar/cik.htm. In the UK this information would usually appear in the body of the main report under the heading 'Report of the Directors on Remuneration'.

The quality of financial reports varies from company to company. The Investor Relations Society (go to www.irs.org.uk and click on 'IR Best Practice') makes an award each year to the company producing the best (in other words, 'complete' and 'clear') set of reports and accounts.

Chapter 2

How Investors Read a Financial Report

*I*n reading financial reports, directors, managers, business owners and investors need to know how to navigate through the financial statements to find the vital signs of progress and problems. The financial statement ratios explained in this chapter point the way – these ratios are signposts on the financial information highway. You can also keep abreast of business affairs by reading financial newspapers and investment magazines, and investment newsletters are very popular. These sources of financial information refer to the ratios discussed in this chapter on the premise that you know what the ratios mean. Most managers or individual investors in public companies don't have the time or expertise to study a financial report thoroughly enough to make decisions based on the report, so they rely on stockbrokers, investment advisers and publishers of credit ratings (like Standard & Poor's) for interpretations of financial reports. The fact is that the folks who prepare financial reports have this kind of expert audience in mind; they don't include explanations or mark passages with icons to help *you* understand the report.

Sure, you may have your own accountant or investment adviser on tap, so why should you bother reading this chapter if you rely on others to interpret financial reports anyway? Well, the more you understand the factors that go into interpreting a financial report, the better prepared you are to evaluate the commentary and advice of stock analysts and other investment experts. If you can at least nod intelligently while your stockbroker talks about a business's P/E and EPS, you'll look like a savvy investor – and may get more favourable treatment. (P/E and EPS, by the way, are two of the key ratios we explain later in the chapter.)

This chapter gives you the basics for comparing companies' financial reports, including the points of difference between private and public companies, the important ratios that you should know about and the warning signs to look out for on audit reports. In this chapter, we also suggest how to sort through the footnotes that are an integral part of every financial report, to identify those that have the most importance to you. Believe us, the pros read the footnotes with a keen eye.

Financial Reporting by Private versus Public Businesses

The main impetus behind the continued development of generally accepted accounting principles (GAAP) has been the widespread public ownership and trading in the securities (stocks and bonds) issued by thousands of companies. The 1929 stock market crash and its aftermath plainly exposed the lack of accounting standards, as well as many financial reporting abuses and frauds. Landmark federal securities laws were passed in the US in 1933 and 1934, and a federal regulatory agency with broad powers – the Securities and Exchange Commission (SEC) – was created and given jurisdiction over trading in corporate securities. In the UK, the government has enacted a series of Companies Acts, culminating in one consolidated act in 2006, that have strengthened the protection for shareholders. Financial reports and other information must be filed with the London Stock Exchange or the relevant authorities elsewhere, such as the SEC in the US, and made available to the investing public.

Accounting standards aren't limited to public companies whose securities are traded on public exchanges, such as the London and New York Stock Exchanges and NASDAQ. These financial accounting and reporting standards apply with equal force and authority to private businesses whose ownership shares aren't traded in any open market. When the shareholders of a private business receive its periodic financial reports, they're entitled to assume that the company's financial statements and footnotes are prepared in accordance with the accounting rules in force at the time. Even following the rules leave a fair amount of wriggle room – look back to Book V, Chapter 2 if you need a refresher on this subject. So it always pays to check over the figures yourself to be sure of what's really going on. The bare-bones content of a private business's annual financial report includes the three primary financial statements (Balance Sheet, Profit and Loss statement, and cash flow statement) plus several footnotes. We've seen many private company financial reports that don't even have a letter from the chairman – just the three financial statements plus a few footnotes and nothing more. In fact, we've seen financial reports of private businesses (mostly small companies) that don't even include a cash flow statement; only the Balance Sheet and Profit and Loss statement are presented. Omitting a cash flow statement violates the rules – but the company's shareholders and its lenders may not demand to see the cash flow statement, so the company can get away with it.

Publicly owned businesses must comply with an additional layer of rules and requirements that don't apply to privately owned businesses. These rules are issued by the Stock Exchange, the agency that regulates financial reporting and trading in stocks and bonds of publicly owned businesses. The Stock Exchange has no jurisdiction over private businesses; those businesses need only worry about GAAP, which don't have many hard-and-fast rules about financial report formats. Public businesses have to file financial reports and other forms with the Stock Exchange that are made available to the public. These filings are available to the public on the London Stock Exchange's website (www.londonstockexchange.com) or for US companies on the Securities Exchange Commission's (SEC's) EDGAR database at the SEC's website (www.sec.gov/edgar/quickedgar.htm).

Book VI

Accountants: Working with the Outside World

The best known of these forms is the annual 10-K, which includes the business's annual financial statements in prescribed formats with all the supporting schedules and detailed disclosures that the SEC requires.

Here are some (but not all) of the main financial reporting requirements that publicly owned businesses must adhere to. (Private businesses may include these items as well if they want, but they generally don't.)

- ✔ **Management discussion and analysis (MD&A) section:** Presents the top managers' interpretation and analysis of a business's profit performance and other important financial developments over the year.

- ✔ **Earnings per share (EPS):** The only ratio that a public business is *required* to report, although most public businesses do report a few other ratios as well. See 'Earnings per share, basic and diluted', later in this chapter. Note that private businesses' reports generally don't include any ratios (but you can, of course, compute the ratios yourself).

- ✔ **Three-year comparative Profit and Loss statements:** See Book IV, Chapter 1 for more information about Profit and Loss statements.

Note: A publicly owned business can make the required filings with the Stock Exchange or SEC and then prepare a different annual financial report for its shareholders, thus preparing two sets of financial reports. This is common practice. However, the financial information in the two documents can't differ in any material way. A typical annual financial report to shareholders is a glossy booklet with excellent art and graphic design including high-quality photographs. The company's products are promoted and its people are featured in glowing terms that describe teamwork, creativity and innovation – we're sure you get the picture. In contrast, the reports to the London Stock Exchange or SEC look like legal briefs – nothing fancy in these filings. The core of financial statements and footnotes (plus certain other information) is the same in both the Stock Exchange filings and the annual reports to shareholders. The Stock Exchange filings contain more information about certain expenses and require much more disclosure about the history of the business, its main markets and competitors, its principal officers, any major changes on the horizon and so on. Professional investors and investment managers read the Stock Exchange filings.

Most public companies solicit their shareholders' votes in the annual election of persons to the board of directors (whom the business has nominated) and on other matters that must be put to a vote at the annual shareholders' meeting. The method of communication for doing so is called a *proxy statement* – the reason being that the shareholders give their votes to a *proxy*, or designated person, who actually casts the votes at the annual meeting. The Stock Exchange requires many disclosures in proxy statements that aren't found in annual financial reports issued to shareholders or in the business's annual accounts filed at Companies House. For example, compensation paid to the top-level officers of the business must be disclosed, as well as their shareholdings. If you own shares in a public company, take the time to read through all the financial statements you receive through the post and any others you can get your hands on.

Analysing Financial Reports with Ratios

Financial reports have lots of numbers in them. (Duh!) The significance of many of these numbers isn't clear unless they're compared with other numbers in the financial statements to determine the relative size of one number to another number. One very useful way of interpreting financial reports is to compute *ratios* – that is, to divide a particular number in the financial report by another. Financial report ratios are also useful because they enable you to compare a business's current performance with its past performance or with another business's performance, regardless of whether sales revenue or net profit was bigger or smaller for the other years or the other business. In other words, using ratios cancels out size differences.

The following sections explain the ten financial statement ratios that you're most likely to run into. Here's a general overview of why these ratios are important:

- ✔ **Gross margin ratio and profit ratio:** You use these ratios to measure a business's profit performance with respect to its sales revenue. Sales revenue is the starting point for making profit; these ratios measure the percentage of total sales revenue that is left over as profit.

- ✔ **Earnings per share (EPS), price/earnings (P/E) ratio and dividend yield:** These three ratios revolve around the market price of shares, and anyone who invests in publicly owned businesses should be intimately familiar with them. As an investor, your main concern is the return you receive on your invested capital. Return on capital consists of two elements:

  - Periodic **cash dividends** distributed by the business

  - Increase (or decrease) in the **market price** of the shares

  Dividends and market prices depend on earnings – and there you have the relationship among these three ratios and why they're so important to you, the investor. Major newspapers report P/E ratios and dividend yields in their stock market activity tables; stockbrokers' investment reports focus mainly on forecasts of EPS and dividend yield.

- ✔ **Book value per share and return on equity (ROE):** Shares for private businesses have no ready market price, so investors in these businesses use the ROE ratio, which is based on the value of their ownership equity reported in the Balance Sheet, to measure investment performance. Without a market price for the shares of a private business, the P/E ratio can't be determined. EPS can easily be determined for a private business but doesn't have to be reported in its Profit and Loss statement.

- ✔ **Current ratio and acid-test ratio:** These ratios indicate whether a business should have enough cash to pay its liabilities.

- ✔ **Return on assets (ROA):** This ratio is the first step in determining how well a business is using its capital and whether it's earning more than the interest rate on its debt, which causes financial leverage gain (or loss).

To demonstrate these ratios, we use the Profit and Loss statement (shown in Figure 2-1) and the Balance Sheet of a business (shown in Figure 2-2). Notice that a cash flow statement isn't presented here – mainly because no ratios are calculated from data in the cash flow statement. (Refer to the sidebar, 'The temptation to compute cash flow per share: Don't give in!') The footnotes to the company's financial statements aren't presented here, but the use of footnotes is discussed in the following sections.

(Amounts in thousands, except per share amounts)

Profit and Loss Account for Year

Sales Revenue	£ 52,000
Cost of Goods Sold Expense	31,200
Gross Margin	£ 20,800
Sales, Administration, and General Expenses	15,600
Depreciation Expense	1,650
Earnings Before Interest and Tax	£ 3,550
Interest Expense	750
Earnings Before Tax	£ 2,800
Corporation Tax Expense	900
Net Profit	£ 1,900
Earnings Per Share	£ 2.39

Figure 2-1:
A sample Profit and Loss statement.

(Amounts in thousands)

Balance Sheet at End of Year

Assets		
Cash	£ 3,500	
Debtors	5,000	
Stock	7,800	
Prepaid Expenses	900	
Current Assets		£ 17,200
Fixed Assets	£ 19,500	
Accumulated Depreciation	(6,825)	12,675
Total Assets		£ 29,875
Liabilities		
Creditors	£ 1,500	
Accrued Expenses Payable	2,400	
Tax Payable	75	
Overdraft	4,000	
Current Liabilities		£ 7,975
Long-term Loans		6,000
Owners' Equity		
Share Capital (795,000 shares)	£ 4,000	
Retained Earnings	11,900	15,900
Total Liabilities and Owners' Equity		£ 29,875

Figure 2-2:
A sample Balance Sheet.

Gross margin ratio

Making bottom-line profit begins with making sales and earning enough gross margin from those sales, as explained in Book V, Chapter 3. In other words, a business must set its sales prices high enough over product costs to yield satisfactory gross margins on its products, because the business has to worry about many more expenses of making sales and running the business, plus interest expense and income tax expense. You calculate the *gross margin ratio* as follows:

Gross margin ÷ Sales revenue = Gross margin ratio

So a business with a £20.8 million gross margin and £52 million in sales revenue (refer to Figure 2-1) ends up with a 40 per cent gross margin ratio. Now, if the business had only been able to earn a 41 per cent gross margin, that one additional point (one point is 1 per cent) would have caused a jump in its gross margin of £520,000 (1 per cent × £52 million sales revenue) – which would have trickled down to earnings before income tax. Earnings before income tax would have been 19 per cent higher (a £520,000 bump in gross margin ÷ £2.8 million income before income tax). Never underestimate the impact of even a small improvement in the gross margin ratio!

Outside investors know only the information disclosed in the external financial report that the business releases. They can't do much more than compare the gross margin for the two- or three-yearly Profit and Loss statements included in the annual financial report. Although publicly owned businesses are required to include a management discussion and analysis (MD&A) section that should comment on any significant change in the gross margin ratio, corporate managers have wide latitude in deciding what exactly to discuss and how much detail to go into. You definitely should read the MD&A section, but it may not provide all the answers you're looking for. You have to search further in stockbroker releases, in articles in the financial press or at the next professional business meeting you attend.

As explained in Book V, Chapter 3, managers focus on *contribution margin per unit* and *total contribution margin* to control and improve profit performance business. Contribution margin equals sales revenue minus product cost and other variable operating expenses of the business. Contribution margin is profit before the company's total fixed costs for the period are deducted. Changes in the contribution margins per unit of the products sold by a business and changes in its total fixed costs are extremely important information in managing profit.

However, businesses don't disclose contribution margin information in their *external* financial reports – they wouldn't even think of doing so. This information is considered to be proprietary in nature; it should be kept confidential and out of the hands of its competitors. In short, investors don't have access to information about the business's contribution margin. Neither accounting standards nor the Stock Exchange requires that such information be disclosed. The external Profit and Loss statement discloses gross margin and operating profit, or earnings before interest and income tax expenses. However, the expenses between these two profit lines in the Profit and Loss statement aren't separated between variable and fixed (refer to Figure 2-1).

Profit ratio

Business is motivated by profit, so the *profit ratio* is very important to say the least. The profit ratio indicates how much net profit was earned on each £100 of sales revenue:

Net profit ÷ Sales revenue = Profit ratio

For example, the business in Figure 2-1 earned £1.9 million net profit from its £52 million sales revenue, so its profit ratio is 3.65 per cent, meaning that the business earned £3.65 net profit for each £100 of sales revenue.

A seemingly small change in the profit ratio can have a big impact on the bottom line. Suppose that this business had earned a profit ratio of 5 per cent instead of 3.65 per cent. That increase in the profit ratio translates into a £700,000 increase in bottom-line profit (net profit) on the same sales revenue.

Profit ratios vary widely from industry to industry. A 5–10 per cent profit ratio is common in most industries, although some high-volume retailers, such as supermarkets, are satisfied with profit ratios around 1 per cent or 2 per cent.

You can turn any ratio upside down and come up with a new way of looking at the same information. If you flip the profit ratio over to be sales revenue divided by net profit, the result is the amount of sales revenue needed to make £1 profit. Using the same example, £52 million sales revenue ÷ £1.9 million net profit = 27.37 to 1 upside-down profit ratio, which means that this business needs £27.37 in sales to make £1 profit. So you can say that net profit is 3.65 per cent of sales revenue, or you can say that sales revenue is 27.37 times net profit – but the standard profit ratio is expressed as net profit divided by sales revenue.

Earnings per share, basic and diluted

Publicly owned businesses, according to generally accepted accounting principles (GAAP), must report *earnings per share (EPS)* below the net profit line in their Profit and Loss statements – giving EPS a certain distinction among the ratios. Why is EPS considered so important? Because it gives investors a means of determining the amount the business earned on its share investments: EPS tells you how much net profit the business earned for each share you own. The essential equation for EPS is as follows:

Net profit ÷ Total number of capital stock shares = EPS

For the example in Figures 2-1 and 2-2, the company's £1.9 million net profit is divided by the 795,000 shares of stock the business has issued to compute its £2.39 EPS.

Note: Private businesses don't have to report EPS if they don't want to. Considering the wide range of issues covered by GAAP, you find surprisingly few distinctions between private and public businesses – these authoritative accounting rules apply to all businesses. But EPS is one area where GAAP makes an exception for privately owned businesses. EPS is extraordinarily important to the shareholders of businesses whose shares are publicly traded. These shareholders focus on market price *per share*. They want the total net profit of the business to be communicated to them on a per-share basis so that they can easily compare it with the market price of their shares. The shares of privately owned companies aren't actively traded, so there's no readily available market value for their shares. The thinking behind the rule that privately owned businesses shouldn't have to report EPS is that their shareholders don't focus on per share values and are more interested in the business's total net profit performance.

Book VI

Accountants: Working with the Outside World

The business in the example is too small to be publicly owned. So we turn here to a larger public company example. This publicly owned company reports that it earned £1.32 billion net profit for the year just ended. At the end of the year, this company has 400 million shares *outstanding*, which refers to the number of shares that have been issued and are owned by its shareholders. Thus, its EPS is £3.30 (£1.32 billion net profit ÷ 400 million stock shares). But here's a complication: the business is committed to issuing additional capital shares in the future for share options that the company has granted to its managers, and it has borrowed money on the basis of debt instruments that give the lenders the right to convert the debt into its capital stock. Under terms of its management share options and its convertible debt, the business could have to issue 40 million additional capital shares in the future. Dividing net profit by the number of shares outstanding plus the number of shares that could be issued in the future gives the following computation of EPS:

£1.32 billion net profit ÷ 440 million capital stock shares = £3.00 EPS

This second computation, based on the higher number of shares, is called the *diluted* earnings per share. (*Diluted* means thinned out or spread over a larger number of shares.) The first computation, based on the number of shares actually outstanding, is called *basic* earnings per share. Publicly owned businesses have to report two EPS figures – unless they have a *simple capital structure* that doesn't require the business to issue additional shares in the future. Generally, publicly owned companies have *complex capital structures* and have to report two EPS figures. Both are reported at the bottom of the Profit and Loss statement. So the company in this example reports £3.30 basic EPS and £3.00 diluted EPS. Sometimes it's not clear which of the two EPS figures is being used in press releases and in articles giving investment advice. Fortunately, *The Financial Times* and most other major financial publications leave a clear trail of both EPS figures.

Calculating basic and diluted EPS isn't always as simple as our examples may suggest. An accountant would have to adjust the EPS equation for the following complicating things that a business may do:

- ✔ Issue additional shares during the year and buy back some of its shares (shares of its stock owned by the business itself that aren't formally cancelled are called *treasury stock*).

- ✔ Issue more than one class of share, causing net profit to be divided into two or more pools – one pool for each class of share.

- ✔ Go through a merger (business combination) in which a large number of shares are issued to acquire the other business.

The shareholders should draw comfort from the fact that the top management of many businesses in which they invest are probably just as anxiously reviewing EPS performance as they are. This extract from Tesco's annual accounts reveals much:

> Annual bonuses based on achieving stretching EPS growth targets and specific corporate objectives.

> Annual bonuses are paid in shares. On award, the Executive can elect to defer receipt of the shares for a further two years, which is encouraged, with additional matching share awards.

> Longer-term bonus based on a combination of relative total shareholder return, and the achievement of stretching EPS growth targets and specific corporate objectives. Longer-term bonuses are paid in shares, which must be held for a further four years. Executive Directors are encouraged to hold shares for longer than four years with additional matching share awards. Further details are provided below.

Share options are granted to Executive Directors at market value and can only be exercised if EPS growth exceeds Retail Price Index (RPI) plus 9 per cent over any three years from grant.

Executive Directors are required to build and hold a shareholding with a value at least equal to their basic salary; full participation in the Executive Incentive scheme is conditional upon meeting this target.

Price/earnings (P/E) ratio

The *price/earnings (P/E) ratio* is another ratio that's of particular interest to investors in public businesses. The P/E ratio gives you an idea of how much you're paying in the current price for the shares for each pound of earnings, or net profit, being earned by the business. Remember that earnings prop up the market value of shares, not the book value of the shares that's reported in the Balance Sheet. (Read on for the book value per share discussion.)

The P/E ratio is, in one sense, a reality check on just how high the current market price is in relation to the underlying profit that the business is earning. Extraordinarily high P/E ratios are justified only when investors think that the company's EPS has a lot of upside potential in the future.

The P/E ratio is calculated as follows:

Current market price of stock ÷ Most recent trailing 12 months diluted EPS = P/E ratio

If the business has a simple capital structure and doesn't report a diluted EPS, its basic EPS is used for calculating its P/E ratio. (See the earlier section 'Earnings per share, basic and diluted'.)

Assume that the stock shares of a public business with a £3.65 diluted EPS are selling at £54.75 in the stock market. *Note:* From here forward, we'll use the briefer term EPS in reference to P/E ratios; we assume you understand that it refers to diluted EPS for businesses with complex capital structures and to basic EPS for businesses with simple capital structures.

The actual share price bounces around day to day and is subject to change on short notice. To illustrate the P/E ratio, we use this price, which is the closing price on the latest trading day in the stock market. This market price means that investors trading in the stock think that the shares are worth 15 times diluted EPS (£54.75 market price ÷ £3.65 diluted EPS = 15). This value may be below the broad market average that values shares at, say, 20 times EPS. The outlook for future growth in its EPS is probably not too good.

Book VI

Accountants: Working with the Outside World

Market cap – not a cap on market value

One investment number you see a lot in the financial press is the *market cap*. No, this doesn't refer to a cap, or limit, on the market value of a company's capital shares. The term is shorthand for *market capitalisation*, which refers to the total market value of the business that is determined by multiplying the stock's current market price by the total number of shares issued by the company. Suppose a company's stock is selling at £50 per share in the stock market and it has 200 million shares outstanding. Its market cap is £10 billion. Another business may be willing to pay higher than £50 per share for the company. Indeed, many acquisitions and mergers involve the acquiring company paying a hefty premium over the going market price of the shares of the company being acquired.

Dividend yield

The *dividend yield* tells investors how much *cash flow income* they're receiving on their investment. (The dividend is the cash flow income part of investment return; the other part is the gain or loss in the market value of the investment over the year.)

Suppose that a stock of a public company that is selling for £60 paid £1.20 cash dividends per share over the last year. You calculate dividend yield as follows:

£1.20 annual cash dividend per share ÷ £60 current market price of stock = 2% dividend yield

You use dividend yield to compare how your stock investment is doing to how it would be doing if you'd put that money in corporate or Treasury bonds, gilt-edged stock (UK government borrowings) or other debt securities that pay interest. The average interest rate of high-grade debt securities has recently been three to four times the dividend yields on most public companies; in theory, market price appreciation of the shares over time makes up for that gap. Of course, shareholders take the risk that the market value won't increase enough to make their total return on investment rate higher than a benchmark interest rate. (At the time of writing, this yield gap has shrunk to nothing and is causing an agonising reappraisal of the value of equities in relation to debt as an investment medium.)

Assume that long-term government gilt-edged stock is currently paying 6 per cent annual interest, which is 4 per cent higher than the business's 2 per cent dividend yield in the example just discussed. If this business's shares don't increase in value by at least 4 per cent over the year, its investors would have been better off investing in the debt securities instead. (Of course, they wouldn't have had all the perks of a share investment, like those heartfelt letters from the chairman and those glossy financial reports.) The market price of publicly traded debt securities can fall or rise, so things get a little tricky in this sort of investment analysis.

Book value per share

Book value per share is one measure, but it's certainly not the only amount, used for determining the value of a privately owned business's shares. The asset values that a business records in its books (also known as its *accounts*) are *not* the amounts that a business could get if it put its assets up for sale. Book values of some assets are generally lower than what the cost would be for replacing the assets if a disaster (such as a flood or a fire) wiped out the business's stock or equipment. Recording current market values in the books is really not a practical option. Until a seller and a buyer meet and haggle over price, trying to determine the market price for a privately owned business's shares is awfully hard.

You can calculate book value per share for publicly owned businesses too. However, market value is readily available, so shareholders (and investment advisers and managers) don't put much weight on book value per share. EPS is the main factor that affects the market prices of stock shares of public companies – not the book value per share. We should add that some investing strategies, known as *value investing*, search out companies that have a high book value per share compared to their going market prices. But by and large, book value per share plays a secondary role in the market values of stock shares issued by public companies.

Although book value per share is generally not a good indicator of the market value of a private business's shares, you do run into this ratio, at least as a starting point for haggling over a selling price. Here's how to calculate book value per share:

Total owners' equity ÷ Total number of stock shares = Book value per share

The business shown in Figure 2-2 has issued 795,000 shares: its £15.9 million total owners' equity divided by its 795,000 shares gives a book value per share of £20. If the business sold off its assets exactly for their book values and paid all its liabilities, it would end up with £15.9 million left for the shareholders, and it could therefore distribute £20 per share. But the company won't go out of business and liquidate its assets and pay off its liabilities. So book value per share is a theoretical value. It's not totally irrelevant, but it's not all that definitive, either.

Return on equity (ROE) ratio

The *return on equity (ROE) ratio* tells you how much profit a business earned in comparison to the book value of shareholders' equity. This ratio is useful for privately owned businesses, which have no way of determining the current value of owners' equity (at least not until the business is actually sold). ROE is also calculated for public companies, but, just like book value per share, it plays a secondary role and isn't the dominant factor driving market prices. (Earnings are.) Here's how you calculate this key ratio:

Net profit ÷ Owners' equity = ROE

The owners' equity figure is at book value, which is reported in the company's Balance Sheet.

The business whose Profit and Loss statement and Balance Sheet are shown in Figures 2-1 and 2-2 earned £1.9 million net profit for the year just ended and has £15.9 million owners' equity. Therefore, its ROE is 11.95 per cent (£1.9 million net profit ÷ £15.9 million owners' equity = 11.95 per cent). ROE is net profit expressed as a percentage of the amount of total owners' equity of the business, which is one of the two sources of capital to the business, the other being borrowed money, or interest-bearing debt. (A business also has non-interest-bearing operating liabilities, such as creditors.) The cost of debt capital (interest) is deducted as an expense to determine net profit. So net profit 'belongs' to the owners; it increases their equity in the business, so it makes sense to express net profit as the percentage of improvement in the owners' equity.

Gearing or leverage

Your company's liquidity keeps you solvent from day to day and month to month, and we come to that next when we look at the current ratio and acid test. But what about your ability to pay back long-term debt year after year? Two financial ratios indicate what kind of shape you're in over the long term.

If you've read this chapter from the beginning, you may be getting really bored with financial ratios by now, but your lenders – bankers and bondholders, if you have them – find these long-term ratios to be incredibly fascinating, for obvious reasons.

The first ratio gauges how easy it is for your company to continue making interest payments on the debt:

> Times interest earned = Earnings before interest and taxes ÷ Interest expense

Don't get confused – earnings before any interest expense and taxes are paid (EBIT) is really just the profit that you have available to make those interest payments in the first place. Figure 2-1, for example, shows an EBIT of £3.55Million and an interest expense of £750,000 this year for a times-interest-earned ratio of 4.73. In other words, this business can meet its interest expense 4.73 times over.

You may also hear the same number called an *interest coverage*. Lenders get mighty nervous if this ratio ever gets anywhere close to 1.0, because at that point, every last penny of profits goes for interest payments on the long-term debt.

The second ratio tries to determine whether the principal amount of your debt is in any danger:

> Debt-to-equity ratio = Long-term liabilities ÷ Owners' equity

The debt-to-equity ratio says a great deal about the general financial structure of your company. After all, you can raise money to support your company in only two ways: borrow it and promise to pay it back with interest, or sell pieces of the company and promise to share all the rewards of ownership. The first method is debt; the second, equity.

Figure 2-2, for example, shows a debt-to-equity ratio of £6,000 divided by £15,900, or 0.38. This ratio means that the company has around three times more equity financing than it does long-term debt.

Lenders love to see lots of equity supporting a company's debt because then they know that the money they loan out is safer. If something goes wrong with the company, they can go after the owners' money. Equity investors, on the other hand, actually want to take on some risk. They like to see relatively high debt-to-equity ratios because that situation increases their leverage and (as the following section points out) can substantially boost their profits. So the debt-to-equity ratio that's just right for your company depends not only on your industry and how stable it is, but also on who you ask.

Current ratio

The *current ratio* is a test of a business's *short-term solvency* – its capability to pay off its liabilities that come due in the near future (up to one year). The ratio is a rough indicator of whether cash on hand plus the cash flow from collecting debtors and selling stock will be enough to pay off the liabilities that will come due in the next period.

As you can imagine, lenders are particularly keen on punching in the numbers to calculate the current ratio. Here's how they do it:

Current assets ÷ Current liabilities = Current ratio

Note: Unlike with most of the other ratios, you don't multiply the result of this equation by 100 and represent it as a percentage.

Businesses are expected by their creditors to maintain a minimum current ratio (2.0, meaning a 2-to-1 ratio, is the general rule) and may be legally required to stay above a minimum current ratio as stipulated in their contracts with lenders. The business in Figure 2-2 has £17.2 million in current assets and £7,975,000 in current liabilities, so its current ratio is 2.16 and it shouldn't have to worry about lenders coming by in the middle of the night to break its legs.

How much working capital, ready or nearly ready money do you need to ensure survival? Having the liquid assets available when you absolutely need them to meet short-term obligations is called *liquidity*. You don't have to have cash in the till to be liquid. Debtors (that is, people who owe you money and can be reasonably expected to cough up soon) and stock ready to be sold are both part of your liquid assets. You can use several financial ratios to test a business's liquidity, including the current ratio and the acid test. You can monitor these ratios year by year and measure them against your competitors' ratios and the industry averages.

Acid-test ratio

Most serious investors and lenders don't stop with the current ratio for an indication of the business's short-term solvency – its capability to pay the liabilities that will come due in the short term. Investors also calculate the *acid-test ratio* (also known as the *quick ratio* or the *pounce ratio*), which is a more severe test of a business's solvency than the current ratio. The acid-test ratio excludes stock and prepaid expenses, which the current ratio includes, and limits assets to cash and items that the business can quickly convert to cash. This limited category of assets is known as *quick* or *liquid* assets.

You calculate the acid-test ratio as follows:

Liquid assets ÷ Total current liabilities = Acid-test ratio

Note: Unlike most other financial ratios, you don't multiply the result of this equation by 100 and represent it as a percentage.

For the business example shown in Figure 2-2, the acid-test ratio is as follows:

Cash	£3,500,000
Marketable securities	none
Debtors	5,000,000
Total liquid assets	£8,500,000
Total current liabilities	£7,975,000
Acid-test ratio	1.07

A 1.07 acid-test ratio means that the business would be able to pay off its short-term liabilities and still have a little bit of liquid assets left over. The general rule is that the acid-test ratio should be at least 1.0, which means that liquid assets equal current liabilities. Of course, falling below 1.0 doesn't mean that the business is on the verge of bankruptcy, but if the ratio falls as low as 0.5, that may be cause for alarm.

This ratio is also known as the *pounce ratio* to emphasise that you're calculating for a worst-case scenario, where a pack of wolves (more politely known as *creditors*) has pounced on the business and is demanding quick payment of the business's liabilities. But don't panic. Short-term creditors don't have the right to demand immediate payment, except under unusual circumstances. This is a very conservative way to look at a business's capability to pay its short-term liabilities – too conservative in most cases.

Keeping track of stock and debtor levels

Two other areas that effect liquidity need to be monitored carefully: how fast your stock is selling out (if your business requires holding goods for sale), and how fast your customers are paying up.

Here's the ratio for stock levels:

Stock turnover = Cost of goods sold ÷ Stock

Stock turnover tells you something about how liquid your stocks really are. This ratio divides the cost of goods sold, as shown in your yearly Profit and

Loss statement, by the average value of your stock. If you don't know the average, you can estimate it by using the stock figure listed in the Balance Sheet at the end of the year.

For the business represented in Figures 2-1 and 2-2, the stock turnover is £31,200 ÷ £7,800, or 4.0. This ratio means that this business turns over its stock four times each year. Expressed in days, the business carries a 91.25-day (365 ÷ 4.0) supply of stock.

Is a 90-day plus inventory good or bad? It depends on the industry and even on the time of year. A car dealer who has a 90-day supply of cars at the height of the season may be in a strong stock position, but the same stock position at the end of the season could be a real weakness. As Just In Time (JIT) supply chains and improved information systems make business operations more efficient across all industries, stock turnover is on the rise, and the average number of days that stock of any kind hangs around continues to shrink.

What about debtor levels?

Debtor turnover = Sales on credit ÷ Debtors

Debtor turnover tells you something about liquidity by dividing the sales that you make on credit by the average debtors. If an average isn't available, you can use the debtors from a Balance Sheet.

If the business represented in Figures 2-1 and 2-2 makes 80 per cent of its sales on credit, its debtor turnover is (£52,000 multiplied by 0.8) divided by £5,000, or 8.3. In other words, the company turns over its debtors 8.3 times per year, or once every 44 days, on average. That's not too bad: payment terms are 30 days. But remember, unlike fine wine, debtors don't improve with age.

Return on assets (ROA) ratio

One factor affecting the bottom-line profit of a business is whether it used debt to its advantage. For the year, a business may have realised a *financial leverage gain* – it earned more profit on the money it borrowed than the interest paid for the use of that borrowed money. So a good part of its net profit for the year may be due to financial leverage. The first step in determining financial leverage gain is to calculate a business's *return on assets (ROA) ratio*, which is the ratio of EBIT (earnings before interest and tax) to the total capital invested in operating assets.

Here's how to calculate ROA:

EBIT ÷ Net operating assets = ROA

Note: This equation calls for *net operating assets*, which equals total assets less the non-interest-bearing operating liabilities of the business. Actually, many stock analysts and investors use the total assets figure because deducting all the non-interest-bearing operating liabilities from total assets to determine net operating assets is, quite frankly, a nuisance. But we strongly recommend using net operating assets because that's the total amount of capital raised from debt and equity.

Compare ROA with the interest rate: if a business's ROA is 14 per cent and the interest rate on its debt is 8 per cent, for example, the business's net gain on its debt capital is 6 per cent more than what it's paying in interest. There's a favourable spread of 6 points (one point = 1 per cent), which can be multiplied by the total debt of the business to determine how much its total earnings before income tax is traceable to financial leverage gain.

In Figure 2-2, notice that the company has £10 million total interest-bearing debt (£4 million short-term plus £6 million long-term). Its total owners' equity is £15.9 million. So its net operating assets total is £25.9 million (which excludes the three short-term non-interest-bearing operating liabilities). The company's ROA, therefore, is

£3.55 million earnings before interest and tax ÷ £25.9 million net operating assets = 13.71% ROA

The business earned £1,371,000 (rounded) on its total debt – 13.71 per cent ROA times £10 million total debt. The business paid only £750,000 interest on its debt. So the business had £621,000 financial leverage gain before income tax (£1,371,000 less £750,000). Put another way, the business paid 7.5 per cent interest on its debt but earned 13.71 per cent on this money for a favourable spread of 6.21 points – which, when multiplied by the £10 million debt, yields the £621,000 pre-tax financial gain for the year.

ROA is a useful earnings ratio, aside from determining financial leverage gain (or loss) for the period. ROA is a *capital utilisation* test – how much profit before interest and tax was earned on the total capital employed by the business. The basic idea is that it takes money (assets) to make money (profit); the final test is how much profit was made on the assets. If, for example, a business earns £1 million EBIT on £20 million assets, its ROA is only 5 per cent. Such a low ROA signals that the business is making poor use of its assets and will have to improve its ROA or face serious problems in the future.

Using combined ratios

You wouldn't use a single ratio to decide whether one vehicle was a better or worse buy than another. Miles per Gallon (MPG), Miles per hour (MPH), annual depreciation percentage and residual value proportion are just a handful of the ratios that you'd want to review. So it is with a business. You can use a combination of ratios to form an opinion on the financial state of affairs at any one time.

The best known of these combination ratios is the Altman Z-Score (www.creditguru.com/CalcAltZ.shtml) that uses a combined set of five financial ratios derived from eight variables from a company's financial statements linked to some statistical techniques to predict a company's probability of failure. Entering the figures into the onscreen template at this website produces a score and an explanatory narrative giving a view on the businesses financial strengths and weaknesses.

Appreciating the limits of ratios

A danger with ratios is to believe that because you have a precise number, you have a right figure to aim for. For example, a natural feeling with financial ratios is to think that high figures are good ones, and an upward trend represents the right direction. This theory is, to some extent, encouraged by the personal feeling of wealth that having a lot of cash engenders.

Unfortunately, no general rule exists on which way is right for financial ratios. In some cases a high figure is good; in others, a low figure is best. Indeed, in some circumstances, ratios of the same value aren't as good as each other. Look at the two working capital statements in Table 2-1.

Table 2-1	Difficult Comparisons				
	1				*2*
Current Assets					
Stock	10,000				22,990
Debtors	13,000				100
Cash	100	23,100	10		23,100
Less Current Liabilities					
Overdraft	5,000		90		
Creditors	1,690	6,690	6,690		6,690
Working Capital		16,410			16,410
Current Ratio		3.4:1			3.4:1

The amount of working capital in examples 1 and 2 is the same, £16,410, as are the current assets and current liabilities, at £23,100 and £6,690 respectively. It follows that any ratio using these factors would also be the same. For example, the current ratios in these two examples are both identical, 3.4:1, but in the first case there's a reasonable chance that some cash will come in from debtors, certainly enough to meet the modest creditor position. In the second example there's no possibility of useful amounts of cash coming in from trading, with debtors at only £100, while creditors at the relatively substantial figure of £6,600 will pose a real threat to financial stability.

So in this case the current ratios are identical, but the situations being compared are not. In fact, as a general rule, a higher working capital ratio is regarded as a move in the wrong direction. The more money a business has tied up in working capital, the more difficult it is to make a satisfactory return on capital employed, simply because the larger the denominator, the lower the return on capital employed.

In some cases the right direction is more obvious. A high return on capital employed is usually better than a low one, but even this situation can be a danger signal, warning that higher risks are being taken. And not all high profit ratios are good: sometimes a higher profit margin can lead to reduced sales volume and so lead to a lower return on capital employed (ROCE).

In general, business performance as measured by ratios is best thought of as lying within a range; liquidity (current ratio), for example, staying between 1.2:1 and 1.8:1. A change in either direction may represent a cause for concern.

The Biz/ed (www.bized.co.uk/compfact/ratios/index.htm) website contains free tools that calculate financial ratios from company accounts. It also provide useful introductions to ratio analysis and definitions of each ratio and the formula used to calculate it.

By registering (for free) with the ProShare website (go to www.proshareclubs.co.uk and click on 'Research Centre' and 'Performance Tables'), you have access to a number of tools that crunch public company ratios for you. Select the companies you want to look at, and then the ratios you're most interested in (EPS, P/E, ROI, Dividend Yield and so on). All is revealed within a couple of seconds. You can then rank the companies by performance in more or less any way you want. You can find more comprehensive tools on the Internet, on the websites of share traders for example, but ProShare is a great site to cut your teeth on – and the price is right!

The temptation to compute cash flow per share: Don't give in!

Businesses are prohibited from reporting a *cash flow per share* number on their financial reports. The accounting rule book specifically prohibits very few things, and cash flow per share is on this small list of contraband. Why? Because – and this is somewhat speculative on our part – the powers that be were worried that the cash flow number would usurp net profit as the main measure for profit performance. Indeed, many writers in the financial press were talking up the importance of cash flow from profit, so we see the concern on this matter. Knowing how important EPS is for market value of stocks, the authorities declared a similar per share amount for cash flow out of bounds and prohibited it from being included in a financial report. Of course, you could compute it quite easily – the rule doesn't apply to how financial statements are interpreted, only to how they're reported.

Should we dare give you an example of cash flow per share? Here goes: a business with £42 million cash flow from profit and 4.2 million total capital stock shares would end up with £10 cash flow per share. Shhh. One final sidebar, and you can call it quits — okay?

Frolicking through the Footnotes

Reading the footnotes in annual financial reports is no picnic. The investment pros have to read them, because in providing consultation to their clients they're required to comply with due diligence standards, or because of their legal duties and responsibilities of managing other peoples' money.

We suggest you do a quick read-through of the footnotes and identify the ones that seem to have the most significance. Generally, the most important footnotes are those dealing with the following matters:

- ✔ **Share options awarded by the business to its executives:** The additional shares issued under share options dilute (thin out) the earnings per share of the business, which in turn puts downside pressure on the market value of its shares, everything else being the same.

- ✔ **Pending legal actions, litigation and investigations by government agencies:** These intrusions into the normal affairs of the business can have enormous consequences.

- ✔ **Segment information for the business:** Most public businesses have to report information for the major segments of the organisation – sales and operating profit by territories or product lines. This gives a better glimpse of the different parts making up the whole business. (However, segment information may be reported elsewhere in an annual financial report than in the footnotes.)

These are just three of the many important pieces of information you should look for in footnotes. But you have to stay alert for other critical matters that a business may disclose in its footnotes – scan each and every footnote for potentially important information. You may find a footnote that discusses a major lawsuit against the business, for example, that makes the shares too risky for your portfolio.

Checking for Ominous Skies on the Audit Report

The value of analysing a financial report depends directly and entirely on the accuracy of the report's numbers. Top management wants to present the best possible picture of the business in its financial report (which is understandable, of course). The managers have a vested interest in the profit performance and financial condition of the business.

Independent auditors are like umpires in the financial reporting process. The auditor comes in, does an audit of the business's accounting system and procedures, and gives a report that's attached to the company's financial statements. You should check the audit report included with the financial report. Publicly owned businesses are required to have their annual financial reports audited by an independent accountancy firm, and many privately owned businesses have audits done too because they know that an audit report adds credibility to the financial report.

What if a private business's financial report doesn't include an audit report? Well, you have to trust that the business prepared accurate financial statements that follow generally accepted accounting principles and that the footnotes to the financial statements provide adequate disclosure.

Unfortunately, the audit report gets short shrift in financial statement analysis, maybe because it's so full of technical terminology and accountant doublespeak. But even though audit reports are a tough read, anyone who reads and analyses financial reports should definitely read the audit report. Book VI, Chapter 3 provides a lot more information on audits and the auditor's report.

The auditor judges whether the business used accounting methods and procedures in accordance with accepted accounting principles. In most cases, the auditor's report confirms that everything is hunky-dory, and you can rely on the financial report. However, sometimes an auditor waves a yellow flag – and in extreme cases, a red flag. Here are the two most important warnings to watch out for in an audit report:

   ✔ The business's capability to continue normal operations is in doubt because of what are known as *financial exigencies*, which may mean a low cash balance, unpaid overdue liabilities or major lawsuits that the business doesn't have the cash to cover.

   ✔ One or more of the methods used in the report isn't in line with the prevailing accounting body rules, leading the auditor to conclude that the numbers reported are misleading or that disclosure is inadequate.

Although auditor warnings don't necessarily mean that a business is going down the tubes, they should turn on that light bulb in your head and make you more cautious and sceptical about the financial report. The auditor is questioning the very information on which the business's value is based, and you can't take that kind of thing lightly.

In very small businesses it's likely that the accounts won't be independently audited and their accounts come with a rather alarming caveat, running something like this: *These accounts have been prepared on the basis of information provided by the owners and have not been independently verified.* A full audit is an expensive process and few businesses that don't have to will go to the expense and trouble just to be told what they probably already know anyway.

Just because a business has a clean audit report doesn't mean that the financial report is completely accurate and above board. As discussed in Book VI, Chapter 3, auditors don't necessarily catch everything. Keep in mind that the accounting rules are pretty flexible, leaving a company's accountants with room for interpretation and creativity that's just short of *cooking the books* (deliberately defrauding and misleading readers of the financial report). Window dressing and profit smoothing – two common examples of massaging the numbers – are explained in Book VI, Chapter 1.

Finding Financial Facts

Understanding how to calculate financial ratios and how to interpret that data is all fine and dandy, but before you can do anything useful you need to get a copy of the accounts in the first place. Seeing the accounts for your own business shouldn't be too much of a problem. If you're the boss, the accounts should be on your desk right now; if you're not the boss, try snuggling up to the accounts department. If they're too coy to let you have today's figures, the latest audited accounts are in the public domain anyway filed away at Companies House (www.companieshouse.gov.uk), as required by law.

Public company accounts

Most companies make their glossy annual financial reports available to download from their websites, which you can find by typing the company name into an Internet search engine. You need to have Adobe Acrobat Reader on your computer to open the files. No problem, though: Adobe Acrobat Reader is free and you can easily download the program from Adobe's website (http://get.adobe.com/uk/reader).

Yahoo has direct online links to several thousand public company reports and accounts and performance ratios at http://uk.finance.yahoo.com. (Enter the name of the company you're looking for in the box on the left of the screen under Investing. It appears after you've entered about three letters; click and follow the threads). Paying this site a visit saves you the time and trouble of hunting down company websites.

Private company accounts

Finding financial information on private companies is often a time-consuming and frustrating job. Not for nothing do these companies call themselves 'private'. Businesses, and particularly smaller businesses, can be very secretive about their finances and have plenty of tricks to hide information from prying eyes. Many smaller businesses can elect to file abbreviated accounts with Companies House that provide only the barest details. The accounts of very small companies don't need to be audited, so the objective reliability of the scant data given may be questionable. Having said that, tens of thousands of private companies file full and generally reliable accounts.

Two fruitful sources of private company accounts exist:

✔ **Companies House** (www.companieshouse.gov.uk) is the official repository of all company information in the UK. Its WebCHeck service offers a free Company Names and Address Index that covers 2 million companies, searchable either by company name or by company registration numbers. You can use WebCHeck to purchase (at a cost of £1 per document) a company's latest accounts that give details of sales, profits, margins, directors, shareholders and bank borrowings.

✔ **Keynote** (www.keynote.co.uk) offers business ratios and trends for 140 industry sectors and provides information to assess accurately the financial health of each industry sector. This service enables you to find out how profitable a business sector is and how successful the main companies operating in each sector are. Executive summaries are free, but expect to pay between £400 and £600 for most reports.

Scoring credit

If all you want is a quick handle on whether a company is likely to be around long enough to pay its bills, including a dividend to shareholders, then a whole heap of information exists about credit status for both individual sole traders and companies of varying complexity. Expect to pay anywhere from £5 for basic information up to £200 for a very comprehensive picture of a company's credit status, so you can avoid trading unknowingly with individuals or businesses that pose a credit risk.

Experian (www.ukexperian.com), Dun & Bradstreet (www.dnb.com), Creditgate.com (www.creditgate.com) and Credit Reporting (www.creditreporting.co.uk) are the major agencies compiling and selling credit histories and small-business information. Between them they offer a comprehensive range of credit reports instantly available online that include advice about credit limits.

Using FAME (Financial Analysis Made Easy)

FAME (Financial Analysis Made Easy) is a powerful database that contains information on 7 million companies in the UK and Ireland. Typically, the following information is included: contact information including phone, email and web addresses plus main and other trading addresses; activity details; 29 Profit and Loss statement and 63 Balance Sheet items; cash flow and ratios; credit score and rating; security and price information (listed companies only); names of bankers, auditors, previous auditors and advisers; details of holdings and subsidiaries (including foreign holdings and subsidiaries); names of current and previous directors with home addresses and shareholder indicator; heads of department; and shareholders. You can compare each company with detailed financials with its peer group based on its activity codes and the software lets you search for companies that comply with your own criteria, combining as many conditions as you like. FAME is available in business libraries and on CD from the publishers, who also offer a free trial (www.bvdinfo.com/Products/Company-Information/National/FAME.aspx).

Looking beyond financial statements

Investors can't rely solely on the financial report when making investment decisions. Analysing a business's financial statements is just one part of the process. You may need to consider these additional factors, depending on the business you're thinking about investing in:

✔ Industry trends and problems

✔ National economic and political developments

✔ Possible mergers, friendly acquisitions and hostile takeovers

✔ Turnover of key executives

✔ International markets and currency exchange ratios

✔ Supply shortages

✔ Product surpluses

Whew! This kind of stuff goes way beyond accounting, obviously, and is just as significant as financial statement analysis when you're picking stocks and managing investment portfolios. A good book for new investors to read is *Investing For Dummies* by Tony Levene (John Wiley & Sons).

Have a Go

Use the following Profit and Loss statement and Balance Sheet for Company A to answer the questions in this Have a Go section.

Company A Ltd.

Profit and Loss Account	*£000s*
Sales revenue	110,000
Cost of goods sold	(62,400)
Gross margin	47,600
Sales, admin and general expenses	31,200
Depreciation expense	3,300
Earnings before interest and tax	13,100
Interest expenses	1,500
Earnings before tax	11,600
Corporation tax payable	1,800
Net profit	**9,800**

Earnings per share £6.16 (9,800,000 ÷ 1,590,000 shares)

(continued)

Company A Ltd. (continued)

Balance Sheet	*£000s*	
Fixed Assets	*39,000*	
Accumulated depreciation	13,650	25,350
Current Assets		
Stock	15,600	
Debtors	10,000	
Cash	7,000	
Prepaid expenses	1,500	
	£34,400	
Current Liabilities		
Creditors	3,000	
Accrued expenses	4,800	
Tax payable	150	
Overdraft	8,000	
	15,950	
Net current assets		18,450
Total assets less current liabilities		43,800
Long-term liabilities		12,000
		31,800
Capital		
Share capital		8,000
Retained earnings		23,800
		31,800

1. Calculate the gross profit margin for Company A.

2. Calculate the net profit ratio for Company A.

3. What is the earnings per share (EPS)?

4. What is the price earnings ratio (P/E ratio), given that the market value of the shares is £21?

5. Suppose the stock of a public company is selling at £50 and it offers cash dividends per share of 75p. What is the dividend yield?

6. Calculate the return on equity for Company A.

7. Calculate the current ratio for Company A.

8. Calculate the acid ratio for Company A.

9. Calculate the stock turnover for Company A.

10. Calculate the debtors turnover for Company A. Assume that 80 per cent of sales are on credit.

Answering the Have a Go Questions

1. You calculate the gross profit margin as follows:

   - Gross margin ÷ Sales revenue × 100

   - = 47,600 ÷ 110,000 × 100

   - = **43.27%**

2. You calculate the net profit ratio as follows:

   - Net Profit ÷ Sales Revenue × 100

   - = 9,800 ÷ 110,000 × 100

   - = **8.91%**

3. You calculate the earnings per share as follows:

   - Net profit ÷ Total number of shares

   - = 9,800,000 ÷ 1,590,000

   - = **$6.16**

4. You calculate the P/E ratio as follows:

   - Market value of share ÷ EPS

   - = 21 ÷ 6.16

   - = **$3.41**

5. You calculate the dividend yield as follows:

   - Annual cash dividend ÷ Current market price per share

   - = 75p ÷ 50

   - = **1.5%**

6. **You calculate return on equity as follows:**

   - Net profit ÷ Owners equity

   - = 9,800 ÷ 31,800

   - = **30.8%**

7. **You calculate the current ratio as follows:**

   - Current assets ÷ Current liabilities

   - = 34,400 ÷ 15,950

   - = **2.156**

   Businesses are expected to have a current ratio of approximately 2:1, so this is fine.

8. **You calculate the acid ratio as follows:**

   - Cash + Debtors ÷ Current liabilities

   - = 17,000 (7,000 + 10,000) ÷ 15,950

   - = **1.06**

   The company would be able to pay off its short-term liabilities, so this result is fine.

9. **You calculate the stock turnover as follows:**

   - Cost of goods sold ÷ stock

   - = 62,400 ÷ 15,600

   - = **4**

   This means that the business is turning over its stock four times a year. Expressed in days, you'd say that the business carries 91.25 days' worth of stock (365 ÷ 4).

10. **You calculate the debtors turnover as follows:**

    - Sales on credit ÷ Debtors

    - = 88,000 (110,000 × 0.8) ÷ 10,000

    - = **8.8**

    This means that the company turns over its debt 8.8 times a year, or once every 41 days (365 ÷ 8.8).

Chapter 3

Professional Auditors and Advisers

*I*f we'd written this chapter 50 years ago, we'd have talked almost exclusively about the role of the professional chartered or certified accountant as the *auditor* of the financial statements and footnotes presented in a business's annual financial report to its owners and lenders. Back then, in the 'good old days', audits were a professional accountancy firm's bread-and-butter service – audit fees were a large share of these firms' annual revenue. Audits were the core function that accountants performed then. In addition to audits, accountants provided accounting and tax advice to their clients, and that was pretty much all they did.

Today, accountants do a lot more than auditing. In fact, the profession has shifted away from the expression *auditing* in favour of broader terms like *assurance* and *attestation*. More importantly, accountants have moved into consulting and advising clients on matters other than accounting and tax. The movement into the consulting business while continuing to do audits – often for the same clients – has caused all sorts of problems, which this chapter looks at after discussing audits by accountants.

Why Audits?

When Jane graduated from university, she went to work for a big national accountancy firm. The transition from textbook accounting theory to real-world accounting practice came as a shock. Some of her clients dabbled in window dressing (refer to Book VI, Chapter 1), and more than a few used earnings management tactics. It was a bit of a reality check, to say the least! Jane's experience demonstrates that not everything is pure and straight. Nevertheless, legal and ethical lines of conduct separate what is tolerated and what isn't. If you cross the lines, you're subject to legal sanctions and can be held liable to others. For instance, a business can deliberately deceive its investors and lenders with false or misleading numbers in its financial report. Instead of 'What You See Is What You Get' in its financial statements, you get a filtered and twisted version of the business's financial affairs – more of a 'What I Want You to See Is What You Get' version. That's where audits come in.

Audits are the best practical means for keeping fraudulent and misleading financial reporting to a minimum. A business having an independent accounting professional who comes in once a year to check up on its accounting system is like a person getting a physical exam once a year – the audit exam may uncover problems that the business was not aware of, and knowing that the auditors come in once a year to take a close look at things keeps the business on its toes.

The basic purpose of an annual financial statement audit is to make sure that a business has followed the accounting methods and disclosure requirements required by law – in other words, to make sure that the business has stayed in the ballpark of accounting rules. After completing an audit examination, the accountant prepares a short auditor's report stating that the business has prepared its financial statements according to the rules – or has not, as the case may be. In this way, audits are an effective means of enforcing accounting standards.

An audit by an independent accountant provides assurance (but not an iron-clad guarantee) that the business's financial statements follow accepted accounting methods and provide adequate disclosure. This is the main reason why accountancy firms are paid to do annual audits of financial reports. The auditor must be *independent* of the business being audited. The auditor can have no financial stake in the business or any other relationship with the client that may compromise his objectivity. However, the independence of auditors has come under scrutiny of late. See the section 'From Audits to Advising', later in the chapter.

The core of a business's financial report is its three primary financial statements – the Profit and Loss statement, the Cash Flow statement and the Balance Sheet – and the necessary footnotes to these statements. A financial report may consist of just these statements and footnotes and nothing more. Usually, however, there's more – in some cases, a lot more. Book VI, Chapter 1 explains the additional content of financial reports of public business corporations, such as the transmittal letter to the owners from the chief executive of the business, historical summaries, supporting schedules and listings of directors and top-level managers – items not often included in the financial reports of private businesses.

The auditor's opinion covers the financial statements and the accompanying footnotes. The auditor, therefore, doesn't express an opinion on whether the chairman's letter to the shareholders is a good letter – although if the chairman's claims contradicted the financial statements, the auditor would comment on the inconsistency. In short, auditors audit the financial statements and their footnotes but don't ignore the additional information included in annual financial reports.

Although the large majority of audited financial statements are reliable, a few slip through the audit net. Auditor approval isn't a 100 per cent guarantee that the financial statements contain no erroneous or fraudulent numbers, or that the statements and their footnotes provide all required disclosures, as the all-too-frequent Enron-like events attest.

Who's Who in the World of Audits

To become a qualified accountant, a person usually has to hold a degree, pass a rigorous national exam, have audit experience and satisfy continuing education requirements. Many accountants operate as sole practitioners, but many form partnerships (also called firms). An accountancy firm has to be large enough to assign enough staff auditors to the client so that all audit work can be completed in a relatively short period – financial reports are generally released about four to six weeks after the close of the fiscal year. Large businesses need large accountancy firms, and very large global business organisations need very large international accountancy firms. The public accounting profession consists of four very large international firms, known as 'The Big Four': PricewaterhouseCoopers, Deloitte, KPMG and Ernst & Young. There are also several good-sized second-tier national firms, often with international network arrangements, many regional firms, small local firms and sole practitioners.

All businesses whose ownership units (shares) are traded in public markets in the UK, the US and most other countries with major stock markets are required to have annual audits by independent auditors. Every stock you see listed on the LSE (London Stock Exchange), the NYSE (New York Stock Exchange), NASDAQ (National Association of Securities Dealers Automated Quotations) and other stock-trading markets must be audited by an outside accountancy firm. Accountancy firms are legally organised as limited liability partnerships, so you see *LLP* after their names. For businesses that are legally required to have audits done, the annual audit is a cost of doing business; it's the price they pay for going into public markets for their capital and for having their shares traded in a public marketplace – which provides liquidity for their shares.

Banks and other lenders may insist on audited financial statements. We'd say that the amount of a bank loan, generally speaking, has to be more than £5 million or £10 million before a lender will insist that the business pay for the cost of an audit. If outside non-manager investors – for example, venture capital providers or business angels – have much invested in a business, they almost certainly insist on an annual audit to be carried out by a substantial firm such as those listed earlier.

Instead of an audit, which they couldn't realistically afford, many smaller businesses have an outside accountant come in regularly to look over their accounting methods and give advice on their financial reporting. Unless an accountant has done an audit, he has to be very careful not to express an opinion on the external financial statements. Without a careful examination of the evidence supporting the account balances, the accountant is in no position to give an opinion on the financial statements prepared from the accounts of the business.

In the grand scheme of things, most audits are a necessary evil that doesn't uncover anything seriously wrong with a business's accounting system and the accounting methods it uses to prepare its financial statements. Overall, the financial statements end up looking virtually the same as they'd have looked without an audit. Still, an audit has certain side benefits. In the course of doing an audit, an accountant watches for business practices that could stand some improvement and is alert to potential problems. And fraudsters beware: accountants may face legal action if they fail to report any dodgy dealings they discover.

The auditor usually recommends ways in which the client's *internal controls* can be strengthened. For example, an auditor may discover that accounting employees aren't required to take holidays and let someone else do their jobs while they're gone. The auditor would recommend that the internal control requiring holidays away from the office be strictly enforced. Book II, Chapter 1 explains that good internal controls are extremely important in an accounting system.

What an Auditor Does before Giving an Opinion

An auditor does two basic things: *examines evidence* and *gives an opinion* about the financial statements. The lion's share of audit time is spent on examining evidence supporting the transactions and accounts of the business. A very small part of the total audit time is spent on writing the auditor's report, in which the auditor expresses an opinion on the financial statements and footnotes.

This list gives you an idea of what the auditor does 'in the field' – that is, on the premises of the business being audited:

- ✔ Evaluates the design and operating dependability of the business's accounting system and procedures.

- ✔ Evaluates and tests the business's internal accounting controls that are established to deter and detect errors and fraud.

- ✔ Identifies and critically examines the business's accounting methods – especially whether the methods conform to generally accepted accounting rules, which are the touchstones for all businesses.

- ✔ Inspects documentary and physical evidence for the business's revenues, expenses, assets, liabilities and owners' equities – for example, the auditor counts products held in stock, observes the condition of those products and confirms bank account balances directly with the banks.

Book VI

Accountants: Working with the Outside World

The purpose of all the audit work (examining evidence) is to provide a convincing basis for expressing an opinion on the business's financial statements, attesting that the company's financial statements and footnotes (as well as any directly supporting tables and schedules) can be relied upon – or not, in some cases. The auditor puts that opinion in the auditor's report.

The auditor's report is the only visible part of the audit process to financial statement readers – the tip of the iceberg. All the readers see is the auditor's one-page report (which is based on the evidence examined during the audit process, of course).

What's in an Auditor's Report

The audit report, which is included in the financial report near the financial statements, serves two useful purposes:

- ✔ It reassures investors and creditors that the financial report can be relied upon or calls attention to any serious departures from established financial reporting standards and principles.

- ✔ It prevents (in the large majority of cases, anyway) businesses from issuing sloppy or fraudulent financial reports. Knowing that your report will be subject to an independent audit really keeps you on your toes!

The large majority of audit reports on financial statements give the business a clean bill of health, or a *clean opinion*. At the other end of the spectrum, the auditor may state that the financial statements are misleading and shouldn't be relied upon. This negative audit report is called an *adverse opinion*. That's the big stick that auditors carry: they have the power to give a company's financial statements an adverse opinion, and no business wants that. Notice that we say here that the audit firms 'have the power' to give an adverse opinion. In fact, the threat of an adverse opinion almost always motivates a business to give way to the auditor and change its accounting or disclosure in order to avoid getting the kiss of death of an adverse opinion. An adverse audit opinion, if it were actually given, states that the financial statements of the business are misleading and, by implication, fraudulent. The London Stock Exchange (LSE) and the US's Security & Exchange Commission (SEC) don't tolerate adverse opinions; they'd stop trading in the company's shares if the company received an adverse opinion from its auditor.

Between the two extremes of a clean opinion and an adverse opinion, an auditor's report may point out a flaw in the company's financial statements – but not a fatal flaw that would require an adverse opinion. These are called *qualified opinions*.

The following sections look at the most common type of audit report: the clean opinion, in which the auditor certifies that the business's financial statements conform to the rules and are presented fairly, and the other kind of opinion, which is not quite so squeaky clean!

True and fair: A clean opinion

If the auditor finds no serious problems, the audit firm states that the accounts give a true and fair view of the state of affairs of the company. In the US, the auditor gives the financial report an *unqualified opinion*, which is the correct technical name, but most people call it a *clean opinion*. This expression has started to make its way in UK accounting parlance as the auditing business becomes more international. The clean-opinion audit report runs to about 100 words and three paragraphs, with enough defensive legal language to make even a seasoned accountant blush. This is a clean, or unqualified, opinion in the standard three-paragraph format:

In our opinion:

> *The financial statements give a true and fair view of the state of affairs of the company and the Group at 22 February 2012 and of the profit and cash flows of the Group for the year then ended;*

> *The financial statements have been properly prepared in accordance with the Companies Act 1985; and*

> *Those parts of the Directors' remuneration report required by Part 3 of Schedule 7A to the Companies Act 1985 have been properly prepared in accordance with the Companies Act 1985.*

1st paragraph	We did the audit, but the financial statements are the responsibility of management; we just express an opinion on them.
2nd paragraph	We carried out audit procedures that provide us a reasonable basis for expressing our opinion, but we didn't necessarily catch everything.
3rd paragraph	The company's financial statements conform to generally accepted accounting principles and aren't misleading.

Figure 3-1 presents a clean opinion but in a *one*-paragraph format – given by PricewaterhouseCoopers on one of Caterpillar's financial statements. For many years, Price Waterhouse (as it was known before its merger with Coopers) was well known for its maverick one-paragraph audit report.

REPORT OF INDEPENDENT ACCOUNTANTS

PRICEWATERHOUSE(COOPERS ⬚

To the Board of Directors and Stockholders of Caterpillar Inc.: We have audited, in accordance with auditing standards generally accepted in the United States, the consolidated financial position of Caterpillar Inc. and its subsidiaries as of December 31, 1999, 1998 and 1997, and the related consolidated results of their operations and their consolidated cash flow for each of the three years in the period ended December 31, 1999, (not presented herein); and in our report dated January 21, 2000, we expressed an unqualified opinion on those consolidated financial statements.

In our opinion, the information set forth in the accompanying condensed consolidated financial statements is fairly stated, in all material respects, in relation to the consolidated financial statements from which it has been derived.

Pricewaterhouse Coopers LLP

Peoria, Illinois
January 21, 2000

Figure 3-1:
A one-paragraph audit report.

Other kinds of audit opinions

An audit report that does *not* give a clean opinion may look very similar to a clean-opinion audit report to the untrained eye. Some investors see the name of an audit firm next to the financial statements and assume that everything is okay – after all, if the auditor had seen a problem, the cops would have pounced on the business and put everyone in jail, right? Well, not exactly.

How do you know when an auditor's report may be something other than a straightforward, no-reservations clean opinion? *Look for a fourth paragraph*; that's the key. Many audits require the audit firm to add additional, explanatory language to the standard, unqualified (clean) opinion.

One modification to an auditor's report is very serious – when the audit firm expresses the view that it has substantial doubts about the capability of the business to continue as a going concern. A *going concern* is a business that has sufficient financial wherewithal and momentum to continue its normal operations into the foreseeable future and would be able to absorb a bad turn of events without having to default on its liabilities. A going concern doesn't face an imminent financial crisis or any pressing financial emergency. A business could be under some financial distress, but overall still be judged a going concern. Unless there is evidence to the contrary, the auditor assumes that the business is a going concern.

But in some cases, the auditor may see unmistakable signs that a business is in deep financial waters and may not be able to convince its creditors and lenders to give it time to work itself out of its present financial difficulties. The creditors and lenders may force the business into involuntary bankruptcy, or the business may make a pre-emptive move and take itself into voluntary bankruptcy. The equity owners (shareholders of a company) may end up holding an empty bag after the bankruptcy proceedings have concluded. (This is one of the risks that shareholders take.) If an auditor has serious concerns about whether the business is a going concern, these doubts are spelled out in the auditor's report.

Auditors also point out any accounting methods that are inconsistent from one year to the next, whether their opinion is based in part on work done by another audit firm, on limitations on the scope of their audit work, on departures from the rules (if they're not serious enough to warrant an adverse opinion) or on one of several other more technical matters. Generally, businesses – and auditors too – want to end up with a clean bill of health; anything less is bound to catch the attention of the people who read the financial statements. Every business wants to avoid that sort of attention if possible.

Do Audits Always Catch Fraud?

Business managers and investors should understand one thing: having an audit of a business's financial statements doesn't guarantee that all fraud, embezzlement, theft and dishonesty will be detected. Audits have to be cost-effective; auditors can't examine every transaction that occurred during the year. Instead, auditors carefully evaluate businesses' internal controls and rely on sampling – they examine only a relatively small portion of transactions closely and in depth. The sample may not include the transactions that would tip off the auditor that something is wrong, however. Perpetrators of fraud and embezzlement are usually clever in concealing their wrongdoing and often prepare fake evidence to cover their tracks.

Looking for errors and fraud

Auditors look in the high-risk areas where fraud and embezzlement are most likely to occur and in areas where the company's internal controls are weak. But again, auditors can't catch everything. High-level management fraud is extraordinarily difficult to detect because auditors rely a great deal on management explanations and assurances about the business. Top-level executives may lie to auditors, deliberately mislead them and conceal things that they don't want auditors to find out about. Auditors have a particularly difficult time detecting management fraud.

Under tougher auditing standards adopted recently, auditors have to develop a detailed and definite plan to search for indicators of fraud, and they have to document the search procedures and findings in their audit working papers. Searching is one thing, but actually finding fraud is quite another. In many cases high-level management fraud went on for some time before it was discovered, usually not by auditors. The new auditing standard was expected to lead to more effective audit procedures that would reduce undetected fraud.

Unfortunately, it doesn't appear that things have improved. Articles in the financial press since then have exposed many cases of accounting and management fraud that weren't detected or, if known about, weren't objected to by the auditors. This is most disturbing. It's difficult to understand how these audit failures and breakdowns happened. The trail of facts is hard to follow in each case, especially by just reading what's reported in the press. Nevertheless, we'd say that two basic reasons explain why audits fail to find fraud.

First, business managers are aware that an audit relies on a very limited sampling from the large number of transactions. They know that only a needle-in-the-haystack chance exists of fraudulent transactions being selected for an in-depth examination by the auditor. Second, managers are in a position to cover their tracks – to conceal evidence and to fabricate false evidence. In short, well-designed and well-executed management fraud is extraordinarily difficult to uncover by ordinary audit procedures. Call this *audit evidence failure*; the auditor didn't know about the fraud.

In other situations, the auditor did know what was going on but didn't act on it – call this an *audit judgement failure*. In these cases, the auditor was overly tolerant of wrong accounting methods used by the client. The auditor may have had serious objections to the accounting methods, but the client persuaded the auditor to go along with the methods.

What happens when auditors spot fraud

In the course of doing an audit, the audit firm may make the following discoveries:

- ✔ **Errors in recording transactions:** These honest mistakes happen from time to time because of inexperienced bookkeepers, or poorly trained accountants, or simple failure to pay attention to details. No one is stealing money or other assets or defrauding the business. Management wants the errors corrected and wants to prevent them from happening again.

- ✔ **Theft, embezzlement and fraud against the business:** This kind of dishonesty takes advantage of weak internal controls or involves the abuse of positions of authority in the organisation that top management didn't know about and wasn't involved in. Management may take action against the guilty parties.

- ✔ **Accounting fraud (also called financial fraud or financial reporting fraud):** This refers to top-level managers who know about and approve the use of misleading and invalid accounting methods for the purpose of disguising the business's financial problems or artificially inflating profit. Often, managers benefit from these improper accounting methods – by propping up the market price of the company's shares to make their stock options more valuable, for example.

- ✔ **Management fraud:** In the broadest sense this includes accounting fraud, but in a more focused sense it refers to high-level business managers engaging in illegal schemes to line their pockets at the business's expense or knowingly violating laws and regulations that put the business at risk of large criminal or civil penalties. A manager may conspire with competitors to fix prices or divide the market, for example. Accepting kickbacks or bribes from customers is an example of management fraud – although most management fraud is more sophisticated than taking under-the-table payments.

When the first two types of problems are discovered, the auditor's follow-up is straightforward. Errors are corrected, and the loss from the crime against the business is recorded. (Such a loss may be a problem if it's so large that the auditor thinks it should be disclosed separately in the financial report but the business disagrees and doesn't want to call attention to the loss.) In contrast, the auditor is between a rock and a hard place when accounting or management fraud is uncovered.

When an auditor discovers accounting or management fraud, the business has to clean up the fraud mess as best it can – which often involves recording a loss. Of course, the business should make changes to prevent the fraud from occurring again. And it may request the resignations of those responsible or even take legal action against those employees. Assuming that the fraud loss is recorded and reported correctly in the financial statements, the auditor then issues a clean opinion on the financial statements. But auditors can withhold a clean opinion and threaten to issue a qualified or adverse opinion if the client does not deal with the matter in a satisfactory manner in its financial statements. That's the auditor's real clout.

The most serious type of accounting fraud occurs when profit is substantially overstated, with the result that the market value of the corporation's shares was based on inflated profit numbers. Another type of accounting fraud occurs when a business is in deep financial trouble but its Balance Sheet disguises the trouble and makes things look much better than they really are. The business may be on the verge of financial failure, but the Balance Sheet gives no clue. When the fraud comes out into the open, the market value takes a plunge, and the investors call their lawyers and sue the business and the auditor.

Investing money in a business or shares issued by a public business involves many risks. The risk of misleading financial statements is just one of many dangers that investors face. A business may have accurate and truthful financial statements but end up in the tank because of bad management, bad products, poor marketing or just bad luck.

All in all, audited financial statements that carry a clean opinion (the best possible auditor's report) are reliable indicators for investors to use – especially because auditors are held accountable for their reports and can be sued for careless audit procedures. (In fact, accountancy firms have had to pay many millions of pounds in malpractice lawsuit damages over the past 30 years, and Arthur Andersen was actually driven out of business.) Auditors usually handle clients for years, if not decades – PricewaterhouseCoopers LLP have been Sainsbury's auditors since 1995 – so if anyone knows where the bodies are it's the auditor. Therefore, don't overlook the audit report as a tool for judging the reliability of a business's financial statements. When you read the auditor's report on the annual financial statements from your pension fund manager, hopefully you'll be very reassured! That's your retirement money they're talking about, after all.

Auditors and the Rules

In the course of doing an audit, the accountant often catches certain accounting methods used by the client that violate the prevailing approved and authoritative methods and standards laid down by law that businesses must follow in preparing and reporting financial statements. All businesses are subject to these ground rules. An auditor calls to the attention of the business any departures from the rules, and he helps the business make adjustments to put its financial statements back on the right track. Sometimes a business may not want to make the changes that the auditor suggests because its profit numbers would be deflated. Professional standards demand that the auditor secure a change (assuming that the amount involved is material). If the client refuses to make a change to an acceptable accounting method, the accountant warns the financial report reader in the auditor's report.

Auditors don't allow their good names to be associated with financial reports that they know are misleading if they can possibly help it. Every now and then we read in the financial press about an audit firm walking away from a client ('withdraws from the engagement' is the official terminology). As mentioned earlier in this chapter, everything the auditor learns in the course of an audit is confidential and can't be divulged beyond top management and the board of directors of the business. A *confidential relationship* exists between the auditor and the client – although it's not equal to the privileged communication between lawyers and their clients.

If an auditor discovers a problem, he has the responsibility to move up the chain of command in the business organisation to make sure that one level higher than the source of the problem is informed of the problem. But the board of directors is the end of the line. The auditor doesn't inform the LSE, the SEC or another regulatory agency of any confidential information learned during the audit.

However, most outside observers will work on the 'no smoke without fire' principle. No firm, yet alone an accountancy partnership with their partnership profit share on the line, willingly gives up a lucrative client.

Auditors, on the other hand, are frequently being replaced, often for cost reasons – auditing is a negotiable deal too – but also because the firm being audited may have simply outgrown the auditor. This happens fairly frequently when a business is going for a public listing of its shares. The guy round the corner, who was cheap and competent, cuts no ice with the big wheels at the LSE and the placing houses that have to sell the shares. They want a big name auditor to help the PR push.

We can't exaggerate the importance of reliable financial statements that are prepared according to uniform standards and methods for measuring profit and putting values on assets, liabilities and owners' equity. Not to put too fine a point on it, the flow of capital into businesses and the market prices of shares traded in the public markets (the LSE, the NYSE and over the NASDAQ network) depend on the information reported in financial statements.

Smaller, privately owned businesses would have a difficult time raising capital from owners and borrowing money from banks if no one could trust their financial statements. Generally accepted accounting principles, in short, are the gold standard for financial reporting. When financial reporting standards have been put into place, how are the standards enforced? To a large extent, the role of auditors is to do just that – to enforce the rules. The main purpose of having annual audits, in other words, is to keep businesses on the straight-and-narrow path and to prevent businesses from issuing misleading financial statements. Auditors are the guardians of the financial reporting rules. We think most business managers and investors agree that financial reporting would be in a sorry state if auditors weren't around.

From Audits to Advising

If accountant Rip van Winkle woke up today after his 20-year sleep, he'd be shocked to find that accountancy firms make most of their money not from doing audits but from advising clients. A recent advertisement by an international accountancy firm listed the following services: 'assurance, business consulting, corporate finance, eBusiness, human capital, legal services, outsourcing, risk consulting and tax services'. (Now, if the firm could only help you with your back problems!) Do you see audits in this list? No? Well, it's under the first category – assurance. Why have accountancy firms moved so far beyond audits into many different fields of consulting?

We suspect that many businesses don't view audits as adding much value to their financial reports. True, having a clean opinion by an auditor on financial statements adds credibility to a financial report. At the same time, managers tend to view the audit as an intrusion, and an override on their prerogatives regarding how to account for profit and how to present the financial report of the business. Most audits, to be frank about it, involve a certain amount of tension between managers and the audit firm. After all, the essence of an audit is to second-guess the business's accounting methods and financial reporting decisions. So it's quite understandable that accountancy firms have looked to other types of services they can provide to clients that are more value-added and less adversarial – and that are more lucrative.

Nevertheless, many people have argued that accountancy firms should get out of the consulting and advising business – at least to the same clients they audit. For the first years of this millennium, things seemed to be moving in this direction, and new legislation gave them a none-too-gentle prod. Arthur Andersen only just split its consultancy business off before it went under itself. Luckily, it changed the name of the consulting business from Andersen to Accenture, ditching a fair amount of the bad odour that attached itself to the accountancy practice's name. Now the pendulum is swinging back and big accountancy firms are pushing an integrated approach, arguing that clients don't want to have to explain largely the same business facts to different teams of 'visiting firemen'. Although the Big Four are back in the consulting game, figures from the Management Consultancies Association suggest that accountancy firms have only 16 per cent of the market for consultancy services, right now at least.

Sometimes we take the pessimistic view that in the long run accountants will abandon audits and do only taxes and consulting. Who will do audits then? Well, a team of governmental auditors could take over the task – but we don't think this would be too popular.

Index

About the Authors

Jane Kelly trained as a Chartered Management Accountant while working in industry. Her roles ranged from Company Accountant in a small advertising business to Financial Controller for a national house builder. For the last few years Jane has specialised in using Sage accounting software and has taught a wide variety of small businesses and employees the benefits of using Sage. More recently Jane has been involved in writing *For Dummies* books, including *Bookkeeping For Dummies*, 3rd Edition, *Sage One For Dummies and Sage 50 Accounts For Dummies*.

Colin Barrow was until recently Head of the Enterprise Group at Cranfield School of Management, where he taught entrepreneurship on the MBA and other programmes and where he is still a visiting fellow. He is also a visiting professor at business schools in the US, Asia, France and Austria. His books on entrepreneurship and business have been translated into over twenty languages including Russian and Chinese. He worked with Microsoft to incorporate the business planning model used in his teaching programmes into the software program, Microsoft Business Planner, bundled with Office. He is a regular contributor to newspapers, periodicals and academic journals such as *The Financial Times, The Guardian, Management Today* and the *International Small Business Journal.*

Thousands of students have passed through Colin's start-up and business growth programmes, raising millions in new capital and going on to run successful and thriving enterprises. Some have made it to *The Sunday Times* Rich List. He has been a non-executive director of two venture capital funds, on the board of several small businesses, and serves on a number of Government Task Forces. Currently he is a non-executive director in several private firms and works with family businesses in the Middle East on succession planning.

Paul Barrow trained and qualified as a Chartered Accountant with Deloitte & Touche before obtaining his MBA at Bradford University. As a senior consultant with Ernst & Young he was responsible for managing and delivering quality consulting assignments.

Paul is a Visiting Fellow at Cranfi eld University where he teaches on the Business Growth Programme. This programme is designed specifically for owner managers who want to grow and improve their businesses. He also teaches at Warwick University and Oxford Brookes on similar programmes.

Paul has written several other business books aimed at owner managers trying to grow and improve their businesses: *The Business Plan Workbook* and *Raising Finance* (both Kogan Page/Sunday Times); *The Best Laid Business Plans* and *The Bottom Line* (both Virgin Books).

Lita Epstein, who earned her MBA from Emory University's Goizueta Business School, enjoys helping people develop good financial, investing, and tax planning skills. She designs and teaches online courses on topics such as investing for retirement, getting ready for tax time, and finance and investing for women. She's written more than ten books, including *Streetwise Retirement Planning* and *Trading For Dummies*.

John A Tracy is Professor of Accounting, Emeritus, in the College of Business and Administration at the University of Colorado in Boulder. Before his 35-year tenure at Boulder he was on the business faculty for four years at the University of California in Berkeley. He has served as staff accountant at Ernst & Young and is the author of several books on accounting, including *The Fast Forward MBA in Finance, How To Read a Financial Report* and *Accounting For Dummies*. Dr Tracy received his MBA and PhD degrees from the University of Wisconsin and is a CPA in Colorado.

Publisher's Acknowledgements

We're proud of this book; please send us your comments at http://dummies.custhelp.com. For other comments, please contact our Customer Care Department within the U.S. at 877-762-2974, outside the U.S. at (001) 317-572-3993, or fax 317-572-4002.

Some of the people who helped bring this book to market include the following:

Acquisitions, Editorial and Vertical Websites

Commissioning Editor: Annie Knight

Proofreader: Charlie Wilson

Publisher: Miles Kendall

Front Cover Photos: ©iStock.com/Bas Slabbers Photography

Notes

Notes

Take Dummies with you everywhere you go!

Whether you're excited about e-books, want more from the web, must have your mobile apps, or swept up in social media, Dummies makes everything easier.

FOR DUMMIES®

A Wiley Brand

BUSINESS

978-1-118-73077-5

978-1-118-44349-1

978-1-119-97527-4

MUSIC

978-1-119-94276-4

978-0-470-97799-6

978-0-470-49644-2

DIGITAL PHOTOGRAPHY

978-1-118-09203-3

978-0-470-76878-5

978-1-118-00472-2

Algebra I For Dummies
978-0-470-55964-2

Anatomy & Physiology For Dummies, 2nd Edition
978-0-470-92326-9

Asperger's Syndrome For Dummies
978-0-470-66087-4

Basic Maths For Dummies
978-1-119-97452-9

Body Language For Dummies, 2nd Edition
978-1-119-95351-7

Bookkeeping For Dummies, 3rd Edition
978-1-118-34689-1

British Sign Language For Dummies
978-0-470-69477-0

Cricket for Dummies, 2nd Edition
978-1-118-48032-8

Currency Trading For Dummies, 2nd Edition
978-1-118-01851-4

Cycling For Dummies
978-1-118-36435-2

Diabetes For Dummies, 3rd Edition
978-0-470-97711-8

eBay For Dummies, 3rd Edition
978-1-119-94122-4

Electronics For Dummies All-in-One For Dummies
978-1-118-58973-1

English Grammar For Dummies
978-0-470-05752-0

French For Dummies, 2nd Edition
978-1-118-00464-7

Guitar For Dummies, 3rd Edition
978-1-118-11554-1

IBS For Dummies
978-0-470-51737-6

Keeping Chickens For Dummies
978-1-119-99417-6

Knitting For Dummies, 3rd Edition
978-1-118-66151-2

FOR DUMMIES
A Wiley Brand

SELF-HELP

978-0-470-66541-1

978-1-119-99264-6

978-0-470-66086-7

LANGUAGES

978-0-470-68815-1

978-1-119-97959-3

978-0-470-69477-0

HISTORY

978-0-470-68792-5

978-0-470-74783-4

978-0-470-97819-1

Laptops For Dummies 5th Edition
978-1-118-11533-6

Management For Dummies, 2nd Edition
978-0-470-97769-9

Nutrition For Dummies, 2nd Edition
978-0-470-97276-2

Office 2013 For Dummies
978-1-118-49715-9

Organic Gardening For Dummies
978-1-119-97706-3

Origami Kit For Dummies
978-0-470-75857-1

Overcoming Depression For Dummies
978-0-470-69430-5

Physics I For Dummies
978-0-470-90324-7

Project Management For Dummies
978-0-470-71119-4

Psychology Statistics For Dummies
978-1-119-95287-9

Renting Out Your Property For Dummies, 3rd Edition
978-1-119-97640-0

Rugby Union For Dummies, 3rd Edition
978-1-119-99092-5

Stargazing For Dummies
978-1-118-41156-8

Teaching English as a Foreign Language For Dummies
978-0-470-74576-2

Time Management For Dummies
978-0-470-77765-7

Training Your Brain For Dummies
978-0-470-97449-0

Voice and Speaking Skills For Dummies
978-1-119-94512-3

Wedding Planning For Dummies
978-1-118-69951-5

WordPress For Dummies, 5th Edition
978-1-118-38318-6

Think you can't learn it in a day? Think again!

The *In a Day* e-book series from *For Dummies* gives you quick and easy access to learn a new skill, brush up on a hobby, or enhance your personal or professional life — all in a day. Easy!